Italian Popular Tales

ABC≈CLIO CLASSIC FOLK AND FAIRY TALES

Jack Zipes, Series Editor

Collectors in the nineteenth and early twentieth centuries unearthed a wealth of stories from around the world and published them in English translations for the delight of general readers, young and old. Most of these anthologies have been long out of print.

The ABC-CLIO Classic Folk and Fairy Tales series brings back to life these key anthologies of traditional tales from the golden age of folklore discovery. Each volume provides a freshly typeset but otherwise virtually unaltered edition of a classic work and each is enhanced by an authoritative introduction by a top scholar. These insightful essays discuss the significance of the collection and its original collector; the original collector's methodology and translation practices; and the original period context according to region or genre.

Certain to be of interest to folklorists, these classic collections are also meant to serve as sources for storytellers and for sheer reading pleasure, reviving as they do hundreds of folk stories, both reassuringly familiar and excitingly strange.

FORTHCOMING TITLES:

Creation Myths of Primitive America, by Jeremiah Curtin;
Introduction by Karl Kroeber

English Fairy Tales and More English Fairy Tales, by Joseph Jacobs;
Introduction by Donald Haase

Folktales from Northern India, by William Crooke and
Pandit Ram Gharib Chaube;
Introduction by Sadhana Naithani

Old Deccan Days or Hindoo Fairy Legends, by Mary Frere;
Introduction by Kirin Narayan

Popular Tales and Fictions, by William Alexander Clouston;
Introduction by Christine Goldberg

Popular Tales of Ancient Egypt, by Gaston Maspero;
Introduction by Hasan El-Shamy

ITALIAN POPULAR TALES

୬

THOMAS FREDERICK CRANE

EDITED AND WITH AN INTRODUCTION BY

JACK ZIPES

A B C 🌑 C L I O

Santa Barbara, California
Denver, Colorado   Oxford, England

Library of Congress Cataloging-in-Publication Data

Crane, Thomas Frederick, 1844-1927
  Italian popular tales / Thomas Frederick Crane; with an Introduction by Jack Zipes.
    p. cm. – (ABC-CLIO classic folk and fairy tales)
Includes bibliographical references and index.
  ISBN 1-57607-272-X (hardcover); 1-57607-553-2 (e-book)
  1. Tales—Italy. I. Title. II. Series.
GR176 .C7 2001
398,2'0945—dc21

2001004558

06 05 04 03 02 01   10 9 8 7 6 5 4 3 2 1 (cloth)

This edition reprints in its entirety and retains the original chapter sequence of *Italian Popular Tales*, by Thomas Frederick Crane, A.M., published by The Riverside Press, Cambridge, and printed by Houghton, Mifflin and Company, 1885. The text of the 1885 edition has been altered only to fit an increased page dimension and to reflect contemporary conventions.

ABC-CLIO, Inc.
130 Cremona Drive, P.O. Box 1911
Santa Barbara, California 93116–1911

This book is also available on the World Wide Web as an e-book. Visit www.abc-clio.com for details.

Contents

Preface to this Edition — VII

Thomas F. Crane: The Uncanny Career
of a Folklorist — IX

Bibliography of the Writings of
Thomas F. Crane — XXV

Italian Popular Tales

Preface — XLVII

Introduction — XLIX

Bibliography — LVII

List of Stories — LXV

  I. Fairy Tales — 3

  II. Fairy Tales Continued — 79

  III. Stories of Oriental Origin — 119

  IV. Legends and Ghost Stories — 149

  V. Nursery Tales — 193

  VI. Stories and Jests — 221

Notes — 255

List of Works Referred To — 309

Index — 311

꙳

PREFACE TO THIS EDITION

Italian Popular Tales is a treasure for folklorists, storytellers, and literary critics. More than the Grimm Brothers' *Children's and Household Tales* and Afanasyev's *Russian Fairy Tales*, which have unfortunately, I believe, dominated our contemporary imagination of what folk and fairy tales were like in the nineteenth century, Thomas Frederick Crane's collection of different nineteenth-century Italian tale types offers a much more complex and rich selection of oral and literary tales with multiple versions from different centuries and countries and exhaustive notes. In fact, one might consider *Italian Popular Tales* a correction to many misconceptions of *popular* storytelling and literary publications of the nineteenth century that stem from the emphasis that has been placed on the Grimms and Afanasyev as European models.

Crane worked assiduously to document all the tales from his collection, which were taken from over forty different works, and to demonstrate the fluid flow between the oral and literary traditions. He covers a wide range of tale types including the fairy tale, Oriental tales, legends, ghost stories, nursery tales and rhymes, jests, and anecdotes. Unlike the Grimms and Afanasyev, he does not "clean up" or modify all the tales that he translates from different regions of Italy. The tales deal openly and frankly with such subjects as murder, adultery, incest, child abuse, brutal vengeance, robbery, cheating, and exploitation. Many of the morals are dubious. In fact, numerous tales might be considered "immoral" today, for they depict simply that crime pays, might makes right, and cunning is necessary to survive in a dog-eat-dog world. The realism of the tales is uncanny.

The language and style of the different texts vary depending on the collector and the storyteller. Many of the stories were recorded in standard Italian after they were heard in dialect; some were printed in dialect, especially those from Giuseppe Pitrè's Sicilian collections; many were taken from German translations that were originally told in an Italian dialect. As Crane, who did all the translating from the Italian, German, and French, makes clear, all these tales have unique histories and can be traced to similar narratives in the Orient and in Europe. He does not deal with American folklore and the transmission of the tales to North America or the parallels between Native American and indigenous European tales. Crane was very much the Europhile with a comprehensive knowledge of Oriental folklore. Though he participated in the founding of the American Folklore Association at the end of the nineteenth century, he appears to have distanced himself from the association and its focus on North American folklore soon after its establishment.

Crane's translations are remarkably accurate. Somehow he mastered different Italian dialects and slang, and though his nineteenth-century English is somewhat archaic and quaint, and his punctuation uneven, there is a "raw" quality to his literal translations that gives to them a more "authentic" ring than would a smooth contemporary translation. His notes are still valuable, and in some cases, present minor discoveries such as his remarks on the diffusion of *Petit-Poucet* (*Little Tom Thumb*) and his translation of rare versions of this tale type. For the most part, very few changes in the original text of Crane's book were made in the ABC-CLIO reprint. Since Crane was a prolific and significant folklorist and literary historian, I have included his own mammoth bibliography that he composed and printed privately right before his death. Otherwise, I have made only minor orthographic and factual corrections in his book.

I am deeply grateful to Todd Hallman, who helped initiate and develop the ABC-CLIO Classic Folk and Fairy Tales series, and I am very much in debt to Martha Whitt, who has done a superb job in overseeing the editing of *Italian Popular Tales*, which, I hope, will not only reawaken an interest in Crane and Italian folklore but also inaugurate a series of significant collections of folk and fairy tales that will appeal not only to specialists but also to the general public that still constitutes the original audience of the tales.

—*Jack Zipes*
Minneapolis
September 5, 2001

INTRODUCTION
Thomas F. Crane:
The Uncanny Career of a Folklorist

IT IS generally believed that Italo Calvino's book of Italian folktales, *Fiabe Italiane*, published in 1956, was the first comprehensive collection of stories from all over Italy, composed in the manner of the Brothers Grimm, to celebrate the rich tradition of Italian folklore. But the fact is that the American scholar Thomas Frederick Crane was really the first to produce a monumental anthology of tales, in 1885, dedicated to establishing the significance of Italian folklore in the English-speaking world. It is somewhat of a mystery as to why and how Crane did this, and it is a story worth telling before I turn to discussing the nature and importance of his edition of *Italian Popular Tales*.

Though Crane was one of the leading folklorists and professors of medieval literature in the nineteenth century and one of the founders of the *Journal of American Folklore*, very little is known about him, and the papers that he deposited at Cornell University do not provide abundant information about his life, his training, and his contacts with other folklorists. Nevertheless, the materials at Cornell and his voluminous published works are sufficient enough to draw a brief portrait of an amazingly prolific, meticulous, and imaginative scholar, who had little preparation for the great career that he made for himself in the fields of folklore and medieval literature.

Born in New York City on July 12, 1844, Crane was the oldest son of Thomas Sexton and Charlotte (Nuttman) Crane. His father was a merchant, and soon after Crane was born, the family moved to New Orleans. He learned to read before the time he was five and developed an early interest in literature. Due to the nomadic life of his family, Crane was sent in 1853 to live with his father's mother in Ithaca, New York, and was educated at a public school and Ithaca Academy. Early in 1856, his father retired from business, and his parents moved to Elizabeth, New Jersey, where his mother died the next year. In 1858, his father summoned him to Elizabeth, and Crane wrote that "not having the advantage of school athletics my health was not strong, and my father insisted on my abandoning my studies entirely and spending a year on the farm. I draw a veil over that period. For years I could not behold a potato or a kernel of corn without a back ache!"[1]

Evidently there was some tension between son and father, who was not entirely supportive of his son's intellectual proclivities. However, he did allow Crane to return to a New Jersey private school in 1859, and the following year his father granted him permission to attend Princeton College. Crane's description of his four years at Princeton reveals a great deal about the educational climate of those times:

> So to college I went, and during four years studied the classics, philosophy, and every species of mathematics then known to the civilized world. I know it will sound incredible, but it is true: there was no elective system, and no elective studies, except, I believe, that more mathematics could be substituted for Greek in the senior year. There was no English literature in the course, no history, no modern languages. Otherwise the place was an educational paradise. There were no fraternities, no musical or dramatic clubs, no athletics, nor even a Minor Sports Association, no Junior Week! We had absolutely nothing to do but to study and dissipate. It was before the days of large fortunes and there was no display of any kind. Men were ranked according to their intellectual and social qualities and the hero of those times was the one who could write well, speak well, talk well and was moreover a good fellow.[2]

By the time Crane graduated in 1864, at the age of twenty, he had developed a great love for literature and a strong interest in foreign languages, even though he had only studied some French outside the normal curriculum. It never occurred to him to teach because most of the professors at that time were clergymen who were not particularly stimulating or dedicated to scholarly pursuits, and most of the students had a vague idea of becoming lawyers. Since Crane's father also wanted him to study law, Crane enrolled at Columbia law school in the fall of 1864, but his passion for literature had not abated, and he also began studying German, Spanish, and Italian on his own. Early in January 1865, he was obliged to return to Ithaca due to the sickness of a relative, and while he was there, he met with a well-established lawyer by the name of F. M. Finch, who advised him to leave Columbia and take a position in his firm. At that time it was not necessary to complete three years of university study, and an apprenticeship at a law firm was sufficient to prepare a young man to take the law examinations. So, in June of 1865, Crane moved back to Ithaca, which he was to make his home for the rest of his life, and began working for Finch, who was to become the dean of the Cornell Law School. By May of 1866, he was admitted to the bar, and aside from practicing law, he also held the position of assistant deputy collector of internal revenue.

But Crane was not destined to follow a career in law, nor did he particularly want to do this. He had continued studying German and French on his own, and he had made the acquaintance of Ezra Cornell, who was in the process of making plans to found Cornell University, which he did in 1868. Crane also met the man who was to become the first president of Cornell, Andrew D. White. In addition to acquiring substantial knowledge of German and French, Crane started learning Spanish with Edward Curtis Guild, the new Unitarian pastor in Ithaca, and became involved in politics. One day, while he was studying Spanish, A. B. Cornell, a son of Ezra Cornell, came into his office and suggested that he apply for a professorship in Spanish at the new university. When Crane eventually summoned the courage to apply for this position, President White could not promise him anything and gently persuaded him to return to the profession of law. However, Crane did not abandon his private studies of literature and languages and was even asked by *The Nation* to review important books on Spanish topics.

In the meantime, White discovered that the founding of a university and the commencement of classes in the fall of 1868 presented unforeseeable problems, and one of them was to alter Crane's destiny. When White learned that the professor whom he had hired to teach German, a certain Mr. Fiske, would not return from Europe to Ithaca until January of 1869, he approached Crane and asked him to organize the department and to maintain the teaching of German until Fiske's return. This offer changed the course of Crane's life. As he writes,

> I helped examine the entering class in the basement of the Cornell Library and took their matriculation fees. I attended the first Faculty meeting in Mr. Cornell's office which

had once been my law office for a winter. I sat on the plat-
form in the Assembly Room at the top of Morrill Hall
when in turn the new Faculty announced to the students
(the one room then held them all) their books and lessons
for the next day, and the following morning, in a little
room just over my present dean's office, I started the beginning classes in Otto's German Grammar and the advanced
class in Nathan der Weise. *I had become a professor.*[3]

It was indeed only because of a remarkable set of coincidences that Crane
had embarked on a career as a professor, and once he began, he was total-
ly dedicated to his research and teaching. When Fiske returned to Cornell in January of 1869, Crane was eager to train himself more diligently
in foreign languages, and he set sail for Europe with the intention of pur-
suing his studies in Spanish with an expert in the field, Dr. Mahn, who
was living in Berlin. Crane studied Provençal, Gothic, Italian, and Spanish texts with Mahn in Berlin until June, when he planned to go to Italy
and Spain. However, when the Franco-Prussian War made travel difficult, he decided to spend the remainder of his European stay in Wölfen-
buttel, famous for its library of ancient texts. By September, Crane
returned to Ithaca to begin teaching in the Department of Romance
Languages.

Within three years, he was made professor of Italian and Spanish, and
in 1884, Crane became the head of the Department of Romance Languages. He was also dean of the Faculty of Arts and Sciences from 1896
to 1902 and of the University Faculty from 1902 to 1909. Twice he served
as acting president of the university, in 1899 and between 1912 and 1913.
He was a member of the Finnish Society of Letters, the American Philosophical Society, the Modern Language Association of America, and the
Royal Academy of Sciences and Arts of Palermo. A regular reviewer for
The Nation, mainly of books dealing with folklore, from 1868 until his
death in 1924, he also founded and helped to establish the *Journal of
American Folklore* and was a contributor to other magazines and journals
such as *Modern Philology, Folk-Lore,* and *Modern Language Notes.*

How and why Crane developed such a passion for folklore and
medieval literature is difficult to say, but his papers and notes at Cornell's
Carl A. Kroch Library reveal that he commenced a serious study of
medieval texts and storybooks in the late 1860s and focused on European
studies of folklore in numerous reviews for *The Nation.* The boxes of his

materials contain numerous annotated cards with references to sources and analogues in the oral and literary traditions as well as copious notes and comments based on his research in American libraries. His knowledge of European scholarship in folklore and medieval and Renaissance literature was prodigious, and he evidently saw part of his role as a mediator between Europe and the United States. In this respect, he was a pioneer in America of the comparative method of the oral and literary tradition with a strong emphasis on sociocultural contexts and history. More than any other American scholar of the late nineteenth century, he introduced the most significant scholarly works on folklore from Europe, as well as translations of texts, to an American public. His first major work was a short talk, "Medieval Sermon-Books and Stories," published by the Folk-Lore Society in 1883, and he gave indication from the very beginning of his career that he would be a pioneer, not only in the field of medieval literature but also in folklore. Crane believed deeply that the oral tradition of the people had been unduly neglected in the study of literature, and he explored the popular sources of the literature that emanated from this tradition in such key works as *The Exempla of Jacques Vitry* (1890), "Medieval Story-Books" (1911), and "New Analogues of Old Tales" (1913). The essay on medieval storybooks contains an interesting comment that sums up his critical perspective:

> The innate love of mankind for stories and story-telling
> has always been freely gratified, but, as its manifestations
> lie largely outside of literary expression, they have often
> been forgotten. It is difficult to distinguish the popular
> element in the Greek romances or to estimate exactly the
> influence of the latter upon the Christian entertaining lit-
> erature which was rapidly taking their place. The legends
> of the fifth century *Vitae Patrum* exhibit every variety of
> romantic plot found in the Greek Romances together with
> specific Christian supernatural elements. The vogue of this
> collection was enormous and it retained its well-deserved
> popularity through the Reformation period. The change in
> Christian thought and dogma during the sixth and sev-
> enth centuries is clearly shown in the only rival of the
> *Vitae Patrum,* the *Dialogues* of Gregory the Great. The
> romantic element of the former has disappeared, the most
> childish miracles abound, and, above all, the fourth book
> introduces the sombre literature of visions. These two
> works constituted for many centuries the magazines of

entertaining and edifying stories, which were diffused
throughout the world by a channel to be mentioned
presently.[4]

This channel is constituted by the clergy, the pulpit, sermons, and public readings. Crane was fascinated by what texts reveal about the interaction between the oral and literary traditions. Throughout his life, he excavated and recuperated neglected tales, stories, poems, songs, and texts that provided evidence of customs and mores of the people in specific societies at particular times. In this regard, he was a "populist," that is, he understood the term "popular" in its more traditional etymological sense, stemming from the Latin *popularis* or *populus,* pertaining to and consisting of the common people, or the people as a whole. His last great work, *Italian Social Customs of the Sixteenth Century, and Their Influence on the Literatures of Europe* (1920), reveals to what extent his interest in literature extended beyond the texts to comprehend the relationship between habits, rituals, superstitions, material living conditions, and literature. In this respect, Crane was greatly influenced by the work of the formidable Sicilian folklorist Giuseppe Pitrè, to whom Crane dedicated *Italian Popular Tales.*

In his introduction to *Italian Popular Tales,* Crane points out that Pitrè began collecting and publishing his various collections of tales, legends, superstitions, proverbs, and historical studies of customs when there had been more Italian folktales translated into English and German than there were in Italian. Inspired by Pitré, Crane ironically continued this "tradition," for his *English* collection of Italian tales was the very first cross-section of tales from different regions of Italy ever to be published in the world. His introduction is short and provides significant historical background information on the development of collections of folktales in Italy. He does not intend to explain the derivation of the tales, nor does he want to elaborate a theoretical position with regard to the origins of the tales. As a comparative folklorist, he wants to provide a sampling of tales that can be found throughout Italy, tales that have parallels in many different countries. At times, however, he makes some misleading statements. For instance, he maintains that "from their very nature the stories we are now considering were long confined to the common people, and were preserved and transmitted solely by oral tradition."[5] Yet, he does not consider that many educated people maintained these stories in the oral tradition as well and that these tales were in part kept alive through the writing and publishing of texts in different forms, something that he actually demonstrated in his studies of sermons and the exempla. Another minor mistake concerns his assertion that the first fairy tale to appear in France was "L'Adroite Princesse," when it was actually "L'Île de la félicité," incorporated by Mme. d'Aulnoy in her novel *Comte Duglas* in 1690.

Crane's comparative perspective is at times strange, if not contradictory. For example, he states: "If we turn our attention now to the contents of our stories we shall find that they do not differ materially from those of the rest of Europe, and the same story is found, with trifling variations, all over Italy. There is but little local coloring in the fairy tales, and they are chiefly interesting for purposes of comparison." Yet, when we compare the tales, especially when we compare them in Italian and in their dialects, it is obvious that the expressions, proverbs, motifs, characters, and plots do reflect local and regional differences, and the changes (especially in time) reveal a great deal about customs, mores, and thought in particular societies—factors that Crane himself studied very carefully. Indeed, he relates the rise of interest in Italian folktales to the rise of nationalism in the nineteenth century, and there are some interesting parallels here with other European countries with regard to the rise of interest in folklore and the rise of nationalism. In particular, the vital connection to Germany is clear.

In the late eighteenth century, Johann Gottfried Herder was the stimulating force behind the romantic interest in German folklore, and by the beginning of the nineteenth century, Achim von Arnim and Clemens Brentano had produced their famous collection of folksongs, *Des Knaben Wunderhorn* (1803); Joseph von Görres had published *Die teutschen Volksbücher* (1807), a huge compendium of folklore; and, of course, the Brothers Grimm had issued their two volumes of *Kinder- und Hausmärchen* in 1812 and 1815. However, it was not just the literary and philosophical influence of Herder that mattered for the production of their works but the rise of national consciousness and call for a German nation during the Napoleonic Wars, a time when Germany was divided and partially occupied by French forces. Politically and socially there was a movement toward establishing a German nation and cultural understanding about the essence of German identity. The strong interest that the Grimms generated in German folklore, mythology, philology, and history was connected to a profound belief in the rich culture of the common people and a common feeling that cultural ties needed to be explored and tightened if the German people were going to grasp that they belonged to one nation. At the same time, the Grimms were aware of the cross-cultural ties with Asia, Africa, and other European countries and the regional differences in Germany itself. They realized that the so-called German soul, or the essence of German culture, could only be distinguished through a comparative mythological approach to folklore. Hence, analogues were important for the distinction of individual cultural traditions. Ultimately, they hoped that the German people would take pride in their own culture through a more comprehensive knowledge of folklore.

This goal was shared by other folklorists throughout Europe, particularly in Italy during the nineteenth century, when the country was divided and partially occupied by the Spanish, French, and Austrians. Ironically, the Germans provided a good deal of the national impulse to recover the Italian "national" soul through collecting folklore and producing collections of tales, songs, proverbs, riddles, and myths. Many Italian philologists and folklorists studied in Germany, and Germans, Austrians, and Swiss writers and scholars traveled to Italy, where they, under the influence of the Brothers Grimm, began collecting Italian tales and taking notes about Italian folklore. In 1860, one year after he had published his significant study *La poesia popolare italiana,* Alessando D'Ancona (1835–1914), who was a professor at Pisa and director of the Florentine daily newspaper *La Nazione,* called for Italian scholars to begin collecting Italian folktales in the manner of the Brothers Grimm. One response was by a teacher by the name of Temistocle Gradi (1824–1887), who published a school text, *Saggio di letture varie per i giovani* (1865), which included 143 proverbs, seven literary Tuscan tales, and four translations from the collection of the Brothers Grimm. About the same time two Germans, Georg Widter and Adam Wolf, published a small collection, *Volksmärchen aus Venetien* (Folktales from Venice), in the journal *Jahrbuch für Romanische und Englische Literatur* in 1866, and they were quickly followed by Hermann Knust, a German professor of Romance languages who published twelve tales from Livorno in the same journal, and Christian Schneller (1831–1908), who published *Märchen und Sagen aus Wälschtirol* (1867), sixty-nine tales from the Italian Tirol. Though these tales (some of which Crane translated for his edition) were in German, they were based on notes that Widter, Wolf, Knust, and Schneller had taken in German and Italian, and they reflected the enormous interest that both foreigners and Italians were now taking in Italian folklore just at a time when the national liberation movement was gathering momentum. It is to Crane's credit that he translated some of this early work for his collection, and he manages to include most of the other important Italian and foreign folklorists and scholars who participated in the folklore renascence in Italy, such as Angelo De Gubernatis, Laura Gonzenbach, Domenico Giuseppe Bernoni, Vittorio Imbriani, Rachel Harriet Busk, Domenico Comparetti, Gherardo Nerucci, Giuseppe Morosi, Carolina Coronedi Berti, Emilio Teza, Francesco Corazzini, Giovanni Papante, Antonio Ive, Isaia Visentini, and last but not least Giuseppe Pitré. Crane even translates an older version of "Puss in Boots" from Giovan Francesco Straparola's important book of tales *Le piacevoli Notti* (The Pleasant Nights, 1550–1553). But almost all the others are from the *Risorgimento* period of the nineteenth century, and their collections reflect a deep concern on the part of scholars to keep alive if not save the great tradition of Italian lore. Since Crane does not provide much background material on these collectors, I should like to discuss their work briefly to place Crane's anthology in a historical context.

Angelo De Gubernatis (1840–1913), who had studied in Berlin and represented yet another connection with German folklorists and philologists, was a professor of Sanskrit and comparative linguistics at the universities of Florence and Rome. His important work in the field of folklore was *Le Novelline di Santo Stefano* (1869), which was a collection of thirty-five folktales from the town of Santo Stefano. Influenced by Adalbert Kuhn and Max Müller, he sought to trace the Indo-Germanic mythic sources in each of the tales. Among his other accomplishments were the two ethnological studies *Storia comparata degli usi nuziali in Italia e presso gli altri popoli indo-europei* (1869) and *Storia popolare degli usi funebri indo-europei* (1873).

Soon after De Gubernatis's collection appeared, Laura Gonzenbach (1842–1878), daughter of the Swiss consul in Messina, surprised Italian folklorists with her remarkable two-volume collection, *Sicilianische Märchen* (Sicilian Folktales), published in Leipzig. She was assisted in her endeavor by the librarian Otto Hartwig, who wrote the historical introduction, and Reinhold Köhler, a meticulous scholar, who provided the notes for the ninety-two tales. Gonzenbach, fluent in many different languages and dialects, had gathered the tales largely from peasant women. Though she made some slight changes in her transcription of the tales into German, as did Hartwig and Köhler, her texts reveal a close approximation to the oral tradition and are a rich source for understanding Sicilian folk customs.

Not as well known as De Gubernatis or Gonzenbach, Domenico Giuseppe Bernoni, born 1828 in Asola (date of death unknown), had a clear impact on Italian folklore. A council member at the prefecture of Venice, Bernoni was also a popular writer who began collecting proverbs, fairy tales, and folk songs in Venetian dialect in the 1860s and 1870s. His most important work is *Fiabe e novelli poplari veneziane* (1873), and the tales were gathered mainly from women. His work had a large influence on Vittorio Imbriani.

Indeed, it was not until Vittorio Imbriani (1840–1886) published his collection *La novellaja fiorentina* (1871) that Italian folklorists produced prose texts in dialects closer to the oral renditions. Imbriani, a professor of German literature in Naples who had studied in Switzerland and Germany, wrote down oral tales from Tuscan storytellers in shorthand, but he, too, was prone to making stylistic changes, as he did in his Milanese collection, *La novellaja milanese,* published the following year. Nevertheless, his tales are among the best representations of oral storytelling of this period since Imbriani was concerned with recapturing the "authentic" tone of his informants.

The same cannot be said for the texts of Rachel Harriet Busk (1831–1907), who translated her texts into English. Though she is not included in Crane's collection, she should be mentioned here because her accomplishments are remarkable. Born in London and educated privately by her father, the poet Hans Busk, she converted to the Catholic faith in 1858 and moved to Rome in 1862, where she worked as a journalist for the *Westminster Gazette.* Fluent in Spanish, French, German, and Italian, Busk began to collect folktales in Italy, Spain, and Austria during the 1860s. Strongly influenced by the Brothers Grimm and the mythological school of folklore, she took careful notes about her sources and background and context for her tales. Nevertheless, there are some indications that she censored many of her tales so as not to offend proper taste of her times. Her best work is in the field of Italian folklore: *The Folk-Lore of Rome* (1874), *The Valleys of Tirol* (1874), and *The Folk-Songs of Italy* (1887), which was a collaboration with Pitré.

While Busk was more like Crane, a mediator between the English-speaking world and Italian culture, the Italian folklorists were turning more toward the task of representing "authentic" Italian popular culture to an educated reading audience. Here Domenico Comparetti (1835–1927) played an important role in preserving Italian folklore. He was a professor of ancient Greek literature at the universities of Pisa, Florence, and

Rome and was regarded as one of the foremost pioneers of literary criticism and philology in Italy. Ahead of his times, Comparetti took an interdisciplinary approach to literature and had a profound knowledge of narrative theory, archaeology, classical philology, and history. His first important book was *Edipo e la mitologia comparata* (1867), in which he analyzed the Oedipus myth from a comparative perspective. He is best known, however, for his study *Virgilio nel medio-evo* (1872), which traced Virgil's history as a legendary figure back to Neopolitan folk origins. Comparetti was also one of the first scholars to write an exhaustive analysis of the contents and form of the *Kalevala* in 1890. Between 1870 and 1871 he edited a series entitled *Canti e racconti del popolo italiano* (Songs and stories of the Italian people), in which he published *Novelline popolari italiene* (1875), a book that Crane used. Though there are no annotations, this collection is valuable because it contains seventy folktales collected in dialect from different regions of Italy, and Comparetti translated them into standard Italian.

Another scholar, equally as important as Comparetti, was Gherardo Nerucci (1828–1906), a philologist, translator, and high school teacher from Pistoia. His major collection of tales was *Sessanta novelle popolari montalesi* (1880), and in his introduction to these tales from northern Tuscany, he notes that, when he had begun collecting tales in the fall of 1868, he had done so without writing down when and where he had heard them, and some of his early tales were actually taken from the collections of Imbriani and Comparetti. But during the next decade, he concentrated on collecting tales from the oral sources and started taking notes about his informants. Altogether he gathered fifty-eight texts, of which forty-eight were told by women. He translated them from the dialect and sought to develop (as did the Brothers Grimm) a unique folk style in order to replicate the mood and atmosphere of the oral storytelling. Nerucci was of the opinion that many of the oral tales had literary models as their sources, and in this respect he was one of the early folklorists who was interested in the interaction between the literary and oral traditions.

All the other important collectors represented in Crane's book— Giuseppe Morosi, 1844–1871 (*Studi sui Dialetti Greci della Terra d'Otranto*, 1870), Carolina Coronedi Berti, 1821–? (*Novelle popolari bolognesi*, 1874), Emilio Teza, 1831–1921 (*La Tradizione dei Sette Savi nelle novelline magiare di E. Teza*, 1874), Francesco Corazzini, 1832–c.1914 (*I Componimenti minori della letteratura popolare italiana nei principali dialetti o saggio di letteratura dialettale comparata*, 1877), Giovanni Papanti, 1830–1893

(*Novelline popolari livornesi*, 1877), Antonio Ive, 1851–1937 (*Fiabe popolari rovignesi*, 1878), and Isaia Visentini, 1843-? (*Fiabe Mantovane*, 1879)—paid great attention to the dialects in which the tales were told, often reproducing them in the vernacular with notes. Unfortunately, there is very little background material about their lives and working conditions.

This is, of course, not the case with Giuseppe Pitrè(1841–1916), the folklorist whose work and method Crane admired most and who left an indelible mark on Crane's concept for *Italian Popular Tales*. When Pitrè died in 1916, Crane wrote a moving obituary in which he compares Pitrè to the Brothers Grimm and points out an essential difference between them and the remarkable Italian doctor.

> But these [the Grimms] were essentially scholars and their lives were largely spent in the seclusion of their study. Besides, as wide as was the scope of their labors, it did not equal in extent the field cultivated by Pitrè, and after the "Kinder- und Hausmärchen" and the "Deutsche Sagen" the interests of the brothers became almost exclusively linguistic and lexicographical. Pitrè, on the other hand, was all his life a practicing physician, and took a prominent part in the civic affairs of Palermo, being Syndic, or Mayor, for many years. The Grimms were chiefly concerned with the tales and legends of Germany and its medieval literature: Pitrè throughout his long life devoted himself to every branch of folk-lore—popular tales, legends, songs, children's games, proverbs, riddles, customs, etc.—and collected himself an astounding mass of material, only a part of which is represented in the twenty-five volumes of the "Bibiloteca delle traditioni popolari sicilliane" (Palermo, 1871–1914).[6]

Pitrè began collecting proverbs and peculiar expressions of sailors as a young man while studying medicine at the University of Palermo. Since he came from a seafaring family, it was almost natural for him to occupy himself with sea-lore. What was extraordinary, however, was his rise from a humble family to become one of the most celebrated and prominent scholars in Sicily. Once he completed his university studies, he taught for a while at a high school and then abandoned teaching to pursue his profession as a doctor. At the same time, his interest in folklore grew, and he expanded his collecting to include popular tales, songs, customs, costumes, and artifacts. His three greatest accomplishments consisted of founding the journal *Archivio per lo studio delle tradizioni popolari*, which was begun in 1882 and lasted until 1907; establishing the massive series *Curiosità popolari tradizionali*, sixteen volumes of popular tales, songs, customs, and proverbs, which he edited from 1885 to 1890; and producing the *Biblioteca delle tradizioni popolari siciliane*, twenty-five volumes published between 1871 and 1914, comprising every branch of Sicilian folklore. For Crane the four volumes of folktales, *Fiabe, novelle e racconti popolari siciliani* (1875), in the *Biblioteca* are the most important source for his translations. Pitrè recorded most of the 300 narratives in dialect mainly from old women all over the island and provided background notes. The eighteenth volume of 1888 also contains 157 folktales and legends of the saints. Unlike most collectors, Pitrè, who had help from a daughter and dedicated assistants, refrained from making major stylistic changes in the tales he collected, and consequently they are often repetitious and monotonous. Nevertheless, they have a "raw" quality and historical value that still makes for interesting reading, and Crane's translations capture the simple meter and phraseology of the informants.

Pitrè was important for Crane not simply because of the enormous number of tales, songs, and proverbs that he collected, but because of his method and understanding of popular customs. As Crane noted in "The Diffusion of Popular Tales," published in the first issue of *The Journal of American Folk-Lore* in 1888, "the widespread interest in popular tales, which has produced within the last twenty-five years an amazing number of collections from all parts of the world, is not wholly due to their intrinsic worth, great though in some cases it may be (notably in the collections of the Grimms and of Asbjörnsen and Moe), but largely to the fact that they are supposed to possess a scientific value for the comparative mythologist, ethnologist, and student of comparative literature."[7] For Crane, the value of collecting, translating, and reproducing folktales lay in their "inter-nationalism," that is, in revealing to us how the peculiar narratives and customs of a particular society or group, no matter how unique, were somehow linked to many other cultures. Crane was an international humanist at heart, who saw the tales of the people as a means for bringing about greater understanding and respect of the common people and peoples throughout the world. He sought the universal in the particular, and his attraction to Pitrè and the great folklore scholarship of Europe reflected his desire to introduce European methods that could be applied to the understanding of Native American folklore in the United States. Here, too, he was a pioneer, although he seems to have withdrawn early from the ethnographical work that had begun in America. He never did any fieldwork and was more interested in European folklore and literature and seeking to grasp the cultural bonds between Europeans. Therefore, he was devastated when World War I erupted and wrote a letter to *The Nation* in which he decried the violence and intolerance that had arisen during the international conflict.[8] To the end of his life, he remained dedicated to international understanding through folklore. There is very little known about the latter part of his life except that he lived in Ithaca as a revered professor and kept working assiduously until his death.

His book *Italian Popular Tales,* unjustly neglected for over 115 years, was his major endeavor to bring together tales that he believed originated in the Orient and were diffused in unpredictable and marvelous ways through Italy down to his times. He played an important part in the nineteenth-century folklorist movement that sought to establish criteria for determining the origins, diffusion, and value of oral folktales. Like many scholars of his time, he sought to create the grounds for allowing the folk to speak and to present their "authentic" tales. The categories he established in *Italian Popular Tales* preceded Antti Aarne's *The Types of the Folktale* (1910), developed by the Finnish School at the beginning of the twentieth century, and are often imprecise and misleading. Nevertheless, Crane does foster a certain type of tale that Germans call the *Buchmärchen* (book tale) when describing the accomplishments of the Brothers Grimm. I prefer the term "literary folktale" rather than "book tale" because Crane and other important folklorists and collectors of the nineteenth century relied heavily on the oral tradition of tales that stemmed from a broad spectrum of people, and they transformed and translated the tales through various literary styles intended to evoke a rustic and natural atmosphere, as though one could hear the teller speak. They wanted in some way to remain "true" to the people or to their personal image of the folk and their heritage. These are the tales of different types that one can find in Crane's admirable translations in *Italian Popular Tales.*

Crane believed that these tales enriched not only Italian culture but civilization in general, and he modestly wanted to preserve them for future generations. The result is a collection of intriguing literary folktales that combine the efforts of both common people and sophisticated collectors. It is thanks to Crane's career as an uncanny folklorist that we can gain a sense of how Italian storytellers and their collectors of the nineteenth century endeavored to convey the wisdom and customs of their times that continue to speak to us in the present.

Works Consulted

Cocchiara, Giuseppe. *The History of Folklore in Europe.* Trans. John N. McDaniel. Philadelphia: Institute for the Study of Human Issues, 1981.

Crane, Thomas Frederick. "How I Became a Professor," *The Cornell Era* 41 (January, 1909): 149–158.

———. "Scholars and the War—Now and Then." *The Nation* 103 (1916): 107–108.

———. "The Diffusion of Popular Tales." *The Journal of American Folk-Lore* 1 (1888): 8–15.

———. "Giuseppe Pitrè and Sicilian Folk-Lore." *The Nation* 103 (1916): 234–236.

Schenda, Rudolf. *Folklore e Letteratura Popolare: Italia—Germania—Francia.* Trans. Maria Chiara Figliozzi and Ingeborg Walter. Rome: Istituto della Enciclopedia Italiana, 1986.

Notes

1. Thomas F. Crane, "How I Became a Professor," *The Cornell Era* 41 (January, 1909): 151–152.

2. *Ibid.*, 152.

3. *Ibid.*, 158

4. Thomas F. Crane, "Medieval Story-Books and Stories," in Rare and Manuscript Collections, Carl A. Kroch Library, Cornell University, 14/18/36.

5. Thomas F. Crane, *Italian Popular Tales* (Boston: Houghton, Mifflin, 1885): x.

6. Thomas F. Crane, "Giuseppe Pitrè and Sicilian Folk-Lore," *The Nation* 103 (1916): 234.

7. Thomas F. Crane, "The Diffusion of Popular Tales," *The Journal of American Folk-Lore* 1 (1888): 9.

8. Thomas F. Crane, "Scholars and the War—Now and Then," *The Nation* 103 (1916): 107–108.

ॐ

BIBLIOGRAPHY OF THE WRITINGS OF
THOMAS FREDERICK CRANE
Professor Emeritus
Romance Languages
Cornell University
1868–1924

In an article in *The Cornell Era*, January 1909, "How I became a Professor," I mentioned the fact of writing fiction while in college. Some of these youthful works were printed later. They are not entered in this Bibliography, but for the sake of completeness are mentioned in this note. "The Emerald Beetles" in *The Galaxy*, vol. I, pp. 589–599 (Aug. 1866). This was reprinted at about the same date in the Saturday issue of *The Albany Evening Journal*. "Aunt Maria and the Autophone," *Harper's Magazine*, vol. LXVII, July 1883, pp. 296–298, not signed. Reprinted with name in *Humorous Masterpieces from American Literature*, Edited by E. T. Mason, 3 vols. N. Y. and London, G. P. Putnam's Sons, 1886, vol. III, pp. 163–172. "Six of One and Half a Dozen of the Other," *Harper's Magazine*, vol. LXVIII, April, 1884, pp. 765–768, not signed.

1868

1   A. Helps, Spanish Conquest. 4 vols. New York. Harper & Bros. 1868.
      The Nation, Vol. VII, pp. 133–134. R.*

2   D. F. McCarthy, [Translations of Calderon]: Mysteries of Corpus Christi. From the Spanish. Dublin and London, 1867.—Circe; or Love the Greatest Enchantment. From the Spanish. London, 1861.
      The Nation, Vol. VII, pp. 233–234. R.

3   R. Major, Life of Prince Henry of Portugal, surnamed the Navigator, and its results. London, 1868.
      The Nation, Vol. VII, p. 534. N.

1870

4   A Day's Ride in Spain.
      The Cornell Era, pp. 49–50.

*The reviews in *The Nation* are not signed, and fall into two classes; longer notices or reviews, and notes or minor notices. These are designated by R(eviews) and N(otes).

1872

5   History of Spanish Literature. By George Ticknor. Fourth American edition.
    3 vols. Boston, 1872.
    The Nation, Vol. XIV, pp. 377–378. R.

1874

6   The Troubadours. By John Rutherford. London, 1873.
    The Nation, Vol. XVIII, pp. 107–108. R.

7   K. A. F. Mahn, Werke der Troubadours. Berlin, 1856–73.—H. Bischoff,
    Biographie des Troubadours: Bernhard von Ventadorn. Berlin, 1873.—P.
    Meyer, Recueil d'anciens Textes. Paris, 1874.—A. Stimming, Der Troubadour
    Jaufre Rudel sein Leben und seine Werke, Kiel. 1873.
    The Nation, Vol. XVIII, pp. 283–284. N.

8   A. Bartoli, I primi due Secoli della Letteratura italiana. Fasc. 1–10.
    The Nation, Vol. XVIII, pp. 332–333. N.

9   G. Papanti, Dante secondo la Tradizione e i Novellatori. Leghorn, 1873.
    The Nation, Vol. XVIII, p. 413. N.

10 A. Scheffer-Boichorst, Florentiner Studien. Leipzig, 1874.
    The Nation, Vol. XIX, p. 332. N.

11 F. Gregorovius, Lucrezia Borgia. Stuttgart, 1874.
    The Nation, Vol. XIX, p. 352. N.

12 A. Ebert, Geschichte der Literatur des Mittelalters im Abendlande. I.
    Leipzig, 1874,—Italia, vol. I.—Rivista di Filologia Romanza, vol. I.
    The Nation, Vol. XIX, pp. 399–400. N.

13 [Fifth Centenary of Petrarch's Death.]
    The Nation, Vol. XIX, p. 439. N.

1875

14 G. A. Scartazzini, Dante, Divina Commedia. Vol. I. Leipzig, 1874.—J. Jacob,
    Die Bedeutung der Führer Dante's in der Divina Comedia. Leipzig, 1874.—
    D'Ancona, I Precursori di Dante. Firenze, 1874.
    The Nation, Vol. XX, p. 26. N.

15 L. Geiger, Petrarch. Leipzig, 1874.
    The Nation, Vol. XX, p. 79. N.

16 Jahrbuch für romanische und englische Sprache und Literatur. N. F. Band II,
    Heft 1, 1875.
    The Nation, Vol. XX, p. 97. N.

17 A. von Reumont, Lorenzo de' Medici il Magnifico. Leipzig, 1874.
    The Nation, Vol. XX, p. 97. N.

18 Italia, II.
    The Nation, Vol. XX, p. 152. N.

19 A. Brachet, Morceaux choisis des grands Ecrivains du XVIe siècle. Paris,
    1875.—Early French Text Society.
    The Nation, Vol. XX, p. 174. N.

20 [Spanish Reformers] E. Boehmer, Bibliotheca Wiffeniana. 1874.
    The Nation, Vol. XX, pp. 192–193. R.

21 J. L. Klein, Geschichte des Dramas. 11 vols. Leipzig, 1865–1875.
    The Nation, Vol. XX, p. 224. N.

22 Henri de Bornier, La Fille de Roland. Paris, [1875].
    The Nation, Vol. XX, p. 260. N.

23 [Appearances of the Virgin in Elsass.]
    The Nation, Vol. XX, p. 276. N.

24 A. Mussafia, Ein Betrag zur Kunde der norditalienischen Mundarten im XV.
    Jahrhundert. Vienna, 1873.—Ueber eine altveronesichen Version der Katharin-
    enlegende. 1874.—Ueber die provenzalischen Liederhandschriften des Gio-
    vanni Maria Barbieri. 1874.—Fünf neue in einer Handschrift der Wiener
    Hofbibliothek aufgefundene Sonette. 1874.—La Curne de Sainte-Pelaye, Dic-
    tionnaire historique de l'ancien language françois, ou Glossaire de la langue
    françoise depuis son origine jusqu'au siècle de Louis XIV. Vol. I. Paris, 1875.
    The Nation, Vol. XX, p. 295. N.

25 A. Mussafia, Zur Katharinenlegende; and the Provençal MS. of Barbieri.
    Vienna, 1875.
    The Nation, Vol. XX, p. 315. N.

26 M. Landau, Beiträge zur Geschichte der Italienischen Novelle. Vienna, 1875.
    The Nation, Vol. XX, p. 347. N.

27 Modern Latin Poetry in the Rivista Europea.
    The Nation, Vol. XX, p. 348. N.

28 Prospectus of Sainte-Pelaye's Dictionnaire Historique.
    The Nation, Vol. XX, p. 397. N.

29 A. Cantù, Commento storico ai Promessi Sposi. Milano, 1874.
    The Nation, Vol. XX, p. 397. N.

30 G. Garducci, Studi Litterari. Leghorn, 1874.
    The Nation, Vol. XX, p. 425. N.

31 An inedited Sonnet of Michael Angelo.
    The Nation, Vol. XXI, p. 28. N.

32 Gino Capponi, storia della Republica di Firenze. 2 vols. Firenze, 1875.
    The Nation, Vol. XXI, p. 42. N.

33 Rivista di Filologia Romanza II, 1, 1875.
    The Nation, Vol. XXI, p. 73. N.

34 G. Pitrè, Biblioteca delle Tradizioni Popolari Siciliane, I-VII. Palermo,
    1871–1875.
    The Nation, Vol. XXI, p. 103. N.

35 C. Tomlinson, The Sonnet. London, 1874.
    The Nation, Vol. XXI, p. 138. N.

36 Rivista di Filologia Romanza, II, 2, 1875.
    The Nation, Vol. XXI, p. 181. N.

37 John Addington Symonds, Renaissance in Italy, Age of the Despots. London,
    1875.
    The Nation, Vol. XXI, p. 249. R.

38 P. Fanfani, Dino Compagni vendicato dalla Calumnia di Scrittore della Cron-
    ica. Milan, 1875.—O. Hartwig, Quellen und Forschungen zur ältesten
    Geschichte der Stadt Florenz. Marburg, 1875.
    The Nation, Vol. XXI, pp. 372–373. N.

39 Calderon, Autos Sacramentales.
    The Catholic World, Vol. XXI, pp. 32–40; 213–222.

40 The Roman Campagna.
    The New York Tribune.

41 Norse Mythology.
    Lippincott's Magazine, Vol. XVI, pp. 646–648.

42 F. Gregorovius, Lucrezia Borgia. 2 vols. Stuttgart, 1874.
    The North American Review, Vol. CXXI, pp. 229–234.

43 Gino Capponi, Storia della Republica di Firenze. 2 vols. Firenze, 1875.
    The North American Review, Vol. CXXI, pp. 450–456.

44 Adolf Ebert, Allgemeine Geschichte der Literatur des Mittelalters im Abendlande. I. Leipzig, 1874.
    The North American Review, Vol. CXXI, pp. 457–461.

1876

45 L. Bruyere, Contes Populaires de la Grande Bretagne. Paris, 1875.
    The Nation, Vol. XXII, pp. 47–48. N.

46 G. Paris, Le Petit Poucet et la Grande Ourse. Paris, 1875.
    The Nation, Vol. XXII, p. 48. N.

47 Rivista Europea. Dec. 1875.
    The Nation, Vol. XXII, p. 64. N.

48 D. Comparetti, Virgilio nel Medio Evo. Firenze, 1872.
    The Nation, Vol. XXII, p. 147. N.

49 A. von Reumont, Geschichte Toscana's seit dem Ende des florentinischen Freistaates. Gotha, 1876.
    The Nation, Vol. XXII, p. 147. N.

50 Romania. Nos. 15–17.
    The Nation, Vol. XXII, p. 195. N.

51 Jahrbuch für Romanische und Englische Literatur. N. F. vols. II-III, 1875–6.
    The Nation, Vol. XXII, p. 211. N.

52 T. Tasso, Gerusalemme Liberata, Cantos, 1.2. Edited by H. B. Cotterill. London, 1875.
    The Nation, Vol. XXII, p. 229. N.

53 W. Lang, Transalpinische Studien. Leipzig, 1875.
    The Nation, Vol. XXII, p. 386. R.

54 J. L. Klein, Geschichte des Dramas, XIV. Leipzig, 1876.
    The Nation, Vol. XXIII, pp. 258–9. N.

55 A. De Gubernatis, Matériaux pour server à l'histoire des Etudes orientales en Italie. Paris, 1876.
    The Nation, Vol. XXIII, p. 301. N.

56 T. Benfey, Kalilag und Damnaj. Alte syrische Uebersetzung des Indischen Fürstenspiegels. Leipzig, 1876.
    The Nation, Vol. XXIII, p. 314. N.

57 [Appearances of the Virgin in Elsass].
    The Nation, Vol. XXIII, pp. 315–6. N.

58 C. Faccioli, Enoc Arden, Idilli, Liriche, Miti e Leggende di Alfredo Tennyson. Verona, 1876.
    The Nation, Vol. XXIII, p. 315. N.

59 Old French Text Society. Chansons du XVe siècle, editeur G. Paris. Paris, 1876.—Les plus anciens Monuments de la Langue française (IXe, Xe siècle). ed. A. Gevaert, Paris, 1876.
    The Nation, Vol. XXIII, p. 384. N.

60 G. D. Rossetti, Dante and his Circle. Boston, 1876.
    Lippincott's Magazine, Vol. XVII, pp. 262–263.

61 Lucrezia Borgia.
    Harper's Magazine, Vol. LII, pp. 498–502.

62 A. von Reumont, Lorenzo de' Medici il Magnifico, 2 vols. Leipzig, 1874.
    North American Review, vol. CXXII, pp. 437–446.

63 A Nursery Tale.
    The Cornell Era, May, 1876.

64 Italian Popular Tales. L. Gonzenbach, Sicilianische Märchen. 2 vols. Leipzig, 1870.—G. Pitrè, Biblioteca delle tradizioni popolari siciliane. IV-VII. Palermo, 1875.—R. H. Busk, The Folk Lore of Rome. London, 1874.—A. De Gubernatis, Le Novelline de Santo Stefano. Torino, 1869.—T. Gradi, La Vigilia di Pasqua di Ceppo. Torino, 1860.—T. Gradi, Saggio di letture varie per igiovani. Torino, 1865.—C. Coronedi-Berti, Novelle popolari bolognese. Bologna, 1874.—G. Bernoni, Fiabe fantastiche popolari veneziane. Venezia, 1875.—C. Scheller, Märchen und Sagen aus Wälschtirol. Innsbruck, 1867.—D. Comparetti ed A. D'Ancona, Canti e racconti del popolo italiano. Novelline popolari italiane. Torino, 1874, etc.
    North American Review, Vol. CXXIII, pp. 25–60. Translated in *Giornale di Sicilia*, Palermo, Aug.–Oct., 1877.

65 Sicilian Folk-Lore.
    Lippincott's Magazine, October, 1876. pp. 433–443. Translated in *Nuove Effemeridi Siciliane*, Palermo, 1877.

1877

66 A. Mussafia, Die catalanische mertische Version der sieben weisen Meister. Vienna, 1875.
    The Nation, Vol. XXIV, p. 14. N.

67 Italia, III.
    The Nation, Vol. XXIV, p. 118. R.

68 Miss H. W. Preston, The Troubadours and Trouvères. Boston, 1876.
    The Nation, Vol. XXIV, pp. 118–119. R.

69 Rivista di Filologia Romanza, II, 3.
    The Nation, Vol. XXIV, p. 164. N.

70 K. Witte, Dante's Vita Nuova. Leipzig, 1876.
    The Nation, Vol. XXIV, pp. 177–178. N.

71 W. R. S. Ralston, Russian Folk-Tales. New York, [1877].
    The Nation, Vol. XXIV, p. 182. R.

72 Old French Text Society. Brun de la Montagne, ed. P. Meyer. Paris, 1875.
    The Nation, Vol. XXIV, p. 195. N.

73 H. C. Prime, Holy Cross. New York, 1877.
    The Nation, Vol. XXIV, p. 240. R.

74 Mélusine, I, 1–6.
    The Nation, Vol. XXIV, p. 265. N.

75 N. B. Dennys, The Folk-Lore of China. London, 1876.
    The Nation, Vol. XXIV, p. 270. R.

76 Rivista di Literatura popolare, I, 1.
    The Nation, Vol. XXIV, p. 265. N.

77 A. Bartoli, I Precursori del Boccaccio e alcune delle sue Fonti. Firenze, 1876.
    The Nation, Vol. XXIV, pp. 265–6. N.

78 P. Rajna, Le fonti dell' Orlando Furioso. Firenze, 1876.
    The Nation, Vol. XXIV, p. 266. N.

79 Fernan Caballero.
    The Nation, Vol. XXIV, p. 339. N.

80 Zeitschrift für romanische Philologie, I, 1, 1877.
    The Nation, Vol. XXIV, p. 367. N.

81 W. Webster, Basque Legends. London, 1877.
    The Nation, Vol. XXV, p. 15. R.

82 V. Imbriani, La Novellaja Fiorentina. Livorno, 1877.
    The Nation, Vol. XXV, p. 26. N.

83 A. von Reumont, Geschichte Toscana's unter dem Hause Lothringen-Habs-
    burg, 1737–1859. Gotha, 1877.
    The Nation, Vol. XXV, p. 27. N.

84 P. Meyer, Recueil d'anciens texts, II. Paris, 1877.
    The Nation, Vol. XXV, pp. 41–2. N.

85 M. Landau, Giovanni Boccaccio, sein Leben und seine Werke. Stuttgart, 1877.
    The Nation, Vol. XXV, p. 42. N.

86 Per le Nozze Pirè-Vitrano. Palermo, 1877.
    The Nation, Vol. XXV, p. 91. N.

87 Romania No. 22.
    The Nation, Vol. XXV, p. 169. N.

88 Mrs. Oliphant, Dante. Philadelphia, 1877.
    The Nation, Vol. XXV, p. 354. R.

89 Romania No. 23.
    The Nation, Vol. XXV, p. 366. N.

90 Zeitschrift für romanische Philologie, I, 2–3.
    The Nation, Vol. XXV, p. 381. N.

91 [Galileo's Trial.]
    The Nation, Vol. XXVI, p. 43. N.

92 Mélusine, I.
    The Nation, Vol. XXVI, p. 79. N.

93 P. Villari, Machiavelli e i suoi tempi, I. Firenze, 1877.
    The Nation, Vol. XXVI, p. 98. N.

94 Old French Text Society, II. Miracles de Nostre Dame, ed., G. Paris et V.
    Robert, I. Paris, 1876.—Guillaume de Palerne, ed., H. Michelant. Paris, 1876.—
    Deux Rédactions du Roman des Sept Sages de Rome, ed. G. Paris. Paris, 1876.
    The Nation, Vol. XXVI p. 309. N.

95 Romania, No. 24, and Zeitschrift für Romanische Philologie, VI.
    The Nation, Vol. XXVI, p. 135. N.

96 Jahrbuch der deutschen Dante Gesellschaft, IV, 1877.
    The Nation, Vol. XXVI, p. 243. N.

97   C. Lenient, La Satire en France au Moyen Âge. Paris, 1877.
       The Nation, Vol. XXVI, p. 425. R.

98   Fernan Caballero, Cuentos, Oraciones, Adivinas y Refranes populares e infan-
       tiles. Leipzig, 1878.
       The Nation, Vol. XXVII, p. 26. N.

99   H. Breymann, Friederich Diez, sein Leben, seine Werke und deren Bedeu-
       tung für die Wissenschaft. Munich, 1878.
       The Nation, Vol. XXVII, p. 70. N.

100   Giornale di Filologia Romanza I, 1.
       The Nation, Vol. XXVII, p. 71. N.

101   J. Burckhardt, Die Kultur der Renaissance in Italien, 3d ed. I. Leipzig, 1877.
       The Nation, Vol. XXVII, p. 99. N.

102   A. Bartoli, I Precursori del Rinascimento. Firenze, 1877.
       The Nation, Vol. XXVII, p. 99. N.

103   F. Hueffer, The Troubadours. London, 1878.
       The Nation, Vol. XXVII, p. 103. R.

104   M. Gisi, Der Troubadour Guillem Anelier von Toulouse. Solothurn, 1877.
       The Nation, Vol. XXVII, p. 131. N.

105   A. D'Ancona, La Poesia popolare italiana. Livorno, 1878.—E. Rubieri, Storia
       della poesia popolare italiana. Firenze, 1877.—A. Ive, Canti popolari. Torino,
       1877.—S. A. Guastella, Canti populari. Modica, 1876.
       The Nation, Vol. XXVII, pp. 178–9. N.

106   F. Corazzini, Componimenti minori della litteratura popolare italiana nei
       pricipali dialetti. Benevento, 1877.
       The Nation, Vol. XXVII, p. 286. N.

107   A. Birch-Hirschfeld, Ueber die den provenzalischen Troubadours del XII,
       und XIII. Jahrhunderts bekannten epischen Stoffe. Halle, 1878.
       The Nation, Vol. XXVII, p. 335. N.

108   A. D'Ancona, Origini del Teatro in Italia. 2 vols. Firenze, 1877.
       The North American Review, Vol. CXXVII, pp. 169–171.

109   P. Villari, Niccolò Machiavelli e i suoi tempi. Firenze, 1877.
       The North American Review, Vol. CXXVII, pp. 337–339.

110   A. D'Ancona, La poesia popolare italiana. Livorno, 1878.
       The North American Review, Vol. CXXVII, pp. 515–518.

111   Mélusine, I, 1878.
       The North American Review, Vol. CXXVII, pp. 518–520.

112   F. Hueffer, The Troubadours. London, 1878.
       The North American Review, Vol. CXXVII, pp. 520–521.

113   Italian Fairy Tales.
       St. Nicholas, Dec. 1878, pp. 101–107.

114   G. Pitrè, Popular Marriage Customs. [Translated by T. F. Crane.]
       Lippincott's Magazine, Vol. XXII, pp. 89–96.

115   A Spanish Story Teller: Antonio de Trueba.
       Lippincott Magazine, Vol. XXII, pp. 730–738.

116   The Style is the Man; a Story from the Spanish of Don Antonio de Trueba.
       Cornell Review, November and December, 1878.

1879

117 Poggio Bracciolini, Les Facéties de Pogge. Lisieux and Paris, 1878.
The Nation, Vol. XXVIII, p. 53. N.

118 A. De Gubernatis, La Mythologie des Plantes ou les Légendes du Règne Végétal. Paris, 1871.
The Nation, Vol. XXVIII, p. 85. N.

119 A. D'Ancona, Origini del Teatro in Italia. 2 vols. Firenze, 1877.
The Nation, Vol. XXVIII, p. 268. N.

120 M. Sepet, Le Drame chrétien au Moeyn-Age. Paris, 1878.
The Nation, Vol. XXVIII, p. 268. N.

121 R. W. Church, Dante: An Essay. To which is added a translation of De Monarchia by F. G. Church. London and New York, 1878.
The Nation, Vol. XXVIII, pp. 340–341. R.

122 K. Hegel, Ueber den historischen Werth der älteren Dante-Commentare. Leipzig, 1878.
The Nation, Vol. XXVIII, p. 406. N.

123 A. Bartoli, Caratteri Fondimentali della Letteratura Italiana. Firenze, 1879.
The Nation, Vol. XXVIII, p. 436. N.

124 Rivista di Letteratura Popolare, I.
The Nation, Vol. XXIX, p. 28. N.

125 V. Balaguer, Historia Politica y Literaria de los Trovadores, I-II. Madrid, 1878–79.
The Nation, Vol. XXIX, p. 97. N.

126 J. L. Whitney, Catalogue of the Spanish Library and of the Portuguese Books bequeathed by George Ticknor to the Boston Public Library. Boston, 1879.
The Nation, Vol. XXIX, p. 116. R.

127 F. Baethgen, Sindban, oder die Sieben Weisen Meister, Syrisch und Deutsch. Leipzig, 1878.
The Nation, Vol. XXIX, p. 227. N.

128 Mediaeval French Literature. Ch. Aubertin, Histoire de la Langue et de la Littérature française au Moyen-Âge. 2 vols. Paris, 1876–78.—L. Gautier, Les Epopées françaises. 2 ième Ed., I. Paris, 1878.—M. Sepet, Le Drame Chrétien au Moyen-Âge. Paris, 1878.—Société des anciens Textes français. Guillaume de Palerne, 1876; Les Sept Sages de Rome, 1876; Miracles de Nostre Dame, I–II, 1876–77; Aiol, 1877.
The North American Review, Vol. CXXVIII, pp. 213–220.

129 Basque Legends.
International Review, Vol. VI, pp. 386–404.

1880

130 E. J. Hasell, Calderon. Philadelphia, 1879.
The Nation, Vol. XXX, p. 104. R.

131 A. Graf, La Leggenda del Paradiso Terrestre. Torino, 1878.
The Nation, Vol. XXX, p. 119. N.

132 South African Folk-Lore Society Journal, Parts 1–5.
The Nation, Vol. XXX, p. 154. N.

133 A. De Gubernatis, Alessandro Manzoni: Studio biografico. Firenze, 1879.

The Nation, Vol. XXX, p. 156. N.

134 J. Brander Matthews, Comedies for Amateur Acting. New York, 1880.
The Nation, Vol. XXX, p. 201. N.

135 Sir G. W. Cox and E. H. Jones, Popular romances of the Middle Ages. New York, 1880.
The Nation, Vol. XXX, p. 478. R.

136 R. Reinsch, Die Pseudo-Evangelien von Jesu und Maria's Kindheit in der romanischen und germanischen Literatur. Halle, 1879.
The Nation, Vol. XXXI, p. 61. N.

137 [Recent Collections of Italian Popular Tales]. G. Nerucci, Sessanta novelle popolari Montalesi. Firenze, 1880.—Tuscan Fairy Tales, taken down from the Mouths of the People. London, 1880.
The Nation, Vol. XXXI, p. 63. N.

138 A. Bartoli, I primi due secoli della letteratura italiana. Milano, 1880.
The Nation, Vol. XXXI, p. 154. N.

139 R. C. Trench, Essay on the Life and Genius of Calderon. London, 1880.
The Nation, Vol. XXXI, p. 157. N.

140 A. De Gubernatis, Il Manzoni ed il Fauriel studiati nel loro carteggio inedito. Roma, 1880.
The Nation, Vol. XXXI, p. 188. N.

141 A. Ebert, Allgemeine Geschichte der Literatur des Mittelalters im Abendlande, II. Leipzig, 1880.
The Nation, Vol. XXXI, p. 255. N.

142 G. Pitrè, Biblioteca delle tradizoni popolari siciliane. VIII–XI. Palermo, 1880.
The Nation, Vol. XXXI, p. 411. N.

143 The Lovers of Provence. Aucassin et Nicolette. [Translation by] A. R. Macdonough. New York, 1880.
The Nation, Vol. XXXI, p. 432.

144 H. Cruel, Geschichte der deutschen Predigt im Mittelalter. Detmold, 1870.
The Nation, Vol. XXXI, p. 464. N.

145 G. Saintsbury, Primer of French Literature. New York, 1880.
The Nation, Vol. XXXI, pp. 468–9. R.

146 An Episcode of Spanish Chivalry.
Lippincott's Magazine, Vol. XXVII, pp. 747–755.

147 Italian Popular Poetry.
International Review, Vol. IX, pp. 155–170.

148 Recent European Publications. A. De Gubernatis, Il Manzoni e il Fauriel studiati nel loro carteggio. Roma, 1880.—R. C. Trench, An Essay on the Life and Genius of Calderon. 2d Ed. London, 1880.—K. Hase, Miracle Plays and Sacred Dramas. London and Boston, 1880.—The Purgatory of Dante Alighieri. Edited with Translation and notes by A. G. Butler. London, 1880.
The North American Review, Vol. CXXXI, pp. 457–463.

1881

149 L. Gautier, Epopées Françaises. 2d Ed. III. Paris, 1880.
The Nation, Vol. XXXII, p. 29. N.

150 G. Milchsack, Die Oster-und Passionspiele. Wolfenbüttel, 1880.

The Nation, Vol. XXXII, p. 29. N.

151 A. D'Ancona, Studj di Critica e Storia letteraria. Bologna, 1880.
The Nation, Vol. XXXII, p. 133. N.

152 Mrs. Oliphant, Cervantes. Philadelphia, 1881.
The Nation, Vol. XXXII, p. 193. R.

153 G. Paris, Le Juif Errant. Paris, 1880.
The Nation, Vol. XXXII, p. 221. N.

154 C. N. Caix, Le Origini della lingua poetica italiana. Firenze, 1880.
The Nation, Vol. XXXII, p. 261. N.

155 W. Kaden, Unter den Olivenbäume. Leipzig, 1880.
The Nation, Vol. XXXII, p. 351. N.

156 P. Villari, Niccolò Machiavelli e i suoi Tempi. II. Firenze, 1881.
The Nation, Vol. XXXII, pp. 352–3. N.

157 K. Vollmöller, Ein Spanisches Steinbuch. Heilbronn, 1880.
The Nation, Vol. XXXII, p. 390. N.

158 F. Castets, Historia Karoli Magni et Rotholandi. Paris, 1880.
The Nation, Vol. XXXII, p. 408. N.

159 M. A. Chassang, New Etymological French Grammar. Paris and London, 1881.
The Nation, Vol. XXXII, p. 425. N.

160 S. Prato, Quattro novelline popolari. Spoleto, 1880.
The Nation, Vol. XXXII, p. 443. N.

161 G. Pitrè, Spettacoli e Feste. Biblioteca delle Tradizioni Popolari Siciliane, XII, Palermo, 1881.
The Nation, Vol. XXXII, p. 460. N.

162 G. Biagi, Le Novelle Anitche. Firenze, 1880.
The Nation, Vol. XXXIII, p. 10. N.

163 G. Finamore, Vocabolario dell' Uso Abruzzese. Lanciano, 1880.
The Nation, Vol. XXXIII, p. 35. N.

164 S. Solomone-Marino, Leggende popolari siciliane in poesia. Palermo, 1880.
The Nation, Vol. XXXIII, p. 118. N.

165 Plantation Folk-Lore. Review of Joel Chandler Harris's Uncle Remus.
Popular Science Monthly, Vol. XVIII, pp. 824–833.

1882

166 E. Monaci, Facsimili di antichi manoscritti per uso delle scuole di filologia neolatina. Fasc. 1. Roma, 1882.
The Nation, Vol. XXXIV, p. 298. N.

167 Les Littératures Populaires de Toutes les Nations, I–V, Paris, (1881).
The Nation, Vol. XXXIV, p. 402. N.

168 G. Finamore, Tradizioni popolari Abruzzese. Lanciano, 1882.
The Nation, Vol. XXXIV, p. 423. N.

169 F. Metcalfe, Passio et Miracula Beati Olaui. Oxford, 1881.
The Nation, Vol. XXXIV, p. 425. N.

170 Archivio per lo Studio delle Tradizioni Popolari, I. 1. 1882.
The Nation, Vol. XXXIV, p. 465. N.

171 Romanische Forschungen, I. 1–2.
The Nation, Vol. XXXV, p. 54. N.

172   E. Stengel, Ausgaben und Abhandlungen aus dem Gebiete der romanischen Philologie, I–III. Marburg, 1881–2.
      The Nation, Vol. XXXV, p. 54. N.

173   F. A. von Schiefner, Tibetan Tales derived from Indian Sources. [Translated by] W. R. S. Ralston. Boston, 1882.
      The Nation, Vol. XXXV, p. 227. R.

174   The Legendary Dante.
      The Cornell Review, Vol. IX, pp. 189–200.

175   Denis Florence MacCarthy.
      The Catholic World, August, 1882, pp. 659–677.

176   A Roumanian Folk-Tale.
      The Cornell Era, Vol. XV, pp. 75–77.

1883

177   A. De Gubernatis, La Mythologie des Plantes, II. Paris, 1882.
      The Nation, Vol. XXXVI, p. 363. N.

178   W. W. Newell, Games and Songs of American Children. New York, 1883.
      The Nation, Vol. XXXVI, p. 495. R. (Also printed in *The* [New York] *Evening Post*, June 7.)

179   A. De Gubernatis, Storia universale della Letteratura, I–II. Milano, 1883.
      The Nation, Vol. XXXVII, p. 57. N.

180   M. N. Cantù, Alessandro Manzoni; riminiscenze. 2 vols. Milano, 1882.
      The Nation, Vol. XXXVII, p. 142. N.

181   Mediaevel Sermon-Books and Stories. Read before the American Philosophical Society, March 16, 1883. Printed in the Proceedings of the American Philosophical Society. XXI, 114, pp. 49–78.
      Rev. by E. Stengel in *Literaturblatt f. germ. u. roman. Philol.*, Dec., 1883, iv, 12, 481–3; by Philipp Strauch in *Zs. f. deutsches Alterthum*, xxviii. Anzeiger, x., pp. 286–8; in *Giornale Storico della Letteratura Italiana*, 1884, iv, 269–71; in *Romania*, 1883, xii, 416; by H. Gaidoz in *Mélusine*, Nov. 20, 1885, ii, 538.

182   A Celebrated Poison, Acqua Tofana.
      The [New York] *Evening Post*, May 16, 1883.

1884

183   John Addington Symonds, Wine, Women, and Song. New York, 1884.
      The Nation, Vol. XXXIX, p. 530. R.

184   Tableaux de la Révolution Française. An Historical French Reader. Edited with Notes by T. F. Crane, A. M., and S. J. Brun, B. S. With an Introduction by Andrew D. White, LL. D. G. P. Putnam's Sons. New York, 1884. 16 mo. pp. XV, 311. A sixth edition was published in 1892, an eighth impression in 1900, and a ninth revised edition in 1907.

1885

185   The University Library.
      The [New York] *Evening Post*.

186   Sicilian Proverbs.
      Lippincott's Magazine, Vol. XXXV (N. S. IX), pp. 309–313.

187   W. F. Shaw, The Preacher's Promptuary of Anecdote. London, 1885.
      The Academy, April 11, pp. 255–6.

188 Two Mediaeval Folk-Tales.
Germania, XVIII, N. F., pp. 203–205.

189 Italian Popular Tales. Boston, Houghton, Mifflin and Co. (London, Macmillan and Co.) 8vo, pp. XXXIV, 389. Written February to September, 1880. Went to press June, 1885. Published November 14, 1885.
Rev. in *The Hartford Courant,* Nov. 21, 1885; by S. A. U. in *The Index* (Boston), Nov. 26, 1885, in *The Boston Daily Advertiser,* Nov. 27, 1885; in *The Worcester Daily Spy,* Nov. 28, 1885; in *The* [New York] *Evening Post,* Nov. 30, 1885 (same in *The Nation,* Nov. 26, 1885, xli, 451–2); in *The New York Commercial,* Dec. 1, 1885; in *The New York Christian Advocate,* Dec. 3, 1885, lx, 785; in *The Christian Union,* Dec. 24, xxxii, 1885, 26–30; in *The Independent,* Dec. 31, 1885, xxxvii, 1713; in *The New York Times,* reprinted in *The Literary News,* Jan., 1886, pp. 11–12; in *The Dial,* Jan., 1886, vi, 256; in *The Literary News,* Christmas Number, 1885; in *The* [Cincinnati] *Graphic,* Jan. 23, 1886; in *The Critic,* Jan. 16, 1886, viii, 29–30; in *The Literary World,* Jan. 23, 1886, xvii, 24; by Margaret J. Preston in *The Home Journal,* March 10, 1886; in *The Atlantic Monthly,* March, 1886, lvii, 431; by [Eugene Schuyler] in same, pp. 419–23; in *De Portefeuille* (Amsterdam), March 6, 1886; in *The British Quarterly Rev.,* Jan., 1886, lxxxiii, 207–8; in *The Folk-Lore Journal,* Jan.–March, 1886, iv, 89–94; by W. R. S. Ralston in *The Academy,* Jan. 9, 1886, xxix, 21–2; [by W. R. S. R.] in *The Athenaeum,* Feb. 13, 1886, p. 226; in *Galignani's Messenger,* Paris, Feb. 22, 1886 (the first two paragraphs lifted from the *Athenaeum* review!); in *The Spectator,* June 5, 1886, lix, 760; in *The Saturday Rev.,* March 27, 1886, lxi, 452–3; in *The Washington Rev.,* Apr., 1886, cxxv, 590; by Theodore Stanton in *The American Register* (Paris), Dec. 4, 1886; in *The Guardian,* Aug. 4, 1886; by A. D'Ancona in *Fanfulla della Domenica,* Rome, Jan. 10, 1886; by G. Pitrè in *Archivo per le Tradizioni Popolari,* 1886, iv, 606–8; by Felix Liebrecht in *Literaturblatt f. german. u. roman. Philol.,* July, 1886, vii, 291–2; by H. G. [aidoz] in *Mélusine,* June 6, 1886, iii, 144; by Reinhold Köhler in *Literarisches Centralblatt,* Apr. 23, 1887, xxxviii, 580–1; in *Ethnologische Mitteilungen aus Ungarn,* Budapest, June 1, 1887; by Robert Lee Vance in *The Critic,* Jan. 14, 1888, xii, 13–14.

1886

190 Isabel F. Hapgood, Epic Songs of Russia. New York, 1886.—Countess Evelyn Martinengo-Caesaresco, Essays in the Study of Folk-Songs. New York, 1886.
The Nation, Vol. XLII, p. 494. R.

191 Some Forgotten Italian Story-Tellers.
The Academy, Jan. 20, pp. 78–79.

192 Liber de Abundantia Exemplorum.
The Academy, Feb. 20, p. 133.

193 The Death of Pope Alexander VI.
Harper's Magazine, Vol. LXXIII, pp. 120–125.

194 M. Monteiro, Legends and Popular Tales of the Basque People. New York, 1887.
The Nation, Vol. XL, p. 195. R.

195 E. J. W. Gibbs, History of the Forty Vezirs. London and New York, 1886.

The Nation, Vol. XLIV, p. 324. R.

196 W. A. Clouston, Popular Tales and Fictions. 2 vols. London and New York, 1887.
The Nation, Vol. XLV, p. 15. R.

197 A. De Nino, Ovidio nella Tradizione Popolare di Sulmona. Casalbordino, 1886.
The Nation, Vol. XLV, p. 54. N.

198 Lady Wilde, Ancient Legends, etc. of Ireland. 2 vols. Boston, 1887.
The Nation, Vol. XLV, p. 99. R.

199 A. C. Arawiyeh, Tales of the Caliph. London, 1887.
The Nation, Vol. XLV, p. 99. N.

200 A. De Nino, Sacre Leggende Abruzzesi. 2 vols. Firenze, 1887.
The Nation, Vol. XLV, p. 174. N.

201 C. P. Caspari, Eine Augustin fälschlich beteilegte Homilia de Sacrilegiis. Christiania, 1886.
The Nation, Vol. XLV, p. 235. N.

202 Annuaire de la Société des Traditions Populaires, 1887.
The Nation, Vol. XLV, p. 419. N.

203 Zeitschrift für vergleichende Litteraturgeschichte I, (1886–7).
The Nation, Vol. XLV, p. 527. N.

204 French Folk-Tales. E. Cosquin, Contes populaires de Lorraine. 2 vols. Paris, 1886.
Modern Language Notes, II, 1887, pp. 174–181.

205 Le Romantisme Français. A Selection from Writers of the French Romantic School, 1824–1848. By Thomas Frederick Crane, A. M. 16 mo., pp. xlvii, 362. New York, G. P. Putnam's Sons, 1887. a fifth revised edition was issued in 1907. Rev. by Melville B. Anderson in *The Dial*, Feb., 1887, vii, 252; in *The Critic*, March 26, 1887, N. S. vii, 150–51; in *The Literary World*, Apr. 16, 1887, xviii, 119; in *The Saturday Rev.*, Apr. 2, 1887, lxiii, 494; [by F. Bôcher] in *The Nation*, Apr. 28, 1887, xliv, 371; in *The Academy*, May 28, 1887, xxxi, 377.

1888

206 A. Lang, Myth, Ritual and Religion. 2 vols. London and New York, 1887.
The Nation, Vol. XLVI, pp. 36–37. R.

207 Alma Strettell, Spanish and Italian Folk-Songs. London and New York, 1887.
The Nation, Vol. XLVI, p. 220. R. (Also in *Semi-Weekly Post*, April 3.)

208 A. Lang, Perrault's Popular Tales. Oxford, 1888.—The Most Pleasant and Delectable Tale of the Marriage of Cupid and Psyche. Done in English by William Addington of University College in Oxford. London, 1887.
The Nation, Vol. XLVI, pp. 347–348. R.

209 A. Ebert, Allgemeine Geschichte der Literatur des Mittelalters im Abend-lande. 3 vols. Leipzig, 1874–1887.
The Nation, Vol. XLVI, pp. 412–413. R.

210 G. Pitrè, Biblioteca delle Tradizioni popolari siciliani, XVIII.
The Nation, Vol. XLVI, p. 430. N.

211 Catalan Folk-Lore. Pau Bertran y Bros, Rondallistica: Estudi de Leteratura Popular ab mostres catalanes inédites. Barcelona, 1888.

The Nation, Vol. XLVI, p. 500. N.

212 The Diffusion of Popular Tales.
Journal of American Folk-Lore, Vol. I, pp. 8–15.

213 Annuaire des traditions populaires. Paris, 1887.
Journal of American Folk-Lore, Vol. I, p. 87.

214 W. A. Clouston, Popular Tales and Fictions: Their Migrations and Transformations. 2 vols. London and New York, 1887.
Journal of American Folk-Lore, Vol. I, pp. 87–88.

215 C. Perrault, Popular Tales. Edited from the Original Editions, with Introduction, etc., by A. Lang. Oxford, 1888.
Journal of American Folk-Lore, Vol. I, p. 88.

216 The Most Pleasant and Delectable Tale of the Marriage of Cupid and Psyche. Done into English by William Addington. With a Discourse on the Fable by A. Lang. London, 1887.
Journal of American Folk-Lore, Vol. I, pp. 88–89.

217 Select Tales from the Gesta Romanorum. Translated from the Latin with preliminary observations and notes by the Rev. C. Swan. New York and London, 1887.
Journal of American Folk-Lore, Vol. I, p. 89.

218 The Less Known Libraries of New York.
The Evening Post, May 8, 1888; *Semi-Weekly,* May 10, 1888.

1889

219 J. S. Tunison, Master Virgil. Cincinnati, 1888.
The Nation, Vol. XLVIII, p. 36. R.

220 A. Lecoy de la Marche, L'Esprit de nos Aïeux. Paris, 1889.
The Nation, Vol. XLIX, p. 337. R.

221 T. North, Fables of Bidpai. Edited by J. Jacobs. The Earliest English Version of the Fables of Bidpai, "The Morall Philosophie of Doni." London, 1889.
The Nation, Vol. XLIX, pp. 373–4. R.

222 Recent Folk-Lore Publications. W. B. Yeats, Fairy and Folk Tales of the Irish Peasantry. London and New York, 1888.—Sir G. W. Dasent, Popular Tales from the Norse. 3d ed. Edinburgh and New York, 1888.—A. Fortier, Bits of Louisiana Folk-Lore. Baltimore, 1887.—F.-J. de Santa-Anna Nery, Folk-Lore Brésilien. Paris, 1889.—T. F. Thistledon Dyer, The Folk-Lore of Plants. New York, 1889.—C. De B. Mills, The Tree of Mythology, its Growth and Fruitage. Syracuse, N. Y., 1889.
The Nation, Vol. XLVIII, p. 451. R.

223 G. Pitrè, Biblioteca delle Tradizioni popolari siciliane, XIV–XVII. Palermo, 1889.
The Nation, Vol. XLIX, pp. 195–196. N.

224 A. Morel-Fatio, Etudes sur l'Espagne, I. Paris, 1889.
The Nation, Vol. XLIX, pp. 235–236. R.

225 W. A. Clouston, A Group of Eastern Romances. London, 1889.
The Nation, Vol. XLIX, p. 313. N.

226 Fables of Bidpai. North's Translation. Ed. By J. Jacobs. London, 1888.
Journal of American Folk-Lore, I. 1888, p. 243.

227 A. Fortier, Bits of Louisiana Folk-Lore. Baltimore, 1888.
Journal of American Folk-Lore, II. 1889, p. 78.

228 F.-J. de Santa-Anna Nery, Folk-Lore Brésilien. Paris, 1889.
Journal of American Folk-Lore, II, p. 79.

229 J. S. Tunison, Master Virgil. Cincinnati, 1888.
Journal of American Folk-Lore, II, p. 83.

230 G. W. Dasent, Popular Tales from the Norse. Edinburgh, 1888.
Journal of American Folk-Lore, II, p. 84.

231 C. Nigra, Canti popolari del Piemonte. Turin, 1888; G. Giannini, Canti popolari della Montagna Lucchese. Turin, 1889.
Journal of American Folk-Lore, II. 1889, pp. 316–318.

232 A Vagabond Volume.
The Cornell Magazine, Vol. II, pp. 1–8.

233 La Société Française au XVIIe siècle. New York, 1889. G. P. Putnam's Sons. 16 mo., pp. lvii, 342. Second revised edition with bibliography brought down to date was reissued in 1907.
Rev. in *The* [New York] *Sun*, June 22, 1889; in *The New York Times*, June 24, 1889; in *The Congregationalist*, July 18, 1889; in *The Nation*, July 4, 1889, xlix, 19, and in *The Evening Post*, July 29, 1889; in *Galignani's Messenger*, Paris, Sept. 9, 1889; in *The Atlantic Monthly*, Sept., 1889, lxiv, 432; in *The Christian Union*, Aug. 8, 1889, xl, 169; in *The Unitarian Rev.*, Sept., 1889, xxxii, 280–81; in *The Literary World*, Sept. 14, 1889, xx, 306; in *The Critic*, Oct. 19, 1889, N. S. xii, 186; in *The Saturday Rev.*, Sept. 7, 1889, lxviii, 284; by A. Delboulle in *Revue Critique*, Sept. 2–9, 1889, N. S. xxviii, 141–2; in *The Athenaeum*, Nov. 16, 1889, p. 670; in *The Boston Post*, July 18, 1889; by Henry A. Todd in *Mod. Lang. Notes*, Feb., 1890, v, 91–6; Melville B. Anderson in *The Dial*, April, 1890, x, 341; by S. Waetzoldt in *Archiv für das Studium der neueren Sprachen*, 1890, lxxxv, 358–9; by Ph. A. Becker in *Literaturblatt f. german. u. roman. Philol.*, Dec., 1890, xi, 456.

1890
234 La Passione di Gesù Cristo. Edita da V. Promis. Torino, 1888.
The Nation, Vol. L, pp. 185–6. R.

235 Recent Folk-Lore Publications. Folk-Lore and Legends: Germany, Scotland, Ireland, Oriental. New York, 1889.—Lady Wilde, Ancient Cures, Charms, and Usages of Ireland. New York, 1890.—J. Curtin, Myths and Folk-Lore of Ireland. Boston, 1890.—A. H. Wratislaw, Sixty Folk-Tales from Exclusively Slavonic Sources. Boston, 1890.—G. B. Grinnell, Pawnee Hero Stories and Folk-Tales. New York, 1889.—W. A. Clouston, Flowers from a Persian Garden and Other Papers. London, 1890.—Stewart Culin, Chinese Games with Dice. Philadelphia, 1889.
The Nation, Vol. L, pp. 475–476. R.

236 J. Jacobs, Fables of Aesop. 2 vols. London, 1889.
The Nation, Vol. LI, pp. 95–96. R.

237 May M. J. Garnett, Women of Turkey and their Folk-Lore. London, 1890.
The Nation, Vol. LI, p. 387. R.

238 A new mediaeval Legend of Virgil.
The Academy (London), No. 929, Feb. 22.

239 T. Davidson, Folk-Lore, in Chambers' Encyclopaedia, new edition.—H. N. Allen, Korean Folk-Tales. New York, 1889.—E. S. Mason, Songs of Fairy

Land. New York, 1889.—Laura A. Smith, through Romany Song Land. London, 1889.

> *Journal of American Folk-Lore*, Vol. III, pp. 245–250.

240 J. Jacobs, English Fairy Tales. London and New York, 1890.

> *Journal of American Folk-Lore*, Vol. IV, pp. 89–90.

241 The Exempla of Jacques de Vitry. Folk-Lore Society. London, 1890. Publications of the Folk-Lore Society, XXVI. 8vo. pp. CXVI, 303.

> Rev. in *The Athenaeum*, Aug. 1, 1891, pp. 153–4; by Ludwig Fränkel in *Literarisches Centralblatt*, Feb. 6, 1892, xliii, 187–91; in *The New York Times*, May 3, 1891; in *The Saturday Rev.*, March 21, 1891, lxxi, 362–3; in *The Nation*, Jan. 15, 1891, lii, 57–8; in *The Critic*, March 28, 1891, N. S. xv, 163–4; by Hermann Varnhagen in *Literaturblatt f. german. u. roman. Philol.*, March, 1892, xiii, 99–100; by Lucy Toulmin Smith in *Englische Studien*, 1892, xvi, 292–4; by G. R. in *Giornale Storico della Letteratura Italiana*, 1891, xviii, 400–3; by H. G. [aidoz] in *Mélusine*, 1891, v, 239–40; by M. Di Martino in *Archivio per le Tradizioni Popolari*, 1891, x, 137–9; in *The Home Journal*, New York, April 1, 1891; in *The New York Times*, May 3, 1891; by Geo. L. Burr in *The Cornell Magazine*, Apr., 1891, iii, 278–80; by L. J. Vance in *American Notes and Queries*, March 7, 1891, vi, 217–20; by P. M. in *Revue Critique*, Feb. 16, 1891, N. S. xxxi, 127–32; by Ch.-V. Langlois in *Revue des deux Mondes*, Jan., 1893, cxv, 170–201; in *The New York Tribune*, Feb. 6, 1891; by W. W. N [ewell] *in Journal of American Folk-Lore*, 1891, iv, p. 90.

1891

242 G. L. Gomme, Handbook of Folk-Lore. London, 1890.

> *The Nation*, Vol. LII, p. 32. N.

243 J. Curtin, Myths and Folk-Tales of the Russians, Western Slavs, and Magyars. Boston, 1890.

> *The Nation*, Vol. LII, p. 52. N.

244 J. Jacobs, English Fairy Tales. London and New York, 1890.

> *The Nation*, Vol. LII, pp. 368–9. R.

245 Douglas Hyde, Beside the Fire; a Collection of Irish Gaelic Folk Stories. London, 1890.

> *The Nation*, Vol. LII, p. 443. N.

246 E. S. Hartland, Science of Fairy Tales. New York, 1891.

> *The Nation*, Vol. LII, p. 486. R.

247 J. C. Atkinson, Forty Years in a Moorland Parish. London, 1891.

> *The Nation*, Vol. LIII, p. 75. R.

248 May M. J. Garnett, The Women of Turkey and their Folklore. Vol. IV. The Jewish and Moslem Women. London, 1891.

> *The Nation*, Vol. LIII, p. 260. N.

249 J. Jacobs, Celtic Fairy Tales. New York, 1891.

> *The Nation*, Vol. LIII, pp. 453–4. R.

250 Chansons populaires de la France (Knickerbocker Nuggets). New York, G. P. Putnam's Sons, 1891. sq. 24°, pp. XXXIX, 282.

> Rev. in *The New York World*, May 10, 1891, p. 28; in *The New York Tribune*, May 22, 1891, p. 8; in *The Springfield Republican*, May 24, 1891; by H.

G.[aidoz] in *Mélusine*, 1891, v, 263; in *The Philadelphia Press*, May 30, 1891; in *The Levant Herald and Eastern Express*, Constantinople, July 3, 1891; in *The Epoch*, New York, July 24, 1891; by William M. Payne in *The Dial*, Aug., 1891, xii, 112–13; by C. in *Revue Critique*, Aug. 17–24, 1891, N. S. xxxii, 108; by W. Knörich in *Zs. für frz. Sprache u. Litteratur*, 1890, xii, 2. Hälfte, pp. 104–10; by Adolf Tobler in *Archiv für das Studium der neueren Sprachen*, 1891, lxxxvii, 330–332; by G. Pitrè in *Archivo per lo Studio delle Tradizioni Popolari*, 1891, x, 583–4; by W. W. N [ewell] *in Journal of American Folk-Lore*, 1891, iv, p. 282.

1892

251 H. C. Hazlitt, Tales and Legends of National Origin, etc. New York, 1892.
   The Nation, Vol. LIV, p. 271. R.

252 P. Kennedy, Legendary Fictions of the Irish Celts. London and New York, 1891.
   The Nation, Vol. LIV, p. 291–2. R.

253 G. L. Gomme, Ethnology in Folklore. New York, 1892.
   The Nation, Vol. LV, pp. 15–17. R.

254 An ill-used Quotation.
   The Cornell Magazine, Vol. V, pp. 43–45.

255 The Study of Popular Tales.
   The Chautauquan, Vol. XVI, p. 180, ff.

1893

256 International Humor. Edited by W. H. Dircks. The Humor of France. Translated by Elizabeth Lee.—The Humor of Germany. Translated by H. Müller-Casenow.—The Humor of Italy. Translated by A. Werner. 3 vols. New York, 1892.
   The Nation, Vol. LVI, pp. 166–167. R.

257 C. Leland, Etruscan Roman Remains in Popular Tradition. New York, 1892.
   The Nation, Vol. LVI, p. 281. R.

258 Recent Folk-Lore Publications. Mary A. Owen, Voodoo Tales as Told Among the Negroes of the Southwest. New York, 1893.—G. B. Grinnell, Blackfoot Lodge Tales. New York, 1892.—Marian R. Cox, Cinderella. London, 1893.
   The Nation, Vol. LVI, pp. 459–460. R.

1895

259 The Palio at Sienna.
   The Cornell Magazine, Vol. VII, pp. 201–206.

1896–1897

260 Catalan Language and Literature, revised.
   R. Johnson, editor, *Universal Cyclopaedia*. A new edition. New York, 1896. 8 vols. Vol. II, 1897, pp. 116–118.

261 Exempla Books.
   R. Johnson, editor, *Universal Cyclopaedia*, Vol. III, 1896, pp. 245–246.

1902

262 Les Héros de Roman. Dialogue de Nicolas Boileau-Despréaux. Edited with Introduction and Notes. Boston. Ginn and Co. 1902, 16mo, pp. VI, 282.

  Rev. by Paul Selge in *Archiv für das Studium der neueren Sprachen*, 1904, cxii, 236.

1904

263 The Modern Languages in Secondary Schools and Colleges.
  Proceedings of the 18ᵗʰ Annual Convention of Colleges and Preparatory Schools of the Middle States and Maryland, 1904, p. 23.

1906

264 Molière, A Biography by H. C. Chatfield-Taylor. With an Introduction by Thomas Frederick Crane. New York, Duffield & Co., 1906, 8vo., pp. XXV, 446. Introduction, pp. XVII-XXV.

1907

265 Jean Rotrou, Saint Genest and Venceslas. Edited with Introduction and Notes. Ginn & Co. Boston, 1907. 16mo., pp. 433.
  Rev. in *The Dial*, Nov. 1, 1907, xliii, 288–9.

1909

266 How I became a Professor.
  The Cornell Era, Jan., 1909, pp. 149–158.

1911

267 That imaginative Gentleman Don Quixote de la Mancha. By Miguel Cervantes Saavedra. Translated into English by Robinson Smith. New York, 1910.
  The Nation, Vol. XCII, pp. 61–62. R.

268 G. Pitrè, Biblioteca delle tradizioni popolari siciliane, XXIII. Palermo, 1910.
  The Nation, Vol. XCII, p. 120. N.

269 J. A. Herbert, Catalogue of Romances in the Department of Manuscripts in the British Museum, III. London, 1910.
  The Nation, Vol. XCIII, pp. 34–35. R. (Also *The* [New York] *Evening Post*, Aug. 7.)

270 The Legend of the Soul Dispossessed by a Devil.
  The Nation, Vol. XCIII, p. 142, letter.

271 Studies in Honor of A. Marshall Elliott. Baltimore, [1911].
  The Nation, Vol. XCIII, p. 472. R. (Also in *The* [New York] *Evening Post*, Nov. 20.)

272 Miracles of the Virgin.
  Romanic Review, Vol. II, pp. 235–279.

273 Mediaeval Story-Books. J. A. Herbert, Catalogue of Romances, III. London, 1910.
  Modern Philology, Vol. IX, pp. 225–237.

1912

274 G. Papini, La Leggenda di Dante. Lanciano, 1911.
  Modern Language Notes, Vol. XXVII, pp. 112–115.

275 J. A. Mosher, The Exemplum in the early religious and didactic literature of England. New York, 1911.
Modern Language Notes, Vol. XXVII, pp. 213–216.

276 Phi Beta Kappa Address, May 25.
Bulletin of the University of Rochester, viii.

1913

277 New Analogues of Old Tales. J. Klapper, Exempla aus Handschriften des Mittelalters. Hilka, Sammlung, 2.
Modern Philology, Vol. X, pp. 301–316.

1914

278 J. Th. Welter, Le Speculum Laicorum. Paris, 1914.
The Nation, Vol. XCIX, p. 475. N.

279 Address before New England Society of Pennsylvania. Philadelphia, Dec. 22, 1914. "Three New England Professors: George Ticknor, Henry W. Longfellow, James Russell Lowell." pp. 68–82.

1915

280 Abigail Adams and Suffrage.
The Nation, Vol. C, pp. 355–356, letter.

281 That Imaginative Gentleman Don Quixote de la Mancha. By Miguel de Cervantes Saavedra. Translated into English by Robinson Smith, second edition, with a new Life of Cervantes. New York, 1914.
The Nation, Vol. C, pp. 510–511. R.

282 "Preparedness" and " A Telegu Tale," also "An Ancient Pacifist."
The Nation, Vol. CI, p. 465, letter.

283 Don Quixote Three Hundred Years Old.
The New York Times, Sunday, Jan. 31, 1915, letter.

284 Address at the unveiling of the statue of Andrew D. White, June 16, 1914. Published by Cornell University.

285 J. Klapper, Exempla aus Handschriften des Mittelalters. Heidelberg, 1911.—A. Hilka, Neue Beiträge zur Erzählungsliteratur des Mittelalters. (Die Compilatio Singularis Exemplorum der Hs. Tours 468, ergänzt durch eine Schwesterschrift Bern 679.) Breslau, 1913.—J. Th. Welter, Thesaurus Exemplorum, Fasc. V: Le Speculum Laicorum. Paris, 1914.—J. Greven, Die Exempla aus den Sermones feriales et communes des Jakob von Vitry. Heidelberg, 1914.—G. Frenken, Die Exempla des Jakob von Virty. Munich, 1914.
Romanic Review, Vol. VI, pp. 219–236. R.

286 The Story of the "Wine Tasters" in Don Quixote.
The [New York] *Evening Post*, Nov. 6.

1916

287 Joseph Salathiel Tunison.
The Nation, Vol. CII, pp. 645–646.

288 Scholars and the War—Now and Then.
The Nation, Vol. CIII, pp. 107–108.

289 Giuseppe Pitrè and Sicilian Folk-Lore.
The Nation, Vol. CIII, pp. 234–236.

290 Studies in Folk-Lore: F F Communications, 17, 22, 23.
   The Nation, Vol. CIII, p. 6 (The Nation Supplement, Essays and Letters.)

291 J. Bolte and G. Polívka, Anmerkungen zu den Kinderund Hausmärchen der Brüder Grimm, I–II.
   Modern Language Notes, Vol. XXXI, pp. 33–42.

292 F F Communications, Nos. 1–21. Helsingfors, 1911–1915.
   The Romanic Review, Vol. VIII, pp. 110–125.

293 Introduction to Selections from the Cornell Era: Above Cayuga's Waters. A Collection of articles which have appeared in The Cornell Era from its first publication in Nov., 1868, to the present day, Ithaca, N. Y. (1916). pp. IX-XII.

1917

294 Axel Olrik.
   The Nation, Vol. CIV, pp. 540–541.

295 J. Klapper, Erzählungen des Mittelalters in deutscher Uebersetzung und lateinischem Urtext. Breslau, 1914.
   Modern Language Notes, Vol. XXXII, pp. 26–40.

296 The External History of the Kinder-und Hausmärchen of the Brothers Grimm.
   Modern Philology, Vol. XIV, pp. 65–77, 355–383.

297 Mediaeval Sermon-Books and Stories and their Study since 1883. (Read April 12, 1917.)
   Proceedings of the American Philosophical Society, Vol. LVI, pp. 369–402.

1918

298 The Mountain of Nida: An Episode of the Alexander Legend.
   The Romanic Review, Vol. IX, pp. 129–153. (See 1921.)

299 "The Crystal Trench."
   The [New York] *Evening Post*, Sat., June 1, 1918.

300 Response at Alumnae Banquet, Fiftieth Anniversary of the Founding of Wells College. (June 11, 1918.)
   Wells College Bulletin, Vol. IV, pp. 65–67.

301 The Wason Chinese Library.
   Cornell Alumni News, Vol. XX, pp. 464–465.

302 J. Rendel Harris, The Origin of the Cult of Aphrodite. New York, 1917.—J. G. Frazer, Jacob and the Mandrakes. London, 1917.—A. T. Starck, Der Alraun. Baltimore, 1917.
   Modern Language Notes, Vol. XXXIII, pp. 417–421.

303 Andrew Dickson White.
   Cornell Alumni News, Vol. XXI, pp. 88–89.

304 E. Levi, Il Libro dei Cinquanta Miracoli della Vergine. Bologna, 1917.—I Miracoli della Vergine nell' Arte del Medio Evo. Roma, 1918.
   Modern Language Notes, Vol. XXXIII, pp. 481–484.

1919

305 The Epigram in Italy.
   The [London] *Times. Literary Supplement.* May 30, 1919. p. 296. Correspondence.

306 Address at the Unveiling of the Statue of Ezra Cornell, June 22, 1919.
     Published in *Proceedings and Addresses at the Semi-Centennial Celebration of Cornell University*, Ithaca, N. Y., 1919, pp. 78–85.

307 Lope de Vega, "El Peregrino."
     The [London] *Times. Literary Supplement.* Sept. 19, 1919. p. 499. Correspondence.

1920

308 F F Communications. Nos. 17, 22, 23–6, 30–1. Helsingfors, 1915–1919.
     The Romanic Review, Vol. XI, pp. 187–194.

309 Italian Social Customs of the Sixteenth Century and their Influence on the Literatures of Europe. (Cornell Studies in English, vol. 5) 8vo. Pp. XV, 689. New Haven, Yale University Press, 1920.
     Rev. by Clark S. Northup in *The Cornell Alumni News*, May 6, 1920, xxii, 386; in *The* [London] *Times Lit. Supplement*, July 8, 1920, p. 433; by Jean Plattard in *Revue Critique d'Histoire et de Littérature.* 1920, No. 23, Dec. 1, pp. 443–444; in *Literarisches Zentralblatt für Deutschland* Nos. 50–52, 18 Dec., 1920, coll. 972–973; by V. Cian in *Giornale Storico della Letteratura Italiana*, Vol. LXXVII, 1921, fasc. 229, pp. 129–130; in *Deutsche Literaturzeitung*, XXXXII Jahrgang. No. 5, Feb., 1921, col. 76; by Edmund G. Gardner in *The Modern Language Review*, Vol. XVI, No. 2, April, 1921, pp. 184–185; in *Studies in Philology*, Elizabethan Studies. Sixth Series. Vol. XVIII, July, 1921, No. 3, pp. 368–9. Published quarterly by the University of North Carolina, Chapel Hill; in *The English Historical Review*, Vol. XXXVII (1922), pp. 613–614; by Johannes Bolte in *Archiv f. das Studium der neueren Sprachen*, 1922, cxliv, 128–9; by Anna Benedetti in *Nuova Antologia*, Feb. 1, 1922, pp. 293–294.

310 L. De-Mauri, L'Epigramma italiano dal Risorgimento delle Lettere ai Tempi moderni. Milano, 1918.
     The Romanic Review, Vol. XI, pp. 274–282.

311 Doctor Andrew Turnbull and the New Smyrna Colony of Florida.
     The [London] *Times. Literary Supplement*, Aug. 19, 1920, p. 536. Correspondence.

312 J. Bolte and G. Polívka, Anmerkungen zu den Kinder-und Hausmärchen der Brüder Grimm, III. 1918.
     Modern Language Notes, Vol. XXXV, pp. 423–426.

1921

313 The Mountain of Nida. A Postscript.
     The Romanic Review, Vol. XII, pp. 80–83. (See 1918.)

314 The Wason Chinese Library at Cornell University.
     Christian China, Vol. VII, pp. 207–213.

315 J. R. Charbonnel, La Pensée italienne au XVIe siècle et le courant libertine. Paris, 1920.
     American Historical Review, vol. XXVI, pp. 504–506.

316 The Sources of Boccaccio's Novella of Mitridanes and Natan (Decameron X. 3).
     The Romanic Review, Vol. XII, pp. 193–215.

317 T. Koch-Grünberg, Indianermärchen aus Südamerika. (Die Märchen der Weltliteratur, herausgegeben von Friedrich von der Leyen und Paul Zaunert). Jena, 1920.
The Journal of American Folk-Lore, Vol. XXXIV, pp. 329–332.

318 Address at the Semi-Centennial of the College of Architecture, Cornell University, Oct. 21, 1921, pp. 10–16. Published by the University.

1922

319 F F Communications, Nos. 32–41. 1920–1.
The Romanic Review, Vol. XIII, pp. 276–278.

320 R. T. Christiansen. Norske Eventyr. (Norske Folkeminner utgivne av Den Norske Historiske Kildeskriftkommission, II.) Kristiania, 1921.
The Romanic Review, Vol. XIII, pp. 278–9.

321 G. C. Trancoso, Histórias de Proveito e Exemplo. Paris and Lisbon, 1921.
The Romanic Review, Vol. XIII, pp. 279–282.

1923

322 A. von Mailly, Sagen aus Friaul und den Jülischen Alpen. Leipzig, 1922.
Modern Language Notes, Vol. XXXVIII, pp. 169–171.

323 H. Ashton, Madame de La Fayette. Cambridge, 1922.
The Literary Review, March 17, 1923, p. 526.

324 A. Wesselski, Die Legende um Dante. Weimar, 1921.
Modern Language Notes, vol. XXXVIII, pp. 293–295.

325 "Trifles and Travels."
The [London] *Times, Literary Supplement,* Thursday, July 5, 1923, p. 456, letter.

326 F F Communications, Nos. 42–50. 1922–23.
The Romanic Review, Vol. XIV, pp. 319–324.

327 Italy, France and Spain.
Auxiliary Educational League.

328 Andrew D. White.
The Cornell Daily Sun, Nov. 8, 1923.

1924

329 "Painting the Town Red."
Scientific Monthly, Vol. XVIII, pp. 605–615.

330 F. A. G. Cowper, Italian Folk Tales and Folk Songs. Chicago, 1923.
Modern Language Notes, Vol. XXXIX, pp. 126–127.

331 J. Pauli, Schimpf und Ernst, Erster Teil, herausgegeben von Johannes Bolte. Berlin, 1924.
Modern Language Notes, Vol. XXXIX, pp. 314–16.

$\mathcal{P}$REFACE

THE growing interest in the popular tales of Europe has led me to believe that a selection from those of Italy would be entertaining to the general reader, and valuable to the student of comparative folk-lore.

The stories which, with but few exceptions, are here presented for the first time to the English reader, have been translated from recent Italian collections, and are given exactly as they were taken down from the mouths of the people, and it is in this sense, belonging to the people, that the word popular is used in the title of this work. I have occasionally changed the present to the past tense, and slightly condensed by the omission of tiresome repetitions;* but otherwise my versions follow the original closely, too closely perhaps in the case of the Sicilian tales, which, when recited, are very dramatic, but seem disjointed and abrupt when read.

The notes are intended to supplement those of Pitrè and Köhler by citing the stories published since the *Fiabe, Novelle e Racconti*, and the *Sicilianische Märchen*, and also to furnish easy reference to the parallel stories of the rest of Europe. As the notes are primarily intended for students I have simply pointed out the most convenient sources of information and those to which I have had access. My space has obliged me to restrict my notes to what seemed to me the most important, and I have as a rule given only references which I have verified myself.

My object has been simply to present to the reader and student unacquainted with the Italian dialects a tolerably complete collection of Italian popular tales; with theories as to the origin and diffusion of popular tales in general, or of Italian popular tales in particular, I have nothing to do at present either in the text or notes. It is for others to draw such inferences as this collection seems to warrant.

It was, of course, impossible in my limited space to do more than give a small selection from the class of Fairy Tales numbering several hundred; of the other classes nearly everything has been given that has been

* Other condensations are indicated by brackets.

published down to the present date. The Fairy Tales were selected to represent as well as possible typical stories or classes, and I have followed in my arrangement, with some modification and condensation, Hahn's *Märchen- und Sagformeln (Griechische und Albanesische Märchen*, vol. i. p. 45), an English version of which may be found in W. Henderson's *Notes on the Folk-lore of the Northern Counties of England and the Borders. With an Appendix on Household Stories*, by S. Baring-Gould. London, 1866.

In conclusion, I must express my many obligations to Dr. Giuseppe Pitrè, of Palermo, without whose admirable collection this work would hardly have been undertaken, and to the library of Harvard College, which so generously throws open its treasures to the scholars of less favored institutions.

T. F. CRANE.
ITHACA, N. Y., *September* 9, 1885.

Introduction

By popular tales we mean the stories that are handed down by word of mouth from one generation to another of the illiterate people, serving almost exclusively to amuse and seldom to instruct. These stories may be roughly divided into three classes: nursery tales, fairy stories, and jests. In countries where the people are generally educated, the first two classes form but one; where, on the other hand, the people still retain the credulity and simplicity of childhood, the stories which with us are confined to the nursery amuse the fathers and mothers as well as the children. These stories were regarded with contempt by the learned until the famous scholars, the brothers Grimm, went about Germany some sixty years ago collecting this fast disappearing literature of the people. The interesting character of these tales, and the scientific value attributed to them by their collectors, led others to follow their footsteps, and there is now scarcely a province of Germany that has not one or more volumes devoted to its local popular tales. The impulse given by the Grimms was not confined to their own country, but extended over all Europe, and within the last twenty years more than fifty volumes have been published containing the popular tales of Iceland, Greenland, Norway, Sweden, Russia, Germany, England, Scotland, France, Biscay, Spain, Portugal, and Greece. Asia and Africa have contributed stories from India, China, Japan, and South Africa. In addition to these we have now to mention what has been done in this field in Italy.

From their very nature the stories we are now considering were long confined to the common people, and were preserved and transmitted solely by oral tradition. It did not occur to any one to write them down from the lips of the people until within the present century. The existence of these stories is, however, revealed by occasional references, and many of them have been preserved, but not in their original form, in books designed to entertain more cultivated readers.[1] The earliest literary collection of stories having a popular origin was made in the sixteenth century by an Italian, Giovan Francesco Straparola, of Caravaggio.[2] It is astonishing that a person of Straparola's popularity should have left behind him nothing but a name. We only know that he was born near the end of the fifteenth century at Caravaggio, now a small town half way between Milan and Cremona, but during the Middle Ages an important city belonging to the duchy of Milan. In 1550 he published at Venice a collection of stories in the style of the Decameron, which was received with the greatest favor. It passed through sixteen editions in twenty years, was translated into French and often printed in that language, and before the end of the century was turned into German. The author feigns that Francesca Gonzaga, daughter of Ottaviano Sforza, Duke of Milan, on account of commotions in that city, retires to the island of Murano, near Venice, and surrounded by a number of distinguished ladies and gentlemen, passes the time in listening to stories related by the company. Thirteen nights are spent in this way, and seventy-four stories are told, when the approach of Lent cuts short the diversion. These stories are of the most varied form and origin; many are borrowed without acknowledgment from other writers, twenty-four, for example, from the little known Morlini, fifteen from Boccaccio, Sachetti, Brevio, Ser Giovanni, the Old-French *fabliaux*, the Golden Legend, and the Romance of Merlin. Six others are of Oriental origin, and may be found in the *Pantschatantra, Forty Viziers, Siddhi Kûr,* and *Thousand and One Nights.*[3] There remain, then, twenty-nine stories, the property of Straparola, of which twenty-two are *Märchen,* or popular tales. We say "the property" of Straparola: we mean they had never appeared before in the literature of Europe, but they were in no sense original with Straparola, being the common property which the Occident has inherited from the Orient. There is no need of mentioning in detail here these stories as they are frequently cited in the notes of the present work, and one, the original of the various modern versions of "Puss in Boots," is given at length in the notes to Chapter I.[4] Two of Straparola's stories have survived their author's oblivion and still live in Perrault's *"Peau d'Ane"* and *"Le Chat Botté,"* while others in the witty versions of Madame D'Aulnoy delighted the romance-loving French society of the seventeenth century.[5] Straparola's work had no influence on contemporary Italian literature, and was soon forgotten—an unjust oblivion, for to him belongs the honor of having introduced the Fairy Tale into modern European literature. He has been criticized for his style and blamed for his immorality. The former, it seems to us, is not bad, and the latter no worse than that of many contemporaneous writers who have escaped the severe judgment meted out to Straparola.

We find no further traces of popular tales until nearly a century later, when the first edition of the celebrated *Pentamerone* appeared at Naples in 1637. Its author, Giambattista Basile (known as a writer by the anagram of his name, Gian Alesio Abbatutis), is but little better known to us than Straparola. He spent his youth in Crete, became known to the Venetians, and was received into the *Academia degli Stravaganti*. He followed his sister Adriana, a celebrated cantatrice, to Mantua, enjoyed the duke's favor, roamed much over Italy, and finally returned to Naples, near where he died in 1632.[6] The *Pentamerone*, as its title implies, is a collection of fifty stories in the Neapolitan dialect, supposed to be narrated, during five days, by ten old women, for the entertainment of the person (Moorish slave) who had usurped the place of the rightful princess.[7] Basile's work enjoyed the greatest popularity in Italy, and was translated into Italian and into the dialect of Bologna. It is worthy of notice that the first fairy tale that appeared in France, and was the *avant-coureur* of the host that soon followed under the lead of Charles Perrault, "*L'Adroite Princesse*," is found in the *Pentamerone*. We know nothing of the sources of Basile's work, but it contains the most popular and extended of all European tales, and must have been in a great measure drawn directly from popular tradition. The style is a wonderful mass of conceits, which do not, however, impair the interest in the material, and it is safe to say that no people in Europe possesses such a monument of its popular tales as the *Pentamerone*.[8] Its influence on Italian literature was not greater than that of Straparola's *Piacevoli Notti*. From the *Pentamerone* Lorenzo Lippi took the materials for the second *cantare* of his *Malmantile Racquistato*, and Carlo Gozzi drew on it for his curious *fiabe*, the earliest dramatizations of fairy tales, which, in our day, after amusing the nursery, have again become the vehicles of spectacular dramas. Although there is no proof that Mlle. Lhéritier and Perrault took their stories from Straparola and the *Pentamerone*, there is little doubt that the French translation of the former, which was very popular (Jannet mentions fourteen editions between 1560 and 1726) awakened an interest in this class of stories, and was thus the origin of that copious French fairy literature, which, besides the names mentioned above, includes such well-known writers as Mme. D'Aulnoy, the Countess Murat, Mlle. De La Force, and Count Caylus, all of whom drew on their Italian prototypes more or less.[9]

Popular as were the two collections above mentioned they produced but one imitation, *La Posillecheata*, a collection of five stories in the Neapolitan dialect and in the style of the *Pentamerone*, by Pompeo Sarnelli, Bishop of Bisceglie, whose anagram is Masillo Reppone. The first edition appeared at Naples in 1684, and it has been republished twice since then at the same place. The work is exceedingly coarse, and has fallen into well-deserved oblivion.[10]

Nearly two centuries elapsed before another collection of Italian tales made its appearance. The interest that the brothers Grimm aroused in Germany for the collection and preservation of popular traditions did not, for obvious reasons, extend to Italy. A people must first have a consciousness of its own nationality before it can take sufficient interest in its popular literature to inspire even its scholars to collect its traditions for the sake of science, to say nothing of collections for entertainment. In 1860, Temistocle Gradi, of Siena, published in his *Vigilia di Pasqua di Ceppo*, eight, and in his *Saggio di Letterature varie*, 1865, four popular tales, as related in Siena. These were collected without any other aim than that of entertainment, but are valuable for purposes of comparison. No attempt at a scientific collection of tales was made until 1869, when Professor De Gubernatis published the *Novelline di Santo Stefano*, containing thirty-five stories, preceded by an introduction on the relationship of the myth to the popular tale. This was the forerunner of numerous collections from the various provinces of Italy, which will be found noted in the bibliography. The attention of strangers was early directed to Italian tales, and the earliest scientific collection was the work of two Germans, Georg Widter and Adam Wolf, who published a translation of twenty-one Venetian tales in the *Jahrbuch für romanische und englische Literatur*, Vol. VII. (1866), pp. 1–36, 121–154, 249–290, with comparative notes by R. Köhler. In the same volume were published, pp. 381–400, twelve tales from Leghorn, collected by Hermann Knust; and finally the eighth volume of the same periodical, pp. 241–260, contains three stories from the neighborhood of Sora, in Naples. In 1867 Schneller published at Innsbruck a German translation of sixty-nine tales, collected by him in the Italian Tyrol. Of much greater interest and importance than any of the above are the two volumes of Sicilian tales, collected and translated into German by Laura Gonzenbach, afterwards the wife of the Italian general, La Racine. There are but two other collections of Italian stories by foreigners: Miss Busk's *Folk-Lore of Rome*, and the anonymous *Tuscan Fairy Tales* recently published.

The number of stories published, in German and English, is about twice as many as those published in Italian before Pitrè's collection, being over four hundred. Pitrè contains more than all the previous Italian publications together, embracing over three hundred tales, etc., besides those previously published by him in periodicals and elsewhere. Since Pitrè's collection, the three works of Comparetti, Visentini, and Nerucci, have added one hundred and eighty tales, not to speak of wedding publications, containing from one to five stories. It is, of course, impossible to examine separately all these collections—we will mention briefly the most important. To Imbriani is due the first collection of tales taken down from the mouths of the people and compared with previously published Italian popular tales. In 1871 appeared his *Novellaja fiorentina*, and in the following year the *Novellaja milanese*. These two have been combined, and published as a second edition of the *Novellaja fiorentina*, containing fifty Florentine and forty-five Milanese tales, besides a number of stories from Straparola, the *Pentamerone*, and the Italian novelists, given by way of illustration. The stories are accompanied by copious references to the rest of Italy, and Liebrecht's references to other European parallels. It is an admirable work, but one on which we have drawn but seldom, restricting ourselves to the stories in the various dialects as much as possible. The Milanese stories are in general very poor versions of the typical tales, being distorted and fragmentary. In 1873 Dr. Giuseppe Pitrè, of Palermo, well known for his collection of popular Sicilian songs, published three specimens of a collection of Sicilian popular tales, and two years later gave to the world his admirable work, *Fiabe, Novelle e Racconti*, forming vols. IV.–VII. of the *Biblioteca delle Tradizioni popolari Siciliane* per cura di Giuseppe Pitrè. It is not, however, numerically that Pitrè's collection surpasses all that has previously been done in this field. It is a monument of patient, thorough research and profound study. Its arrangement is almost faultless, the explanatory notes full, while the grammar and glossary constitute valuable contributions to the philology of the Italian dialects. In the Introduction the author, probably for the first time, makes the Sicilian public acquainted with the fundamental principles of comparative mythology and its relation to folk-lore, and gives a good account of the Oriental sources of the novel. He has, it seems to us, very properly confined his notes and comparisons entirely to Italy, with references of course to Gonzenbach and Köhler's notes to Widter-Wolf when necessary. In other words, his work is a contribution to Italian folk-lore, and the student of comparative Aryan folk-lore must make his own comparisons: a task no longer difficult, thanks to the works of Grimm, Hahn, Köhler, Cox, De Gubernatis, etc. The only other collection that need be mentioned here is the one in the *Canti e Racconti del Popolo italiano,* consisting of the first volume of the *Novellino pop. ital.* pub. ed ill. da Dom. Comparetti, and of Visentini's *Fiabe Mantovane.* The stories in both of the above works are translated into Italian. In the first there is no arrangement by locality or subject; and the annotations, instead of being given with each story, are reserved for one of the future volumes—an unhandy arrangement, which detracts from the value of the work.

We will now turn our attention from the collections themselves to the stories they contain, and examine these first as to their form, and secondly as to their contents.

The name applied to the popular tale differs in various provinces, being generally a derivative of the Latin *fabula.* So these stories are termed *favuli* and *fràuli* in parts of Sicily, *favole* in Rome, *fiabe* in Venice, *foe* in Liguria, and *fole* in Bologna. In Palermo and Naples they are named *cunti, novelle* and *novelline* in Tuscany, *esempi* in Milan, and *storie* in Piedmont." There are few peculiarities of form, and they refer almost exclusively to the beginning and ending of the stories. Those from Sicily begin either with the simple "*cc'era*" (there was), or "*'na vota cc'era*" (there was one time), or "*si raccunta chi 'na vota cc'era*" (it is related that there was one time). Sometimes the formula is repeated, as, "*si cunta e s' arrleuntà*" (it is related and related again), with the addition at times of "*a lor signuri*" (to your worships), or the story about to be told is qualified as "*stu bellissimu cuntu*" (this very fine story). Ordinarily they begin, as do our own, with the formula, "once upon a time there was." The ending is also a variable formula, often a couplet referring to the happy termination of the tale and the relatively unenviable condition of the listeners. The Sicilian ending usually is:—

> "Iddi arristaru filici e cuntenti,
> E nuàtri semu senza nenti."

(They remained happy and contented, and we are without anything.) The last line often is "*E nui semu ccà munnamu li denti.*" (And here we are picking our teeth), or "*Ma a nui 'un ni dèsinu nenti*" (But to us they gave nothing), which corresponds to a Tuscan ending:—

> "Se ne stettero e se la goderono
> E a me nulla mi diedero."

(They stayed and enjoyed it, and gave nothing to me.) A common Tuscan ending is:—

> "In santa pace pia
> Dite la vostra, ch' io detto la mia."

(In holy pious peace tell yours, for I have told mine.) In some parts of Sicily (Polizzi) a similar conclusion is found:—

> "Favula scritta, favula ditta:
> Diciti la vostra, ca la mia è ditta."

(Story written, story told; tell yours, for mine is told.) So in Venice,—

> "Longa la tua, curta la mia;
> Conta la tua, chè la mia xè finla."

(Long yours, short mine; tell yours, for mine is ended.) The first line is sometimes as follows:—

> "Stretto il viuolo, stretta la via:
> Dite la vostra, ch' io detto la mia."

(Narrow the path, narrow the way; tell yours, for I have told mine.) The most common form of the above Tuscan ending is:—

> "Stretta è la foglia è larga è la via,
> Dite la vostra chè ho detto la mia."

(Narrow is the leaf, broad is the way, etc.) This same ending is also found in Rome.[12] These endings have been omitted in the present work as they do not constitute an integral part of the story, and are often left off by the narrators themselves. The narrative is usually given in the present tense, and in most of the collections is animated and dramatic. Very primitive expedients are employed to indicate the lapse of time, either the verb indicating the action is repeated, as, "he walked, and walked, and walked," a proceeding not unknown to our own stories, or such expressions as the following are used: *Cuntu 'un porta tempu*, or *lu cuntu 'un metti tempu*, or *'Ntra li cunti nun cc'è tempu*, which are all equivalent to, "The story takes no note of time." These Sicilian expressions are replaced in Tuscany by the similar one: *Il tempo delle novelle passa presto* ("Time passes quickly in stories"). Sometimes the narrator will bring himself or herself into the story in a very naive manner; as, for example, when a name is wanted. So in telling a Sicilian story which is another version of "The Fair Angiola" given in our text, the narrator, Gna Sabbedda, continues: "The old woman met her once, and said: 'Here, little girl, whose daughter are you?' "Gna Sabbedda's, for example; I mention myself, but, however, I was not there."[13]

If we turn our attention now to the contents of our stories we shall find that they do not differ materially from those of the rest of Europe, and the same story is found, with trifling variations, all over Italy.[14] There is but little local coloring in the fairy tales, and they are chiefly interesting for purposes of comparison. We have given in our text such a copious selection from all parts of the country that the reader can easily compare them for himself with the tales of other lands in their more general features. If they are not strikingly original they will still, we trust, be found interesting variations of familiar themes; and we shall perhaps deem less strange to us a people whose children are still amused with the same tales as our own.

BIBLIOGRAPHY

ARCHIVIO per lo Studio delle Tradizioni popolari. Rivista trimestrale diretta da G. Pitrè e S. Salomone-Marino. Palermo, 1882–1885. 8vo.

The following popular tales have been published in the Archivio: *Novelle popolari toscane,* edited by G. Pitrè, vol. I. pp. 35–69, 183–205, 520–540; vol. II. pp. 157–172. *La Storia del Re Crin,* collected by A. Arietti [Piedmont], vol. I. pp. 424–429. *Cuntu di lu Ciropiddhu, novellina popolare messinese,* collected by T. Cannizzaro, vol. I. pp. 518–519. *Novelle popolari sarde,* collected by P. E. Guarnerio, vol. II. pp. 19–38, 185–206, 481–502; vol. III. pp. 233–240. *La Cenerentola a Parma e a Camerino,* collected by Caterina Pigorini-Beri, vol. II. pp. 45–58. *Fiabe popolari crennesi [provincia di Milano],* collected by V. Imbriani, vol. II. pp. 73–81. *Fiaba veneziana [== Pitrè, xxxix.],* collected by Cristoforo Pasqualigo, vol. II. pp. 353–358. *Il Re Porco, novellina popolare marchigiana,* collected by Miss R. H. Busk, vol. II, pp. 403–409. *Tre novellini pugliesi di Cerignola,* collected by N. Zingarelli, vol. III. pp. 65–72. *La Bona Fia, Fiaba veneziana,* collected by A. Dalmedico, vol. III. pp. 73–74. *Tradizioni popolari abruzzesi, Novelle,* collected by G. Finamore, vol. III. pp. 359–372, 331–350. *I Tre Maghi ovverosia Il Merlo Bianco, novella popolare montalese,* collected by G. Nerucci, vol. III. pp. 373–388, 551–568.

BARTOLI, A., E G. SANSONI

Una novellina e una poesia popolare gragnolesi. Florence, 1881. 8°. Pp. 15. Per le Nozze Biagi-Piroli. Edizione di 100 copie numerate.

The *novellina* is a version of Pitrè, Nos. 159, 160 ("The Treasure of Rhampsinitus").

BASILE, GIAMBATTISTA

Lo Cunto de li Cunti. Overo Lo Trattenemiento de Peccerille. De Gian Alesio Abbattutis. Iornate Cinco. Naples, Per Camillo Cavallo. 1644. 12°.

Il conto de' conti trattenimento a' fanciulli. Trasportato dalla Napolitana all' Italiana favella, cd adornato di bellissime Figure. Naples, 1784.

La Chiaqlira dla Banzola o per dir mli Fol divers traduit dal parlar Napulitan in lengua Bulgnesa per rimedi innucent dla sonn, e dla malincunj. Dedicà al merit singular dl gentilessem sgnori d' Bulogna. Bologna, 1813. 4°.

Der Pentamerone oder: Das Märchen aller Märchen von Giambattista Basile. Aus dem Neapolitanischen übertragen von Felix Liebrecht. Nebst einer Vorrede von Jacob Grimm. 2 vols. Breslau, 1846. 8°.

The Pentamerone, or the Story of Stories, Fun for the Little Ones, By Giambattista Basile. Translated from the Neapolitan by John Edward Taylor. With Illustrations by George Cruikshank. Second edition. London, 1850. 8°.

Archiv für das Studium der neueren Sprachen und Literaturen. Herausgegeben von Ludwig Herrig. Vol. XLV. p. 1, Eine neapolitanische Märchen-sammlung aus der ersten Hälfte des XVII. Jahrhunderts—Pentamerone des Giambattista Basile.

BASILE, GIAMBATTISTA Archivio di Letteratura popolare. Naples, 1883–85.
    A monthly periodical devoted to popular literature. The volumes which have already appeared contain a large number of popular tales collected at Naples or in the vicinity.

BERNONI, DOM. GIUSEPPE
    Fiabe popolari veneziane raccolte da Dom. Giuseppe Bernoni. Venice, 1875. 8°.

    Leggende fantastiche popolari veneziane raccolte da Dom. Giuseppe Bernoni. Venice, 1873. 8°.

    Le Strighe: Leggende popolari veneziane raccolte da Dom. Giuseppe Bernoni. Venice, 1874. 16°.

    Tradizioni popolari veneziane raccolte da Dom. Giuseppe Bernoni. Puntate I.–IV. Venice, 1875–77.

BOLOGNINI, DR. NEPOMUCENO
    Fiabe e Legende della Valle di Rendena nel Trentino. Rovereto, 1881. 8°. Pp. 50. [Estratto dal VII. Annuario della Società degli Alpinisti Tridentini.]

BUSK, R. H.
    Household Stories from the Land of Hofer; or, Popular Myths of Tirol, including the Rose-Garden of King Lareyn. London, 1871. 8°.

    The Folk-Lore of Rome. Collected by word of mouth from the people. By R. H. Busk. London, 1874. 8°.

CANTI E RACCONTI DEL POPOLO ITALIANO
    See Comparetti and Visentini.

COMPARETTI, DOMENICO
    Novelline popolari italiane pubblicate ed illustrate da Domenico Comparetti. Vol. I. Turin, 1875. 8°.
    In Canti e Racconti del Popolo italiano. Pubblicati per cura di D. Comparetti ed A. D'Ancona. Vol. VI.

COOTE, HENRY CHARLES
    Some Italian Folk-Lore, Folk-Lore Record, I., pp. 187–215.
    Notice of Comparetti's Nov. pop. ital., with translations.

CORAZZINI, FRANCESCO
    I Componimenti minori della letteratura popolare italiana nei principali dialetti o saggio di letteratura dialettale comparata. Benevento, 1877. 8°.
    Novelle toscane, beneventane, apicese (Benvento), bolognese, bergamasca e vicentina. Pp. 409–489.

CORONEDI-BERTI, CAROLINA

Novelle popolari bolognesi raccolte da Carolina Coronedi-Berti. Bologna, 1874. 8°.

La Fola del Muretein, Novellina popolare Bolognese. Estratto dalla Rivista Europea. Florence, 1873, 8°. Pp. 9.

CRANE, T. F.

A Nursery Tale. The Cornell Review, May, 1876, pp. 337–347.

Italian Fairy Tales. St. Nicholas, December, 1878, pp. 101–107.

Italian Popular Tales. North American Revlew, July, 1876, pp. 25–60.

Le Novelle Popolari Italiane. In Giornale di Sicilia. Palermo. Nos. 186–188, 190, 195, 206, 207, 216, 225, 236, 239, 240. Aug.–Oct., 1877.

Italian translation of above Article.

Recent Italian Popular Tales. The Academy, London, March 22, 1879, pp. 262–263.

Sicilian Folk-Lore. Lippincott's Magazine, October, 1876, pp. 433–443.

Devoted to Pitrè's collection.

La Novellistica Popolare di Sicilia per T. F. Crane. Versione dall' Inglese per F. Polacci Nuccio. Estratto dalle Nuove Effemeridi Siciliane, Vol. VI. Palermo, 1877. 8°. Pp. 26.

Italian translation of above Article.

DE GUBERNATIS, A.

Le Novelline di Santo Stefano raccolte da Angelo De Gubernatis e precedute da una introduzione sulla parentela del mito con la novella. Turin, 1869. 8°.

See Rivista di Letteratura Popolare.

Zoölogical Mythology, or the Legends of Animals. By Angelo De Gubernatis. 2 vols. London, 1872. 8°.

DE NNO, ANTONIO

Usi e Costumi Abruzzesi. Vol. III. Fiabe. Florence, 1883. 16°.

FINAMORE, GENNARO

Tradizioni popolari abruzzesi. Vol. 1. Novelle. Prima Parte, Lanciano, 1882. 8°. Parte seconda, Lanciano, 1885.

FRIZZI, GIUSEPPE

Novella montanina, Florence, 1876. 8°. Pp. 36. Edizione di 150 esemplari.

GARGIOLLI, CARLO

Novelline e Canti popolari delle Marche. Fano, 1878. 8°. Pp. 18.

Per le Nozze Imbriani-Rosnati.

GIANANDREA, ANTONIO

Biblioteca delle Tradizioni popolari marchigiane. Novelline e Fiabe popolari marchigiane raccolte e annotate da Antonio Gianandrea. Jesi, 1878. 12°. Punt. I. pp. 32.

See Academy, March 22, 1879, pp. 262.

Della novella del Petit Poucet. In Giornale di Filologia Romanza, II., pp. 231–234.

A few copies were printed separately.

BIBLIOGRAPHY

GONZENBACH, LAURA

Sicilianische Märchen. Aus dem Volksmund gesammelt von Laura Gonzen-bach. Mit Anmerkungen Reinhold Köhler's und einer Einleitung heraus-gegeben von Otto Hartwig. 2 vols. Leipzig, 1870. 8°.

GRADI, TEMISTOCLE

Saggio di Letture varie per i Giovani di Temistocle Gradi da Siena. Turin, 1865. 8°.

La Vigilia di Pasqua di Ceppo. Otto Novelle di Temistocle Gradi. Coll'aggiunta di due racconti. Turin, 1860. 8°.

GUARNERIO, P. E.

Una novellina nel dialetto di Luras in Gallura (Sardinia). Milan, 1884. Per le Nozze Vivante-Ascoli. Edizione di soli L. esemplari.

An incomplete version of the Cupid and Psyche myth.

IMBRIANI, VITTORIO

La Novellaja fiorentina cioè fiabe e novelline stenografate in Firenze dal dettato popolare e corredate di qualche noterella da Vittorio Imbriani. Naples, 1871. Esemplari 150. 16°.

La Novellaja milanese, esempii e panzane lombarde raccolte nel Milanese da Vittorio Imbriani. Bologna, 1872. Esemplari 40. 8°.

Paralipomeni alla Novellaja milanese. Bologna, pp. 9. Tratura a parte del Propug-natore, Vol. VI. Esemplari 30.

'A 'Ndriana Fata. Cunto pomiglianese. Per nozze. Pomigliano d' Arco, 1875. 8°. Pp. 14. 250 esemplari fuori di commercio.

Due Fiabe Toscane annotate da V. I. Esemplari 100. Naples, 1876. 8°. Pp. 23.
   These *fiabe* are also in Nerucci, pp. 10, 18.

Dodici conti pomiglianesi con varianti avellinesi, montellesi, bagnolesi, milanesi, toscane, leccesi, ecc. Illustrati da Vittorio Imbriani. Naples, 1877. 8°.

'E Sette Mane-Mozze. In dialetto di Avellino. Principato Ulteriore. Pomigliano d' Arco, 1877. 8° Per le nozze Pitrè-Vitrano. Esemplari cc. Fuori commercio.

La Novellaja Fiorentina. Fiabe e Novelline stenografate in Firenze dal dettato popolare da Vittorio Imbriani. Ristampa accresciuta di molte novelle inedite, di numerosi riscontri e di note, nelle quali è accolta integralmente La Novellaja Milanese dello stesso raccoglitore. Leghorn, 1877. 8°.

IVE, ANTONIO

Fiabe popolari rovignesi. Per le Nozze Ive-Lorenzetto. XXVIII. Novembre, 1877. Vienna, 1877. 8°. Pp. 32. Edizione fuori di commercio di soli 100 esemplari.
   See Academy, March 22, 1879, p. 262.

Fiabe popolari rovignesi raccolte ed annotate da Antonio Ive. Per le Nozze Ive-Rocco. Vienna, 1878. 8°. Pp. 26, Edizione fuori di commercio di soli 100 esemplari.
   See Academy, March 22, 1879, p. 262.

KADEN, WOLDEMAR

Unter den Olivenbäumen. Süditalienische Volksmärchen. Nacherzählt, Leipzig, 1880. 8°.

Of the forty-four stories in this work thirty-four are translated from Pitrè's Fiabe, six from Comparetti's Nov. pop. ital., and three from Imbriani's XII. Conti pomig., without any acknowledgment. This plagiarism was first exposed by R. Köhler in the Literarisches Centralblatt, 1881, vol. XXXII. p. 337, and afterwards by Pitrè in the Nuove Effemeridi Sicilians, 1881.

KNUST, HERMANN

Italienische Märchen. (Leghorn.) In Jahrbuch für romanische und englische Literatur. Leipzig, 1866. Vol. VII. Pp. 381–401.

KOEHLER, REINHOLD

Italienische Volksmärchen. (Sora). In Jahrbuch für romanische und englische Literatur. Leipzig, 1867. Vol. VIII. Pp.241–260.

MARC-MONNIER

Les Contes de Nourrice de la Sicile, d'après des recueils nouveaux publiés récemment in Italie. Revue des Deux Mondes, 15 Aug., 1875.

Devoted to Pitrè's collection.

Les Contes de Pomigliano et la filiation des Mythes populaires. Revue des Deux Mondes, 1 Nov., 1877.

Contes populaires de l'Italie. Les Contes de Toscane et de Lombardie. Revue des Deux Mondes, 1 Dec., 1879.

Devoted to the Novellaja Fiorentina of Imbriani.

Les Contes populaires en Italie. Paris, 1880. 16°.

Reprint of the above articles.

MOROSI, PROF. DOTT. GIUSEPPE

Studi sui Dialetti Greci della Terra d' Otranto. Preceduto da una raccolta di Canti, Leggende, Proverbi, e Indovinelli. Lecce, 1870. 4°. Leggende, pp. 73–77.

NERUCCI, PROF. GHERARDO

Sessanta novelle popolari montalesi (Circondario di Pistoja). Florence, 1880. 12°.

Cincelle da Bambini in nella stietta parlatura rustica d' i' Montale Pistolese. Pistoia, 1881. 8°.

ORTOLI, J. B. FRÉDÉRIC

Les Contes populaires de l'Ile de la Corse. Paris, 1883. 8°.

Vol. XVI. of Littératures populaires de toutes les Nations, Paris, Maisonneuve.

PANZANEGA D' ON RE. In dialetto di Crenna [Provincia di Milano]. Rome, 1876. 8°. Pp. 15. 200 esemplari fuori di commercio.

PAPANTI, GIOVANNI

Novelline popolari livornesi raccolte e annotate da Giovanni Papanti. Leghorn, 1877. 8°. Pp. 29.

Per le nozze Pitrè-Vitrano. Edizione fuori di commercio di soli 150 esemplari.

PELLIZZARI, P.

Fiabe e Canzoni popolari del Contado di Maglie in Terra d' Otranto. Fasc. I. Maglie, 1884. 8°. Pp. 143.

PITRÈ, GIUSEPPE

Saggio (Primo) di Fiabe e Novelle popolari Siciliane raccolte da Giuseppe Pitrè. Palermo, 1873. 8°. Pp. 16.

Nuovo Saggio (Secundo) di Fiabe e Novelle popolari Siciliane raccolte ed illustrate da Giuseppe Pitrè. Estratto dalla Rivista di Filologia Romanza, vol. I. fasc. II. e III. Imola, 1873. 8°. Pp. 34.

Otto Fiabe (Terzo Saggio) e Novelle Siciliane raccolte dalla bocca del Popolo ed annotate da Giuseppe Pitrè. Bologna, 1873. Estratto dal Propugnatore, Vol. VI. 8°. Pp. 42.

Novelline popolari siciliane raccolte in Palermo ed annotate da Giuseppe Pitrè. Palermo, 1873. 8°.
   Edizione di soli 100 esemplari.

Fiabe, Novelle e Racconti. 4 vols. Palermo, 1875. 8°.*   Biblioteca delle tradizioni popolari siciliane per cura di Giuseppe Pitrè. Vols. IV.–VII.

La Scatola di Cristallo. Novellina popolare senese raccolta da Giuseppe Pitrè. Palermo, 1875. 8°.
   Per le Nozze Montuoro-Di Giovanni.

Cinque novelline popolari siciliane ora per la prima volta pubblicate da G. Pitrè. Palermo, 1878. 8°.
   Per le Nozze Salomone Marino-Abate. Ediz. di 50 esemplari. See Academy, March 22, 1879, p. 262.

Novelline popolari toscane ora per la prima volta pubblicate da G. Pitrè. Il Medico grillo. Vocaboli. La Gamba. Serpentino. Palermo, 1878. 8°. Pp. 16.
   Per le Nozze Imbriani-Rosnati. Tirato a soli 25 esemplari.

Una variante toscana della novella del Petit Poucet. 8°. Pp. 6.
   Estratto dalla Rivista di Lett. Pop. Vol. I. pp. 161–166.

La Tinchina dell' alto Mare. Fiaba toscana raccolta ed illustrata da Giuseppe Pitrè. Quattrasteriscopoli, 1882. 8°. Pp. 14.
   Per le Nozze Papanti-Giraudini. Esemplari novanta.

Il Zoccolo di Legno, Novella popolare fiorentina. In Giornale Napoletano della Domenica, 2 July, 1882. [== Pitrè, Fiabe, No. XIII.]

I tre pareri. Novella popolare toscana di Pratovecchio nel Cosentino. In Giornale Napoletano della Domenica, 20 August, 1882. [==Pitrè, Fiabe, No. CXCVII.]

Novelle popolari toscane. Florence, 1885. 16°.
   Collected by Giovanni Siciliano. A few of the stories in this collection have already been published in the Archivio per lo Studio delle Tradizioni popolari.

PRATO, STANISLAO

La Leggenda Indiana di Nala in una Novellina. popolare Pitiglianese. 8°. Pp. 8. Extract from I Nuovi Goliardi.

---

* When Pitrè is mentioned without any other qualification than that of a numeral, this work is understood.

La Leggenda del Tesoro di Rampsinite nelle varie redazioni Italiane e Straniere. Como, 1882. 8°. Pp. xii., 51. Edizione di soli 100 esemplari numerati.

Una Novellina popolare monferrina. Como, 1882. 8°. Pp. 67. Edizione di soli 80 esemplari.

Quattro Novelline popolare livornesi accompagnate da varianti umbre raccolte, pubblicate ed illustrate con note comparative. Spoleto, 1880. Gr. 8°. Pp. 168.

L'Uomo nella Luna. Fol. pp. 4. Estratto dalla rivista di Ancona: Il Preludio, del 30 gennaio, 1881.

L' Orma del Leone, un racconto orientale nella tradizione popolare. Romania XII., pp. 535–565.

RALSTON, W. R. S.
Sicilian Fairy Tales. Fraser's Magazine, New Series, vol. XIII 1876, pp. 423–433.

RIVISTA DI LETTERATURA POPOLARE DIRETTA DA G. PITRÈ, F. SABATINI. ROME, 1877.
Vol. I., pp. 81–86, contains *Novelline di Sto. Stefano di Calcinaia* in continuation of *Le Novelline di Santo Stefano*, see De Gubernatis; p. 161, G. Pitrè, *Una variante toscana della novella del Petit Poucet*; p. 213, R. Köhler *Das Räthselmärchen von dem ermordeten Geliebten;* p. 266, G. Pitrè, *La Lucerna, nov, pop. tosc.;* p. 288, F. Sabatini, *La Lanterna, nov. pop. bergamasca.*

ROMANE, QUATTRO NOVELLINE POPOLARI. Nel giornale Il Manzoni (Spoleto), No. I, 1 Marzo, 1880.

SABATINI, FRANCESCO
La Lanterna. Novella popolare siciliana pubblicata ed illustrata a cura di Francesco Sabatini. Imola, 1878. 8°. Pp. 19.
Per le nozze Salomone-Marino-Abate. Edizione di soli 180 esemplari. See Academy, March 22, 1879, p. 262.

SARNELLI, POMPEO, BISHOP OF BISCEGLIE
La Posillecheata de Masillo Reppone di Gnanopole. Naples, 1789. In Collezione di tutti li poeti in lingua Napoletana. 28 vols. 12°. Naples, 1789.

SCALAGERI DELLA FRATTA, CAMILLO
Sette novellette, non più ristampate da oltre due secoli, ripubblicate da V. Imbriani. Pomigliano d' Arco, 1875. 8°. Pp. 15. Soli 150 esemplari.

SCHNELLER, CHRISTIAN
Märchen und Sagen aus Wälschtirol. Ein Beitrag zur deutschen Sagenkunde. Gesammelt von Christian Schneller. Innsbruck, 1867. 8°.

SOMMA, MICHELE
Cento Racconti per divertire gli amici nelle ore oziose e nuovi brindisi per spasso nelle tavole e nelle conversazioni. Messina, 1883. 16°.
The book really contains one hundred and thirty-one stories, and deserves mention hero solely for its relation to the class of stories discussed in Chapter VI.

BIBLIOGRAPHY

STRAPAROLA, GIOVAN FRANCESCO

Piacevoli Notti di M. Giovan Francesco Straparola da Caravagio, Nelle quali si contengono Le Favole con i loro Enimmi da dieci donne, et da duo giovani raccontate. 2 vols. Venice, Per Comin da Trino di Monferrato, 1562. 8°.

Le Tredici Piacevolissime Notte di M. Gio: Francesco Straparola da Caravaggio. Divise in due libri . . . con licenza de' superiori. Venice, 1604. Appresso Zanetto Zanetti. 8°. Con figure.

Les Facetieuses Nuits de Straparole. Traduites par Jean Louveau et Pierre de Larivey. 2 vols. Palis, 1857. 8°.
Bibliothèque elzeverienne.

Die Märchen des Straparola. Aus dem Italienischen, mit Anmerkungen von Dr. F. W. V. Schmidt. Berlin, 1817. 8°. In Märchen-Saal. Sammlung alter Märchen mit Anmerkungen; herausgegeben von Dr. F. W. V. Schmidt. Erster Band.

Giovan Francesco Straparola da Caravaggio. Inaugural-Dissertation zur Erlangung der philosophischen Doctorwürde in Göttingen von F. W. J. Brakelmann. Göttingen, 1867. 8°.

TEZA, E.

La Tradizione dei Sette Savi nelle novelline magiare di E. Teza. Bologna, 1874. Pp. 56. Contains: *Mila e Buccia, novellina, veneziana,* p. 26; *La Novellina del Papagallo, novellina toscana,* p. 52.

TUSCAN FAIRY TALES (Taken down from the Mouths of the People). With sixteen illustrations by J. Stanley, engraved by Edmund Evans. London, 1880. 16°.

VENETIAN POPULAR LEGENDS

The Cornhill Magazine, July, 1875, pp. 80–90.
Devoted to Bernoni's collections.

VISENTINI, ISAIA

Fiabe Mantovane raccolte da Isaia Visentini. Turin, 1879. In Canti e Racconti del Popolo italiano. Vol. VII.

WIDTER-WOLF

Volksmärchen aus Venetian. Gesammelt und herausgegeben von Georg Widter und Adam Wolf. Mit Nachweisen und Vergleichungen verwandter Märchen von Reinhold Köhler. In Jahrbuch für romanische und englische Literatur. Leipzig, 1866. VII. vol., pp. 1–36; 121–154; 249–290.

~

LIST OF STORIES

Those marked with an * are translated from the dialect; those in italics are found in the notes.

I. * THE KING OF LOVE. (Sicilian, Pitrè, No. 18, *Lu Re d'Amuri*) 3

II. ZELINDA AND THE MONSTER. (Tuscan, Nerucci, No. I, *Zelinda e il Mostro*) 8

II. * KING BEAN. (Venetian, Bernoni, *Fiabe*, No. 17, *El Re de Fava*) 11

IV. * THE DANCING WATER, THE SINGING APPLE, AND THE SPEAKING BIRD. (Sicilian, Pitrè, No. 36, *Li Figghi di lu Cavuliciddaru*) 16

V. THE FAIR ANGIOLA. (Sicilian, Gonzenbach, No. 53, *Von der schönen Angiola*) 22

VI. THE CLOUD. (Tuscan, Comparetti, No. 32, *La Nuvolaccia*) 25

VII. * THE CISTERN. (Sicilian, Pitrè, No. 80, *La Jisterna*) 30

VIII. * THE GRIFFIN. (Neapolitan, Imbriani, *Pomiglianesi*, p. 195, *L'Auciello Crifone*) 33

IX. CINDERELLA. (Tuscan, *Novellaja fiorentina*, p. 151, *La Cenerentola*) 35

X. * FAIR MARIA WOOD. (Vincenza, Corazzini, p. 484, *La Bela Maria del Legno*) 39

XI. * THE CURSE OF THE SEVEN CHILDREN. (Bolognese, Coronedi-Berti, No. 19, *La Malediziôn di Sèt Fiù*) 44

XII. ORAGGIO AND BIANCHINETTA. (Tuscan, *Novellaja fiorentina*, p. 314, *Oraggio e Bianchinetta*) 47

XIII. THE FAIR FIORITA. (Basilicata, Comparetti, No. 20, La Bella Fiorita) 49

XIV. * Bierde. (Istrian, Ive, 1877, p. 13, Bierde) 55

XV. * SNOW-WHITE-FIRE-RED. (Sicilian, Pitrè, No. 13, B*ianca-comu-nivi-russa-comu-focu*) 58

XVI. HOW THE DEVIL MARRIED THREE SISTERS. (Venetian, Widter-Wolf, No. II, *Der Teufel heirathet drei Schwestern*) 63

XVII. IN LOVE WITH A STATUE. (Piedmontese, Comparetti, No. 29, *L'Innamorato d' una Statua*) 69

XVIII. * THIRTEENTH. (Sicilian, Pitrè, No. 33, *Tridicinu*) 72

XIX. * THE COBBLER. (Milanese, *Novellaja fiorentina*. p. 575, *El Sciavattin*) 75

XX. *Sir Fiorante, Magician.* (Tuscan, De Gubernatis, *Sto. Stefano*, No. 14, *Sor Fiorante mago*) 257

XXI. *The Crystal Casket.* (Tuscan, *La Scatola di Cristallo raccolta da* G. Pitrè) 261

XXII. * *The Stepmother.* (Sicilian, Pitrè, No. 283, *La Parrastra*) 265

XXIII. * *Water and Salt.* (Sicilian, Pitrè, No. 10, *L'Acqua e lu Salì*) 266

XXIV. * *The Love of the Three Oranges.* (Istrian, Ive, 1878, p. 3, *L'Amur dei tri Narançi*) 270

XXV. THE KING WHO WANTED A BEAUTIFUL WIFE. (Sicilian, Gonzenbach, No. 73, *Von dem Könige, der eine schöne Frau wollte*) 79

XXVI. * THE BUCKET. (Milanese, *Novellaja fiorentina*, p. 190, *El Sidellin*) 81

XXVII. THE TWO HUMPBACKS. (Tuscan, *Novellaja fiorentina*, p. 559, *I due Gobbi*) 83

XXVIII. THE STORY OF CATHERINE AND HER FATE. (Sicilian, Gonzenbach, No. 21, *Die Geschichte von Caterina und ihrem Schicksal*) 85

XXIX. * THE CRUMB IN THE BEARD. (Bolognese, Coronedi-Berti, No. 15, *La Fola d' Brisla in Barba*) 89

XXX. * THE FAIRY ORLANDA. (Neapolitan, *Novellaja fiorentina*, p. 333, *'A Fata Orlanna*) 93

XXXI. THE SHEPHERD WHO MADE THE KING'S DAUGHTER LAUGH. (Sicilian, Gonzenbach, No. 31, *Von dem Schäfer der die Königstochter zum Lachen brachte*) 96

XXXII. THE ASS THAT LAYS MONEY. (Tuscan, Nerucci, No. 43, *Il Ciuchino caca-zecchini*) 100

XXXIII. * DON JOSEPH PEAR. (Sicilian, Pitrè, No. 88, *Don Giuseppi Piru*) 102

XXXIV. PUSS IN BOOTS. (Straparola, XI. 1.) 278

XXXV. * FAIR BROW. (Istrian, Ive, 1877, p. 19, *Biela Fronte*) 106

XXXVI. LIONBRUNO. (Basilicata, Comparetti, No. 41, *Lionbruno*) 109

XXXVII. * THE PEASANT AND THE MASTER. (Sicilian, Pitrè, No. 194, *Lu Burgisi e lu Patruni*) 119

XXXVIII. THE INGRATES. (Piedmontese, Comparetti, No. 67, *Gli Ingrati*) 120

XXXIX. * THE TREASURE. (Sicilian, Pitrè, No. 138, *La Truvatura*) 124

XL. * THE SHEPHERD. (Milanese, *Novellaja fiorentina*, p. 572, *El Pegorée*) 125

XLI. * THE THREE ADMONITIONS. (Sicilian, Pitrè, No. 197, *Li tri Rigordi*) 125

XLII. * VINEYARD I WAS AND VINEYARD I AM. (Venetian. Bernoni, *Trad. pop. venez., Punt.* I. p. 11, *Vigna era e Vigna son*) 127

XLIII. THE LANGUAGE OF ANIMALS. (Piedmontese, Comparetti, No. 56, *Il Linguaggio degli Animali*) 129

XLIV. * THE MASON AND HIS SON. (Sicilian, Pitrè, No. 160, *Lu Muratu ri e sò Figghiu*) 130

XLV. THE PARROT. FIRST VERSION. (Tuscan, Comparetti, No. 1, *Il Papagallo*) 134

XLVI. THE PARROT. SECOND VERSION. (Tuscan, Teza, *La Tradizione dei Sette Savi*, etc., p. 52, *La Novellina del Papagallo*) 135

XLVII. * THE PARROT WHICH TELLS THREE STORIES. THIRD VERSION. (Sicilian, Pitrè, No. 2, *Lu Papagaddu chi cunta tri cunti*) 138

First Story of the Parrot 140

Second Story of the Parrot 142

Third Story of the Parrot 144

XLVIII. * TRUTHFUL JOSEPH. (Neapolitan, *Pomiglianesi*, p. 1, *Giuseppe 'A Veretà*)   147

XLIX. *The Man, the Serpent, and the Fox.* (Otranto, Morosi, p. 75)   283

L. * THE LORD, ST. PETER, AND THE APOSTLES. (Sicilian, Pitrè, No. 123, *Lu Signuri, S. Petru e li Apostuli*)   150

LI. THE LORD, ST. PETER, AND THE BLACKSMITH. (Venetian, Widter-Wolf, No. 5, *Der Herrgott, St. Peter und der Schmied*)   151

LII. * IN THIS WORLD ONE WEEPS AND ANOTHER LAUGHS. (Sicilian, Pitrè, *Cinque nov. pop. sicil.*, p. 7, *A stu munnu cu' chianci e cu' ridi*)   153

LIII. * THE ASS. (Sicilian, Pitrè, *Cinque nov. pop, sicil.*, p. 8, *Lu Sceccu*)   153

LIV. ST. PETER AND HIS SISTERS. (Tyrolese, Schneller, p. 6, *St. Petrus und seine Schwestern*)   155

LV. * PILATE. (Sicilian, Pitrè, No. 119, *Pilatu*)   156

LVI. * THE STORY OF JUDAS. (Sicilian, Pitrè, vol. I. p, cxxxviii., *Lu Cuntu di Giuda*)   157

LVII. * DESPERATE MALCHUS. (Sicilian, Pitrè, No. 120, *Marcu dispiratu*)   158

LVIII. * MALCHUS AT THE COLUMN. (Venetian, Bernoni, *Preghiere pop. veneziane*, p. 18, *Malco a la Colona*)   158

LIX. * THE STORY OF BUTTADEU. (Sicilian, Pitrè, vol. I. p. cxxxiii., *La Storia di Buttadeu*)   159

LX. THE STORY OF CRIVÒLIU. (Sicilian, Gonzenbach, No. 85, *Vom Crivòliu*)   160

LXI. THE STORY OF ST. JAMES OF GALICIA. (Sicilian, Gonzenbach, No. 90, *Die Geschichte von San Japicu alla Lizia*)   163

LXII. * THE BAKER'S APPRENTICE. (Sicilian, Pitrè, No. 111, *Lu Giuvini di lu Furnaru*)   170

LXIII. * OCCASION. (Sicilian, Pitrè, No. 124, *Accaciùni*)   173

LXIV. * BROTHER GIOVANNONE. (Sicilian, Pitrè, No. 125, *Fra Giugannuni*)   175

LXV. GODFATHER MISERY. (Tuscan, De Gubernatis, *Sto. Stefano*, No. 32, *Compar Miseria*)   177

LXVI. BEPPO PIPETTA. (Venetian, Widter-Wolf, No.7, *Beppo Pipetta*)   179

LXVII. * THE JUST MAN. (Venetian, Bernoni, *Trad. pop. venez.*, Punt. I. p. 6, *El Giusto*)   182

LXVIII. * OF A GODFATHER AND A GODMOTHER OF ST. JOHN WHO MADE LOVE. (Venetian, Bernoni, *Leggende*, p. 3, *De una comare e un compare de San Zuane che i conversava in fra de lori*)   184

LXIX. * THE GROOMSMAN. (Venetian, Bernoni, *Leggende*, p. 7, *De un compare de l' anelo ch' el gà strucà la man a la sposa co cativa intenzion*)   186

LXX. * THE PARISH PRIEST OF SAN MARCUOLA. (Venetian, Bernoni, *Leggende*, p. 17, *De un piovan de San Marcuola, che gà dito che i morti in dove che i xè i resta*)   188

LXXI. * THE GENTLEMAN WHO KICKED A SKULL. (Venetian, Bernoni, *Leggende*, p. 19, *De un signor che gà dà 'na peada a un cragno da morto*)   189

LXXII. * *The Gossips of St. John.* (Sicilian, Pitrè, No.110, *Li Cumpari di S. Giuvanni*)   295

LXXIII. * SADDAEDDA. (Sicilian, Pitrè, No. 128, *Saddaedda*)   191

LXXIV. * MR. ATTENTIVE. (Venetian, Bernoni, *Punt.* II. p. 53, *Sior Intento*)   193

LXXV. * THE STORY OF THE BARBER. (Sicilian, Pitrè, No. 141, *Lu Cuntu di lu Varveri*)   194

LXXVI. * DON FIRRIULIEDDU. (Sicilian, Pitrè, No. 130, *Don Firriulieddu*)   194

LXXVII. LITTLE CHICK-PEA. (Tuscan, *Rivista di Lett. pop.* I. p. 161, *Cecino*)   195

LXXVIII. * PITIDDA. (Sicilian, Pitrè, No. 131, *Pitidda*)   200

LXXIX. * THE SEXTON'S NOSE. (Sicilian, Pitrè, No. 135, *Lu Nasu di lu Sagristanu*)   201

LXXX. * THE COCK AND THE MOUSE. (Principato Ulteriore, Imbriani, *Pomiglianesi*, p. 239, *'O Gallo e 'o Sorece*)   203

LXXXI. * GODMOTHER FOX. (Sicilian, Pitrè, No. 132, *Cummari Vurpidda*)   204

LXXXII. * THE CAT AND THE MOUSE. (Sicilian, Pitrè, No. 134, *La Gatta e lu Surci*)   207

LXXXIII. * A FEAST DAY. (Venetian, Bernoni, *Fiabe*, No. 4, *'Na Giornada de Sagra*)   210

LXXXIV. * THE THREE BROTHERS. (Venetian, Bernoni, *Trad. pop. venez.*, *Punt.* I. p. 18, *I tre Fradei*)   212

LXXXV. BUCHETTINO. (Tuscan, Papanti, *Novelline pop. livornesi*, p. 25, *Buchettino*)   213

LXXXVI. * THE THREE GOSLINGS. (Venetian, Bernoni, *Trad. pop. venez.*, *Punt.* III. p. 65, *Le Tre Ochete*)   215

LXXXVII. * THE COCK. (Venetian, Bernoni, *Trad. pop. venez.*, *Punt.* III. p. 69, *El Galo*)   218

LXXXVIII. THE COCK THAT WISHED TO BECOME POPE. (Sicilian, Gonzenbach, No. 66, *Von dem Hahne, der Pabst werden wollte*)   219

LXXXIX. THE GOAT AND THE FOX. (Otranto, Morosi, p. 73)   300

XC. THE ANT AND THE MOUSE. (Otranto, Morosi, p. 73)   302

XCI. * THE COOK. (Milan, *Novellaja fiorentina*, p. 621, *El Coeugh*)   221

XCII. * THE THOUGHTLESS ABBOT. (Sicilian, Pitrè, No. 97, *L'Abbati senza Pinseri*)   222

XCIII. * BASTIANELO. (Venetian, Bernoni, *Fiabe*, No. 6, *Bastianelo*)   224

XCIV. * CHRISTMAS. (Neapolitan, Imbriani, *Pomiglianesi*, p. 226, *Natale*)   227

XCV. * THE WAGER. (Venetian, Bernoni, *Fiabe*, No. 13, *La Scomessa*)   228

XCVI. * SCISSORS THEY WERE. (Sicilian, Pitrè, No. 257, *Fòrfici fòro*)   229

XCVII. * THE DOCTOR'S APPRENTICE. (Sicilian, Pitrè, No. 180, *L'Apprinnista di lu Medicu*)   230

XCVIII. * FIRRAZZANU'S WIFE AND THE QUEEN. (Sicilian, Pitrè, No. 156, *La Mugghieri di Firrazzanu e la Riggina*)   231

XCIX. * GIUFÀ AND THE PLASTER STATUE. (Sicilian, Pitrè, No. 190, 1, *Giufà e la statua di ghissu*)   234

C. * GIUFÀ AND THE JUDGE. (Sicilian, Pitrè, No. 190, 3, *Giufà e lu Judici*)   235

CI. THE LITTLE OMELET. (Tuscan, *Novellaja fiorentina*, p. 545, *La. Fritatina*)   236

CII. * EAT, MY CLOTHES! (Sicilian, Pitrè, No. 190, 9, *Manciaiti, rubbiceddi mei!*)   238

LIST OF STORIES

CIII. GIUFÀ's EXPLOITS. (Sicilian, Gonzenbach, No. 37, *Giufà*)   239

CIV. * THE FOOL. (Venetian, Bernoni, *Fiabe,* No. 11, *El Mato*)   243

CV. * UNCLE CAPRIANO. (Sicilian, Pitrè, No. 157, *Lu Zu Crapianu*)   244

CVI. * *Peter Fullone and the Egg.* (Sicilian, Pitrè, No. 200, *Petru Fudduni e l'ovu*)   305

CVII. THE CLEVER PEASANT. (Sicilian, Gonzenbach, No. 50, *Vom Klugen Bauer*)   249

CVIII. THE CLEVER GIRL. (Tuscan, Comparetti, No. 43, *La Ragazza astuta*) 250

CIX. CRAB. (Mantuan, Visentini, No. 41, *Gámbara*)   253

ITALIAN POPULAR TALES

჻

CHAPTER I

FAIRY TALES

THE most wide-spread and interesting class of Fairy Tales is the one in which a wife endeavors to behold the face of her husband, who comes to her only at night. She succeeds, but her husband disappears, and she is not reunited to him until she has expiated her indiscretion by weary journeys and the performance of difficult tasks. This class, which is evidently the popular form of the classic myth of Cupid and Psyche, may for convenience be divided into four classes. The first turns on the punishment of the wife's curiosity; the second, on the husband's (Melusina); in the third the heroine is married to a monster, is separated from him by her disobedience, but finally is the means of his recovering his human form; the fourth class is a variant of the first and third, the husband being an animal in form, and parted from his wife by the curiosity or disobedience of the latter or of her envious sisters.

To illustrate the first class, we select, from the large number of stories before us, a Sicilian tale (Pitrè, No. 18) entitled:

✣ I. The King of Love ✣

Once upon a time there was a man with three daughters, who earned his living by gathering wild herbs. One day he took his youngest daughter with him. They came to a garden, and began to gather vegetables. The daughter saw a fine radish, and began to pull it up, when suddenly a Turk appeared, and said: "Why have you opened my master's door? You must come in now, and he will decide on your punishment."

They went down into the ground, more dead than alive; and when they were seated they saw a green bird come in and bathe in a pan of milk, then dry itself, and become a handsome youth. He said to the Turk: "What do these persons want?" "Your worship, they pulled up a radish, and opened the door of the cave." "How did we know," said the father, "That this was Your Excellency's house? My daughter saw a fine radish; it pleased her, and she pulled it up." "Well, if that's the case," said the master, "your daughter shall stay here as my wife; take this sack of gold and go; when you want to see your daughter, come and make yourself at home." The father took leave of his daughter and went away.

When the master was alone with her, he said: "You see, Rosella (Rusidda), you are now mistress here," and gave her all the keys. She was perfectly happy (literally, "Was happy to the hairs of her head"). One day, while the green bird was away, her sisters took it into their heads to visit her, and asked her about her husband. Rosella said she did not know, for he had made her promise not to try to find out who he was. Her sisters, however, persuaded her, and when the bird returned and became a man, Rosella put on a downcast air. "What is the matter?" asked her husband. "Nothing." "You had better tell me." She let him question her a while, and at last said: "Well, then, if you want to know why I am out of sorts, it is because I wish to know your name." Her husband told her that it would be the worse for her, but she insisted on knowing his name. So he made her put the gold basins on a chair, and began to bathe his feet. "Rosella, do you really want to know my name?" "Yes." And the water came up to his waist, for he had become a bird, and had got into the basin. Then he asked her the same question again, and again she answered yes, and the water was up to his mouth. "Rosella, do you really want to know my name?" "Yes, yes, yes!" "Then know that I am called THE KING OF LOVE!" And saying this he disappeared, and the basins and the palace disappeared likewise, and Rosella found herself alone out in an open plain, without a soul to help her. She called her servants, but no one answered her. Then she said: "Since my husband has disappeared, I must wander about alone and forlorn to seek him!"

The poor woman, who expected before long to become a mother, began her wanderings, and at night arrived at another lonely plain; then she felt her heart sink, and, not knowing what to do, she cried out:—

> "Ah! King of Love,
> You did it, and said it.
> You disappeared from me in a golden basin,
> And who will shelter to-night
> This poor unfortunate one?"

When she had uttered these words an ogress appeared and said: "Ah! Wretch, how dare you go about seeking my nephew?" and was going to eat her up; but she took pity on her miserable state, and gave her shelter for the night. The next morning she gave her a piece of bread, and said: "We are seven sisters, all ogresses, and the worst of all is your mother-in-law; look out for her!"

To be brief, the poor girl wandered about six days, and met all six of the ogresses who treated her in the same way. The seventh day, in great distress, she uttered her usual lament, and the sister of the King of Love appeared and said, "Rosella, while my mother is out, come up!" And she lowered the braids of her hair, and pulled her up. Then she gave her something to eat, and told her how to seize and pinch her mother until she cried out: "Let me alone for the sake of my son, the King of Love!"

Rosella did as she was told, but the ogress was so angry she was going to eat her. But her daughters threatened to abandon her if she did. "Well, then, I will write a letter, and Rosella must carry it to my friend." Poor Rosella was disheartened when she saw the letter, and, descending, found herself in the midst of a plain. She uttered her usual complaint, when the King of Love appeared, and said: "You see your curiosity has brought you to this point!" Poor thing! When she saw him she began to cry, and begged his pardon for what she had done. He took pity on her, and said: "Now listen to what you must do. On your way you will come to a river of blood; you must bend down and take some up in your hands, and say: 'How beautiful is this crystal water! Such water as this I have never drunk!' Then you will come to another stream of turbid water, and do the same there. Then you will find yourself in a garden where there is a great quantity of fruit; pick some and eat it, saying: 'What fine pears! I have never eaten such pears as these.' Afterward, you will come to an oven that bakes bread day and night, and no one buys any. When you come there, say: 'Oh, what fine bread! Bread like this I have never eaten,' and eat some. Then you will come to an entrance guarded by two hungry dogs; give them a piece of bread to eat. Then you will come to a doorway all dirty and full of cobwebs; take a broom and sweep it clean. Halfway up the stairs you will find two giants, each with a dirty piece of meat by his side; take a brush and clean it for them. When you have entered the house, you will find a razor, a pair of scissors, and a knife; take something and polish them. When you have done this, go in and deliver your letter to my mother's friend. When she wants to make you enter, snatch up a little box on the table, and run away. Take care to do all the things I have told you, or else you will never escape alive."

5

Rosella did as she was told, and while the ogress was reading the letter Rosella seized the box and ran for her life. When the ogress had finished reading her letter, she called: "Rosella! Rosella!" When she received no answer, she perceived that she had been betrayed, and cried out: "Razor, Scissors, Knife, cut her in pieces!" They answered: "As long as we have been razor, scissors, and knife, when did you ever deign to polish us? Rosella came and brightened us up." The ogress, enraged, exclaimed: "Stairs, swallow her up!" "As long as I have been stairs, when did you ever deign to sweep me? Rosella came and swept me." The ogress cried in a passion: "Giants, crush her!" "As long as we have been giants, when did you ever deign to clean our food for us? Rosella came and did it."

Then the furious ogress called on the entrance to bury her alive, the dogs to devour her, the furnace to burn her, the fruit-tree to fall on her, and the rivers to drown her; but they all remembered Rosella's kindness, and refused to injure her.

Meanwhile Rosella continued her way, and at last became curious to know what was in the box she was carrying. So she opened it, and a great quantity of little puppets came out; some danced, some sang, and some played on musical instruments. She amused herself some time with them; but when she was ready to go on, the little figures would not return to the box. Night approached, and she exclaimed, as she had so often before:—

"Ah! King of Love," etc.

Then her husband appeared and said, "Oh, your curiosity will be the death of you!" And commanded the puppets to enter the box again. Then Rosella went her way, and arrived safely at her mother-in-law's. When the ogress saw her she exclaimed: "You owe this luck to my son, the King of Love!" And was going to devour poor Rosella, but her daughters said: "Poor child! She has brought you the box; why do you want to eat her?" "Well and good. You want to marry my son, the King of Love; then take these six mattresses, and go and fill them with birds' feathers!" Rosella descended, and began to wander about, uttering her usual lament. When her husband appeared Rosella told him what had happened. He whistled and the King of the Birds appeared, and commanded all the birds to come and drop their feathers, fill the six beds, and carry them back to the ogress, who again said that her son had helped Rosella. However, she went and made up her son's bed with the six mattresses, and that very day she made him marry the daughter of the King of Portugal. Then she called Rosella, and, telling her that her son was married, bade her kneel before the nuptial bed, holding two lighted torches. Rosella obeyed, but soon the King of Love, under the plea that Rosella was not in a condition to hold the torches any longer, persuaded his bride to change places with her. Just as the queen took the torches in her hands, the earth opened and swallowed her up, and the king remained happy with Rosella.

When the ogress heard what had happened she clasped her hands over her head, and declared that Rosella's child should not be born until she unclasped her hands. Then the King of Love had a catafalque erected, and stretched himself on it as though he were dead, and had all the bells tolled, and made the people cry, "How did the King of Love die?" The ogress heard it, and asked: "What is that noise?" Her daughters told her that their brother was dead from her fault. When the ogress heard this she unclasped her hands, saying, "How did my son die?" At that moment Rosella's child was born. When the ogress heard it she burst a blood-vessel (in her heart) and died. Then the King of Love took his wife and sisters, and they remained happy and contented.[1]

THERE is another version of this story in Pitrè (No. 281) entitled, "The Crystal King," which resembles more closely the classic myth.

A father marries the youngest of his three daughters to a cavalier (the enchanted son of a king) who comes to his wife at night only. The cavalier once permits his wife to visit her sisters, and they learn from her that she has never seen her husband's face. The eldest gives her a wax candle, and tells her to light it when her husband is asleep, and then she can see him and tell them what he is like. She did so, and beheld at her side a handsome youth; but while she was gazing at him some of the melted wax fell on his nose. He awoke, crying, "Treason! Treason!" and drove his wife from the house. On her wanderings she meets a hermit, and tells him her story. He advises her to have made a pair of iron shoes, and when she has worn them out in her travels she will come to a palace where they will give her shelter, and where she will find her husband. The remainder of the story is of no interest here.[2]

In the second class of stories belonging to this myth it is the curiosity of the husband which is punished, the best known example of this class, out of Italy, being the beautiful French legend of Melusina.[3] A Sicilian story in Gonzenbach, No. 16, "The Story of the Merchant's Son Peppino," is a very close counterpart of "The King of Love," above given. Peppino is wrecked on a rock in the sea; the rock opens, fair maidens come out and conduct Peppino to a beautiful castle in the cave. There a maiden visits him at night only. After a time Peppino wishes to see his parents, and his wife allows him to depart, with the promise to return at a certain date. His parents, after hearing his story, give him a candle with which to see his wife. Everything happens as in the first story; the castle disappears, and Peppino finds himself on the top of a snow-covered mountain. He recovers his wife only after the lapse of many years and the accomplishment of many difficult tasks.[4]

The third class, generally known by the title of "Beauty and the Beast," is best represented by a story from Montale (near Pistoia), called:

✦ II. Zelinda and the Monster ✦

There was once a poor man who had three daughters; and as the youngest was the fairest and most civil, and had the best disposition, her other two sisters envied her with a deadly envy, although her father, on the contrary, loved her dearly. It happened that in a neighboring town, in the month of January, there was a great fair, and that poor man was obliged to go there to lay in the provisions necessary for the support of his family; and before departing he asked his three daughters if they would like some small presents in proportion, you understand, to his means. Rosina wished a dress, Marletta asked him for a shawl, but Zelinda was satisfied with a handsome rose. The poor man set out on his journey early the next day, and when he arrived at the fair quickly bought what he needed, and afterward easily found Rosina's dress and Marletta's shawl; but at that season he could not find a rose for his Zelinda, although he took great pains in looking everywhere for one. However, anxious to please his dear Zelinda, he took the first road he came to, and after journeying a while arrived at a handsome garden enclosed by high walls; but as the gate was partly open he entered softly. He found the garden filled with every kind of flowers and plants, and in a corner was a tall rosebush full of beautiful rosebuds. Wherever he looked no living soul appeared from whom he might ask a rose as a gift or for money, so the poor man, without thinking, stretched out his hand, and picked a rose for his Zelinda.

Mercy! Scarcely had he pulled the flower from the stalk when there arose a great noise, and flames darted from the earth, and all at once there appeared a terrible Monster with the figure of a dragon, and hissed with all his might, and cried out, enraged at that poor Christian: "Rash man! What have you done? Now you must die at once, for you have had the audacity to touch and destroy my rosebush." The poor man, more than half dead with terror, began to weep and beg for mercy on his knees, asking pardon for the fault he had committed, and told why he had picked the rose; and then he added: "Let me depart; I have a family, and if I am killed they will go to destruction." But the Monster, more wicked than ever, responded: "Listen; one must die. Either bring me the girl that asked for the rose or I will kill you this very moment." It was impossible to move him by prayers or lamentations; the Monster persisted in his decision, and did not let the poor man go until he had sworn to bring him there in the garden his daughter Zelinda.

Imagine how downhearted that poor man returned home! He gave his oldest daughters their presents and Zelinda her rose; but his face was distorted and as white as though he had arisen from the dead; so that the girls, in terror, asked him what had happened and whether he had met with any misfortune. They were urgent, and at last the poor man, weeping bitterly, related the misfortunes of that unhappy journey and on what condition he had been able finally to return home. "In short," he exclaimed, "either Zelinda or I must be eaten alive by the Monster." Then the two sisters emptied the vials of their wrath on Zelinda, "Just see," they said, "That affected, capricious girl! She shall go to the Monster! She who wanted roses at this season. No, indeed! Papa must stay with us. The stupid creature!" At all these taunts Zelinda, without growing angry, simply said: "It is right that the one who has caused the misfortune should pay for it. I will go to the Monster's. Yes, Papa, take me to the garden, and the Lord's will be done."

The next day Zelinda and her sorrowful father began their journey and at nightfall arrived at the garden gate. When they entered they saw as usual no one, but they beheld a lordly palace all lighted and the doors wide open. When the two travelers entered the vestibule, suddenly four marble statues, with lighted torches in their hands, descended from their pedestals, and accompanied them up the stairs to a large hall where a table was lavishly spread. The travelers, who were very hungry, sat down and began to eat without ceremony; and when they had finished, the same statues conducted them to two handsome chambers for the night. Zelinda and her father were so weary that they slept like dormice all night.

At daybreak Zelinda and her father arose, and were served with everything for breakfast by invisible hands. Then they descended to the garden, and began to seek the Monster. When they came to the rose-bush he appeared in all his frightful ugliness. Zelinda, on seeing him, became pale with fear, and her limbs trembled, but the Monster regarded her attentively with his great fiery eyes, and afterward said to the poor man: "Very well; you have kept your word, and I am satisfied. Now depart and leave me alone here with the young girl." At this command the old man thought he should die; and Zelinda, too, stood there half stupefied and her eyes full of tears; but entreaties were of no avail; the Monster remained as obdurate as a stone, and the poor man was obliged to depart, leaving his dear Zelinda in the Monster's power.

When the Monster was alone with Zelinda he began to caress her, and make loving speeches to her, and managed to appear quite civil. There was no danger of his forgetting her, and he saw that she wanted nothing, and every day, talking with her in the garden, he asked her: "Do you love me, Zelinda? Will you be my wife?" The young girl always answered him in the same way: "I like you, sir, but I will never be your wife." Then the Monster appeared very sorrowful, and redoubled his caresses and attentions, and, sighing deeply, said: "But you see, Zelinda, if you should marry me wonderful things would happen. What they are I cannot tell you until you will be my wife."

Zelinda, although in her heart not dissatisfied with that beautiful place and with being treated like a queen, still did not feel at all like marrying the Monster, because he was too ugly and looked like a beast, and always answered his requests in the same manner. One day, however, the Monster called Zelinda in haste, and said: "Listen, Zelinda; if you do not consent to marry me it is fated that your father must die. He is ill and near the end of his life, and you will not be able even to see him again. See whether I am telling you the truth." And, drawing out an enchanted mirror, the Monster showed Zelinda her father on his deathbed. At that spectacle Zelinda, in despair and half mad with grief, cried: "Oh, save my father, for mercy's sake! Let me be able to embrace him once more before he dies. Yes, yes, I promise you I will be your faithful and constant wife, and that without delay. But save my father from death."

Scarcely had Zelinda uttered these words when suddenly the Monster was transformed into a very handsome youth. Zelinda was astounded by this unexpected change, and the young man took her by the hand, and said: "Know, dear Zelinda, that I am the son of the King of the Oranges. An old witch, touching me, changed me into the terrible Monster I was, and condemned me to be hidden in this rosebush until a beautiful girl consented to become my wife."

THE remainder of the story has no interest here. Zelinda and her husband strive to obtain his parents' consent to his marriage. They refuse and the young couple run away from the royal palace and fall into the power of an ogre and his wife, from whom they at last escape.[5]

A characteristic trait of this class of stories is omitted in the above version, but found in a number of others. In a Sicilian version (Pitrè, No. 39, "The Empress Rosina") the monster permits Rosina to visit her family, but warns her that if she does not return at the end of nine days he will die. He gives her a ring the stone of which will grow black in that event. The nine days pass unheeded, and when Rosina looks at her ring it is as black as pitch. She returns in haste, and finds the monster writhing in the last agony under the rosebush. Four days she rubbed him with some ointment she found in the palace, and the monster recovered. As in the last story, he resumes his shape when Rosina consents to marry him. In one of Pitrè's variants the monster allows Elizabeth to visit her dying father, if she will promise not to tear her hair. When her father dies she forgets, in her grief, her promise, and tears out her hair. When she returns to the palace the monster has disappeared. She seeks him, exclaiming:—

> "Fierce animal mine,
> If I find thee alive
> I will marry thee although an animal."

She finds him at last, and he resumes his form.[6]

The fourth class consists of stories more or less distantly connected with the first and third classes above mentioned, and which turn on the heroine's separation from, and search after, her lost husband, usually an animal in form.

The example we have selected from this class is from Venice (Bernoni, XVII.), and is as follows:—

ꙮ III. King Bean ꙮ

There was once an old man who had three daughters. One day the youngest called her father into her room, and requested him to go to King Bean and ask him whether he wished her for his wife. The poor old man said: "You want me to go, but what shall I do; I have never been there?" "No matter," she answered; "I wish you to obey me and go." Then he started on his way, and asked (for he did not know) where the king lived, and they pointed out the palace to him. When he was in the king's presence he said: "Your Majesty's servant." The king replied: "What do you want of me, my good old man?" Then he told him that his daughter was in love with him, and wanted to marry him. The king answered: "How can she be in love with me when she has never seen or known me?" "She is killing herself with weeping, and cannot stand it much longer." The king replied: "Here is a white handkerchief; let her dry her tears with it."

The old man took back the handkerchief and the message to his daughter, who said: "Well, after three or four days you must go back again, and tell him that I will kill myself or hang myself if he will not marry me."

The old man went back, and said to the king: "Your Majesty, do me the favor to marry my daughter; if not, she will make a great spectacle of herself." The king replied: "Behold how many handsome portraits I have held, and how many beautiful young girls I have, and not one of them suits me." The old man said: "She told me also to say to you that if you did not marry her she would kill herself or hang herself." Then the king gave him a knife and a rope, and said: "Here is a knife if she wants to kill herself, and here is a rope if she wants to hang herself."

The old man bore this message back to his daughter, who told her father that he must go back to the king again, and not leave him until he obtained his consent. The old man returned once more, and, falling on his knees before the king, said: "Do me this great favor: take my daughter for your wife; do not say no, for the poor girl is beside herself." The king answered: "Rise, good old man, and I will consent, for I am sorry for your long journeys. But hear what your daughter must do first. She must prepare three vessels: one of milk and water, one of milk, and one of rosewater. And here is a bean; when she wants to speak with me, let her go out on the balcony and open the bean, and I will come."

The old man returned home this time more satisfied, and told his daughter what she must do. She prepared the three vessels as directed, and then opened the bean on the balcony, and saw at once something flying from a distance towards her. It flew into the room by the balcony, and entered the vessel of water and milk to bathe, then it hastened into the vessel of milk, and finally into that containing the rosewater. And then there came out the handsomest youth that was ever seen, and made love to the young girl. Afterward, when they were tired of their love-making, he bade her good-night, and flew away.

After a time, when her sisters saw that she was always shut up in her room, the oldest said: "Why does she shut herself up in her room all the time?" The other sister replied: "Because she has King Bean, who is making love to her." The oldest said: "Wait until she goes to church, and then we will see what there is in her room." One day the youngest locked her door, and went to church. Then the two sisters broke open the door, and saw the three vessels prepared, and said: "This is the vessel in which the king goes to bathe." The oldest said; "Let us go down into the store, and get some broken glass, and put a little in each of the three vessels; and when the king bathes in them, the glass will pierce him and cut all his body."

They did so, and then left the room looking as it did first. When the youngest sister returned, she went to her room, and wished to talk with her husband. She opened the balcony, and then she opened the bean, and saw at once her husband come flying from a distance, with his arms open to embrace her. He flew on to the balcony, and threw himself into the vessel of milk and water, and the pieces of glass pierced his body; then he entered the vessel of milk and that of rosewater, and his body was filled with the fragments of glass. When he came out of the rosewater, he flew away. Then his wife hastened out on the balcony, and saw a streak of blood wherever he had flown. Then she looked into the vessels, and saw all three full of blood, and cried: "I have been betrayed! I have been betrayed!"

She called her father, and told him that she had been betrayed by her sisters, and that she wished to go away and see whether she could cure her husband. She departed, and had not gone far when she found herself in a forest. There she saw a little house, with a little bit of a door, at which she knocked, and heard a voice saying, "Are you Christians?" She replied, "Yes." Then the door opened, and she saw a holy hermit, who said; "Blessed one, how did you get here? In a moment the witches will come who might bewitch you." She replied: "Father, I am seeking King Bean, who is ill." The hermit said: "I know nothing about him. Climb that tree; the witches will soon come, and you will learn something from them. If you want anything afterward, come to me, and I will give it to you."

When she was up the tree she heard a loud noise and the words, "Here we are! Here we are!" And all the witches run and seat themselves on the ground in the midst of the forest, and begin to say: "The cripple is not here! Where has that cursed cripple gone?" Some one answered: "Here she is coming!" Another said: "You cursed cripple, where have you been?" The cripple answered: "Be still; I will tell you now. But wait a moment until I shake this tree to see whether there is any one in it." The poor girl held on firmly so as not to fall down. After she had shaken it this cripple said to her companions: "Do you want me to tell you something? King Bean has only two hours to live." Another witch said: "What is the matter with him?" The cripple answered: "He had a wife, and she put some broken glass in the three vessels, and he filled his body with it." Another witch asked: "Is there nothing that can cure him?" The cripple replied: "It is very difficult." Another said: "What would be necessary?" The cripple said: "Listen to what it needs. One of us must be killed, and her blood put in a kettle, and have added to it the blood of one of these doves flying about here. When this blood is well mixed, it must be heated, and with this blood the whole body of the king must be anointed. Another thing yet is necessary. Under the stone you see there is a flask of water. The stone must be removed, a bottle of the water must be poured over the king, and all the bits of glass will come out of him, and in five minutes he will be safe and sound."

Then the witches ate and drank until they were intoxicated and tired, and then threw themselves down on the ground to sleep. When the young girl saw that they were asleep, she descended quietly from the tree, knocked at the hermit's door, told him what the witches had said, and asked him for a kettle, knife, and bottle. He gave them to her, and caught a dove, which he killed, bled, and put the blood in a kettle.

The young girl did not know which one of the witches to kill, but finally she decided to kill the cripple who had spoken, and put her blood in the kettle. Afterward she lifted the stone, found the flask of water, and filled her bottle with it. She then returned to the hermit, and told him all she had done. He gave her a physician's dress, which she put on, and went to the palace of King Bean. There she asked the guards to let her pass, for she was going, she said, to see about curing the king. The guards refused at first, but, seeing her so confident, allowed her to enter. The king's mother went to her at once and said: "My good physician, if you can cure my son, you shall mount the throne, and I will give you my crown." "I have come in haste from a distance," said the physician, "and will cure him." Then the physician went to the kitchen, put the kettle on the fire, and afterward entered the room of the king, who had but a few minutes to live, anointed his whole body with the blood, and then poured the bottle of water all over him. Then the glass came out of his body, and in five minutes he was safe and sound. The king said: "Here, physician, is my crown. I wish to put it on your head." The physician answered: "How did your Majesty come to have this slight trouble?" The king said: "On account of my wife. I went to make love to her, and she prepared for me three vessels of water and milk, of milk, and of rosewater, and put broken glass in them, so that I had my body full of it." Said the physician: "See whether it was your wife who worked you this treason! Could it not have been some one else?" "That is impossible," said the king; "for no one entered her room." "And what would you do," said the physician, "If you had her now in your hands?" "I would kill her with a knife." "You are right," said the physician; "Because, if it is true that she has acted thus, she deserves nothing but death."

Then the physician said he must depart; but the king's mother said: "No, no! It shall never be said that after saving my son's life you went away. Here you are, and here I wish you to stay; and, on account of the promise I made you, I wish my crown to come upon your head." "I want but one thing," said the physician. "Command, doctor; only say what you desire." "I wish the king to write on the palm of one of my hands my name and surname, and on the other his name and surname." The king did so, and the physician said: "Now I am going to make some visits, then I will return."

Instead of returning, the pretended physician went to her own home, and threw away the water and milk in the three vessels, and put in other pure water and milk and rosewater. Then she went out on the balcony, and opened the bean. The king, who felt his heart opened, seized his dagger, and hastened to his wife to kill her. When she saw the dagger, she raised her hands, and the king beheld his name and hers. Then he threw his dagger away, bathed in the three vessels, and then threw his arms about his wife's neck, and exclaimed: "If you are the one who did me so much harm, you are also the one who cured me." She answered: "It was not I. I was betrayed by my sisters." "If that is so," said he, "come at once to my parents' house, and we will be married there." When she arrived at the king's palace, she related everything to his parents, and showed them her hands with her name and surname. Then the king's parents embraced her, and gave her a wedding, and she and the king loved each other as long as they lived.[7]

THE NEXT class to which we shall direct our attention is the one in which jealous relatives (usually envious sisters or mother-in-law), steal a mother's new-born children, who are exposed and afterwards rescued and brought up far from their home by some childless person; or the mother is accused of having devoured them, and is repudiated or punished, and finally delivered and restored to her former position by her children, who are discovered by their father.[8]

The following story, belonging to this class, is from Pitrè (No. 36), slightly condensed.

↶ IV. The Dancing Water, the Singing Apple, and the Speaking Bird[9] ↶

There was once an herb-gatherer who had three daughters who earned their living by spinning. One day their father died and left them all alone in the world. Now the king had a habit of going about the streets at night, and listening at the doors to hear what the people said of him. One night he listened at the door of the house where the three sisters lived, and heard them disputing about something. The oldest said: "If I were the wife of the royal butler, I would give the whole court to drink out of one glass of water, and there would be some left." The second said: "If I were the wife of the keeper of the royal wardrobe, with one piece of cloth I would clothe all the attendants, and have some left." The youngest said: "Were I the king's wife, I would bear him three children: two sons with apples in their hands, and a daughter with a star on her brow."

The king went back to his palace, and the next morning sent for the sisters, and said to them: "Do not be frightened, but tell me what you said last night." The oldest told him what she had said, and the king had a glass of water brought, and commanded her to prove her words. She took the glass, and gave all the attendants to drink, and there was some water left. "Bravo!" cried the king, and summoned the butler. "This is your husband. Now it is your turn," said the king to the next sister, and commanded a piece of cloth to be brought, and the young girl at once cut out garments for all the attendants, and had some cloth left. "Bravo!" cried the king again, and gave her the keeper of the wardrobe for her husband. "Now it is your turn," said the king to the youngest. "Your Majesty, I said that were I the king's wife, I would bear him three children: two sons with apples in their hands, and a daughter with a star on her brow." The king replied: "If that is true, you shall be queen; if not, you shall die," and straightway he married her.

Very soon the two older sisters began to be envious of the youngest. "Look," said they, "she is going to be queen, and we must be servants!" And they began to hate her. A few months before the queen's children were to be born, the king declared war, and was obliged to depart; but he left word that if the queen had three children: two sons with apples in their hands and a girl with a star on her brow, the mother was to be respected as queen; if not, he was to be informed of it, and would tell his servants what to do. Then he departed for the war.

When the queen's children were born, as she had promised, the envious sisters bribed the nurse to put little dogs in the place of the queen's children, and sent word to the king that his wife had given birth to three puppies. He wrote back that she should be taken care of for two weeks, and then put into a tread-mill.

Meanwhile the nurse took the little babies, and carried them out of doors, saying: "I will make the dogs eat them up," and she left them alone. While they were thus exposed, three fairies passed by and exclaimed: "Oh how beautiful these children are!" And one of the fairies said: "What present shall we make these children?" One answered: "I will give them a deer to nurse them." "And I a purse always full of money." "And I," said the third fairy, "will give them a ring which will change color when any misfortune happens to one of them."

The deer nursed and took care of the children until they grew up. Then the fairy who had given them the deer came and said: "Now that you have grown up, how can you stay here any longer?" "Very well," said one of the brothers, "I will go to the city and hire a house." "Take care," said the deer, "That you hire one opposite the royal palace." So they all went to the city and hired a palace as directed, and furnished it as if they had been royal personages. When the aunts saw these three youths, imagine their terror! "They are alive!" they said. They could not be mistaken, for there were the apples in their hands, and the star on the girl's brow. They called the nurse and said to her: "Nurse, what does this mean? Are our nephews and niece alive?" The nurse watched at the window until she saw the two brothers go out, and then she went over as if to make a visit to the new house. She entered and said: "What is the matter, my daughter; how do you do? Are you perfectly happy? You lack nothing. But do you know what is necessary to make you really happy? It is the Dancing Water. If your brothers love you, they will get it for you!" She remained a moment longer and then departed.

When one of the brothers returned, his sister said to him: "Ah! My brother, if you love me go and get me the Dancing Water." He consented, and next morning saddled a fine horse, and departed. On his way he met a hermit, who asked him, "Where are you going, cavalier?" "I am going for the Dancing Water." "You are going to your death, my son; but keep on until you find a hermit older than I." He continued his journey until he met another hermit, who asked him the same question, and gave him the same direction. Finally he met a third hermit, older than the other two, with a white beard that came down to his feet, who gave him the following directions: "You must climb yonder mountain. On top of it you will find a great plain and a house with a beautiful gate. Before the gate you will see four giants with swords in their hands. Take heed; do not make a mistake; for if you do that is the end of you! When the giants have their eyes closed, do not enter; when they have their eyes open, enter. Then you will come to a door. If you find it open, do not enter; if you find it shut, push it open and enter. Then you will find four lions. When they have their eyes shut, do not enter; when their eyes are open, enter, and you will see the Dancing Water." The youth took leave of the hermit, and hastened on his way.

Meanwhile the sister kept looking at the ring constantly, to see whether the stone in it changed color; but as it did not, she remained undisturbed.

A few days after leaving the hermit the youth arrived at the top of the mountain, and saw the palace with the four giants before it. They had their eyes shut, and the door was open. "No," said the youth, "That won't do." And so he remained on the lookout a while. When the giants opened their eyes, and the door closed, he entered, waited until the lions opened their eyes, and passed in. There he found the Dancing Water, and filled his bottles with it, and escaped when the lions again opened their eyes.

The aunts, meanwhile, were delighted because their nephew did not return; but in a few days he appeared and embraced his sister. Then they had two golden basins made, and put into them the Dancing Water, which leaped from one basin to the other. When the aunts saw it they exclaimed: "Ah! How did he manage to get that water?" and called the nurse, who again waited until the sister was alone, and then visited her. "You see," said she, "how beautiful the Dancing Water is! But do you know what you want now? The Singing Apple." Then she departed. When the brother who had brought the Dancing Water returned, his sister said to him: "If you love me you must get for me the Singing Apple." "Yes, my sister, I will go and get it."

Next morning he mounted his horse, and set out. After a time he met the first hermit, who sent him to an older one. He asked the youth where he was going, and said: "It is a difficult task to get the Singing Apple, but hear what you must do: climb the mountain; beware of the giants, the door, and the lions; then you will find a little door and a pair of shears in it. If the shears are open, enter; if closed, do not risk it." The youth continued his way, found the palace, entered, and found everything favorable. When he saw the shears open, he went in a room and saw a wonderful tree, on top of which was an apple. He climbed up and tried to pick the apple, but the top of the tree swayed now this way, now that. He waited until it was still a moment, seized the branch, and picked the apple. He succeeded in getting safely out of the palace, mounted his horse, and rode home, and all the time he was carrying the apple it kept making a sound.

The aunts were again delighted because their nephew was so long absent; but when they saw him return, they felt as though the house had fallen on them. Again they summoned the nurse, and again she visited the young girl, and said: "See how beautiful they are, the Dancing Water and the Singing Apple! But should you see the Speaking Bird, there would be nothing left for you to see." "Very well," said the young girl; "We will see whether my brother will get it for me."

When her brother came she asked him for the Speaking Bird, and he promised to get it for her. He met, as usual on his journey, the first hermit, who sent him to the second, who sent him on to a third one, who said to him: "Climb the mountain and enter the palace. You will find many statues. Then you will come to a garden, in the midst of which is a fountain, and on the basin is the Speaking Bird. If it should say anything to you, do not answer. Pick a feather from the bird's wing, dip it into a jar you will find there, and anoint all the statues. Keep your eyes open, and all will go well."

The youth already knew well the way, and soon was in the palace. He found the garden and the bird, which, as soon as it saw him, exclaimed: "What is the matter, noble sir; have you come for me? You have missed it. Your aunts have sent you to your death, and you must remain here. Your mother has been sent to the tread-mill." "My mother in the tread-mill?" cried the youth, and scarcely were the words out of his mouth when he became a statue like all the others.

When the sister looked at her ring she saw that it had changed its color to blue. "Ah!" she exclaimed, and sent her other brother after the first. Everything happened to him as to the first. He met the three hermits, received his instructions, and soon found himself in the palace, where he discovered the garden with the statues, the fountain, and the Speaking Bird.

Meanwhile the aunts, who saw that both their nephews were missing, were delighted; and the sister, on looking at her ring, saw that it had become clear again.

Now when the Speaking Bird saw the youth appear in the garden it said to him: "What has become of your brother? Your mother has been sent to the tread-mill." "Alas, my mother in the tread-mill!" And when he had spoken these words he became a statue.

The sister looked at her ring, and it had become black. Poor child! Not having anything else to do, she dressed herself like a page and set out.

Like her brothers, she met the three hermits, and received their instructions. The third concluded thus: "Beware, for if you answer when the bird speaks you will lose your life." She continued her way, followed exactly the hermit's directions, and reached the garden in safety. When the bird saw her it exclaimed: "Ah! You here, too? Now you will meet the same fate as your brothers. Do you see them? One, two, and you make three. Your father is at the war. Your mother is in the tread-mill. Your aunts are rejoicing." She did not reply, but let the bird sing on. When it had nothing more to say it flew down, and the young girl caught it, pulled a feather from its wing, dipped it into the jar, and anointed her brothers' nostrils, and they at once came to life again. Then she did the same with all the other statues, with the lions and the giants, until all became alive again. Then she departed with her brothers, and all the noblemen, princes, barons, and kings' sons rejoiced greatly. Now when they had all come to life again the palace disappeared, and the hermits disappeared, for they were the three fairies.

The day after the brothers and sister reached the city where they lived, they summoned a goldsmith, and had him make a gold chain, and fasten the bird with it. The next time the aunts looked out they saw in the window of the palace opposite the Dancing Water, the Singing Apple, and the Speaking Bird. "Well," said they, "the real trouble is coming now!"

The bird directed the brothers and sister to procure a carriage finer than the king's, with twenty-four attendants, and to have the service of their palace, cooks and servants, more numerous and better than the king's. All of which the brothers did at once. And when the aunts saw these things they were ready to die of rage.

At last the king returned from the war, and his subjects told him all the news of the kingdom, and the thing they talked about the least was his wife and children. One day the king looked out of the window and saw the palace opposite furnished in a magnificent manner. "Who lives there?" he asked, but no one could answer him. He looked again and saw the brothers and sister, the former with the apples in their hands, and the latter with the star on her brow. "Gracious! If I did not know that my wife had given birth to three puppies, I should say that those were my children," exclaimed the king. Another day he stood by the window and enjoyed the Dancing Water and the Singing Apple, but the bird was silent. After the king had heard all the music, the bird said: "What does your Majesty think of it?" The king was astonished at hearing the Speaking Bird, and answered: "What should I think? It is marvelous." "There is something more marvelous," said the bird; "just wait." Then the bird told his mistress to call her brothers, and said: "There is the king; let us invite him to dinner on Sunday. Shall we not?" "Yes, yes," they all said. So the king was invited and accepted, and on Sunday the bird had a grand dinner prepared and the king came. When he saw the young people, he clapped his hands and said: "I cannot persuade myself; they seem my children."

He went over the palace and was astonished at its richness. Then they went to dinner, and while they were eating the king said: "Bird, every one is talking; you alone are silent." "Ah! Your Majesty, I am ill; but next Sunday I shall be well and able to talk, and will come and dine at your palace with this lady and these gentlemen." The next Sunday the bird directed his mistress and her brothers to put on their finest clothes; so they dressed in royal style and took the bird with them. The king showed them through his palace and treated them with the greatest ceremony: the aunts were nearly dead with fear. When they had seated themselves at the table, the king said: "Come, bird, you promised me you would speak; have you nothing to say?" Then the bird began and related all that had happened from the time the king had listened at the door until his poor wife had been sent to the tread-mill; then the bird added: "These are your children, and your wife was sent to the mill, and is dying." When the king heard all this, he hastened to embrace his children, and then went to find his poor wife, who was reduced to skin and bones and was at the point of death. He knelt before her and begged her pardon, and then summoned her sisters and the nurse, and when they were in his presence he said to the bird: "Bird, you who have told me everything, now pronounce their sentence." Then the bird sentenced the nurse to be thrown out of the window, and the sisters to be cast into a cauldron of boiling oil. This was at once done. The king was never tired of embracing his wife. Then the bird departed and the king and his wife and children lived together in peace.[10]

WE NEXT pass to the class of stories in which children are promised by their parents to witches or the Evil One. The children who are thus promised are often unborn, and the promise is made by the parents either to escape some danger with which they are threatened by witch or demon, or in return for money. Sometimes there is a misunderstanding, as in Grimm's story of the "Handless Maiden," where the Miller, in return for riches, promises the Evil One to give him "what stands behind his mill." The Miller supposes his apple-tree is meant, but it is his daughter, who happened to be behind the mill when the compact was made. The most usual form of the story in Italian is this: A woman who expects to give birth to a child is seized with a great longing for some herb or fruit (generally parsley) growing in the witch's garden. The witch (ogress) catches her picking it, and only releases her on condition that she shall give her the child after it is born and has reached a definite age. The following Sicilian story from Gonzenbach (No. 53) will illustrate this class sufficiently:

༖ V. The Fair Angiola ༖

Once upon a time there were seven women, neighbors, all of whom were seized with a great longing for some jujubes which only grew in a garden opposite the place where they all lived, and which belonged to a witch. Now this witch had a donkey that watched the garden and told the old witch when any one entered. The seven neighbors, however, had such a desire for the jujubes that they entered the garden and threw the donkey some nice soft grass, and while he was eating it they filled their aprons with jujubes and escaped before the witch appeared. This they did several times, until at last the witch noticed that some one had been in her garden, for many of the jujubes were gone. She questioned the donkey, but he had eaten the nice grass and noticed nothing. Then she resolved the third day to remain in the garden herself. In the middle of it was a hole, in which she hid and covered herself with leaves and branches, leaving only one of her long ears sticking out. The seven neighbors once more went into the garden and began picking jujubes, when one of them noticed the witch's ear sticking out of the leaves and thought it was a mushroom and tried to pick it. Then the witch jumped out of the hole and ran after the women, all of whom escaped but one. The witch was going to eat her, but she begged hard for pardon and promised never to enter the garden again. The witch finally forgave her on the condition that she would give her her child, yet unborn, whether a boy or girl, when it was seven years old. The poor woman promised in her distress, and the witch let her go.

Some time after the woman had a beautiful little girl whom she named Angiola. When Angiola was six years old, her mother sent her to school to learn to sew and knit. On her way to school she had to pass the garden where the witch lived. One day, when she was almost seven, she saw the witch standing in front of her garden. She beckoned to Angiola and gave her some fine fruits and said: "You see, fair Angiola, I am your aunt. Tell your mother you have seen your aunt, and she sends her word not to forget her promise." Angiola went home and told her mother, who was frightened and said to herself: "Ah! The time has come when I must give up my Angiola." Then she said to the child: "When your aunt asks you tomorrow for an answer, tell her you forgot her errand." The next day she told the witch as she was directed. "Very well," she replied, "Tell her today, but don't forget." Thus several days passed; the witch was constantly on the watch for Angiola when she went to school, and wanted to know her mother's answer, but Angiola always declared that she had forgotten to ask her. One day, however, the witch became angry and said: "Since you are so forgetful, I must give you some token to remind you of your errand." Then she bit Angiola's little finger so hard that she bit a piece out. Angiola went home in tears and showed her mother her finger. "Ah!" Thought her mother, "There is no help for it. I must give my poor child to the witch, or else she will eat her up in her anger." The next morning as Angiola was going to school, her mother said to her: "Tell your aunt to do with you as she thinks best." Angiola did so, and the witch said: "Very well, then come with me, for you are mine."

So the witch took the fair Angiola with her and led her away to a tower which had no door and but one small window. There Angiola lived with the witch, who treated her very kindly, for she loved her as her own child. When the witch came home after her excursions, she stood under the window and cried: "Angiola, fair Angiola, let down your pretty tresses and pull me up!" Now Angiola had beautiful long hair, which she let down and with which she pulled the witch up.

Now it happened one day when Angiola had grown to be a large and beautiful maiden, that the king's son went hunting and chanced to come where the tower was. He was astonished at seeing the house without any door, and wondered how the people got in. Just then the old witch returned home, stood under the window, and called: "Angiola, fair Angiola, let down your beautiful tresses and pull me up." Immediately the beautiful tresses fell down, and the witch climbed up by them. This pleased the prince greatly, and he hid himself near by until the witch went away again. Then he went and stood under the window and called: "Angiola, fair Angiola, let down your beautiful tresses and pull me up." Then Angiola let down her tresses and drew up the prince, for she believed it was the witch. When she saw the prince, she was much frightened at first, but he addressed her in a friendly manner and begged her to fly with him and become his wife.

She finally consented, and in order that the witch should not know where she had gone she gave all the chairs, tables, and cupboards in the house something to eat; for they were all living beings and might betray her. The broom, however, stood behind the door, so she did not notice it, and gave it nothing to eat. Then she took from the witch's chamber three magic balls of yarn, and fled with the prince. The witch had a little dog that loved the fair Angiola so dearly that it followed her.

Soon after they had fled, the witch came back, and called: "Angiola, fair Angiola, let down your beautiful tresses and draw me up." But the tresses were not let down for all she called, and at last she had to get a long ladder and climb in at the window. When she could not find Angiola, she asked the tables and chairs and cupboards: "Where has she fled?" But they answered: "We do not know." The broom, however, called out from the corner: "The fair Angiola has fled with the king's son, who is going to marry her." Then the witch started in pursuit of them and nearly overtook them. But Angiola threw down behind her one of the magic balls of yarn, and there arose a great mountain of soap. When the witch tried to climb it she slipped back, but she persevered until at last she succeeded in getting over it, and hastened after the fugitives. Then Angiola threw down the second ball of yarn, and there arose a great mountain covered all over with nails small and large. Again the witch had to struggle hard to cross it; when she did she was almost flayed. When Angiola saw that the witch had almost overtaken them again, she threw down the third ball, and there arose a mighty torrent. The witch tried to swim across it, but the stream kept increasing in size until she had at last to turn back. Then in her anger she cursed the fair Angiola, saying: "May your beautiful face be turned into the face of a dog!" And instantly Angiola's face became a dog's face.

The prince was very sorrowful and said: "How can I take you home to my parents? They would never allow me to marry a maiden with a dog's face." So he took her to a little house, where she was to live until the enchantment was removed. He himself returned to his parents; but whenever he went hunting he visited poor Angiola. She often wept bitterly over her misfortunes, until one day the little dog that had followed her from the witch's said: "Do not weep, fair Angiola. I will go to the witch and beg her to remove the enchantment." Then the little dog started off and returned to the witch and sprang up on her and caressed her. "Are you here again, you ungrateful beast?" cried the witch, and pushed the dog away. "Did you leave me to follow the ungrateful Angiola?" But the little dog caressed her until she grew friendly again and took him up on her lap. "Mother," said the little dog, "Angiola sends you greeting; she is very sad, for she cannot go to the palace with her dog's face and cannot marry the prince." "That serves her right," said the witch. "Why did she deceive me? She can keep her dog's face now!" But the dog begged her so earnestly, saying that poor Angiola was sufficiently punished, that at last the witch gave the dog a flask of water, and said: "Take that to her and she will become the fair Angiola again." The dog thanked her, ran off with the flask, and brought it safely to poor Angiola. As soon as she washed in the water, her dog's face disappeared and she became beautiful again, more beautiful even than she had been before. The prince, full of joy, took her to the palace, and the king and queen were so pleased with her beauty that they welcomed her, and gave her a splendid wedding, and all remained happy and contented.[11]

An interesting class of stories is the one in which the heroes are twin brothers (sometimes three born at the same time, or a larger number) who are born in some unusual manner, generally in consequence of the mother's partaking of some magic fruit or fish. One of the brothers undertakes some difficult task (liberation of princess, etc.) and falls into great danger; the other brother discovers the fact from some sympathetic object and proceeds to rescue him. The following story from Pisa (Comparetti, No. 32) will give a good idea of the Italian stories of this class:

✣ VI. The Cloud ✣

Once upon a time there was a fisherman who had a wife and many children. Now it happened that the fisherman did not catch any fish for a time and did not know how to support his family. One day he cast his net and drew out a large fish which began to talk: "Let me go and cast in your net again and you will catch as many fish as you wish." The fisherman did so and caught more fish than he remembered to have taken before. But in a few days the fish were gone and the fisherman cast his net again, and again caught the big fish, which said: "I see clearly that I must die, so kill me now, and cut me into pieces. Give half to the king, a piece to your wife, one to your dog, and one to your horse; the bones you will tie to the kitchen rafters; your wife will bear sons, and when anything happens to one of them the fish-bone will sweat drops of blood." The fisherman did as he was told, and in due time his wife gave birth to three sons, the dog to three puppies, and the horse to three colts. The boys grew up and went to school and learned much and prospered. One day the oldest said: "I want to go and see a little of the world," and took one of the dogs, one of the horses, and some money, and set out, after receiving his father's and mother's blessing. He arrived at a forest, and there saw a lion, an eagle, and an ant which had found a dead ass that they wanted to divide among themselves, but could not agree and so were quarrelling. They saw the youth, and called on him to make the division. He was afraid at first, but took heart and gave the lean meat to the eagle, the brains to the ant, and the rest to the lion. They were all satisfied, and the youth continued his way. After he had gone a few steps the animals called him back, and the lion said: "You have settled our dispute, and we wish to reward you; when you wish to become a lion, you have only to say: 'No more a man, a lion, with the strength of a hundred lions!'" The eagle said: "When you wish to become an eagle, say: 'No more a man, an eagle, with the strength of a hundred eagles!'" The ant, also, gave him power to transform himself into an ant in the same way. The youth thanked them and departed. As he was passing along the shore of the sea, he saw a dog-fish that was out of the water; he put it back into the sea. The fish said: "When you need me, come to the sea and cry: 'Dog-fish, help me!'"

The youth continued his way and arrived at a city all hung with mourning. "What is the matter?" The young man asked. "There is here," they told him, "a big cloud (it was a fairy) that every year must have a young girl. This year the lot has fallen on the king's daughter. If they do not give her up, the cloud will throw so many things into the city that we shall all be killed." The youth asked if he could see how the thing went, and they told him he could. The ceremony began with muffled drums and an escort of soldiers; the king and queen in tears accompanied their daughter, who was taken to the top of a mountain, placed in a chair, and left alone. The youth, who had followed them, hid himself behind a bush. Then the cloud came, took the young girl in her lap, took her finger in her mouth, and began to suck her blood. This was what the cloud lived on. The princess remained half dead, like a log, and then the cloud carried her away. The youth, who had seen all this, cried: "No more a man, an eagle, with the strength of a hundred eagles!" Then he became an eagle and flew after the cloud. They arrived at a palace, the doors flew open and the cloud entered and carried the princess up-stairs. The eagle alighted on a tree opposite and saw a large room all full of young girls in bed. When the cloud entered they exclaimed: "Mamma! Here is our mamma!" The poor girls were always in bed, because the fairy half killed them. She put the princess in a bed, and said to the girls: "I am going to leave you for a few days." She went away and left the girls. The youth was near and heard everything; he said: "No more an eagle, an ant, with the force of a hundred ants!" He became an ant, entered the palace unseen, and went to the room where the young girls were. There he resumed his shape, and the girls were astonished at seeing a man appear so suddenly, and one of them said to him: "Take care, there is a fairy here; if she finds you on her return she will kill you." "Do not be troubled," he answered, "for I wish to see about setting you all free." Then he went to the bed of the king's daughter and asked her if she had some token to send her mother. She gave him a ring, and the youth took it and went to the queen, told her where her daughter was, and asked her to send some food to the poor girl. She did so, and the youth retraced his steps, reached the palace, informed the girls, and drew up the food with ropes. He then said to the girls: "When the fairy returns, ask her what you shall do when she dies; thus you will find out how to kill her." Then he hid himself, and when the fairy returned the girls asked her the question; but she answered: "I shall never die." They urged her to tell them, and the next day she took them out on a terrace, and said: "Do you see that mountain far off there? On that mountain is a tigress with seven heads. If you wish me to die, a lion must fight that tigress and tear off all seven of her heads. In her body is an egg, and if any one hits me with it in the middle of my forehead I shall die; but if that egg falls into my hands the tigress will come to life again, resume her seven heads, and I shall live." "Good!" said the young girls; "certainly our mamma can never die." But in their hearts they were discouraged. When the fairy had departed, the youth came forth and they told him all. "Do not be disheartened," he said, and straightway went to the princess' father, asked him for a room, a pan of bread, a barrel of good wine, and a child seven years old. He took all these things and shut himself up in the room, and said to the child: "Do you want to see something, my child? I am going to turn into a lion." Then he turned into a lion, and the child was afraid; but the youth persuaded him that it was only himself after all, and the child fed him, and was no longer frightened. As soon as he had instructed the child, he took all the things and went to the mountain where the tigress was. Then he filled the pan with bread and wine and said to the child: "I am going to become a lion; when I return give me something to eat." Then he became a lion, and went to fight the tigress. Meanwhile the fairy returned home, saying: "Alas! I feel ill!" The young girls said to themselves, in delight: "Good!" The youth fought until night, and tore off one of the tigress' heads; the second day another, and so on until six heads were gone. The fairy kept losing her strength all the time. The youth rested two days before tearing off the last head, and then resumed the fight. At evening the last head was torn off, and the dead tigress disappeared, but the youth was not quick enough to catch the egg, which rolled from her body into the sea and was swallowed by the dog-fish. Then the youth went to the sea: "Dog-fish, help me!" The fish appeared: "What do you want?" "Have you found an egg?" "Yes." "Give it to me," and the fish gave him the egg. He took it and went in search of the fairy, and suddenly appeared before her with the egg in his hand. The fairy wanted him to give her the egg, but he made her first restore all the young girls to health and send them home in handsome carriages. Then the youth took the egg, struck it on the fairy's forehead, and she fell down dead. When the youth saw that she was really dead, he entered a carriage with the king's daughter and drove to the palace. When the king and queen saw their daughter again, they wept for joy, and married her to her deliverer. The wedding took place with great magnificence, and there were great festivities and rejoicings in the city.

A few days after, the husband looked out of the window and saw at the end of the street a dense fog; he said to his wife: "I will go and see what that fog is." So he dressed for the chase and went away with his dog and horse. After he had passed through the mist, he saw a mountain on which were two beautiful ladies. They came to meet him, and invited him to their palace. He accepted and they showed him into a room, and one of the ladies asked: "Would you like to play a game of chess?" "Very well," he answered, and began to play and lost. Then they took him into a garden where there were many marble statues, and turned him into one, together with his dog and horse. These ladies were sisters of the fairy, and this was the way they avenged her death.

Meanwhile the princess waited and her husband did not return. One morning the father and brothers of the youth found the kitchen full of blood, which dropped from the fishbone. "Something has happened to him," they said, and the second brother started in search of him with another one of the dogs and horses. He passed by the palace of the princess who was at the window, and those brothers looked so much alike that when she saw him, she thought it was her husband and called him. He entered and she spoke to him of the fog, but he did not understand her; he let her talk on, however, imagining that his brother was mixed up in that affair. The next morning he arose and went to see the fog with his dog and horse. He passed through the fog, found the mountain and the two ladies, and, to make the story short, the same thing happened to him that happened to his brother, and he became stone. And the queen waited, and in the father's kitchen the bone dropped blood faster than ever.

The third brother too set out with his dog and horse. When he came to the palace, the princess saw him from the window, took him for her husband, and called him in. He entered and she reproved him for having made her wait so long, and spoke of the mist; but he did not understand her and said: "I did not see very clearly what was in the mist, and I wish to go there again." He departed, and when he had passed through the mist he met an old man who said to him: "Where are you going? Take care, your brothers have been turned into statues. You will meet two ladies; if they ask you to play chess with them, here are two pawns, say that you cannot play except with your own pawns. Then make an agreement with them that, if you win, you can do with them what you please; if they win, they can do what they please with you. If you win, and they beg for mercy, command them to restore to life all the stone statues with which the palace is filled, and when they have done so, you can do what you will with these ladies."

The youth thanked the old man, departed, followed his directions, and won. The two ladies begged for their lives, and he granted their prayer on condition of restoring to life all those stone statues. They took a wand, touched the statues, and they became animated; but no sooner were they all restored to life than they fell on the two ladies and cut them into bits no larger than their ears.

Thus the three brothers were reunited. They related their adventures, and returned to the palace. The princess was astonished when she saw them, and did not know which was her husband. But he made himself known, told her that these were his brothers, and they had their parents come there, and they all lived happily together, and thus the story is ended.[12]

WE NOW pass to the class of stories in which one of several brothers succeeds in some undertaking where the others fail, and thereby draws down on himself the hatred of the others, who either abandon him in a cavern, or kill him and hide his body, which is afterwards discovered by a musical instrument made of one of the bones or of the reeds growing over the grave. The former treatment is illustrated by a Sicilian tale (Pitrè, No. 80) called:

⤞ VII. The Cistern ⤝

There were once three king's sons. Two of them were going hunting one day, and did not want to take their youngest brother with them. Their mother asked them to let him go with them, but they would not. The youngest brother, however, followed them, and they had to take him with them. They came to a beautiful plain, where they found a fine cistern, and ate their lunch near it. After they had finished, the oldest said: "Let us throw our youngest brother into the cistern, for we cannot take him with us." Then he said to his brother: "Salvatore, would you like to descend into this cistern, for there is a treasure in it?" The youngest consented, and they lowered him down. When he reached the bottom, he found three handsome rooms and an old woman, who said to him: "What are you doing here?" "I am trying to find my way out; tell me how to do it." The old woman answered: "There are here three princesses in the power of the magician; take care." "Never mind, tell me what to do; I am not afraid." "Knock at that door." He did so and a princess appeared: "What has brought you here?" "I have come to liberate you; tell me what I have to do." "Take this apple and pass through that door; my sister is there, who can give you better directions than I can."

She gave him the apple as a token. He knocked at that door, another princess appeared, who gave him a pomegranate for a remembrance and directed him to knock at a third door. It opened and the last princess appeared. "Ah! Salvatore" (for she knew who he was), "What have you come for?" "I have come to liberate you; tell me what to do." She gave him a crown, and said: "Take this; when you are in need, say: 'I command!

I command!' and the crown will obey you. Now enter and eat; take this bottle; the magician, you see, is about rising; hide yourself behind this door, and when he awakens he will ask you: 'What are you here for?' You will answer: 'I have come to fight you; but you must agree to take the smaller horse and sword than mine, because I am smaller than you.' You will see there a fountain which will invite you to drink; do not risk it, for all the statues you see there are human beings who have become statues drinking that water; when you are thirsty drink secretly from this bottle."

With these directions the youth went and knocked at the door. Just then the magician arose and said: "What are you here for?" "I have come to fight with you." And he added what the princess had told him. The fountain invited him to drink, but he would not. They began to fight, and at the first blow the youth cut off the magician's head. He took the head and sword, and went to the princesses and said: "Get your things together, and let us go, for my brothers are still waiting at the mouth of the cistern."

Let us now return to the brothers. After they had lowered their youngest brother into the cistern, they turned around and went back to the royal palace. The king asked: "Where is your brother?" "We lost him in a wood, and could not find him." "Quick!" said the king, "go and find my son, or I will have your heads cut off." So they departed, and on their way found a man with a rope and a bell, and took them with them. When they reached the cistern, they lowered the rope with the bell, saying among themselves: "If he is alive he will hear the bell and climb up; if he is dead, what shall we do with our father?" When they lowered the rope, Salvatore made the princesses ascend one by one. As the first appeared, who was the oldest, the oldest brother said: "Oh, what a pretty girl! This one shall be my wife." When the second appeared, the other brother said: "This is mine." The youngest princess did not wish to ascend, and said to Salvatore: "You go up, Salvatore, first; if you do not, your brothers will leave you here." He said he would not; she said he must; finally he prevailed, and she ascended. When she appeared the two brothers took her, and left Salvatore in the cistern, and returned to the palace. When they arrived there, they said to their father: "We have looked for Salvatore, but we could not find him; but we have found these three young girls, and now we wish to marry them." "I," said the oldest brother, "will take this one." "And I," said the second, "take this one. The other sister we will marry to some other youth."

Now let us return to Salvatore, who, when he found himself alone and disconsolate, felt in his pockets and touched the apple. "O my apple, get me out of this place!" And at once he found himself out of the cistern. He went to the city where he lived, and met a silversmith, who took him as an apprentice, feeding and clothing him. While he was with the silversmith, the king commanded the latter to make a crown for his oldest son, who was to be married: "You must make me a royal crown for my son, and tomorrow evening you must bring it to me."

He gave him ten ounces and dismissed him. When he reached home, the silversmith was greatly disturbed, for he had such a short time to make the crown in. Salvatore said: "Grandfather, why are you so disturbed?" The master replied: "Take these ten ounces, for now I am going to seek refuge in a church, for there is nothing else for me to do." (For in olden times the church had the privilege that whoever robbed or killed fled to the church, and they could not do anything with him.) The apprentice replied: "Now I will see if I can make this crown. My master would take refuge in a church for a trifle." So he began to make the crown. What did he do? He took out the apple and commanded it to make a very beautiful crown. He hammered away, but the apple made the crown. When it was finished he gave it to the wife of the silversmith, who took it to her husband. When the latter saw that he need not flee to the church, he went to the king, who, well pleased, invited him to the feast in the evening. When he told this at home, the apprentice said: "Take me to the feast." "How can I take you when you have no clothes fit to wear? I will buy you some, and when there is another feast I will take you." When it struck two, the silversmith departed, and Salvatore took the apple and said: "O my apple, give me clothes and carriages and footmen, for I am going to see my brother married." Immediately he was dressed like a prince, and went to the palace, where he hid in the kitchen, saw his brother married, and then took a big stick and gave the silversmith a sound beating. When the latter reached home, he cried: "I am dying! I am dying!" "What is the matter?" asked the apprentice, and when he learned what had happened, he said: "If you had taken me with you to the feast this would not have happened."

A few days after, the king summoned the silversmith again to make another crown within twenty-four hours. Everything happened as before: the apprentice made a crown handsomer than the first, with the aid of the pomegranate. The smith took it to the king, but after the feast came home with his shoulders black and blue from the beating he received.

After a time they wanted to marry the third sister, but she said: "Who wishes me must wait a year, a month, and a day." And she had no peace wondering why Salvatore did not appear for all he had the apple, the pomegranate, and the crown. After a year, a month, and a day, the wedding was arranged, and the smith had orders to make another crown more beautiful than the first two. (This was so that no one could say that because the young girl was a foreigner they treated her worse than the others.) Again the smith was in despair, and the apprentice had to make, by the aid of his magic crown, a better and larger crown than the others. The king was astonished when he saw the beautiful crown, and again invited the silversmith to the feast. The smith returned home sorrowful, for fear that he should again receive a beating, but he would not take his apprentice with him.

After Salvatore had seen him depart, he took his magic crown and ordered splendid clothes and carriages. When he reached the palace, he did not go to the kitchen, but before the bride and groom could say "yeh," "Stop!" said Salvatore. He took the apple and said: "Who gave me this?" "I did," replied the wife of the oldest brother. "And this?" showing the pomegranate. "I, my brother-in-law," said the wife of the second brother. Then he took out the crown, "Who gave me that?" "I, my husband," said the young girl whom they were marrying. And at once she married Salvatore, "for," said she, "he freed me from the magician."

The bridegroom was fooled and had to go away, and the astonished silversmith fell on his knees, begging for pity and mercy.[13]

In some of the versions of the above story, the hero, after he is abandoned by his brothers in the cistern or cave, is borne into the upper world by an eagle. The rapacious bird on the journey demands from the young man flesh from time to time. At last the stock of flesh with which he had provided himself is exhausted and he is obliged to cut off and give the eagle a piece of his own flesh. In one version (Pitrè, ii. p. 208) he gives the eagle his leg; and when the journey is concluded the bird casts it up, and the hero attaches it again to his body, and becomes as sound as ever.[14]

The class of stories in which the brother is killed and his death made known by a musical instrument fashioned from his body is sufficiently illustrated by a short Neapolitan story (Imbriani, *Pomiglianesi*, p. 195) entitled:

✣ VIII. The Griffin ✣

There was once a king who had three sons. His eyes were diseased, and he called in a physician who said that to cure them he needed a feather of the griffin. Then the king said to his sons: "He who finds this feather for me shall have my crown." The sons set out in search of it. The youngest met an old man, who asked him what he was doing. He replied: "Papa is ill. To cure him a feather of the griffin is necessary. And papa has said that whoever finds the feather shall have his crown." The old man said: "Well, here is some corn. When you reach a certain place, put it in your hat. The griffin will come and eat it. Seize him, pull out a feather, and carry it to papa." The youth did so, and for fear that some one should steal it from him, he put it into his shoe, and started all joyful to carry it to his father. On his way he met his brothers, who asked him if he had found the feather. He said No; but his brothers did not believe him, and wanted to search him. They looked everywhere, but did not find it. Finally they looked in his shoe and got it. Then they killed the youngest brother and buried him, and took the feather to their father, saying that they had found it. The king healed his eyes with it. A shepherd one day, while feeding his sheep, saw that his dog was always digging in the same place, and went to see what it was, and found a bone. He put it to his mouth, and saw that it sounded and said: "Shepherd, keep me in your mouth, hold me tight, and do not let me go! For a feather of the griffin, my brother has played the traitor, my brother has played the traitor."

One day the shepherd, with this whistle in his mouth, was passing by the king's palace, and the king heard him, and called him to see what it was. The shepherd told him the story, and how he had found it. The king put it to his mouth, and the whistle said: "Papa! Papa! Keep me in your mouth, hold me tight, and do not let me go. For a feather of the griffin, my brother has played the traitor, my brother has played the traitor." Then the king put it in the mouth of the brother who had killed the youngest, and the whistle said: "Brother! Brother! Keep me in your mouth, hold me fast, and do not let me go. For a feather of the griffin, you have played the traitor, you have played the traitor." Then the king understood the story and had his two sons put to death. And thus they killed their brother and afterwards were killed themselves.[15]

THE FEMININE counterpart of "Boots," or the successful youngest brother, is Cinderella, the youngest of three sisters who despise and ill-treat her. Her usual place is in the chimney-corner, and her name is derived from the grime of cinders and ashes (her name in German is Aschenputtel). Assisted by some kind fairy who appears in various forms, she reveals herself in her true shape and captivates the prince, who finally recognizes her by the slipper. There are two branches of this story: the one just mentioned, and one where the heroine assumes a repulsive disguise in order to escape the importunities of a father who wishes to marry her. This second branch may be distinguished by the name of "Allerleirauh," the well-known Grimm story of this class. For the first branch of this story we have selected a Florentine story (*Novellaja fior.* p. 151) called:

ᔐ *IX. Cinderella* ᔐ

Once upon a time there was a man who had three daughters. He was once ordered to go away to work, and said to them: "Since I am about to make a journey, what do you want me to bring you when I return?" One asked for a handsome dress, the other, a fine hat and a beautiful shawl. He said to the youngest: "And you, Cinderella, what do you want?" They called her Cinderella because she always sat in the chimney-corner. "You must buy me a little bird Verdeliò." "The simpleton! She does not know what to do with the bird! Instead of ordering a handsome dress, a fine shawl, she takes a bird. Who knows what she will do with it!" "Silence!" She says, "It pleases me." The father went, and on his return brought the dress, hat, and shawl for the two sisters, and the little bird for Cinderella. The father was employed at the court, and one day the king said to him: "I am going to give three balls; if you want to bring your daughters, do so; they will amuse themselves a little." "As you wish," he replies, "Thanks!" And accepts. He went home and said: "What do you think, girls? His Majesty wishes you to attend his ball." "There, you see, Cinderella, if you had only asked for a handsome dress! This evening we are going to the ball." She replied: "It matters nothing to me! You go; I am not coming." In the evening, when the time came, they adorned themselves, saying to Cinderella: "Come along, there will be room for you, too." "I don't want to go; you go; I don't want to." "But," said their father, "let us go, let us go! Dress and come along; let her stay." When they had gone, she went to the bird and said: "O Bird Verdelio, make me more beautiful than I am!" She became clothed in a sea-green dress, with so many diamonds that it blinded you to behold her. The bird made ready two purses of money, and said to her: Take these two purses, enter your carriage, and away!" She set out for the ball, and left the bird Verdelio at home. She entered the ball-room. Scarcely had the gentlemen seen this beautiful lady (she dazzled them on all sides), when the king, just think of it, began to dance with her the whole evening. After he had danced with her all the evening, his Majesty stopped, and she stood by her sisters. While she was at her sisters' side, she drew out her handkerchief, and a bracelet fell out. "Oh, Signora," said the eldest sister, "you have dropped this." "Keep it for yourself," she said. "Oh, if Cinderella were only here, who knows what might not have happened to her?" The king had given orders that when this lady went away, they should find out where she lived. After she had remained a little, she left the ball. You can imagine whether the servants were on the lookout! She entered her carriage and away! She perceives that she is followed, takes the money and begins to throw it out of the window of the carriage. The greedy servants, I tell you, seeing all that money, thought no more of her, but stopped to pick up the money. She returned home and went up-stairs. "O Bird Verdeliò, make me homelier than I am!" You ought to see how ugly, how horrid, she became, all ashes. When the sisters returned, they cried: "Cin-der-ella!" "Oh, leave her alone," said her father; "she is asleep now, leave her alone!" But they went up and showed her the large and beautiful bracelet. "Do you see, you simpleton? You might have had it." "It matters nothing to me." Their father said: "Let us go to supper, you little geese."

Let us return to the king, who was awaiting his servants, who had not the courage to appear, but kept away. He calls them. "How did the matter go?" They fall at his feet. "Thus and thus! She threw out so much money!" "Wretches, you are nothing else," he said, "Were you afraid of not being rewarded? Well! To-morrow evening, attention, under pain of death." The next evening the usual ball. The sisters say: "Will you come this evening, Cinderella?" "Oh," she says, "don't bother me! I don't want to go." Their father cries out to them: "How troublesome you are! Let her alone!" So they began to adorn themselves more handsomely than the former evening, and departed. "Good-by, Cinderella!" When they had gone, Cinderella went to the bird and said: "Little Bird Verdeliò, make me more beautiful than I am!" Then she became clothed in sea-green, embroidered with all the fish of the sea, mingled with diamonds more than you could believe. The bird said: "Take these two bags of sand, and when you are followed, throw it out, and so they will be blinded." She entered her carriage and set out for the ball. As soon as his Majesty saw her he began to dance with her and danced as long as he could. After he had danced as long as he could (she did not grow weary, but he did), she placed herself near her sisters, drew out her handkerchief, and there fell out a beautiful necklace all made of coal. The second sister said: "Signora, you have dropped this." She replied: "Keep it for yourself." "If Cinderella were here, who knows what might not happen to her! To-morrow she must come!" After a while she leaves the ball. The servants (just think, under pain of death!) were all on the alert, and followed her. She began to throw out all the sand, and they were blinded. She went home, dismounted, and went up-stairs. "Little Bird Verdelió, make me homelier than I am!" She became frightfully homely. When her sisters returned they began from below: "Cin-der-ella! If you only knew what that lady gave us!" "It matters nothing to me!" "But tomorrow evening you must go!" "Yes, yes! You would have had it!" Their father says: "Let us go to supper and let her alone; you are really silly!"

Let us return to his Majesty, who was waiting for his servants to learn where she lived. Instead of that they were all brought back blinded, and had to be accompanied. "Rogue!" He exclaimed, "either this lady is some fairy or she must have some fairy who protects her."

The next day the sisters began: "Cinderella, you must go this evening! Listen; it is the last evening; you must come." The father: "Oh let her alone! You are always teasing her!" Then they went away and began to prepare for the ball. When they were all prepared, they went to the ball with their father. When they had departed, Cinderella went to the bird: "Little Bird Verdelió, make me more beautiful than I am!" Then she was dressed in all the colors of the heavens; all the comets, the stars, and moon on her dress, and the sun on her brow. She enters the ball-room. Who could look at her! For the sun alone they lower their eyes, and are all blinded. His Majesty began to dance, but he could not look at her, because she dazzled him. He had already given orders to his servants to be on the lookout, under pain of death, not to go on foot, but to mount their horses that evening. After she had danced longer than on the previous evenings she placed herself by her father's side, drew out her handkerchief, and there fell out a snuff-box of gold, full of money. "Signora, you have dropped this snuff-box." "Keep it for yourself!" Imagine that man; he opens it and sees it full of money. What joy! After she had remained a time she went home as usual. The servants followed her on horseback, quickly; at a distance from the carriage; but on horseback that was not much trouble. She perceived that she had not prepared anything to throw that evening. "Oh!" She cried, "What shall I do?" She left the carriage quickly, and in her haste lost one of her slippers. The servants picked it up, took the number of the house, and went away. Cinderella went up-stairs and said: "Little Bird Verdelió, make me more homely than I am!" The bird does not answer. After she had repeated it three or four times, it answered: "Rogue! I ought not to make you more homely, but . . ." And she became homely and the bird continued: "What are you going to do now? You are discovered." She began to weep in earnest. When her sisters returned, they cried: "Cin-der-ella!" You can imagine that she did not answer them this evening. "See what a beautiful snuff-box. If you had gone you might have had it." "I do not care! Go away!" Then their father called them to supper.

Let us now turn to the servants who went back with the slipper and the number of the house. "To-morrow," said his Majesty, "as soon as it is day, go to that house, take a carriage, and bring that lady to the palace." The servants took the slipper and went away. The next morning they knocked at the door. Cinderella's father looked out and exclaimed: "Oh, Heavens! It is his Majesty's carriage; what does it mean?" They open the door and the servants ascend. "What do you want of me?" asked the father. "How many daughters have you?" "Two." "Well, show them to us." The father made them come in there. "Sit down," they said to one of them. They tried the slipper on her; it was ten times too large for her. The other one sat down; it was too small for her. "But tell me, good man, have you no other daughters? Take care to tell the truth! Because his Majesty wishes it, under pain of death!" "Gentlemen, there is another one, but I do not mention it. She is all in the ashes, the coals; if you should see her! I do not call her my daughter from shame." "We have not come for beauty, or for finery; we want to see the girl!"

Her sisters began to call her: "Cin-der-ella!" but she did not answer. After a time she said: "What is the matter?" "You must come down! There are some gentlemen here who wish to see you." "I don't want to come." "But you must come, you see!" "Very well; tell them I will come in a moment." She went to the little bird: "Ah little Bird Verdeliò, make me more beautiful than I am!" Then she was dressed as she had been the last evening, with the sun, and moon, and stars, and in addition, great chains all of gold everywhere about her. The bird said: "Take me away with you! Put me in your bosom!" She puts the bird in her bosom and begins to descend the stairs. "Do you hear her?" said the father, "do you hear her? She is dragging with her the chains from the chimney-corner. You can imagine how frightful she will look!" When she reached the last step, and they saw her, "Ah!" They exclaimed, and recognized the lady of the ball. You can imagine how her father and sisters were vexed. They made her sit down, and tried on the slipper, and it fitted her. Then they made her enter the carriage, and took her to his Majesty, who recognized the lady of the other evenings. And you can imagine that, all in love as he was, he said to her: "Will you really be my wife?" You may believe she consents. She sends for her father and sisters, and makes them all come to the palace. They celebrate the marriage. Imagine what fine festivals were given at this wedding! The servants who had discovered where Cinderella lived were promoted to the highest positions in the palace as a reward.[16]

IN THE second class of stories alluded to above, the heroine flees in disguise from her home to avoid a marriage with her father or brother. The remainder of the story resembles Cinderella: the heroine reveals herself from time to time in her true form, and finally throws off her disguise. The following story, which illustrates this class, is from the province of Vicenza (Corazzini, p. 484), and is entitled:

ᔈ *X. Fair Maria Wood* ᔈ

There was once a husband and wife who had but one child, a daughter. Now it happened that the wife fell ill and was at the point of death. Before dying she called her husband, and said to him, weeping: "I am dying; you are still young; if you ever wish to marry again, be mindful to choose a wife whom my wedding ring fits; and if you cannot find a lady whom it fits well, do not marry." Her husband promised that he would do so. When she was dead he took off her wedding ring and kept it until he desired to marry again. Then he sought for some one to please him. He went from one to another, but the ring fitted no one. He tried so many but in vain. One day he thought of calling his daughter, and trying the ring on her to see whether it fitted her. The daughter said: "It is useless, dear father; you cannot marry me, because you are my father." He did not heed her, put the ring on her finger, and saw that it fitted her well, and wanted to marry his daughter *nolens volens*. She did not oppose him, but consented. The day of the wedding, he asked her what she wanted. She said that she wished four silk dresses, the most beautiful that could be seen. He, who was a gentleman, gratified her wish and took her the four dresses, one handsomer than the other, and all the handsomest that had ever been seen. "Now, what else do you want?" said he. "I want another dress, made of wood, so that I can conceal myself in it." And at

39

once he had this wooden dress made. She was well pleased. She waited one day until her husband was out of sight, put on the wooden dress, and under it the four silk dresses, and went away to a certain river not far off, and threw herself in it. Instead of sinking and drowning, she floated, for the wooden dress kept her up.

The water carried her a long way, when she saw on the bank a gentleman, and began to cry: "Who wants the fair Maria Wood?" That gentleman who saw her on the water, and whom she addressed, called her and she came to the bank and saluted him. "How is it that you are thus dressed in wood, and come floating on the water without drowning?" She told him that she was a poor girl who had only that dress of wood, and that she wanted to go out to service. "What can you do?" "I can do all that is needed in a house, and if you would only take me for a servant you would be satisfied."

He took her to his house, where his mother was, and told her all that had happened, saying: "If you, dear mother, will take her as a servant, we can try her." In short, she took her and was pleased with this woman dressed in wood.

It happened that there were balls at that place which the best ladies and gentlemen attended. The gentleman who had the servant dressed in wood prepared to go to the ball, and after he had departed, the servant said to his mother: "Do me this kindness, mistress: let me go to the ball too, for I have never seen any dancing." "What, you wish to go to the ball so badly dressed that they would drive you away as soon as they saw you!" The servant was silent, and when the mistress was in bed, dressed herself in one of her silk dresses and became the most beautiful woman that was ever seen. She went to the ball, and it seemed as if the sun had entered the room; all were dazzled. She sat down near her master, who asked her to dance, and would dance with no one but her. She pleased him so much that he fell in love with her. He asked her who she was and where she came from. She replied that she came from a distance, but told him nothing more.

At a certain hour, without any one perceiving it, she went out and disappeared. She returned home and put on her wooden dress again. In the morning the master returned from the ball, and said to his mother: "Oh! If you had only seen what a beautiful lady there was at the ball! She appeared like the sun, she was so beautiful and well dressed. She sat down near me, and would not dance with any one but me." His mother then said: "Did you not ask her who she was and where she came from?" "She would only tell me that she came from a distance; but I thought I should die; I wish to go again this evening." The servant heard all this dialogue, but kept silent pretending that the matter did not concern her.

In the evening he prepared himself again for the ball, and the servant said to him: "Master, yesterday evening I asked your mamma to let me, too, go to the ball, for I have never seen dancing, but she would not; will you have the kindness to let me go this evening?" "Be still, you ugly creature, the ball is no place for you!" "Do me this favor," she said, weeping, "I will stand out of doors, or under a bench, or in a corner so no one shall see me; but let me go!" He grew angry then, and took a stick and began to beat the poor servant. She wept and remained silent.

After he had gone, she waited until his mother was in bed, and put on a dress finer than the first, and so rich as to astonish, and away to the ball! When she arrived all began to gaze at her, for they had never seen anything more beautiful. All the handsomest young men surround her and ask her to dance; but she would have nothing to do with any one but her master. He again asked her who she was, and she said she would tell him later. They danced and danced, and all at once she disappeared. Her master ran here and there, asked one and another, but no one could tell him where she had gone. He returned home and told his mother all that had passed. She said to him: "Do you know what you must do? Take this diamond ring, and when she dances with you give it to her; and if she takes it, it is a sign that she loves you." She gave him the ring. The servant listened, saw everything, and was silent.

In the evening the master prepared for the ball and the servant again asked him to take her, and again he beat her. He went to the ball, and after midnight, as before, the beautiful lady returned more beautiful than before, and as usual would dance only with her master. At the right moment he took out the diamond ring, and asked her if she would accept it. She took it and thanked him, and he was happy and satisfied. Afterward he asked her again who she was and where from. She said that she was of that country

> That when they speak of going to a ball,
> They are beaten on the head;

and said no more. At the usual hour she stopped dancing and departed. He ran after her, but she went like the wind, and reached home without his finding out where she went. But he ran so in all directions, and was in such suffering, that when he reached home he was obliged to go to bed more dead than alive. Then he fell ill and grew worse every day, so that all said he would die. He did nothing but ask his mother and every one if they knew anything of that lady, and that he would die if he did not see her. The servant heard everything; and one day, when he was very ill, what did she think of? She waited until her mistress' eye was turned, and dropped the diamond ring in the broth her master was to eat. No one saw her, and his mother took him the broth. He began to eat it, when he felt something hard, saw something shine, and took it out. . . . You can imagine how he looked at it and recognized the diamond ring! They thought he would go mad. He asked his mother if that was the ring and she swore that it was, and all happy, she said that now he would see her again.

Meanwhile the servant went to her room, took off her wooden dress, and put on one all of silk, so that she appeared a beauty, and went to the room of the sick man. His mother saw her and began to cry: "Here she is; here she is!" She went in and saluted him, smiling, and he was so beside himself that he became well at once. He asked her to tell him her story—who she was, where she came from, how she came, and how she knew that he was ill. She replied: "I am the woman dressed in wood who was your servant. It is not true that I was a poor girl, but I had that dress to conceal myself in, for underneath it I was the same that I am now. I am a lady; and although you treated me so badly when I asked to go to the ball, I saw that you loved me, and now I have come to save you from death." You can believe that they stayed to hear her story. They were married and have always been happy and still are.[17]

IN THE various stories thus far mentioned which involve the family relations, we have had examples of treachery on the part of brothers, ill-treatment of step-children, etc. It remains now to notice the trait of treachery on the part of sister or mother towards brother or son. The formula as given by Hahn (No. 19) is as follows: The hero, who is fleeing with his sister (or mother), overcomes a number of dragons or giants. The only survivor makes love to the sister (or mother), and causes her, for fear of discovery, to send her brother, in order to destroy him, on dangerous adventures, under the pretence of obtaining a cure for her illness. The hero survives the dangers, discovers the deception, and punishes the guilty ones. Traces of this formula are found in several Italian stories,[18] but it constitutes only two entire stories: one in Pitrè (No. 71) the other in Comparetti (No. 54, "The Golden Hair," from Monferrato, Piedmont). The latter is in substance as follows: A king with three sons marries again in his old age. The youngest son falls in love with his stepmother and the jealous father tries to poison her. The son and wife flee together, and fall in with some robbers whom they kill, and set at liberty a princess who has the gift of curing blindness and other diseases. They afterward find a cave containing rooms and all the necessaries of life, but see no one. They spend the night there, and the next morning the youth goes hunting; and as soon as he has departed a giant appears and solicits the step-mother's love, saying that if she will marry him, she will always be healthy and never lose her youth. But first it will be necessary to remove from her step-son's head a golden hair, and then he will become so weak that he can be killed by a blow. She was unwilling at first, because he had saved her life, but finally yielded. First she tried to get rid of him by pretending to be ill, and sending him for some water from a fountain near which was a lion. He obtained the water safely. Then his step-mother, pretending to comb his hair, cut off the golden hair, and the giant dragged him by the feet fifty miles, and let him fall first in the bushes and then on the ground. From the wounds in his head he became blind, but recovered his sight by means of the princess mentioned in the first part of the story, whom he married. After his golden lock had grown out again he returned to the cave and killed the giant, punishing his step-mother by leaving her there without even looking at her.

The story in Pitrè (No. 71, "The Cyclops") is more detailed. A queen who has been unfaithful to her husband is put in confinement, gives birth to a son, and afterward, through his aid, escapes. They encounter some cyclops, a number of whom the son kills; but one becomes secretly the mother's lover. To get rid of her son, she sends him for the water of a certain fountain, which he brings back safely. Finally the mother binds the son fast, under the pretence of playing a game, and delivers him to the cyclops, who kills him and cuts him into small bits, which he loads on his horse and turns him loose. The youth is, however, restored to life by the same water that he had brought back, and kills the cyclops and his mother, finally marrying the princess to whom he owes his life.[19]

IN MARKED contrast to the above class is the one in which a number of brothers owe their deliverance from enchantment to the self-sacrifice of a sister. Generally the sister is the innocent cause of her brothers' transformation. They live far from home, and their sister is not aware for a long time of their existence. When she learns it she departs in search of them, finds them, and, after great risk to herself, delivers them. But two versions of this story have yet been published in Italy: one from Naples

(Pent, IV. 8), the other from Bologna (Coronedi-Berti, No. 19). The latter version we give at length.

✃ XI. The Curse of the Seven Children ✃

There was once a king and a queen who had six children, all sons. The queen was about to give birth to another child, and the king said that if it was not a daughter all seven children would be cursed. Now it happened that the king had to go away to war; and before departing he said to the queen, "Listen. If you have a son, hang a lance out of the window; if a daughter, a distaff; so that I can see as soon as I arrive which it is." After the king had been gone a month, the queen gave birth to the most beautiful girl that was ever seen. Imagine how pleased the queen was at having a girl. She could scarcely contain herself for joy, and immediately gave orders to hang the distaff out of the window; but in the midst of the joyful confusion, a mistake was made, and they put out a lance. Shortly after, the king returned and saw the sign at the window, and cursed all his seven sons; but when he entered the house and the servants crowded around him to congratulate him and tell him about his beautiful daughter, then the king was amazed and became very melancholy. He entered the queen's room and looked at the child, who seemed exactly like one of those wax dolls to be kept in a box; then he looked about him and saw nothing of his sons, and his eyes filled with tears, for those poor youths had wandered out into the world.

Meanwhile the girl grew, and when she was large she saw that her parents caressed her, but always with tears in their eyes. One day she said to her mother: "What is the matter with you, mother, that I always see you crying?" Then the queen told her the story, and said that she was afraid that some day she would see her disappear too. When the girl heard how it was, what did she do? One night she rose softly and left the palace, with the intention of going to find her brothers. She walked and walked, and at last met a little old man, who said to her: "Where are you going at this time of the night?" She answered: "I am in search of my brothers." The old man said: "It will be difficult to find them, for you must not speak for seven years, seven months, seven weeks, seven days, seven hours, and seven minutes." She said: "I will try." Then she took a bit of paper which she found on the ground, wrote on it the day and the hour with a piece of choral, and left the old man and hastened on her way. After she had run a long time, she saw a light and went towards it, and when she was near it, she saw that it was over the door of a palace where a king lived. She entered and sat down on the stairway, and fell asleep. The servants came later to put out the light, and saw the pretty girl asleep on the stone steps; they awakened her, asking her what she was doing there. She began to make signs, asking them to give her a lodging. They understood her, and said they would ask the king. They returned shortly to tell her to enter, for the king wished to see her before she was shown to her room. When the king saw the beautiful girl, with hair like gold, flesh like milk and wine, teeth white as pearls, and little hands that an artist could not paint as beautiful as they were, he suddenly imagined that she must be the daughter of some lord, and gave orders that she should be treated with all possible respect. They showed her to a beautiful room; then a maid came and undressed her and put her to bed. Next morning, Diana, for so she was called, arose, saw a frame with a piece of embroidery in it, and began to work at it. The king visited her, and asked if she needed anything, and she made signs that she did not. The king was so pleased with the young girl that he ended by falling in love with her, and after a year had passed he thought of marrying her. The queen-mother, who was an envious person, was not content with the match, because, said she, no one knows where she came from, and, besides, she is dumb, something that would make people wonder if a king should marry her. But the king was so obstinate that he married her; and when his mother saw that there was no help, she pretended to be satisfied. Shortly after, the queen-mother put into the king's hands a letter which informed him of an imminent war, in which, if he did not take part, he would run the risk of losing his realm. The king went to the war, in fact, with great grief at leaving his wife; and before departing, he commended her earnestly to his mother, who said: "Do not be anxious, my son, I shall do all that I can to make her happy." The king embraced his wife and mother, and departed.

Scarcely had the king gone when the queen-mother sent for a mason, and made him build a wall near the kitchen-sink, so that it formed a sort of box. Now you must know that Diana expected soon to become a mother, and this afforded the queen-mother a pretext to write to her son that his wife had died in giving birth to a child. She took her and put her in the wall she had had built, where there was neither light nor air, and where the wicked woman hoped that she would die. But it was not so. The scullion went every day to wash the dishes at the sink near where poor Diana was buried alive. While attending to his business, he heard a lamentation, and listened to see where it could come from. He listened and listened, until at last he perceived that the voice came from the wall that had been newly built. What did he do then? He made a hole in the wall, and saw that the queen was there. The scullion asked how she came there; but she only made signs that she was about to give birth to a child. The poor scullion had his wife make a fine cushion, on which Diana reposed as well as she could, and gave birth to the most beautiful boy that could be seen. The scullion's wife went to see her every moment, and carried her broth, and cared for the child; in short, this poor woman, as well as her husband, did everything she could to alleviate the poor queen, who tried to make them understand by signs what she needed. One day it came into Diana's head to look into her memorandum book and see how long she still had to keep silent, and she saw that only two minutes yet remained. As soon as they had passed, she told the scullion all that had happened. At that moment the king arrived, and the scullion drew the queen from out the hole, and showed her to the king. You can imagine how delighted he was to see again his Diana, whom he believed to be dead. He embraced her, and kissed her and the child; in short, such was his joy that it seemed as if he would go mad. Diana related everything to him: why she had left her home, and why she had played dumb so long, and finally how she had been treated by the queen-mother, and what she had suffered, and how kind those poor people had been to her. When he had heard all this, he said: "Leave the matter to me; I will arrange it."

The next day the king invited all the nobles and princes of his realm to a great banquet. Now it happened that in setting the tables the servants laid six plates besides the others; and when the guests sat down, six handsome youths entered, who advanced and asked what should be given to a sister who had done so and so for her brothers. Then the king sprang up and said: "And I ask what shall be done to a mother who did so and so to her son's wife?" and he explained everything. One said: "Burn her alive." Another: "Put her in the pillory." Another: "Fry her in oil in the public square." This was agreed to. The youths had been informed by that same old man whom Diana had met, and who was a magician, where their sister was and what she had done for them. Then they made themselves known, and embraced Diana and their brother-in-law the king, and after the greatest joy, they all started off to see their parents. Imagine the satisfaction of the king and queen at seeing again all their seven children. They gave the warmest reception to the king, Diana's husband, and after they had spent some days together, Diana returned with her husband to their city. And all lived there after-ward in peace and contentment.[20]

WE SHALL now turn our attention to another wide-spread story, which may be termed "The True Bride," although the Grimm story of that name is not a representative of it. One of the simplest versions is Grimm's "The Goose-Girl," in which a queen's daughter is betrothed to a king's son who lives far away. When the daughter grew up she was sent to the bridegroom, with a maid to wait upon her. On the journey the maid takes the place of the princess, who becomes a poor goose-girl. The true bride is of course discovered at last, and the false one duly punished. "The White and the Black Bride," of the same collection, is a more complicated version of the same theme. The first part is the story of two sisters (step-sisters) who receive different gifts from fairies, etc.; the second part, that of the brother who paints his sister's portrait, which the king sees and desires to marry the original. The sister is sent for, but on the journey the ugly step-sister pushes the bride into a river or the sea, and takes her place. The true bride is changed into a swan (or otherwise miraculously preserved), and at last resumes her lawful place. In the above stories the substitution of the false bride is the main incident in the story; there are many other tales in which the same incident occurs, but it is subordinate to the others. Examples of this latter class will be given as soon as we reach the story of "The Forgotten Bride."

The first class mentioned is represented in Italy by two versions also. The first is composed of the two traits: "Two Sisters" and "True Bride"; the second, of "Brother who shows beautiful sister's portrait to king." This second version sometimes shows traces of the first. It is with this second version that we now have to do, as in it only is the substitution of the false bride the main incident. Examples of the first version will be found in the notes.[21] The story we have selected to illustrate the second version of this story is from Florence (*Nov. fior.* p. 314), and is entitled:

❧ XII. Oraggio and Bianchinetta ❧

There was once a lady who had two children: the boy was called Oraggio, the girl, Bianchinetta. By misfortunes they were reduced from great wealth to poverty. It was decided that Oraggio should go out to service, and indeed he found a situation as *valet de chambre* to a prince. After a time the prince, satisfied with his service, changed it, and set him to work cleaning the pictures in his gallery. Among the various paintings was one of a very beautiful lady, which was constantly Oraggio's admiration. The prince often surprised him admiring the portrait. One day he asked him why he spent so much time before that picture. Oraggio replied that it was the very image of his sister, and having been away from her some time, he felt the need of seeing her again. The prince answered that he did not believe that picture resembled his sister, because he had a search made, and it had not been possible to find any lady like the portrait. He added: "Have her come here, and if she is as beautiful as you say, I will make her my wife."

Oraggio wrote at once to Bianchinetta, who immediately set out on her journey. Oraggio went to the harbor to await her, and when he perceived the ship at a distance, he called out at intervals: "Mariners of the high sea, guard my sister Bianchina, so that the sun shall not brown her." Now, on the ship where Bianchinetta was, was also another young girl with her mother, both very homely. When they were near the harbor, the daughter gave Bianchinetta a blow, and pushed her into the sea. When they landed, Oraggio could not recognize his sister; and that homely girl presented herself, saying that the sun had made her so dark that she could no longer be recognized. The prince was surprised at seeing such a homely woman, and reproved Oraggio, removing him from his position and setting him to watch the geese. Every day he led the geese to the sea, and every day Bianchinetta came forth and adorned them with tassels of various colors. When the geese returned home, they said:—

> "Crò! Crò!
> From the sea we come,
> We feed on gold and pearls.
> Oraggio's sister is fair,
> She is fair as the sun;
> She would suit our master well."

The prince asked Oraggio how the geese came to repeat those words every day. He told him that his sister, thrown into the sea, had been seized by a fish, which had taken her to a beautiful palace under the water, where she was in chains. But that, attached to a long chain, she was permitted to come to the shore when he drove the geese there. The prince said: "If what you relate is true, ask her what is required to liberate her from that prison."

The next day Oraggio asked Bianchinetta how it would be possible to take her from there and conduct her to the prince. She replied: "It is impossible to take me from here. At least, the monster always says to me:

48

'It would require a sword that cuts like a hundred, and a horse that runs like the wind.' It is almost impossible to find these two things. You see, therefore, it is my fate to remain here always." Oraggio returned to the palace, and informed the prince of his sister's answer. The latter made every effort, and succeeded in finding the horse that ran like the wind, and the sword that cut like a hundred. They went to the sea, found Bianchinetta, who was awaiting them. She led them to her palace. With the sword the chain was cut. She mounted the horse, and thus was able to escape. When they reached the palace the prince found her as beautiful as the portrait Oraggio was always gazing at, and married her. The other homely one was burned in the public square, with the accustomed pitch-shirt; and they lived content and happy.[22]

WE HAVE already encountered the trait of "Thankful Animals," who assist the hero in return for kindness he has shown them. What is merely an incident in the stories above alluded to constitutes the main feature of a class of stories which may be termed "Animal Brothers-in-law." The usual formula in these stories is as follows: Three princes, transformed into animals, marry the hero's sisters. The hero visits them in turn; they assist him in the performance of difficult tasks, and are by him freed from their enchantment. This formula varies, of course. Sometimes there are but two sisters, and the brothers-in-law are freed from their enchantment in some other way than by the hero. A good specimen of this class is from the south of Italy, Basilicata (Comparetti, No. 20), and is called:

✕ XIII. The Fair Fiorita ✕

There was once a king who had four children: three daughters and a son, who was the heir to the throne. One day the king said to the prince: "My son, I have decided to marry your three sisters to the first persons who pass our palace at noon." At that time there first passed a swineherd, then a huntsman, and finally a grave-digger. The king had them all three summoned to his presence, and told the swine-herd that he wished to give him his oldest daughter for a wife, the second to the huntsman, and the third to the grave-digger. Those poor creatures thought they were dreaming. But they saw that the king spoke seriously, or rather commanded. Then, all confused, but well pleased, they said: "Let your Majesty's will be done." The prince, who loved his youngest sister dearly, was deeply grieved that she should become a grave-digger's wife. He begged the king not to make this match, but the king would not listen to him.

The prince, grieved at his father's caprice, would not be present at his sisters' wedding, but took a walk in the garden at the foot of the palace. Now, while the priest in the marriage hall was blessing the three brides, the garden suddenly bloomed with the fairest flowers, and there came forth from a white cloud a voice which said: "Happy he who shall have a kiss from the lips of the fair Fiorita!" The prince trembled so that he could hardly stand; and afterward, leaning against an olive-tree, he began to weep for the sisters he had lost, and remained buried in thought many hours. Then he started, as if awakening from a dream, and said to himself: "I must flee from my father's house. I will wander about the world, and will not rest until I have a kiss from the lips of the fair Fiorita."

He travelled over land and sea, over mountains and plains, and found no living soul that could give him word of the fair Fiorita. Three years had elapsed, when one day, leaving a wood and journeying through a beautiful plain, he arrived at a palace before which was a fountain, and drew near to drink. A child two years old, who was playing by the fountain, seeing him approach, began to cry and call its mother. The mother, when she saw the prince, ran to meet him, embraced him, and kissed him, crying: "Welcome, welcome, my brother!" The prince at first did not recognize her; but looking at her closely in the face, he saw that it was his oldest sister, and embracing her in turn, exclaimed: "How glad I am to see you, my sister!" And they rejoiced greatly. The sister invited him to enter the palace, which was hers, and led him to her husband, who was much pleased to see him, and all three overwhelmed with caresses the child who, by calling his mother, had been the cause of all that joy.

The prince then asked about his other two sisters, and his brother-in-law replied that they were well, and lived in a lordly way with their husbands. The prince was surprised, and his brother-in-law added that the fortunes of the three husbands of his sisters had changed since they had been enchanted by a magician. "And cannot I see my other two sisters?" asked the prince. The brother-in-law replied: "Direct your journey towards sunrise. After a day you will find your second sister; after two days, the third." "But I must seek the way to the fair Fiorita, and I do not know whether it is towards sunrise or sunset." "It is precisely towards sunrise; and you are doubly fortunate: first, because you will see your two sisters again; secondly, because from the last you can receive information about the fair Fiorita. But before departing I wish to give you a remembrance. Take these hog's bristles. The first time you encounter any danger from which you cannot extricate yourself, throw them on the ground, and I will free you from the danger." The prince took the bristles, and after he had thanked his brother-in-law, resumed his journey.

The next day he arrived at the palace of his second sister; was received there also with great joy, and this brother-in-law, too, wished to give him a memento before he departed; and because he had been a huntsman, presented him with a bunch of birds' feathers, telling him the same thing that the other brother-in-law had. He thanked him and departed. The third day he came to his youngest sister's, who, seeing the brother who had always loved her more dearly than his other sisters, welcomed him more warmly, as did also her husband. The latter gave him a little human bone, giving him the same advice as the other brothers-in-law had. His sister then told him that the fair Fiorita lived a day's journey from there, and that he could learn more about her from an old woman who was indebted to her, and to whom she sent him.

As soon as the prince arrived at the fair Fiorita's country (she was the king's daughter), he went to the old woman. When she heard that he was the brother of the one who had been so kind to her, she received him like a son. Fortunately, the old woman's house was exactly opposite that side of the king's palace where there was a window to which the fair Fiorita came every day at dawn. Now one morning at that hour she appeared at the window, scarcely covered by a white veil. When the prince saw that flower of beauty, he was so agitated that he would have fallen had not the old woman supported him. The old woman attempted to dissuade him from the idea of marrying the fair Fiorita, saying that the king would give his daughter only to him who should discover a hidden place, and that he killed him who could not find it, and that already many princes had lost their lives for her. But, notwithstanding, he answered that he should die if he could not obtain possession of the fair Fiorita. Having learned afterward from the old woman that the king bought for his daughter the rarest musical instruments, hear what he devised! He went to a cymbal-maker and said: "I want a cymbal that will play three tunes, and each tune to last a day, and to be made in such a way that a man can be hidden inside of it; and I will pay you a thousand ducats for it. When it is finished I will get in it; and you must go and play it in front of the king's palace; and if the king wishes to buy it you will sell it to him on condition that you shall take it every three days to fix it." The cymbal-maker consented, and did all that the prince commanded him. The king purchased the cymbal with the maker's condition, had it carried to his daughter's bed-chamber, and said to her: "See, my daughter, I do not wish you to lack any diversion, even when you are in bed and cannot sleep."

Next to the fair Fiorita's chamber slept her maids of honor. In the night when all were asleep, the prince, who was hidden in the cymbal, came out and called: "Fair Fiorita! Fair Fiorita!" She awoke in a fright and cried: "Come, my maids of honor, I hear some one calling me." The maids of honor came quickly, but found no one, for the prince hid himself suddenly in the instrument. The same thing happened twice, and the maids coming and finding no one, the fair Fiorita said: "Well, it must be my fancy. If I call you again, do not come, I command you." The prince, within the cymbal, heard this. Scarcely had the maids of honor fallen asleep again, when the prince approached the fair one's bed and said: "Fair Fiorita, give me, I beg you, a kiss from your lips; if you do not, I shall die." She, all trembling, called her maids; but obeying her command, they did not come. Then she said to the prince: "You are fortunate and have won. Draw near." And she gave him the kiss, and on the prince's lips there remained a beautiful rose. "Take this rose," she said, "and keep it on your heart, for it will bring you good luck." The prince placed it on his heart, and then told his fair one all his history from the time he had left his father's palace until he had introduced himself into her chamber by the trick with the cymbal. The fair Fiorita was well pleased, and said that she would willingly marry him; but to succeed, he must perform many difficult tasks which the king would lay upon him. First he must discover the way to a hiding-place where the king had concealed her with a hundred damsels; then he must recognize her among the hundred damsels, all dressed alike and veiled. "But," she said, "you need not trouble yourself about these difficulties, for the rose you have taken from my lips, and which you will always wear over your heart, will draw you like the loadstone, first to the hiding-place, and afterward to my arms. But the king will set you other tasks, and perhaps terrible ones. These you must think of yourself. Let us leave it to God and fortune."

The prince went at once to the king, and asked for the fair Fiorita's hand. The king did not refuse it, but made the same conditions that the princess had told him of. He consented, and by the help of the rose quickly performed the first tasks. "Bravo!" exclaimed the king, when the prince recognized the fair Fiorita among the other damsels: "But this is not enough." Then he shut him up in a large room all full of fruit, and commanded him, under pain of death, to eat it all up in a day. The prince was in despair, but fortunately he remembered the hog's bristles and the advice which his first brother-in-law had given him. He threw the bristles on the ground, and there suddenly came forth a great herd of swine which ate up all the fruit and then disappeared. This task was accomplished. But the king proposed another. He wished the prince to retire with his bride, and cause her to fall asleep at the singing of the birds which are the sweetest to hear and the most beautiful to see. The prince remembered the bunch of feathers given him by his brother-in-law the huntsman, and threw them on the ground. Suddenly there appeared the most beautiful birds in the world, and sang so sweetly that the king himself fell asleep. But a servant awakened him at once, because he had commanded it, and he said to the prince and his daughter: "Now you can enjoy your love at liberty. But to-morrow, on arising, you must present me with a child two years old, who can speak and call you by name. If not, you will both be killed." "Now let us retire, my dear wife," said the prince to the fair Fiorita. "Between now and to-morrow some saint will aid us." The next morning the prince remembered the bone which his brother-in-law the grave-digger had given him. He rose and threw it to the ground, and lo! A beautiful child, with a golden apple in his right hand, who cried papa and mamma. The king entered the room, and the child ran to meet him, and wished to put the golden apple on the crown which the king wore. The king then kissed the child, blessed the pair, and taking the crown from his head, put it on his son-in-law's, saying: "This is now yours." Then they gave a great feast at the court for the wedding, and they invited the prince's three sisters, with their husbands. And the prince's father, receiving such good news of the son whom he believed lost, hastened to embrace him, and gave him his crown too. So the prince and the fair Fiorita became king and queen of two realms, and from that time on were always happy.[23]

IN THE above story the wife is won by the performance of difficult tasks by the suitor. A somewhat similar class of stories is the one in which the bride is won by the solution of a riddle. The riddle, or difficult question, is either proposed by the bride herself, and the suitor who fails to answer it is killed, or the suitor is obliged to propose one himself, and if the bride fails to solve it, she marries him; if she succeeds, the suitor is killed. The first of the above two forms is found in three Italian stories, two of which resemble each other quite closely.

In the Pentamerone (I. 5, "The Flea"), the King of High-Hill, "being bitten by a flea, caught him by a wonderful feat of dexterity; and seeing how handsome and stately he was, he could not in conscience pass sentence on him upon the bed of his nail. So he put him into a bottle, and feeding him every day with the blood of his own arm, the little beast grew at such a rate that at the end of seven months it was necessary to shift his quarters, for he was grown bigger than a sheep. When the king saw this, he had him flayed, and the skin dressed. Then he issued a proclamation, that whoever could tell to what animal this skin had belonged should have his daughter to wife." The question is answered by an ogre, to whom the king gives his daughter rather than break his promise. The hapless wife is afterward rescued by an old woman's seven sons, who possess remarkable gifts. In Gonz. (No. 22, "The Robber who had a Witch's Head"), a king with three daughters fattens a louse and nails its skin over the door as in the Pentamerone. A robber, who had a witch's head that told him everything he wanted to know, answers the question, and receives in marriage the king's eldest daughter. He takes her home and leaves her alone for a time, and on his return learns from the witch's head that his wife has reviled him. He kills her and marries the second sister, whom he kills for the same reason, and marries the youngest. She is more discreet, and the witch's head can only praise her. One day she finds the head and throws it in the oven; and the robber, whose life was in some way connected with it, died. The wife then anointed her sisters with a life-giving salve, and all three returned to their father's house, and afterward married three handsome princes. The third story, from the Tyrol (Schneller, No. 31, "The Devil's Wife"), is connected with the Bluebeard story which will be mentioned later. A king and queen had an only daughter, who was very pretty and fond of dress. One day she found a louse; and as she did not know what kind of an animal it was, she ran to her mother and asked her. Her mother told her and said: "Shut the louse up in a box and feed it. As soon as it is very large, we will have a pair of gloves made of its skin; these we will exhibit, and whoever of your suitors guesses from the skin of what animal they are made, shall be your husband." The successful suitor is no other than the Devil, who takes his wife home and forbids her to open a certain room. One day, while he is absent, she opens the door of the forbidden chamber, and sees from the names and condemned souls who her husband is. She is so frightened that she becomes ill, but manages to send word to her father by means of a carrier-pigeon. The king sets out with many brave men to deliver her; on the way he meets three men who possess wonderful gifts (far seeing, sharp ear, great strength), and with their aid rescues his daughter.

More frequently, however, this class of stories turns on a riddle proposed by the suitor himself, and which the bride is unable to solve.

The following story, which illustrates the latter version, is from Istria (Ive, 1877, p. 13), and is entitled:

℘ *XIV. Bierde* ℘

Once upon a time there was a mother who had a son, who went to school. One day he came home and said to his mother: "Mother, I want to go and seek my fortune." She replied: "Ah, my son, are you mad? Where do you want to seek it?" "I want to wander about the world until I find it." Now he had a dog whose name was Bierde. He said: "To-morrow morning bake me some bread, put it into a bag, give me a pair of iron shoes, and I and Bierde will go and seek our fortune." His mother said: "No, my son, don't go, for I shall not see you again!" And she wept him as dead. After she was quieted she said to him: "Well, if you will go, to-morrow I will bake you some bread, and I will make you a bread-cake." She made the bread-cake, and put some poison in it; she put the bread and the bread-cake in the bag, and he went away. He walked and walked and walked until he felt hungry, and said to the dog: "Ah, poor Bierde, how tired you are, and how hungry, too! Wait until we have gone a little farther, and then we will eat." He went on, tired as he was, and at last seated himself under a tree, with the dog near him. He said: "Oh, here we are; now we will eat. Wait, Bierde; I will give you a piece of the bread-cake so that you, too, can eat." He broke off a piece of the cake, and gave it to him to eat. The dog was so hungry that he ate it greedily. After he had eaten it he took two or three turns, and fell dead on the ground, with his tongue sticking out. "Ah, poor Bierde!" said his master. "You have been poisoned! My mother has done it! The wretch! She has put poison in the cake in order to kill me!" He kept weeping and saying: "Poor Bierde, you are dead, but you have saved my life!" While he was weeping three crows passed, alighted, and pecked at the tongue of the dog, and all three died. Then he said: "Well, well! *Bierde dead has killed three crows!* I will take them with me." So he took them and continued his journey. He saw at a distance a large fire; he approached and heard talking and singing, and beheld seven highwaymen, who had eaten a great many birds, and who had a great deal of meat still left. He said to himself: "Poor me! Now I shall have to die; there is no escape; they will certainly take me and kill me!" Then he said: "Enough; I will go ahead." As soon as they saw him they cried: "Stop! Your money or your life!" The poor fellow said: "Brothers, what would you have me give you? Money I have not. I am very hungry. I have nothing but these three birds. If you want them I will give them to you." "Very well," they said, "eat and drink; we will eat the birds." They took the birds, picked them, skinned them, roasted them over the coals, and said to the youth: "We will not give you any of these; you can eat the others." They ate them, and all seven fell down dead. When the youth saw that they did not stir, but were dead, he said: "Well, well! *Bierde dead has killed three, and these three have killed seven!*" He rose and went away after he had made a good meal. On the way he felt hungry again, and sat down under a tree, and began to eat. When he got up he saw a beautiful canary-bird on the top of another tree. He took up a stone and threw at it. The bird flew away. Now, behind this tree was a hare, big with young, and it happened that the stone fell on it and killed it. The youth went to see where the stone fell, and when he saw the dead hare he said: "Well, well! *I threw it at the canary-bird and the stone killed the hare!* I will take it with me. If I had the fire that those robbers left I would cook it." He went on until he came to a church, in which he found a lighted lamp and a missal. So he skinned the hare, and made a fire with the missal, and roasted and ate the hare. Then he continued his journey until he came to the foot of a mountain, where the sea was. On the shore he saw two persons with a boat, who ferried over those who wished to reach the other shore, because one could not go on foot on account of the great dust, which was suffocating. The price for crossing was three *soldi*. The youth said to the owners of the bark: "How much do you want to set me down on the other bank?" "Three *soldi*." "Take me across, brothers; I will give you two, for I have no more." They replied: "*Two do not enter if there are not three.*" He repeated his offer and they made the same answer. Then he said: "Very well. I will stay here." And he remained there. In a moment, however, there came up a shower, and laid the dust, and he went on. He reached a city, and found it in great confusion. He asked: "What is the matter here, that there are so many people?" They answered: "It is the governor's daughter, who guesses everything. He whose riddle she cannot guess is to marry her; but he whose riddle she guesses is put to death." He asked: "Could I, too, go there?" "What, you go, who are a foolish boy! So many students have abstained, and you, so ignorant, wish to go! You will certainly go to your death!" "Well," he said, "my mother told me that she would never see me again, so I will go." He presented himself to the governor and said: "Sir governor, I wish to go to your daughter and see whether she can guess what I have to tell her." "Do you wish," he replied, "to go to your death? So many have lost their lives, do you, also, wish to lose yours?" He answered: "Let me go and try." He wished to go and see for himself. He entered the hall where the daughter was. The governor summoned many gentlemen to hear. When they were all there the governor again said that the youth should reflect that if she guessed what he had to say that he would lose his life. He replied that he had thought of that. The room was full of persons of talent, and the youth presented himself and said:—

"Bierde dead has killed three."

She said to herself: "How can it be that one dead should kill three?"

"And three have killed seven."

She said: "Here is nothing but dead and killed; what shall I do?" She was puzzled at once, and felt herself perplexed. He continued:—

"I threw where I saw, and reached where I
did not expect to.
I have eaten that which was born, and that
which was not born.
It was cooked with words.
Two do not enter if there are not three;
But the hard passes over the soft."

When she heard this the governor's daughter could not answer. All the others were astonished likewise, and said that she must marry him. Then he told them all that had happened, and the marriage took place.[24]

We shall now direct our attention to a class of stories found in all lands, and which may, from one of its most important episodes, be called "The Forgotten Bride." In the ordinary version, the hero, in consequence of some imprecation, sets out in search of the heroine, who is either the daughter or in the custody of ogre or ogress. The hero, by the help of the heroine, performs difficult tasks imposed upon him by her father or mother, etc., and finally elopes with her. The pursuit of father or mother, etc., is avoided by magic obstacles raised in their way, or by transformations of the fugitives. The hero leaves his bride, to prepare his parents to receive her; but at a kiss, usually from his mother, he entirely forgets his bride until she recalls herself to his memory, and they are both united. The trait of difficult tasks performed by the hero is sometimes omitted, as well as flight with magic obstacles or transformations. All the episodes of the above story, down to the forgetting bride at mother's kiss, are found in many stories; notably in the class "True Bride," already mentioned.

A Sicilian story (Pitrè, No. 13) will best illustrate this class. It is entitled:

✤ XV. Snow-White-Fire-Red ✤

There was once a king and queen who had no son, and they were always making vows to obtain one; and they promised that if they had a son, or even a daughter, they would maintain two fountains for seven years: one running wine, the other oil. After this vow the queen gave birth to a handsome boy.

As soon as the child was born, the two fountains were erected, and everybody went and took oil and wine. At the end of seven years the fountains began to dry up. An ogress, wishing to collect the drops that still fell from the fountain, went there with a sponge and pitcher. She sopped up the drops with the sponge and then squeezed it in the pitcher. After she had worked so hard to fill this pitcher, the little son of the king, who was playing ball, from caprice threw a ball and broke the pitcher. When the old woman saw this, she said: "Listen. I can do nothing to you, for you are the king's son; but I can bestow upon you an imprecation: May you be unable to marry until you find Snow-white-fire-red!" The cunning child took a piece of paper and wrote down the old woman's words, put it away in a drawer, and said nothing about it. When he was eighteen the king and queen wished him to marry. Then he remembered the old woman's imprecation, took the piece of paper, and said: "Ah! If I do not find Snow-white-fire-red I cannot marry!" When it seemed fit, he took leave of his father and mother, and began his journey entirely alone. Months passed without meeting any one. One evening, night overtook him, tired and discouraged, in a plain in the midst of which was a large house.

At daybreak he saw an ogress coming, frightfully tall and stout, who cried: "Snow-white-fire-red, lower your tresses for me to climb up!" When the prince heard this he took heart, and said: "There she is!" Snow-white-fire-red lowered her tresses, which seemed never to end, and the ogress climbed up by them. The next day the ogress descended, and when the prince saw her depart, he came from under the tree where he had concealed himself, and cried: "Snow-white-fire-red, lower your tresses for me to climb up!" She, believing it was her mother (for she called the ogress mother), lowered her tresses, and the prince climbed boldly up. When he was up, he said: "Ah! My dear little sister, how I have labored to find you!" And he told her of the old woman's imprecation when he was seven years old.

She gave him some refreshments, and then said: "You see, if the ogress returns and finds you here, she will devour you. Hide yourself." The ogress returned, and the prince concealed himself.

After the ogress had eaten, her daughter gave her wine to drink, and made her drunk. Then she said: "My mother, what must I do to get away from here? Not that I want to go, for I wish to stay with you; but I want to know just out of curiosity. Tell me!" "What you must do to get away from here!" said the ogress. "You must enchant everything that there is here, so that I shall lose time. I shall call, and instead of you, the chair, the cupboard, the chest of drawers, will answer for you. When you do not appear, I will ascend. You must take the seven balls of yarn that I have laid away. When I come and do not find you, I shall pursue you; when you see yourself pursued, throw down the first ball, and then the others. I shall always overtake you until you throw down the last ball."

Her daughter heard all that she said, and remembered it. The next day the ogress went out, and Snow-white-fire-red and the prince did what they had to do. They went about the whole house, saying: "Table, you answer if my mother comes; chairs, answer if my mother comes; chest of drawers, answer if my mother comes;" and so she enchanted the whole house. Then she and the prince departed in such a hurry that they seemed to fly. When the ogress returned, she called: "Snow-white-fire-red, let down your tresses that I may climb up!" The table answered: "Come, come, mother!" She waited a while, and when no one appeared to draw her up, she called again: "Snow-white-fire-red, lower your tresses for me to climb up!" The chair answered: "Come, come, mother!" She waited a while, but no one appeared; then she called again, and the chest of drawers replied: "Come, come, mother!" Meanwhile the lovers were fleeing. When there was nothing left to answer, the ogress cried out: "Treason! Treason!" Then she got a ladder and climbed up. When she saw that her daughter and the balls of yarn were gone, she cried: "Ah, wretch! I will drink your blood!" Then she hastened after the fugitives, following their scent. They saw her afar off, and when she saw them, she cried: "Snow-white-fire-red, turn around so that I can see you." (If she had turned around she would have been enchanted.)

When the ogress had nearly overtaken them, Snow-white-fire-red threw down the first ball, and suddenly there arose a lofty mountain. The ogress was not disturbed; she climbed and climbed until she almost overtook the two again. Then Snow-white-fire-red, seeing her near at hand, threw down the second ball, and there suddenly appeared a plain covered with razors and knives. The ogress, all cut and torn, followed after the lovers, dripping with blood.

When Snow-white-fire-red saw her near again, she threw down the third ball, and there arose a terrible river. The ogress threw herself into the river and continued her pursuit, although she was half dead. Then another ball, and there appeared a fountain of vipers, and many other things. At last, dying and worn out, the ogress stopped and cursed Snowwhite-fire-red, saying: "The first kiss that the queen gives her son, may the prince forget you!" Then the ogress could stand it no longer, and died in great anguish.

The lovers continued their journey, and came to a town near where the prince lived. He said to Snow-white-fire-red: "You remain here, for you are not provided with proper clothes, and I will go and get what you need, and then you can appear before my father and mother." She consented, and remained.

When the queen beheld her son, she threw herself on him to kiss him. "Mother," said he, "I have made a vow not to allow myself to be kissed." The poor mother was petrified. At night, while he was asleep, his mother, who was dying to kiss him, went and did so. From that moment he forgot all about Snow-white-fire-red.

Let us leave the prince with his mother, and return to the poor girl, who was left in the street without knowing where she was. An old woman met her, and saw the poor girl, as beautiful as the sun, weeping. "What is the matter, my daughter?" "I do not know how I came here!" "My daughter, do not despair; come with me." And she took her to her house. The young girl was deft with her hands, and could work enchantment. She made things, and the old woman sold them, and so they both lived. One day the maiden said to the old woman that she wanted two bits of old cloth from the palace for some work she had to do. The old woman went to the palace, and began to ask for the bits, and said so much that at last she obtained them. Now the old woman had two doves, a male and a female, and with these bits of cloth Snow-white-fire-red dressed the doves so prettily that all who saw them marveled. The young girl took these doves, and whispered in their ears: "You are the prince, and you are Snow-white-fire-red. The king is at the table, eating; fly and relate all that you have undergone."

While the king, queen, prince, and many others were at the table, the beautiful doves flew in and alighted on the table. "How beautiful you are!" And all were greatly pleased. Then the dove which represented Snow-white-fire-red began: "Do you remember when you were young how your father promised a fountain of oil and one of wine for your birth?" The other dove answered: "Yes, I remember." "Do you remember the old woman whose pitcher of oil you broke? Do you remember?" "Yes, I remember." "Do you remember the imprecation she pronounced on you,—that you could not marry until you found Snow-white-fire-red?" "I remember," replied the other dove. In short, the first dove recalled all that had passed, and finally said: "Do you remember how you had the ogress at your heels, and how she cursed you, saying that at your mother's first kiss you must forget Snow-white-fire-red?" When the dove came to the kiss, the prince remembered everything, and the king and queen were astounded at hearing the doves speak.

When they had ended their discourse, the doves made a low bow and flew away. The prince cried: "Ho, there! Ho, there! See where those doves go! See where they go!" The servants looked and saw the doves alight on a country house. The prince hastened and entered it, and found Snow-white-fire-red. When he saw her he threw his arms about her neck, exclaiming: "Ah! My sister, how much you have suffered for me!" Straightway they dressed her beautifully and conducted her to the palace. When the queen saw her there, she said: "What a beauty!" Things were soon settled and the lovers were married.[25]

As we have remarked above, this story is often found incomplete, the ending—"forgetfulness of bride"—being wanting.

Several of these versions are from Milan (*Nov. fior.* pp. 411, 415, 417). In the first, "The King of the Sun," a trait occurs that is of some interest. The hero plays billiards with the King of the Sun and wins his daughter.

He goes in search of his bride, and at last finds an old man who tells him where the King of the Sun lives, and adds: "In a wood near by is a pond where, in the afternoon, the king's three daughters bathe. Go and carry away their clothes; and when they come and ask for them give them back on condition that they will take you to their father." The hero does as he is told, is taken to the king, and obliged to choose his bride from among the three, with his eyes blindfolded. The remainder of the story consists of the usual flight, with the transformations of the lovers. The incident of the maidens who bathe, and whose clothes the hero steals, is clearly an example of the Swan-maiden myth, and occurs in a few other Italian tales. In a story from the North of Italy (Monferrato, Comparetti, No. 50), "The Isle of Happiness," a poor boy goes to seek his fortune. He encounters an old man who tells him that fortune appears but once in a hundred years, and if not taken then, never is. He adds that this is the very time for fortune to appear—that day or the next—and advises the youth to hide himself in a wood near the bank of a stream, and when three beautiful girls come and bathe, to carry away the clothes of the middle one. He does so, and compels the owner (who is none other than Fortune) to marry him. By his mother's fault he loses his bride, as in the Cupid and Psyche stories, and is obliged to go in search of her to the Isle of Happiness. The same incident occurs in several Sicilian stories. In one (Pitrè, No. 50, "Give me the Veil!") the hero, a poor youth, goes in search of his fortune as in the last story, and meets an old woman who tells him to go to a certain fountain, where twelve doves will come to drink and become twelve maidens "as beautiful as the sun, with veils over their faces," and advises the youth to seize the veil of the most beautiful girl and keep it; for if she obtains it she will become a dove again. The youth does as he is commanded, and takes his wife home, giving the veil to his mother to keep for him. She gives it to the wife, who becomes a dove again, and disappears. The same thing happens twice; the third time the veil is burned, and the wife, who turns out to be the enchanted daughter of the king of Spain, remains with her husband.[26]

There yet remains a large and interesting class of stories to be examined. The class may conveniently be termed "Bluebeard," although, as we shall see, there are three versions of this story, to only one of which the above name properly belongs. These three versions are well represented by the three Grimm stories of "The Feather Bird" (No. 46), "The Robber Bridegroom" (No. 40), and "The Wood-cutter's Child" (No. 3). In the first version, which is, properly speaking, the Bluebeard story, two sisters are married in turn and killed by their husband, because they open the forbidden chamber. The youngest sister, although she opens the forbidden door, manages to escape and deliver her sisters, whom she restores to life. In the second version a robber marries several sisters, whom he kills for disobeying his commands (the trait of forbidden chamber is usually wanting); the youngest sister again manages to escape and restores her dead sisters to life. Generally in this version the husband makes a desperate effort to be revenged on the sister who has escaped from him, but fails in this also. In the third version a young girl is under the guardianship of some supernatural being, who forbids her to open a certain door. The child disobeys, denies her fault, and is sent away in disgrace; she afterward marries and her children are taken from her one by one until she confesses her fault, or, as is the case in an Italian version, persists in her denial to the very end. We shall examine these three versions separately, and first give an example of the first, or Bluebeard, class. It is from Venice (Widter-Wolf, No. 11, *Jahrb.* VII. 148), and is entitled:

✣ XVI. How the Devil Married Three Sisters ✣

Once upon a time the Devil was seized with a desire to marry. He therefore left hell, took the form of a handsome young man, and built a fine large house. When it was completed and furnished in the most fashionable style, he introduced himself to a family where there were three pretty daughters, and paid his addresses to the eldest of them. The handsome man pleased the maiden, her parents were glad to see a daughter so well provided for, and it was not long before the wedding was celebrated.

When he had taken his bride home, he presented her with a very tastefully arranged bouquet, led her through all the rooms of the house, and finally to a closed door. "The whole house is at your disposal," said he, "only I must request one thing of you; that is, that you do not on any account open this door."

Of course the young wife promised faithfully; but equally, of course, she could scarcely wait for the moment to come when she might break her promise. When the Devil had left the house the next morning, under pretence of going hunting, she ran hastily to the forbidden door, opened it, and saw a terrible abyss full of fire that shot up towards her, and singed the flowers on her bosom. When her husband came home and asked her whether she had kept her promise, she unhesitatingly said "Yes," but he saw by the flowers that she was telling a lie, and said: "Now I will not put your curiosity to the test any longer. Come with me. I will show you myself what is behind the door." Thereupon he led her to the door, opened it, gave her such a push that she fell down into hell, and shut the door again.

A few months after he wooed the next sister for his wife, and won her; but with her everything that had happened with the first wife was exactly repeated.

Finally he courted the third sister. She was a prudent maiden, and said to herself: "He has certainly murdered my two sisters; but then it is a splendid match for me, so I will try and see whether I cannot be more fortunate than they." And accordingly she consented. After the wedding the bridegroom gave her a beautiful bouquet, but forbade her, also, to open the door which he pointed out.

Not a whit less curious than her sisters, she, too, opened the forbidden door when the Devil had gone hunting, but she had previously put her flowers in water. Then she saw behind the door the fatal abyss and her sisters therein. "Ah!" She exclaimed, "poor creature that I am; I thought I had marred an ordinary man, and instead of that he is the Devil! How can I get away from him?" She carefully pulled her two sisters out of hell and hid them. When the Devil came home he immediately looked at the bouquet, which she again wore on her bosom, and when he found the flowers so fresh he asked no questions; but reassured as to his secret, he now, for the first time, really loved her.

After a few days she asked him if he would carry three chests for her to her parents' house, without putting them down or resting on the way. "But," She added, "you must keep your word, for I shall be watching you." The Devil promised to do exactly as she wished. So the next morning she put one of her sisters in a chest, and laid it on her husband's shoulders. The Devil, who is very strong, but also very lazy and unaccustomed to work, soon got tired of carrying the heavy chest, and wanted to rest before he was out of the street on which he lived; but his wife called out to him: "Don't put it down; I see you!" The Devil went reluctantly on with the chest until he had turned the corner, and then said to himself: "She cannot see me here; I will rest a little." But scarcely had he begun to put the chest down when the sister inside cried out: "Don't put it down; I see you still!" Cursing, he dragged the chest on into another street, and was going to lay it down on a doorstep, but he again heard the voice: "Don't lay it down, you rascal; I see you still!" "What kind of eyes must my wife have," he thought, "To see around corners as well as straight ahead, and through walls as if they were made of glass!" And thus thinking he arrived, all in a perspiration and quite tired out, at the house of his mother-in-law, to whom he hastily delivered the chest, and then hurried home to strengthen himself with a good breakfast.

The same thing was repeated the next day with the second chest. On the third day she herself was to be taken home in the chest. She therefore prepared a figure which she dressed in her own clothes, and placed on the balcony, under the pretext of being able to watch him better; slipped quickly into the chest, and had the maid put it on the Devil's back. "The deuce!" said he; "This chest is a great deal heavier than the others; and to-day, when she is sitting on the balcony, I shall have so much the less chance to rest." So by dint of the greatest exertions he carried it, without stopping, to his mother-in-law, and then hastened home to breakfast, scolding, and with his back almost broken. But quite contrary to custom, his wife did not come out to meet him, and there was no breakfast ready. "Margerita, where are you?" he cried; but received no answer. As he was running through the corridors he at length looked out of a window, and saw the figure on the balcony. "Margerita, have you gone to sleep? Come down. I am as tired as a dog, and as hungry as a wolf." But there was no reply. "If you do not come down instantly I will go up and bring you down," he cried, angrily; but Margerita did not stir. Enraged, he hastened up to the balcony, and gave her such a box on the ear that her head flew off, and he saw that the head was nothing but a milliner's form, and the body, a bundle of rags. Raging, he rushed down and rummaged through the whole house, but in vain; he found only his wife's empty jewel-box. "Ha!" He cried; "she has been stolen from me, and her jewels, too!" And he immediately ran to inform her parents of the misfortune. But when he came near the house, to his great surprise he saw on the balcony above the door all three sisters, his wives, who were looking down on him with scornful laughter.

Three wives at once terrified the Devil so much that he took his flight with all possible speed.

Since that time he has lost his taste for marrying.[27]

WE HAVE already mentioned, in the class of "Bride Won by Solving Riddle," the story in Gonzenbach of "The Robber who had a Witch's Head." In this story, after the robber has married the first princess, he takes her home, and learns from the witch's head, which hangs over the window in a basket, what his wife says of him in his absence. The counterpart of the witch's head is found in several very curious Italian stories. In these a magician is substituted for the robber, and marries, in the same way, several sisters. In the version in Gonzenbach, No. 23 ("The Story of Ohimè"), Ohimè, the magician, leaves his wife for a few days, and before he goes gives her a human bone, telling her she must eat it before his return. The wife throws the bone away; but when the magician returns he calls out: "Bone, where are you?" "Here I am." "Come here, then." Then the bone came, and the magician murdered his wife because she had not done her duty. The second sister is married and killed in the same way. Then the youngest becomes the magician's bride. In her perplexity and grief at her husband's command to eat a human arm during his absence, she invokes her mother's spirit, which tells her to burn the arm to a coal, powder it, and bind it about her body. When the magician returns and asks the arm where it is, it replies: "In Maruzza's body." Then her husband trusted her, and treated her kindly, showing her, among other things, a closet containing flasks of salve which restored the dead to life. He forbade her, however, to open a certain door. Maruzza could not restrain her curiosity, and the first opportunity she had she opened the door, and found in the room a handsome young prince murdered. She restored him to life, heard his story, and then killed him again, so that her husband would not notice it. Then she extracted from her husband the secret of his life: "I cannot be killed, but if any one sticks a branch of this herb in my ears I shall fall asleep, and not wake up again." Maruzza, of course, throws her husband, as soon as possible, into this magic sleep, restores the prince, flies with him, and marries him.

Some years after, the branch in the magician's ears withered and fell out, and he awakened. Then he desired to be revenged, and traveled about until he found where his wife lived. Then he had a silver statue made in which he could conceal himself, and in which he placed some musical instruments. He shut himself up in it, and had himself and the statue taken to the palace where Maruzza and her husband lived. In the night, when all were asleep, the magician came out of the statue, carried Maruzza to the kitchen, kindled a fire, and put on some oil to boil, into which he intended to throw poor Maruzza. But just as he was about to do it, the flask which he had laid on the king's bed, and which had thrown him into a magic sleep, rolled off, and the king awoke, heard Maruzza's cries, saved her, and threw the magician into the boiling oil. In spite of his assurances he seems to have been very thoroughly killed.[28]

A Florentine story (*Nov. fior.* p. 290), called "The Baker's Three Daughters," is a combination of the Bluebeard and Robber Bridegroom stories. The husband forbids his wife to open a certain door with a gold key, saying: "You cannot deceive me; the little dog will tell me; and, besides, I will leave you a bouquet of flowers, which you must give me on my return, and which will wither if you enter that room." The two sisters yield to their curiosity, and are killed. The third sister kills the treacherous little dog, delivers the prince, as in the last story, flies with him, and the story ends much as the last does. In a Milanese version of this story, with the same title (*Nov. fior.* p. 298), the robber bridegroom takes his wife home, and informs her that it is her duty to watch at night, and open the door to the robbers when they return. The poor wife falls asleep, and is murdered. So with the second sister. The third remains awake, rescues the prince, and flies with him. The rest of the story is as above.

Of the third version of the Bluebeard story there are but two Italian examples: one from Sicily (Gonz. No. 20), and one from Pisa (Comparetti, No. 38). The former is entitled "The Godchild of St. Francis of Paula," and is, briefly, as follows: A queen, through the intercession of St. Francis of Paula, has a girl, whom she names Pauline, from the saint. The saint is in the habit of meeting the child on her way to school, and giving her candy. One day the saint tells her to ask her mother whether it is best to suffer in youth or old age. The mother replies that it is better to suffer in youth. Thereupon the saint carries away Pauline, and shuts her up in a tower, climbing up and down by her tresses, as in other stories we have already mentioned. In the tower the saint instructed Pauline in all that belonged to her rank. One day a king climbs up by the hair, and persuades Pauline to fly with him. She consents and becomes his bride. When her first child was born St. Francis came and took it away, rubbed the mother's mouth with blood, and deprived her of speech. Three times this happened, and then the queen was repudiated and confined in a remote room, where she spent her time in praying to St. Francis.

Meanwhile the queen-mother arranged another marriage for her son; but during the banquet the saint brought Pauline royal robes, and restored her three children to her. Then he led all four to the banquet-hall, and the happy family lived thereafter in peace and happiness.

The "forbidden chamber" is omitted in the above version, but is found in the Pisan story, "The Woodman." The main idea of the story, however, is curiously distorted. A woodman had three daughters whom he cannot support. One day a lady met him in the wood, and offered to take one of his daughters for a companion, giving him a purse of money, and assuring him that he would always find enough wood. The lady took her home, and told her she must not open a certain door during her absence. The girl did so, however, and saw her mistress in a bath, with two damsels reading a book. She closed the door at once; but when the mistress returned and asked her whether she had disobeyed, and what she had seen, she confessed her fault, and told what she saw. Then the lady cut her head off, hung it by the hair to a beam, and buried the body.

The same thing happened to the second sister, who opened the door, and saw the lady sitting at a table with gentlemen. The lady killed her, too, and then took the third sister, who, in spite of having seen her two sisters' heads, could not control her curiosity, and opened the door. She saw her mistress reclining in a beautiful bed. In the evening the lady returned and asked her what she had seen; but she answered: "I have seen nothing." The lady could extort no other answer from her, and finally clothed her in her peasant's dress, and took her back to the wood and left her.

The king of the neighboring city happened to pass by, and fell in love with her, and married her. When her first child was born the lady appeared at her bedside, and said: "Now it is time to tell me what you saw." "I saw nothing," replied the young queen. Then the lady carried away the child, having first rubbed the mother's mouth with blood. This happened a second time, and then the king put her away, and prepared to marry again. The first wife was invited to the wedding feast. While at the table the lady appeared under it, and pulled the first wife's dress, and said: "Will you tell what you saw?" The reply was twice: "Nothing." Then the queen fainted. At that moment a carriage drove up to the palace with a great lady in it, who asked to see the king. She told him that it was she who had carried away his children, and added that from her childhood she had been subjected to an enchantment that was to end when she found a person who should say that she had seen nothing in that room. She then brought back the children, and all lived together in peace and joy.[29]

One of the most beautiful and touching of all fairy tales is the one known to the readers of Grimm's collection by the title of "Faithful John," and which has such a charming parallel in the story of "Rama and Luxman." In Miss Frere's "Old Deccan Days," there are seven Italian versions of this interesting story, which we shall mention briefly, giving first the shortest entire, as a point of departure. It is from the North of Italy (Comparetti, Monferrato, No. 29), and is called:

ᔆ *XVII. In Love with a Statue* ᔆ

There was once a king who had two sons. The eldest did not wish to marry, and the youngest, although he went about everywhere, found no lady to his taste. Now it happened that he once went to a certain city, and there saw a statue with which he fell in love. He bought it, had it carried to his room, and every day embraced and kissed it. One day his father became aware of this, and said to him: "What are you doing? If you want a wife, take one of flesh and bones, and not one of marble." He answered that he would take one exactly like the statue, or none at all. His older brother, who at this time had nothing to do, went out into the world to seek her. On his way he saw in a city a man who had a mouse which danced so that it seemed like a human being. He said to himself: "I will take it home to my brother to amuse himself with." He continued his journey, and arrived in a more distant town, where he found a bird that sang like an angel, and bought that, too, for his brother. He was on the point of returning home, and was passing through a street, when he saw a beggar knocking at a door. A very beautiful girl appeared at the window, who resembled in every respect the prince's statue, and suddenly withdrew. Then he told the beggar to ask alms again; but the beggar refused, because he feared that the magician, who was then absent, would return home and eat him up. But the prince gave him so much money and other things that he knocked again, and the young girl appeared again, and suddenly withdrew. Then the prince went through the streets, saying that he mended and sold looking-glasses. The servant of the young girl, who heard him, told her mistress to go and see the mirrors. She went, but he told her that if she wanted to select the mirrors she would have to go on board his ship. When she was there, he carried her away, and she wept bitterly and sighed, so that he would let her return home, but it was like speaking to the wall.

When they were out at sea, there was heard the voice of a large black bird, saying: "*Ciriù, ciriù!* What a handsome mouse you have! You will take it to your brother; you will turn his head; and if you tell him of it, you will become marble. *Ciriù, ciriù!* A fine bird you have; you will take it to your brother; you will turn his head; and if you tell him, you will become marble. *Ciriù, ciriù!* A fine lady you have; you will take her to your brother; you will turn his head; and if you tell him of it, you will become marble." He did not know how he could tell his brother, because he was afraid of becoming marble. He landed, and took the mouse to his brother; and when he had seen it and wanted it, the elder brother cut off its head. Then he showed him the bird that sang like an angel, and his brother wanted it; but the elder brother again cut off its head. Then he said: "I have something handsomer," and he produced the beautiful girl who looked like the statue. And as the brother who had brought her said nothing, the other feared that he would take her away from him, and had him thrown into prison, where he was a long time; and because he continued to keep silence, he was condemned to death. Three days before he was to die he asked his brother to come and see him, and he consented, although unwillingly. Then the condemned brother said: "A large black bird told me that if I brought you back the dancing mouse, and spoke, I should become a statue," and saying this, he became a statue to the waist. "And if, bringing you the singing bird, I spoke, it would be the same." Then he became a statue to his breast. "And if, bringing you the lady, I spoke, I should become a statue." Then he became a statue all over, and his brother began to lament in despair, and tried to restore him to life. All kinds of physicians came, but none succeeded. Finally there came one who said that he was capable of turning the statue into a man provided they gave him what he needed. The king said he would do so, and the physician demanded the blood of the king's two children; but the mother would on no account consent. Then the king gave a ball, and while his wife was dancing he had the two children killed, and bathed with their blood the statue of his brother, and the statue straightway became a man and went to the ball. The mother, when she beheld him, suddenly thought of her children. She ran to them and found them half dead, and fainted away. All around sought to console and encourage her; but when she opened her eyes and saw the physician, she cried: "Out of my sight, ugly wretch! It is you who have caused my children to be killed." He answered: "Pardon me, my lady, I have done no harm. Go and see whether your children are there!" She ran to see, and found them alive and making a great noise. Then the physician said: "I am the magician, your father, whom you forsook, and I have wished to show you what it is to love one's children." Then they made peace, and remained happy and contented.

IN THE Venetian version (Teza, *La Trad. dei Sette Sari*, p. 26), called "Mela and Buccia," from the names of the prince and his friend, while the two friends are spending the night in a deserted castle, Buccia hears a voice foretelling the dangers to which Mela will be exposed. His horse will throw him if Buccia does not kill it; a dragon will devour him on his wedding night if Buccia does not kill it; and finally, the queen's pet dog will mortally wound him if Buccia does not kill it. If, however, Buccia reveals what he has heard, he will turn to stone. Buccia acts accordingly, and the king forgives him everything but killing the queen's pet dog; for that Buccia is condemned to be hung. Then he relates all, and gradually turns to stone from his feet up. The king, queen, and Buccia's mother are inconsolable until they are informed by an old woman that the blood of the little prince will bring the statue back to life. The faithful friend is by that means restored, and the child also saved. In this version the abduction is wanting, and the last danger is not the one usually threatened.

In a version from Siena (Gradi, *Vigilia*, p. 64), one of two brothers goes in search of the "Princess with Blonde Tresses." He also buys a parrot and a horse, and the dangers are: he who touches the parrot will have his eyes put out; he who mounts the horse will be thrown; he who marries the fair one will be devoured by a dragon; and he who reveals these dangers will become stone. The remainder of the story is like the last version.

The Florentine version (*Nov. fior.* p. 421) is mixed up with a number of other incidents. The dangers from which the prince is saved by his faithful servant are: poisoned apples, poisoned pastry, and a lion in the royal chamber. The servant is turned to stone and restored, as in the other versions.

In a Mantuan story (*Fiabe mant*, No. 9), the dangers are: parrot, horse, and bride; whoever touches these will be devoured by a dragon; whoever reveals these dangers will become stone. The conclusion is the same as above.

The last version we shall mention here is in the Pentamerone (IV. 9), and resembles the one from Monferrato. The elder brother, who goes in search of a bride for his younger brother, buys a falcon and a horse. The first will pick out the younger brother's eyes; the horse will throw him, and finally a dragon will devour him on his wedding night. The remainder of the story is as usual.[30]

We shall conclude this chapter with the class of stories in which giants are outwitted by men. The simplest form is found in two stories which are interesting examples of the survival of classic myths. Both stories are from Sicily, and one was told to Pitrè by a girl eight years old (Pitrè, No. 51). It is entitled "The Little Monk," and is, in substance, as follows: There were once two monks who went begging for the church every year. One was large and the other small. They lost their way once and came to a large cave, in which was a monster (lit. animal, *armalu*), who was building a fire. The two monks, however, did not believe it was a monster, but said: "Let us go and rest there." They entered, and saw the monster killing a sheep and roasting it. He had already killed and cooked twenty.

"Eat!" said the monster to them. "We don't want to eat; we are not hungry." "Eat, I tell you!" After they had eaten the sheep, they lay down, and the monster closed the entrance to the cave with a great stone. Then he took a sharp iron, heated it in the fire, and stuck it in the throat of the larger of the two monks, roasted the body, and wanted the other monk to help eat it. "I don't want to eat," said he; "I am full." "Get up!" said the monster. "If you don't I will kill you."

The wretched monk arose in fright, seated himself at the table, and pretended to eat, but threw the flesh away. In the night the good man took the iron, heated it, and plunged it in the monster's eyes. Then the monk in his terror slipped into the skin of a sheep. The monster felt his way to the entrance of the cave, removed the stone, and let the sheep out one by one; and so the good man escaped and returned to Trapani, and told his story to some fishermen. The monster went fishing, and being blind, stumbled against a rock and broke his head. The other version is from the Albanian colony of Piana de' Greet (Comparetti, No. 70), in Sicily, and is substantially the same as the story just given [31]

Generally, however, the stories in which giants are outwitted by men are more complicated, and may be divided into two classes; one where the giant is outwitted by superior cunning, the other where the giant's stupidity is deceived by the man's braggadocio. The first class may be represented by a Sicilian story (Pitrè, No. 33), entitled:

❧ XVIII. Thirteenth ❧

There was once a father who had thirteen sons, the youngest of whom was named Thirteenth. The father had hard work to support his children, but made what he could gathering herbs. The mother, to make the children quick, said to them: "The one who comes home first shall have herb soup." Thirteenth always returned the first, and the soup always fell to his share, on which account his brothers hated him and sought to get rid of him.

The king issued a proclamation in the city that he who was bold enough to go and steal the ogre's coverlet should receive a measure of gold. Thirteenth's brothers went to the king and said: "Majesty, we have a brother, named Thirteenth, who is confident that he can do that and other things too." The king said: "Bring him to me at once." They brought Thirteenth, who said: "Majesty, how is it possible to steal the ogre's coverlet? If he sees me he will eat me!" "No matter, you must go," said the king. "I know that you are bold, and this act of bravery you must perform." Thirteenth departed and went to the house of the ogre, who was away. The ogress was in the kitchen. Thirteenth entered quietly and hid himself under the bed. At night the ogre returned. He ate his supper and went to bed, saying as he did so:

> "I smell the smell of human flesh;
> Where I see it I will swallow it!"

The ogress replied: "Be still; no one has entered here." The ogre began to snore, and Thirteenth pulled the coverlet a little. The ogre awoke and cried: "What is that?" Thirteenth began to mew like a cat. The ogress said: "Scat! Scat!" And clapped her hands, and then fell asleep again with the ogre. Then Thirteenth gave a hard pull, seized the coverlet, and ran away. The ogre heard him running, recognized him in the dark, and said: "I know you! You are Thirteenth, without doubt!"

After a time the king issued another proclamation, that whoever would steal the ogre's horse and bring it to the king should receive a measure of gold. Thirteenth again presented himself, and asked for a silk ladder and a bag of cakes. With these things he departed, and went at night to the ogre's, climbed up without being heard, and descended to the stable. The horse neighed on seeing him, but he offered it a cake, saying: "Do you see how sweet it is? If you will come with me, my master will give you these always." Then he gave it another, saying: "Let me mount you and see how we go." So he mounted it, kept feeding it with cakes, and brought it to the king's stable.

The king issued another proclamation, that he would give a measure of gold to whoever would bring him the ogre's bolster. Thirteenth said: "Majesty, how is that possible? The bolster is full of little bells, and you must know that the ogre awakens at a breath." "I know nothing about it," said the king. "I wish it at any cost." Thirteenth departed, and went and crept under the ogre's bed. At midnight he stretched out his hand very softly, but the little bells all sounded. "What is that?" said the ogre. "Nothing," replied the ogress; "perhaps it is the wind that makes them ring." But the ogre, who was suspicious, pretended to sleep, but kept his ears open. Thirteenth stretched out his hand again. Alack! The ogre put out his arm and seized him. "Now you are caught! Just wait; I will make you cry for your first trick, for your second, and for your third." After this he put Thirteenth in a barrel, and began to feed him on raisins and figs. After a time he said: "Stick out your finger, little Thirteenth, so that I can see whether you are fat." Thirteenth saw there a mouse's tail, and stuck that out. "Ah, how thin you are!" said the ogre; "and besides, you don't smell good! Eat, my son; take the raisins and figs, and get fat soon!" After some days the ogre told him again to put out his finger, and Thirteenth stuck out a spindle. "Eh, wretch! Are you still lean? Eat, eat, and get fat soon."

At the end of a month Thirteenth had nothing more to stick out, and was obliged to show his finger. The ogre cried out in joy: "He is fat, he is fat!" The ogress hastened to the spot: "Quick, my ogress, heat the oven three nights and three days, for I am going to invite our relatives, and we will make a fine banquet of Thirteenth."

The ogress heated the oven three days and three nights, and then released Thirteenth from the barrel, and said to him: "Come here, Thirteenth; we have got to put the lamb in the oven." But Thirteenth caught her meaning; and when he approached the oven, he said: "Ah, mother ogress, what is that black thing in the corner of the oven?" The ogress stooped down a little, but saw nothing. "Stoop down again," said Thirteenth, "so that you can see it." When she stooped down again, Thirteenth seized her by the feet and threw her into the oven, and then closed the oven door. When she was cooked, he took her out carefully, cut her in two, divided her legs into pieces, and put them on the table, and placed her trunk, with her head and arms, in the bed, under the sheet, and tied a string to the chin and another to the back of her head.

When the ogre arrived with his guests he found the dishes on the table. Then he went to his wife's bed and asked: "Mother ogress, do you want to dine?" Thirteenth pulled the string, and the ogress shook her head. "How are you, tired?" And Thirteenth, who was hidden under the bed, pulled the other string and made her nod. Now it happened that one of her relatives moved something and saw that the ogress was dead, and only half of her was there. She cried in a loud voice: "Treason! Treason!" and all hastened to the bed. In the midst of the confusion Thirteenth escaped from under the bed and ran away to the king with the bolster and the ogre's most valuable things.

After this, the king said to Thirteenth: "Listen, Thirteenth. To complete your valiant exploits, I wish you to bring me the ogre himself, in person, alive and well." "How can I, your Majesty?" said Thirteenth. Then he roused himself, and added: "I see how, now!" Then he had a very strong chest made, and disguised himself as a monk, with a long, false beard, and went to the ogre's house, and called out to him: "Do you know Thirteenth? The wretch! He has killed our superior; but if I catch him! If I catch him, I will shut him up in this chest!" At these words the ogre drew near and said: "I, too, would like to help you, against that wretch of an assassin, for you don't know what he has done to me." And he began to tell his story. "But what shall we do?" said the pretended monk. "I do not know Thirteenth. Do you know him?" "Yes, sir." "Then tell me, father ogre, how tall is he?" "As tall as I am." "If that is so," said Thirteenth, "let us see whether this chest will hold you; if it will hold you, it will hold him." "Oh, good!" said the ogre; and got into the chest. Then Thirteenth shut the chest and said: "Look carefully, father ogre, and see whether there is any hole in the chest." "There is none." "Just wait; let us see whether it shuts well, and is heavy to carry."

Meanwhile Thirteenth shut and nailed up the chest, took it on his back, and hastened to the city. When the ogre cried: "Enough, now!" Thirteenth ran all the faster, and, laughing, sang this song to taunt the ogre:

> "I am Thirteenth,
> Who carry you on my back;
> I have tricked you and am going
> to trick you.
> I must deliver you to the king."

When he reached the king, the king had an iron chain attached to the ogre's hands and feet, and made him gnaw bones the rest of his miserable life. The king gave Thirteenth all the riches and treasures he could bestow on him, and always wished him at his side, as a man of the highest valor.[32]

THE SECOND version of the above story, in which the giant is deceived by the hero's braggadocio, is represented by several Italian stories; the simplest are some Milanese versions (*Nov. fior.* pp. 575-580), one of which (*Ibid.* p. 575) is as follows:

☞ XIX. The Cobbler ☜

There was once a cobbler who one day was so tired of cobbling that he said: "Now I will go and seek my fortune." He bought a little cheese and put it on the table. It got full of flies, and he took an old shoe, and hit the cheese and killed all the flies. He afterward counted them, and five hundred were killed, and four hundred wounded. He then girded on a sword, and put on a cocked hat, and went to the court, and said to the king: "I am the chief warrior of the flies. Four hundred I have killed, and five hundred I have wounded." The king answered: "Since you are a warrior, you will be brave enough to climb that mountain there, where there are two magicians, and kill them. If you kill them, you shall marry my daughter." Then he gave him a white flag to wave when he had killed them. "And sound the trumpet, you will put his head in a bag, both the heads, to show me." The cobbler then departed, and found a house, which was an inn, and the innkeeper and his wife were none other than the magician and his wife. He asked for lodging and food, and all he needed. Afterward he went to his room; but before going to bed, he looked up at the ceiling. There he saw a great stone over the bed. Instead of getting into bed, he got into a corner. When a certain hour struck, the magicians let the stone drop and it crushed the whole bed. The next morning the cobbler went down and said that he could not sleep for the noise. They told him they would change his room. The same thing happened the next night, and in the morning they told him they would give him another room. When it was a certain hour, the husband and wife went to the forest to cut a bundle of fagots. Then the magician went home; and the cobbler, who had made ready a sickle, said: "Wait until I help you to take the bundle off your back." Then he gave the magician a blow with the sickle and cut off his head. He did the same thing when the magician's wife returned. Then he unfurled his flag, and sounded his trumpet, and the band went out to meet him. After he had arrived at the court, the king said to him: "Now that you have killed the two magicians, you shall marry my daughter." But the cobbler had got so used to drawing the thread that he did so in his sleep, and kept hitting his wife, so that she could not rest. Then the king gave him a great deal of money and sent him home.[33]

A MORE detailed version is found in a Sicilian story in Gonzenbach, "The Brave Shoemaker" (No. 41), the first part of which is like the Milanese version. On his way to the giant's, the cobbler makes some balls of plaster of Paris and cream-cheese, and puts them in his pocket. When he heard the giant coming through the woods, he climbed a tree; but the giant scented him, and told him to come down. The cobbler answered that if he did not leave him alone he would twist his neck; and to show him how strong he was, he crushed the balls of plaster of Paris in his hands, telling the giant they were marble. The giant was frightened, and invited the cobbler to remain with him, and took him home. After a while, the giant asked him to bring some water in a pitcher from the well. The cobbler said that if the giant would give him a strong rope he would bring the well itself. The giant in terror took the pitcher, and drew the water himself. Then the giant asked the cobbler to cut some wood, but the latter asked for a strong rope to drag a whole tree to the house with. Then the giant proposed a trial of strength, to see which could carry a heavy stick the longer. The cobbler said that the giant had better wind something about the thick end, for when he, the cob-bler, turned a somersault with it, he might hit the giant. When they went to bed, the giant made the cobbler sleep with him; but the latter crept under the bed, leaving a pumpkin in his place. The giant, who was anxious to get rid of the cobbler, took an iron bar and struck at the pumpkin all night, believing it the cobbler's head. After he had beaten the pumpkin to pieces, the cobbler, under the bed, gave a sigh. "What is the matter with you?" asked the terrified giant. "A flea has just bitten my ear," answered the cobbler. The next day the cobbler proposed to the giant to cook a great ket-tle of macaroni, and after they had eaten it, he would cut open his stomach to show the giant that he had eaten it without chewing it; the giant was to do the same afterward. The cobbler, of course, secretly tied a sack about his neck, and put his macaroni in it; then he took a knife and ripped open the bag, and the macaroni fell out. The giant, in attempting to follow the cob-bler's example, killed himself. Then the cobbler cut his head off, carried it to the king, and claimed his daughter's hand.[34]

THE STORIES given in this chapter constitute, as we have already said in the Introduction, but a small part of Italian fairy tales. They repre-sent, however, as well as our space will allow, the great fairy cycles, so to speak. As our purpose has been to give only those stories which have been taken down from the mouths of the people, we have not drawn, except for purposes of reference, upon the Pentamerone, one of the most original and charming collections of fairy tales in any language. Enough has been given, we trust, to show how the Italians have treated the themes familiar to us from childhood, and to furnish the scholar with additional material for comparison.

༄

CHAPTER II

FAIRY TALES CONTINUED

THE FAIRY tales given in the last chapter belong to what may be called the great fairy tale cycles; that is, to extensive classes that are typical forms. It remains to notice in this chapter those stories which do not belong to any of these typical classes, but constitute, so to speak, independent forms.

The reader has perhaps noticed in the fairy tales of the first chapter the conspicuous absence of the fairies to which we are accustomed in German or Celtic stories. We have met ogres and magicians with magic powers, old men and women, and hermits who have aided the hero and heroine, and played the role of the "good fairy," but the fairy in the bright shape in which we see her in French and Irish stories, for example, has been wanting. It will not be amiss, then, to give a few stories in which the fairies play a more important part. We shall first mention a curious story in which the fairies are represented in one of their most usual rules—that of bestowing good gifts. The story is from Sicily (Gonz. No. 73), and is entitled:

๑ XXV. The King Who Wanted a Beautiful Wife ๑

There was once a king who wanted to marry. But his wife must be more beautiful than the sun, and no matter how many maidens he saw, none was beautiful enough to suit him. Then he called his trusty servant, and commanded him to seek everywhere and see whether he could find a beautiful girl. The servant set out, and wandered through the whole land, but found none who seemed handsome enough to him. One day, however, after he had run about a great deal and was very thirsty, he came to a little house. He knocked and asked for a drink of water. Now there dwelt in the house two very old women—one eighty and the other ninety years old—who supported themselves by spinning. When the servant asked for water, the one eighty years old rose, opened a little wicket in the shutter, and handed him out the water. From spinning so much, her hands were very white and delicate; and when the servant saw them he thought, "It must be a handsome maiden, for she has such a delicate white hand." So he hastened to the king, and said: "Your royal Majesty, I have found what you seek; so and so has happened to me." "Very well," answered the king, "go once more and try to see her."

The servant returned to the little house, knocked, and asked again for some water. The old woman did not open the window, but handed him the pitcher through the little opening in the shutter. "Do you live here all alone?" asked the servant. "No," she answered. "I live here with my sister; we are poor girls and support ourselves by the work of our hands." "How old are you, then?" "I am fifteen and my sister twenty." The servant went back to the king and told him all, and the king said: "I will take the one who is fifteen. Go and bring her to me." When the servant returned to the two old women, and told them that the king wished to elevate the younger to the position of his wife, she answered: "Tell the king I am ready to do his will. Since my birth no ray of the sun has ever struck me, and if a ray of the sun or a beam of light should strike me now, I would become perfectly black. Ask the king, therefore, to send a closed carriage for me at night, and I will come to his palace."

When the king heard this he sent royal apparel and a closed carriage, and at night the old woman covered her face with a thick veil and rode to the palace. The king received her joyfully, and begged her to lay aside the veil. She replied: "There are too many lighted candles here; their light would make me black." So the king married her without having seen her face. When they came into the king's chamber, however, and she removed her veil, the king saw for the first time what an ugly old woman he had married, and in his rage he opened the window and threw her out. Fortunately there was a nail in the wall, on which she caught by her clothes, and remained hanging between heaven and earth. Four fairies chanced to pass by, and when they saw the old woman hanging there, one of them cried: "See, sisters, there is the old woman who cheated the king; shall we wish her dress to tear and let her fall?" "Oh, no! Let us not do that," cried the youngest and most beautiful of the fairies. "Let us rather wish her something good. I wish her youth." "And I, beauty." "And I, prudence." "And I, a good heart." Thus the fairies cried, and while they were yet speaking the old woman became a wondrous fair maiden.

The next morning, when the king looked out of the window and saw the beautiful girl hanging there, he was terrified, and thought: "Unhappy man! What have I done! Had I no eyes last night?" Then he had her carefully taken down with long ladders, and begged her pardon, saying: "Now we will have a great festival and be right happy." So they celebrated a splendid feast, and the young queen was the fairest in the whole city.

But one day the sister ninety years old came to the palace to visit the queen, her sister. "Who is this ugly creature?" asked the king. "An old neighbor of mine who is half-witted," replied the queen, quickly. The old woman kept looking at her rejuvenated sister, and asked: "What did you do to become so young and lovely? I, too, would like to be young and pretty again." She kept asking this the whole day, until the queen finally lost her patience, and said: "I had my old skin taken off, and this new, smooth skin came to light." The old woman went to a barber and said: "I will give you what you will to remove my old skin, so that I may become young and handsome again." "But good old woman, you will surely die if I skin you." The old woman would not listen to him, and at last he had to do her will. He took his knife and made a cut in her forehead. "Oh!" cried the old woman.

> "Who will look fair
> Must grief and pain bear,"

answered the barber. "Then skin away, master," said the old woman. The barber kept cutting on, until all at once the old woman fell down dead.[1]

THIS story leads quite naturally to the class in which gifts, good and bad, are bestowed by the fairies on two persons, one of whom is deserving of good fortune; the other, of punishment or reproof. The simplest form of this story is found in a Milanese tale (*Nov. fior.* p. 190).

ᔓ *XXVI. The Bucket* ᔓ

There was once a mother who had two daughters: one was bad and the other was very good. But the mother loved the bad one more than the good one. She said one day to the bad one: "Go and draw a bucket of water." The bad one did not want to go, and so she would not obey her mother. The good daughter, however, said: "I will go and draw it." She went to draw the water, and the bucket fell down the well. She said: "If I go home now without the bucket, who knows what my mother will do to me?" So she climbed down the well, and at the bottom found a narrow passage, with a door. She knocked at the door. "Have you not found a cord and bucket?" There was a saint there, who answered: "No, my child." She continued her way and found another door. "Have you not found a cord and bucket?" "No!" That was the devil there. He answered her angrily because she was a good girl; he did not say: "My child." She knocked at another door. "Have you not found a cord and bucket?" It was the Madonna who replied: "Yes, my child. Listen. You could do me a pleasure to stay here while I am away. I have my little son here, to whom you will give his soup; you will sweep and put the house in order. When I come home I will give you your bucket." The Madonna went away, and the good girl put the house in order, gave the child his broth, swept the house; and while she was sweeping, instead of finding dirt, she found coral and other beautiful things. She saw that it was not dirt, and put it aside to give the Madonna when she returned. When the Madonna came back, she asked: "Have you done all I told you to do?" The good girl answered: "Yes, but I have kept these things here; I found them on the ground; it is not dirt." "Very well; keep them for yourself. Would you like a dress of calico, or one of silk?" The girl answered: "No, no! A calico dress." Instead of that, the Madonna gave her the silk one. "Do you wish a brass thimble, or a silver one?" "Give me the brass one." "No, take the silver thimble. Here is the bucket and your cord. When you reach the end of this passage, look up in the air." The girl did so, and a beautiful star fell on her brow.

She went home, and her mother ran to meet her to scold her for being away so long; and was about to strike her, when she saw the star on her brow, which shone so that it was beautiful to see, and said: "Where have you been until now? Who put that thing on your forehead?" The girl answered: "I don't know what there is there." Her mother tried to wash it away, but instead of disappearing, it shone more beautiful than ever. Then the girl told what had happened to her, and the other sister wished to go there, too. She went, and did the same as her sister. She let the bucket fall, climbed down, and knocked at the saint's door. "Have you not found a cord and bucket?" "No, my child." She knocked at the next door. "Have you not found a cord and bucket?" The devil answered: "No, I have not found them; but come here, my child, come here." But when she heard that he had not found her bucket, she said: "No, I will go on." She knocked at the Madonna's door. "Have you not found a cord and bucket?" The Madonna said that she had. "I am going away: you will give my son his broth, and then you will sweep. When I return I will give you your bucket." Instead of giving the broth to the child, the bad girl ate it herself. "Oh!" she said, "how good it was!" She swept and found a great deal of dirt. "Oh, poor me! My sister found so many pretty things!" The Madonna returned. "Have you done what I told you?" "Yes." "Do you wish the brass or silver thimble?" "Oh! I want the silver one!" She gave her the brass one. "Do you want the calico dress or the silk one?" "Give me the silk dress." She gave her the calico dress. "Here is your bucket and cord. When you are out of here, look up into the air." When she was out she looked up into the air and there fell on her forehead a lump of dirt that soiled her whole face. She went home in a rage to weep and scold her sister because she had had the star, while she had that dirt on her face. Her mother began to wash her face and rub it; and the more she did so the less the dirt went away. Then the mother said: "I understand; the Madonna has done this to show me that I loved the bad girl and neglected the good one."[2]

IN OTHER versions (mentioned in the note to the above story) the two sisters receive different gifts from the fairies. In a Sicilian tale (Pitrè, No. 62) it is the children of unlike sisters who receive the gifts: the one, beauty. When she combs her hair jewels fall from it; when she washes the water becomes full of fishes; when she opens her mouth flowers fall out; her cheeks are like apples; and finally she can finish her work in a short time. The cousin receives, of course, gifts the very reverse of the above. The story ends with the trait of "True Bride," mentioned at length in Chapter I.

There is still a third version of the above story, which is popular in many lands. The following example is from Florence (*Nov. fior.* p. 559), and is entitled:

☞ *XXVII. The Two Humpbacks* ☜

There were once two companions who were humpbacks, but one more so than the other. They were both so poor that they had not a penny to their names. One of them said: "I will go out into the world, for here there is nothing to eat; we are dying of hunger. I want to see whether I can make my fortune." "Go," said the other. "If you make your fortune, return, and I will go and see if I can make mine." So the humpback set off on his journey. Now these two humpbacks were from Parma. When the humpback had gone a long way, he came to a square where there was a fair, at which everything was sold. There was a person selling cheese, who cried out: "Eat the little Parmesan!" The poor humpback thought he meant him, so he ran away and hid himself in a courtyard. When it was one o'clock, he heard a clanking of chains and the words "Saturday and Sunday" repeated several times. Then he answered: "And Monday." "Oh, heavens!" said they who were singing. "Who is this who has harmonized with our choir?" They searched and found the poor humpback hidden. "O gentlemen!" He said, "I have not come here to do any harm, you know!" "Well! We have come to reward you; you have harmonized our choir; come with us!" They put him on a table and removed his hump, healed him, and gave him two bags of money. "Now," they said, "you can go." He thanked them and went away without his hump. He liked it better, you can believe! He returned to his place at Parma, and when the other humpback saw him he exclaimed: "Does not that look just like my friend? But he had a hump! It is not he! Listen! You are not my friend so and so, are you?" "Yes, I am," he replied. "Listen! Were you not a humpback?" "Yes. They have removed my hump and given me two bags of money. I will tell you why. I reached," he continued, "such and such a place, and I heard them beginning to say, '*Eat the little Parmesan! Eat the little Parmesan!*' I was so frightened that I hid myself." (He mentioned the place—in a court-yard.) "At a certain hour, I heard a noise of chains and a chorus singing: 'Saturday and Sunday.' After two or three times, I said: 'And Monday!' They came and found me, saying that I had harmonized their chorus, and they wanted to reward me. They took me, removed my hump, and gave me two bags of money." "Oh, heavens!" said the other humpback. "I want to go there, too!" "Go, poor fellow, go! Farewell!" The humpback reached the place, and hid himself precisely where his companion had. After a while he heard a noise of chains, and the chorus: "Saturday and Sunday!" Then another chorus: "And Monday!" After the humpback had heard them repeat: "Saturday and Sunday, and Monday!" several times, he added: "And Tuesday!" "Where," they exclaimed, "Is he who has spoiled our chorus? If we find him, we will tear him in pieces." Just think! They struck and beat this poor humpback until they were tired; then they put him on the same table on which they had placed his companion, and said: "Take that hump and put it on him in front." So they took the other's hump and fastened it to his breast, and then drove him away with blows. He went home and found his friend, who cried: "Mercy! Is not that my friend? But it cannot be, for this one is humpbacked in front. Listen," he said, "are you not my friend?" "The same," he answered, weeping. "I did not want to bear my own hump, and now I have to carry mine and yours! And so beaten and reduced, you see!" "Come," said his friend, "come home with me, and we will eat a mouthful together; and don't be disheartened." And so, every day, he dined with his friend, and afterward they died, I imagine.[3]

THERE are a number of Sicilian stories in which one's fate is personified and appears in the role of a guardian angel, or good and bad fairy. In the same way fortune is personified in several stories. The best example of the former class, which has also a point of contact with the latter, is found in Gonzenbach, No. 21, and is entitled:

❧ XXVIII. The Story of Catherine and Her Fate ❧

There was once a merchant who was very rich and had greater treasures than the king. In his reception room stood three wonderfully beautiful seats. One was of silver, the second of gold, and the third of diamonds. This merchant had an only daughter, whose name was Catherine, and who was fairer than the sun.

One day as Catherine was sitting in her chamber, the door suddenly opened of itself, and there entered a tall, beautiful lady, who held in her hand a wheel. "Catherine," said she, "when would you rather enjoy your life, in youth or in old age?" Catherine gazed at her in amazement, and could make no answer. The beautiful lady again asked: "Catherine, when would you rather enjoy your life, in youth or in old age?" Then thought Catherine: "If I say in youth, I must suffer for it in old age; wherefore I will rather enjoy my life in old age, and in youth God's will be done." So she answered: "In old age." "Be it as you have wished," said the beautiful woman, turned her wheel once, and disappeared. Now this beautiful tall lady was poor Catherine's Fate.

A few days later, her father suddenly received news that some of his ships had been wrecked in a storm; a few days after, he learned that several more of his ships had foundered; and to cut the matter short, scarcely a month had passed when he was himself deprived of all his riches. He had to sell all that he had, and this, too, he lost, until at last he remained poor and wretched. From grief he fell ill and died.

So poor Catherine remained all alone in the world, without a penny, and with no one to give her shelter. She thought: "I will go to another city and seek me a place there." So she set out and walked until she came to another city. As she was going through the streets a noble lady happened to be standing by the window, and asked her: "Where are you going, all alone, pretty maiden?" "Ah! Noble lady, I am a poor girl, and would like to find a place to earn my bread. Can you not find use for me?" So the noble lady received her, and Catherine served her faithfully.

Some days later the lady said one evening: "Catherine, I must go out for a time, and will lock the house door." "Very well," said Catherine, and after her mistress had gone she took her work and sat down and sewed. Suddenly the door opened, and her Fate entered. "So?" She cried, "are you here, Catherine? And do you think now that I am going to leave you in peace?" With these words, her Fate ran to all the cupboards, dragged out the linen and clothes of Catherine's mistress, and tore everything into a thousand pieces. Catherine thought: "Woe is me if my mistress returns and finds everything in this condition; she will certainly kill me!" And in her anguish she opened the door and fled. Her Fate, however, gathered up all the torn and ruined things, made them whole, and laid them away in their places. When the mistress returned she called Catherine, but Catherine was nowhere to be seen. "Can she have robbed me?" She thought; but when she looked about, nothing was gone. She was very much astonished, but Catherine did not return, but hastened on until she came to another city. As she was passing through the streets, another lady, standing by the window, asked her: "Where are you going, all alone, pretty maiden?" "Ah! Noble lady, I am a poor girl, and would like a place to earn my bread. Can you not make use of me?" Then the lady took her in, and Catherine served her and thought now she could rest in peace. It lasted, however, but a few days. One evening, when her mistress was out, her Fate appeared again and addressed her harshly: "So, here you are now? Do you think you can escape me?" Then the Fate tore and destroyed everything that it found, so that poor Catherine again fled, in her anguish of heart. To cut the matter short, poor Catherine led this frightful life seven years, flying from one city to another, and everywhere attempting to find a place. Her Fate always appeared after a few days, and tore and destroyed her employers' things, so that the poor girl had to flee.

As soon as she had left the house the Fate restored everything and put it in its place.

Finally, after seven years, her Fate seemed weary of always persecuting the unfortunate Catherine. One day Catherine came again to a city and saw a lady standing at a window, who asked her: "Where are you going, all alone, pretty girl?" "Ah! Noble lady, I am a poor girl, and would like to find a place to earn my bread. Can you not find use for me?" The lady answered: "I will give you a place willingly, but you must perform daily a service, and I do not know whether you have strength for it." "Tell me what it is," said Catherine, "and if I can, I will do it." "Do you see yonder high mountain?" asked the lady. "Every morning you must carry up there a large board covered with fresh bread, and cry with a loud voice: 'O my mistress' Fate! O my mistress' Fate! O my mistress' Fate!' thrice. Then my Fate will appear and receive the bread." "I will do that willingly," said Catherine, and the lady took her into her service.

Now Catherine remained years with this lady, and every morning she took a board with fresh bread and carried it up the mountain, and when she had called three times: "O my mistress' Fate!" there appeared a beautiful tall lady, who received the bread. Catherine often wept when she thought that she, who had once been so rich, must now serve like a poor maid. One day her mistress said to her: "Catherine, why do you weep so much?" Then Catherine told her how ill it had fared with her, and her mistress said: "I will tell you what, Catherine, when you take the bread to the mountain to-morrow, ask my Fate to try and persuade your Fate to leave you now in peace. Perhaps that will do some good." This advice pleased poor Catherine, and the next morning, after she had taken the bread to her mistress' Fate, she disclosed her trouble to her, and said: "O my mistress' Fate, beg my Fate to persecute me no longer." Then the Fate answered: "Ah, poor girl, your Fate is just now covered with seven coverlets, so that she cannot hear you; but when you come to-morrow I will take you to her." After Catherine had returned home, her mistress' Fate went to the young girl's Fate and said: "Dear sister, why are you never weary of making poor Catherine suffer? Permit her again to see some happy days." The Fate answered: "Bring her to me to-morrow and I will give her something that will help her out of all her trouble." When Catherine brought the bread the next morning, her mistress' Fate conducted her to her own Fate, who was covered with seven coverlets. Her Fate gave her a small skein of silk, and said: "Preserve it carefully; it will be of use to you." Then Catherine went home and said to her mistress:

"My Fate has given me a little skein of silk; what shall I do with it? It is not worth three *grani*." "Well," said her mistress, "preserve it; who knows of what use it may be?"

Now it happened, some time after this, that the young king was to marry, and on that account had royal garments made for himself. As the tailor was about to sew a beautiful dress, there was no silk of the same color to be found. So the king proclaimed throughout the whole land that whoever had such silk should bring it to the court and would be well rewarded. "Catherine," said her mistress, "your skein is of that color, take it to the king so that he may make you a handsome present." Then Catherine put on her best clothes, and went to the Court; and when she appeared before the king, she was so beautiful that he could not keep his eyes from her. "Royal Majesty," said she, "I have brought you a little skein of silk, of the color that could not be found." "I will tell you what, royal Majesty," cried one of his ministers, "we will pay the maiden for the silk with its weight in gold." The king was satisfied and they brought a balance; in one scale the king laid the silk, in the other, a gold coin. Now just imagine what happened: no matter how many gold coins the king laid in the scale, the silk was always heavier. Then the king had a larger balance brought, and threw all his treasures into the scale, but the silk still weighed the more. Then the king at last took his crown from his head and placed it with all the other treasures, and behold! The scale with gold sank and weighed exactly as much as the silk. "Where did you get this silk?" asked the king. "Royal Majesty, it was a present from my mistress," answered Catherine. "No, that is impossible," cried the king. "If you do not tell me the truth, I will have your head cut off." Then Catherine related all that had happened to her since she was a rich maiden.

Now there lived at the court a wise lady, who said: "Catherine, you have suffered much, but you will now see happy days; and that it was not until the golden crown was put in the scale that the balance was even, is a sign that you will be a queen." "If she is to be a queen," cried the king, "I will make her one, for Catherine and none other shall be my wife." And so it was; the king informed his betrothed that he no longer wished her, and married the fair Catherine. And after Catherine in her youth had suffered so much, she enjoyed nothing but happiness in her old age, and was happy and contented.[4]

IN THE class of stories of which "The Bucket" is an example, we have seen the good sister rewarded, and the naughty one punished. Another well-known moral story is the one in which a king's daughter is punished for her pride, in refusing to marry a suitable lover, by being made to marry the first one who asks her hand. This is the case in the Grimm story "King Thrush-Beard," or rather the king gives his proud daughter to the first beggar who comes to the palace gate. The same occurs in one of the Italian versions of this story, but usually the haughty princess, after refusing a noble suitor, either falls in love with the same suitor, who has disguised himself as a person of ignoble rank, or she sells herself to the disguised lover for some finery with which he tempts her. At all events, her pride is thoroughly humbled. An example of the more common version is found in Coronedi-Berti's Bolognese tales (No. 15), and is as follows:

✃ XXIX. The Crumb in the Beard ✃

There was once a king who had a daughter whose name was Stella. She was indescribably beautiful, but was so whimsical and hard to please that she drove her father to despair. There had been princes and kings who had sought her in marriage, but she had found defects in them all and would have none of them. She kept advancing in years, and her father began to despair of knowing to whom he should leave his crown. So he summoned his council, and discussed the matter, and was advised to give a great banquet, to which he should invite all the princes and kings of the surrounding countries, for, as they said, there cannot fail to be among so many, some one who should please the princess, who was to hide behind a door, so that she could examine them all as she pleased. When the king heard this advice, he gave the orders necessary for the banquet, and then called his daughter, and said: "Listen, my little Stella, I have thought to do so and so, to see if I can find any one to please you; behold, my daughter, my hair is white, and I must have some one to leave my crown to." Stella bowed her head, saying that she would take care to please him. Princes and kings then began to arrive at the court, and when it was time for the banquet, they all seated themselves at the table. You can imagine what sort of a banquet that was, and how the hall was adorned: gold and silver shone from all their necks; in the four corners of the room were four fountains, which continually sent forth wine and the most exquisite perfumes. While the gentlemen were eating, Stella was behind a door, as has been said, and one of her maids, who was near by, pointed out to her now this one, now that one: "See, your Majesty, what a handsome youth that is there." "Yes, but he has too large a nose." "And the one near your father?" "He has eyes that look like saucers." "And that other at the head of the table?" "He has too large a mouth; he looks as if he liked to eat." In short, she found fault with all but one, who, she said, pleased her, but that he must be a very dirty fellow, for he had a crumb on his beard after eating. The youth heard her say this, and swore vengeance. You must know that he was the son of the king of Green Hill, and the handsomest youth that could be seen. When the banquet was finished and the guests had departed, the king called Stella and asked: "What news have you, my child?" She replied that the only one who pleased her was the one with the crumb in his beard, but that she believed him to be a dirty fellow and did not want him. "Take care, my daughter, you will repent it," answered her father, and turned away.

You must know that Stella's chamber looked into a court-yard into which opened the shop of a baker. One night, while she was preparing to retire, she heard, in the room where they sifted the meal, some one singing so well and with so much grace that it went to her heart. She ran to the window and listened until he finished. Then she began to ask her maid who the person with the beautiful voice could be, saying she would like to know. "Leave it to me, your Majesty," said the maid; "I will inform you to-morrow." Stella could not wait for the next day; and, indeed, early the next day she learned that the one who sang was the sifter. That evening she heard him sing again, and stood by the window until everything became quiet. But that voice had so touched her heart that she told her maid that the next day she would try and see who had that fine voice. In the morning she placed herself by the window, and soon saw the youth come forth. She was enchanted by his beauty as soon as she saw him, and fell desperately in love with him.

Now you must know that this was none other than the prince who was at the banquet, and whom Stella had called "dirty." So he had disguised himself in such a way that she could not recognize him, and was meanwhile preparing his revenge. After he had seen her once or twice he began to take off his hat and salute her. She smiled at him, and appeared at the window every moment. Then they began to exchange words, and in the evening he sang under her window. In short, they began to make love in good earnest, and when he learned that she was free, he began to talk about marrying her. She consented at once, but asked him what he had to live on. "I haven't a penny," said he; "The little I earn is hardly enough to feed me." Stella encouraged him, saying that she would give him all the money and things he wanted. To punish Stella for her pride, her father and the prince's father had an understanding, and pretended not to know about this love affair, and let her carry away from the palace all she owned. During the day Stella did nothing but make a great bundle of clothes, of silver, and of money, and at night the disguised prince came under the balcony, and she threw it down to him. Things went on in this manner some time, and finally one evening he said to her: "Listen. The time has come to elope." Stella could not wait for the hour, and the next night she quietly tied a cord about her and let herself down from the window. The prince aided her to the ground, and then took her arm and hastened away. He led her a long ways to another city, where he turned down a street and opened the first door he met. They went down a long passage; finally they reached a little door, which he opened, and they found themselves in a hole of a place which had only one window, high up. The furniture consisted of a straw bed, a bench, and a dirty table. You can imagine that when Stella saw herself in this place she thought she should die. When the prince saw her so amazed, he said: "What is the matter? Does the house not please you? Do you not know that I am a poor man? Have you been deceived?" "What have you done with all the things I gave you?" "Oh, I had many debts, and I have paid them, and then I have done with the rest what seemed good to me. You must make up your mind to work and gain your bread as I have done. You must know that I am a porter of the king of this city, and I often go and work at the palace. To-morrow, they have told me, the washing is to be done, so you must rise early and go with me there. I will set you to work with the other women, and when it is time for them to go home to dinner, you will say that you are not hungry, and while you are alone, steal two shirts, conceal them under your skirt, and carry them home to me." Poor Stella wept bitterly, saying it was impossible for her to do that; but her husband replied: "Do what I say, or I shall beat you." The next morning her husband rose with the dawn, and made her get up, too. He had bought her a striped skirt and a pair of coarse shoes, which he made her put on, and then took her to the palace with him, conducted her to the laundry and left her, after he had introduced her as his wife, saying that she should remember what awaited her at home. Then the prince ran and dressed himself like a king, and waited at the gate of the palace until it was time for his wife to come. Meanwhile poor Stella did as her husband had commanded, and stole the shirts. As she was leaving the palace, she met the king, who said: "Pretty girl, you are our porter's wife, are you not?" Then he asked her what she had under her skirt, and shook her until the shirts dropped out, and the king cried: "See there! The porter's wife is a thief; she has stolen some shirts." Poor Stella ran home in tears, and her husband followed her when he had put on his disguise again. When he reached home Stella told him all that had happened and begged him not to send her to the palace again; but he told her that the next day they were to bake, and she must go into the kitchen and help, and steal a piece of dough. Everything happened as on the previous day. Stella's theft was discovered, and when her husband returned he found her crying like a condemned soul, and swearing that she had rather be killed than go to the palace again. He told her, however, that the king's son was to be married the next day, and that there was to be a great banquet, and she must go into the kitchen and wash the dishes. He added that when she had the chance she must steal a pot of broth and hide it about her so that no one should see it. She had to do as she was told, and had scarcely concealed the pot when the king's son came into the kitchen and told his wife she must come to the ball that had followed the banquet. She did not wish to go, but he took her by the arm and led her into the midst of the festival. Imagine how the poor woman felt at that ball, dressed as she was, and with the pot of broth! The king began to poke his sword at her in jest, until he hit the pot, and all the broth ran on the floor. Then all began to jeer her and laugh, until poor Stella fainted away from shame, and they had to go and get some vinegar to revive her. At last the king's mother came forward and said: "Enough; you have revenged yourself sufficiently." Then turning to Stella: "Know that this is your mother, and that he has done this to correct your pride and to be avenged on you for calling him dirty." Then she took her by the arm and led her to another room, where her maids dressed her as a queen. Her father and mother then appeared and kissed and embraced her. Her husband begged her pardon for what he had done, and they made peace and always lived in harmony. From that day on she was never haughty, and had learned to her cost that pride is the greatest fault.[5]

A CURIOUS feature in Italian stories is the part played by dolls or puppets. They sometimes serve to represent an absent mistress, or to take her place and receive the brunt of the husband's anger. The most peculiar of these doll-stories are found in the south of Italy; the one that follows is from Naples (*Nov. fior.* p. 333) and is entitled:

♫ *XXX. The Fairy Orlanda* ♫

There was once a merchant who had no children. He was obliged to go away for merchandise. His wife said to him: "Here is a ring; put it on your finger. You must bring me a doll as large as I am; one that can move, sew, and dress herself. If you forget, this ring will turn red, and your steamer will go neither forward nor backward." And so it happened. He forgot the doll, embarked on the steamer, and it would not move. The pilot said: "Sir, have you forgotten anything?" To all the gentlemen who were there. "No, sir; nothing." At the end of the steamer was this merchant. "Sir, have you forgotten anything; for the steamer cannot move?" He looked at his hand and replied: "Yes, I have forgotten something—my wife's doll." He landed, got the doll, reembarked, and the steamer continued its way. On his arrival at Naples, he carried the doll to his wife, well dressed and elegant; it seemed like a very handsome young girl. His wife, well pleased, talked to the doll, and they both worked near the balcony. Opposite lived a king's son, who fell in love with the doll, and became ill from his passion. The queen, who saw that her son was ill, asked: "My son, what is the matter with you? Tell your mamma. To-day or to-morrow we die, and you reign; and if you take an illness and die, who will reign?" He answered: "Mamma, I have taken this illness because there is a young girl, the daughter of the merchant who lives opposite, who is so beautiful that she has enamored me." The queen said: "Yes, my son, I shall marry you to her. Were she the daughter of a scavenger, you shall marry her." "You would do a good thing. Now let us send for the merchant." They sent a servant to the merchant's house. "Her Majesty wishes you at the palace!" "What does she want?" "She must speak with you." The merchant went to the palace, and asked: "Majesty, what do you wish?" "Have you a daughter?" "No, Majesty." "What do you mean? My son has fallen ill from the love he has conceived for your daughter." "Your Majesty, I tell you it is a doll, and not a human being." "I don't want to hear nonsense! If you don't present your daughter to me in a fortnight, your head will fall under the guillotine." (Do you not know what the guillotine is? It is the gallows. He was to be hung if he did not take her his daughter within a fortnight.) The merchant went home, weeping. His wife said: "What is the matter; what has the king said to you at the palace, to make you weep?" "Can you not guess what has happened to me? The king's son has fallen ill for the sake of the doll you have!" "He has fallen ill? Did he not see that it was a doll?" "He would not believe it, and says it is my daughter, and that if I do not bring her to him within a fortnight, my head will fall under the guillotine." "Well," said his wife, "take the doll, and carry her out into the country, and see what will happen." He did so, and while he was going along, all confused, he met an old man who asked him: "Merchant, what are you doing?" "Ah, my old man, why should I tell you?" "I know all." Then said the merchant: "Since you know all, find some remedy for my life." The old man said: "Exactly. Go to such and such a place, where there is a fairy, who is called the fairy Orlanda. She has a palace with no doorkeeper, and no stairway. Here is a violin and a silk ladder. When you reach this palace, begin to play. The fairy and all her twelve maidens will appear at the window. This fairy Orlanda can give you help."

The merchant continued his journey, and found the palace without a doorkeeper, and with no stairway. He began to play the violin, and the fairy and all her twelve damsels appeared and said: "What do you want that you call us?" "Ah! Fairy Orlanda, help me!" "What help do you want?" "I have this doll, and the king's son has fallen in love with it, and is ill. What shall I do? If I do not present her to him in a fortnight my head will be cut off." The fairy Orlanda said: "Put this ladder to the wall. Give me the doll. Wait two hours and I will give her back to you again." He waited two hours and then the fairy appeared: "Here is your daughter. She will speak to all, to the king, to the queen, but not to the prince. Farewell." The fairy Orlanda disappeared within, and the merchant departed with his daughter. He took her home to his wife. The doll said: "Mamma, how do you do?" "I am very well, my daughter. Where have you been?" "I have been into the country with papa, and now I have returned." In a fortnight the merchant dressed her elegantly and carried her to the palace. As soon as the king saw her he said to the queen: "My son was right; she is a beautiful girl!" She went into the gallery and spoke with the king and queen, but did not speak to the prince. The mortified prince thought: "She speaks to papa, she speaks to mamma, but not to me! What does it mean? Perhaps she does not speak to me from embarrassment." They were married, but even then she did not speak to him. So the prince was obliged to separate from her, and they lived in two rooms apart. The prince, meanwhile, courted another princess. One morning, while he was breakfasting with his sweetheart, his wife called a servant: "Come here; is the prince at table?" "Yes, Highness." "Wait!" She cut off her two hands and put them in the oven, and there came out a roast, with ten sausages. "Carry these to the prince." "Prince, the princess sends you this." He asked: "How was it made?" The servant replied: "Prince, she cut off her two hands and put them in the oven. She amazed me." "Enough," said the prince, "let us eat them." His sweetheart said: "I can do it, too." So she cut off her hands and put them in the oven; but they were burned and she died. "Oh, what have you done to me! You have killed one for me!" said the prince. After a time he made love to another. The first time he sat at table with her, the princess called another servant: "Servant, where are you going?" "I am going, Majesty, to the prince's table." "Wait!" She cut off her arms, and put them in the oven, and there came out a roast, with two blood-puddings. She said: "Carry it to the prince, at table." "Prince!" "Go away, I don't want to hear any nonsense." "But listen; let me tell you!" "Well, tell away." So the servant told how the princess had cut off her arms (which had grown out again) and put them in the oven, and the roast and puddings had come out. The second sweetheart tried to do the same and died. After a while the prince fell in love with another, and the same thing was repeated. The princess cut off her legs and put them in the oven, and a large roast came out, with two larded hams. The third sweetheart tried to do the same, and died like the others. Then the prince said: "Ah! She has done it to three for me! Unhappy me! I will not make love to any more."

During the night when the princess had gone to bed, the lamp said: "Lady, I want to drink." "Oil-cruet, give the lamp a drink." "Lady, it has hurt me." "Oil-cruet, why did you hurt the lamp? How beautiful is the fairy Orlanda! How beautiful is the fairy Orlanda! How beautiful is the fairy Orlanda!" So she did all night until day. All these things were enchanted: the lamp and the oil-cruet. The prince, who heard it, said one day to a servant: "This evening you must enter the princess' room. You must spend the night under her bed. You must see what she does in the night." The servant did so, and the same thing was repeated with the lamp and the oil-cruet. The servant told the prince, who said: "To-night, I will go." At night he crept under his wife's bed. The same thing was repeated. The lamp said: "Lady, I want to drink!" "Oil-cruet, give the lamp a drink." "Lady, it has hurt me." "Oil-cruet, why have you hurt the lamp? How beautiful is the fairy Orlanda!" The whole night she repeated: "How beautiful is the fairy Orlanda!" The prince responded: "Blessed be the fairy Orlanda!" " Ah!" said the princess, "did it need so much to say a word?" Then they embraced and kissed each other, and remained contented and happy.[6]

95

WE NOW pass to an amusing class of stories, in which the hero comes in possession of enchanted objects and loses them, finally regaining them in various ways. There are three versions of this class. In the first, the hero loses the objects by the cunning of a woman, and regains them by means of two kinds of fruits, one of which produces some bodily defect and the other cures it. In the second, the episode of the fruits is wanting, and the owner regains his property either by preventing the princess from cheating him at play or by making her fall in love with him. In the third, a person (usually a landlord) substitutes worthless objects for two enchanted ones, which are recovered by means of a third magic object (usually a stick), which beats until the stolen property is restored.[7]

To illustrate the first version, we will give a Sicilian story from Gonzenbach (No. 31), which is entitled:

❧ XXXI. The Shepherd Who Made the King's Daughter Laugh ❧

There was once a king and a queen who had an only daughter, whom they loved very dearly. When she was fifteen years old she became suddenly very sad and would not laugh any more. So the king issued a proclamation that whoever made his daughter laugh, whether he were a prince, peasant, or beggar, should become her husband. Many made the attempt, but none succeeded. Now there was a poor woman who had an only son, who was idle and would not learn any trade; so finally his mother sent him to a farmer to keep his sheep. One day, as he was driving the sheep over the fields, he came to a well, and bent over it to drink. As he did so he saw a handsome ring on the wheel, and as it pleased him, he put it on the ring finger of his right hand. He had scarcely put it on, however, when he began to sneeze violently, and could not stop until he had accidentally removed the ring. Then his sneezing ceased as suddenly as it had begun. "Oh!" Thought he, "If the ring has this virtue, I had better try my fortune with it, and see whether it will not make the king's daughter laugh." So he put the ring on his left hand, and no longer had to sneeze. Then he drove the sheep home, took leave of his master, and set out toward the city where the king lived. He was obliged, however, to pass through a dense forest which was so extensive that it grew dark before he left it. He thought: "If the robbers find me here they will take away my ring, and then I should be a ruined man. I would rather climb a tree and spend the night there." So he climbed a tree, tied himself fast with his belt, and soon fell asleep. Before long, thirteen robbers came and sat down under the tree, and talked so loud that the shepherd awoke. The captain of the robbers said: "Let each relate what he has accomplished to-day;" and each exhibited what he had taken. The thirteenth, however, pulled out a tablecloth, a purse, and a whistle, and said: "I have gained to-day the greatest treasures, for these three things I have taken from a monk, and each of them has a particular virtue. If any one spreads out the tablecloth and says; 'My little table-cloth, give me macaroni, or roast meat,' or whatever one will, he will find everything there immediately. Likewise the purse will give all the money one wants; and whoever hears the whistle must dance whether he will or no." The robbers at once put the power of the tablecloth to the test, and then went to sleep, the captain laying the precious articles near himself. When they were all snoring hard the shepherd descended, took the three articles, and crept away.

The next day he came to the city where the king lived, and went straight to the palace. "Announce me to the king," said he to the servants; "I will try to make the king's daughter laugh." The servants tried to dissuade him, but he insisted on being led before the king, who took him into a large room, in which was the king's daughter, sitting on a splendid throne and surrounded by the whole court. "If I am to make the princess laugh," said the shepherd to the king, "you must first do me the kindness to put this ring on the ring-finger of your right hand." The king had scarcely done so when he began to sneeze violently, and could not stop, but ran up and down the room, sneezing all the time. The entire court began to laugh, and the king's daughter could not stay sober, but had to run away laughing. Then the shepherd went up to the king, took off the ring, and said: "Your Majesty, I have made the princess laugh; to me belongs the reward." "What! You worthless shepherd!" cried the king. "You have not only made me the laughing-stock of the whole court, but now you want my daughter for your wife! Quick! Take the ring from him, and throw him into prison."

While there the wonderful tablecloth provides him and his companions with plenty to eat, and when it is discovered and taken from him by the king's orders, the purse enables them all to live in comfort. That is also discovered, and nothing is left but the whistle. "Well!" thought the shepherd, "If we can't eat any more, we will at least dance," and he pulled out his pipe and began to play on it, and all the prisoners began to dance, and the guards with them, and between them all they made a great noise.

When the king heard it he came running there with his servants, and had to dance like all the rest, but found breath enough to order the pipe to be taken away from the shepherd, and all became quiet again.

So now the shepherd had nothing left, and remained in prison some time, until he found an old file, and one night filed through the iron bars and escaped. He wandered about all day, and at last came to the same forest where he had formerly been. All at once he saw a large fig-tree bearing the most beautiful fruit—on one side black figs, on the other, white ones. "That is something I have never seen," thought the shepherd— "a fig-tree that bears black and white figs at the same time. I must try them." Scarcely had he tasted them when he felt something move on the top of his head, and putting his hand up, found he had two long horns. "Unhappy man!" he cried: "What shall I do?" However, as he was very hungry, he picked some of the white figs and ate them, and immediately one of the horns disappeared, and also the other after he had eaten a few more white figs. "My fortune is made!" He thought. "The king will have to give me all my things back, and his daughter in the bargain."

The shepherd disguised himself and went to the city with two baskets of figs—one of the black and one of the white kind, the former of which he sold to the king's cook, whom he met in the market place. While the king was at the table the servant put the figs before him, and he was much pleased with them, and gave some to his wife and daughter; the rest he ate himself. Scarcely had they eaten them when they saw with terror the long horns that had grown from their heads. The queen and her daughter began to weep, and the king, in a rage, called the cook and asked him who had sold him the figs. "A peasant in the market," answered the cook. "Go at once and bring him here," cried the king.

The shepherd had remained near the palace, and as the cook came out, he went up to him with the basket of white figs in his hand. "What miserable figs did you sell me this morning!" cried out the cook to him. "As soon as the king, queen, and princess had eaten your figs, great horns grew on their heads." "Be quiet," said the shepherd; "I have a remedy here, and can soon remove the horns. Take me to the king." He was led before the king, who asked him what kind of figs he had sold. "Be quiet, your Majesty," said the shepherd, "and eat these figs," at the same time giving him a white one; and as soon as the king had eaten it one of the horns disappeared. "Now," said the shepherd, " before I give you any more of my figs you must give me back my whistle; if not, you may keep your horn." The king in his terror gave up the whistle, and the shepherd handed the queen a fig. When one of the queen's horns had disappeared, he said: "Now give me my purse back, or else I will take my figs away." So the king gave him his purse, and the shepherd removed one of the princess' horns. Then he demanded his tablecloth; and when he had received it he gave the king another fig, so that the second horn disappeared. "Now give me my ring," he said; and the king had to give him his ring before he would remove the queen's horn. The only one left now was the princess, and the shepherd said: "Now fulfill your promise and marry me to the princess; otherwise she may keep her horn as long as she lives." So the princess had to marry him, and after the wedding he gave her another fig to eat, so that her last horn also disappeared. They had a merry wedding, and when the old king died the shepherd became king, and so they remained contented and happy, and we like a bundle of roots.[8]

THE SECOND version of this story is represented by but three examples, none of them worth giving at length. In one (Pomiglianesi, p. 110) the princess wins the magic objects (purse, cloak that renders invisible, and horn that blows out soldiers) at play. The loser disguises himself as a priest and confesses the princess when she is ill, and makes her give back the objects she has won or stolen. In a Florentine version (*Nov. fior.* p. 349), the owner of the objects, a poor shepherd's son, pretends to be the son of the king of Portugal. He plays with the princess and wins, but his true origin is discovered and he is thrown into prison. There he makes use of the magic tablecloth, which he sells to the king for the privilege of passing a night in the princess' room. The same payment is asked for the box that fills itself with money, and the little organ that makes every one dance. The shepherd, of course, becomes the princess' husband and inherits the kingdom when the king dies. In the Sicilian story (Pitrè, No. 26) the fairies give Peter the purse, tablecloth, and violin, and he goes to play chess with the daughter of the king of Spain, who is to marry who- ever beats her at the game. She cheats and wins, and Peter is thrown into prison. There he uses the tablecloth, and when the princess hears of it, she proposes to play for it. Again she cheats by changing a chessman while Peter is looking away, and the loser is thrown into prison again. They play again for the magic violin, and Peter, who has been warned in prison by other losers of the princess' tricks, keeps a sharp lookout, detects, and defeats her. They are married, and Peter releases all the defeated players from jail, and afterward gets rid of them by means of the violin.[9]

The third version is the most popular one; the following example of it is from Nerucci's collection of Montalese tales (No. 43).

ᔕ XXXII. The Ass that Lays Money ᔕ

There was once a poor widow with an only son, and whose brother-in-law was a steward. One day she said to her child: "Go to your uncle and ask him to give you something to keep you from starving." The boy went to the farm and asked his uncle to help him a little. "We are dying of hunger, uncle. My mother earns a little by weaving, and I am too small to find anything. Be charitable to us, for we are your relatives." The steward answered: "Why not? You should have come sooner and I would have helped you the sooner. But now I will give you something to support you always, without need of anything more. I will give you this little ass that lays money. You have only to put a cloth under him, and he will fill it for you with handsome coins. But take care! Don't tell it, and don't leave this animal with anyone." The youth departed in joy, and after he had traveled a long way, he stopped at an inn to sleep, for his house was distant. He said to the landlord: "Give me a lodging, but look! My ass spends the night with me." "What!" said the landlord, "what are you thinking about! It cannot be." The youth replied: "Yes, it can be, because my ass does not leave my side." They disputed a while, until the landlord finally consented; but he had some suspicions; and when the boy and his beast were shut in the room, he looked through the keyhole, and saw that wonder of an ass that laid money in abundance. "Bless me!" cried the host. "I should be a fool, indeed, if I let this piece of good fortune escape my hands!" He at once looked for another ass of the same color and size, and while the lad was asleep, exchanged them. In the morning the boy paid his bill and departed, but on the way, the ass no longer laid any money. The stupefied child did not know what to think at first, but afterward examining it more closely, it appeared to him that the ass was not his, and straightway he returned to the innkeeper, to complain of his deception. The landlord cried out: "I wonder at your saying such a thing! We are all honest people here, and don't steal anything from anybody. Go away, blockhead, or you will find something to remember a while."

The child, weeping, had to depart with his ass, and he went back to his uncle's farm, and told him what had happened. The uncle said: "If you had not stopped at the innkeeper's, you could not have met with this misfortune. However, I have another present to help you and your mother. But take care! Do not mention it to any one, and take good care of it. Here it is. I give you a tablecloth, and whenever you say: *'Tablecloth, make ready,'* after having spread it out, you will see a fine repast at your pleasure." The youth took the tablecloth in delight, thanked his uncle, and departed; but like the fool he was, he stopped again at the same inn. He said to the landlord: "Give me a room and you need not prepare anything to eat. I have all I want with me." The crafty innkeeper suspected that there was something beneath this, and when the lad was in his room, he looked through the key-hole, and saw the tablecloth preparing the supper. The host exclaimed: "What good luck for my inn! I will not let it escape me." He quickly looked for another tablecloth like this one, with the same embroidery and fringe, and while the child was sleeping, he exchanged it for the magic one, so that in the morning the lad did not perceive the knavery. Not until he had reached a forest where he was hungry, did he want to make use of the tablecloth. But it was in vain that he spread it out and cried: *"Tablecloth, make ready."* The tablecloth was not the same one, and made nothing ready for him. In despair the boy went back to the innkeeper to complain, and the landlord would have thrashed him if he had not run away, and he ran until he reached his uncle's. His uncle, when he saw him in such a plight, said: "Oh! What is the matter?" "Uncle!" said the boy, "The same innkeeper has changed the tablecloth, too, for me." The uncle was on the point of giving the dunce a good thrashing; but afterward, seeing that it was a child, he calmed his anger, and said: "I understand; but I will give you a remedy by which you can get back everything from that thief of a landlord. Here it is! It is a stick. Hide it under your bolster; and if any one comes to rob you of it, say to it, in a low voice: *'Beat, beat!'* And it will continue to do so until you say to it, *'Stop.'"*

Imagine how joyfully the boy took the stick! It was a handsome polished stick, with a gold handle, and delighted one only to see it. So the boy thanked his uncle for his kindness, and after he had journeyed a while, he came to the same inn. He said: "Landlord, I wish to lodge here to-night." The landlord at once drew his conclusions about the stick, which the boy carried openly in his hands, and at night when the lad appeared to be sound asleep, but really was on the watch, the landlord felt softly under the bolster and drew out the stick. The boy, although it was dark, perceived the theft and said in a low voice: "Beat, beat, beat!" Suddenly blows were rained down without mercy; everything broken to pieces, the chest of drawers, the looking-glass, all the chairs, the glass in the windows; and the landlord, and those that came at the noise, beaten nearly to death. The landlord screamed to split his throat: "Save me, boy, I am dead!" The boy answered: "What! I will not deliver you, if you do not give me back my property—the ass that lays gold, and the tablecloth that prepares dinner." And if the landlord did not want to die of the blows, he had to consent to the boy's wishes.

When he had his things back, the boy went home to his mother and told her what had happened to him, and then said: "Now, we do not need anything more. I have an ass that lays money, a tablecloth that prepares food at my will, and a stick to defend me from whoever annoys me." So that woman and her son, who, from want had become rich enough to cause every one envy, wished from pride to invite their relatives to a banquet, to make them acquainted with their wealth. On the appointed day the relatives came to the woman's new house; but noon strikes, one o'clock strikes, it is almost two, and in the kitchen the fire is seen extinguished, and there were no provisions anywhere. "Are they playing a joke on us?" said the relatives. "We shall have to depart with dry teeth." At that moment, however, the clock struck two, and the lad, after spreading the cloth on the table, commanded: "Tablecloth, prepare a grand banquet." In short, those people had a fine dinner and many presents in money, and the boy and his mother remained in triumph and joy.[10]

THE NEXT story to which we shall direct our attention is "Puss in Boots," which, in the form known to our children, is of French origin, being one of the tales which Perrault made so popular by his versions. Before Perrault, however, two literary versions of this story existed: one in Straparola and one in the Pentamerone. There are, besides, several popular versions of this story, which are somewhat peculiar. The one that follows is from Sicily (Pitrè, No. 88).

❧ XXXIII. Don Joseph Pear ❧

There were once three brothers who owned a pear-tree and lived on the pears. One day one of the brothers went to pick these pears, and found that they had been gathered. "Oh! My brothers! What shall we do, for our pears have been picked?" So the eldest went and remained in the garden to guard the pear-tree during the night. He fell asleep, however, and the next morning the second brother came and said: "What have you done, my brother? Have you been sleeping? Do you not see that the pears have been picked? To-night I will stay." That night the second brother remained. The next morning the youngest went there and saw more of the pears picked, and said: "Were you the one that was going to keep a good watch? Go, I will stay here to-night; we shall see whether they can cheat me to my face." At night the youngest brother began to play and dance under the pear-tree; while he was not playing, a fox, believing that the youth had gone to sleep, came out and climbed the tree and picked the rest of the pears. When it was coming down the tree, the youth quickly aimed his gun at it and was about to shoot. The fox said: "Don't shoot me, Don Joseph; for I will have you called Don Joseph Pear, and will make you marry the king's daughter." Don Joseph answered: "And where shall I see you again? What has the king to do with you? With one kick that he would give you, you would never appear before him again." However, Don Joseph Pear from pity let her escape. The fox went away to a forest and caught all sorts of game, squirrels, hares, and quails, and carried them to the king; so that it was a sight. "Sir Majesty, Don Joseph Pear sends me; you must accept this game." The king said: "Listen, little fox, I accept this game; but I have never heard this Don Joseph Pear mentioned." The fox left the game there, and ran away to Don Joseph. "Softly, Don Joseph, I have taken the first step; I have been to the king, and carried him the first game; and he accepted it."

A week later the fox went to the forest, caught the best animals, squirrels, hares, birds, and took them to the king. "Sir Majesty, Don Joseph Pear sends me to you with this game." The king said to the fox: "My daughter, I don't know who this Don Joseph Pear is; I am afraid you have been sent somewhere else! I will tell you what: have this Don Joseph Pear come here, so that I can make his acquaintance." The fox wished to leave the game, and said: "I am not mistaken; my master sent me here; and for a token, he said that he wished the princess for his wife."

The fox returned to Don Joseph Pear, and said to him: "Softly, things are going well; after I have been to the king again, the matter is settled." Don Joseph said: "I will not believe you until I have my wife."

The fox now went to an ogress and said: "Friend, friend, have we not to divide the gold and silver?" "Certainly," said the ogress to the fox; "go and get the measure and we will divide the gold from the silver." The fox went to the king and did not say: "The ogress wants to borrow your measure," but she said: "Don Joseph Pear wants to borrow, for a short time, your measure to separate the gold from the silver." "What!" said the king, "has this Don Joseph Pear such great riches? Is he then richer than I?" And he gave the fox the measure. When he was alone with his daughter he said to her, in the course of his conversation: "It must be that this Don Joseph Pear is very rich, for he divides the gold and silver." The fox carried the measure to the ogress, who began to measure and heap up gold and silver. When she had finished, the fox went to Don Joseph Pear and dressed him in new clothes, a watch with diamonds, rings, a ring for his betrothed, and everything that was needed for the marriage. "Behold, Don Joseph," said the fox, "I am going before you now; you go to the king and get your bride and then go to the church." Don Joseph went to the king; got his bride, and they went to the church. After they were married, the princess got into the carriage and the bridegroom mounted his horse. The fox made a sign to Don Joseph and said: "I will go before you; you follow me and let the carriages and horses come after."

They started on their way, and came to a sheep-farm which belonged to the ogress. The boy who was tending the sheep, when he saw the fox approach, threw a stone at her, and she began to weep. "Ah!" She said to the boy; "now I will have you killed. Do you see those horsemen? Now I will have you killed!" The youth, terrified, said: "If you will not do anything to me I will not throw any more stones at you." The fox replied: "If you don't want to be killed, when the king passes and asks you whose is this sheep-farm, you must tell him: 'Don Joseph Pear's,' for Don Joseph Pear is his son-in-law, and he will reward you." The cavalcade passed by, and the king asked the boy: "Whose is this sheep-farm?" The boy replied at once: "Don Joseph Pear's." The king gave him some money.

The fox kept about ten paces before Don Joseph, and the latter did nothing but say in a low tone: "Where are you taking me, fox? What lands do I possess that you can make me believed to be rich? Where are we going?" The fox replied: "Softly, Don Joseph, and leave it to me." They went on and on, and the fox saw another farm of cattle, with the herdsman. The same thing happened there as with the shepherd: the stone thrown and the fox's threat. The king passed. "Herdsman, whose is this farm of cattle?" "Don Joseph Pear's." And the king, astonished at his son-in-law's wealth, gave the herdsman a piece of gold.

Don Joseph was pleased on the one hand, but on the other was perplexed and did not know how it was to turn out. When the fox turned around, Joseph said: "Where are you taking me, fox? You are ruining me." The fox kept on as if she had nothing to do with the matter. Then she came to another farm of horses and mares. The boy who was tending them threw a stone at the fox. She frightened him, and he told the king, when the king asked him, that the farm was Don Joseph Pear's.

They kept on and came to a well, and near it the ogress was sitting. The fox began to run and pretended to be in great terror. "Friend, friend, see, they are coming! These horsemen will kill us! Let us hide in the well, shall we not?" "Yes, friend," said the ogress in alarm. "Shall I throw you down first?" said the fox. "Certainly, friend." Then the fox threw the ogress down the well, and then entered the ogress' palace. Don Joseph Pear followed the fox, with his wife, his father-in-law, and all the riders. The fox showed them through all the apartments, displaying the riches, Don Joseph Pear contented at having found his fortune, and the king still more contented because his daughter was so richly settled. There was a festival for a few days, and then the king, well satisfied, returned to his own country and his daughter remained with her husband. One day the fox was looking out of the window, and Don Joseph Pear and his wife were going up to the terrace. Don Joseph Pear took up a little dust from the terrace and threw it at the fox's head. The fox raised her eyes. "What is the meaning of this, after the good I have done you, miserable fellow?" said she to Don Joseph. "Take care or I will speak!" The wife said to her husband: "What is the matter with the fox, to speak thus?" "Nothing," answered her husband. "I threw a little dust at her and she got angry." Don Joseph took up a little more dust and threw it at the fox's head. The fox, in a rage, cried: "Joe, you see I will speak! And I declare that you were the owner of a pear-tree!" Don Joseph was frightened, for the fox told his wife everything; so he took an earthen jar and threw it at the fox's head, and so got rid of her. Thus—the ungrateful fellow that he was—he killed the one who had done him so much kindness; but nevertheless he enjoyed all his wealth with his wife." [II]

THE STORY we shall next consider is, in some of its versions, legendary in its nature, and might more properly, perhaps, have been treated in chapter IV. Its legendary character, however, is only accidental, and it really belongs to the class of stories discussed in the present chapter. The story in general may be termed "The Thankful Dead," from the most important episode in it. The hero shows some respect to a corpse (paying the debts it incurred when alive, and so obtaining the right of burial for it), the soul of which becomes the hero's good fairy, and assists him when in danger, and finally brings about his good fortune. Around this nucleus have gathered various episodes, which will be mentioned in the notes. As an example of this story, we give, on account of its rarity, the Istrian version (Ive, *Nozze Ive-Lorenzetto,* III. p. 19).

☞ XXXV. Fair Brow ☞

There was once a father who had a son. After this son had passed through school, his father said to him: "Son, now that you have finished your studies, you are of an age to travel. I will give you a vessel, in order that you may load it and unload it, buy and sell. Be careful what you do; take care to make gains!" He gave him six thousand *scudi* to buy merchandise, and the son started on his voyage. On his journey, without having yet purchased anything, he arrived at a town, and on the sea-shore he saw a bier, and noticed that those who passed by left there some a penny, some two; they bestowed alms on the corpse. The traveler went there and asked: "Why do you keep this dead man here? *For the dead desires the grave.*" They replied: "Because he owed a world of debts, and it is the custom here *to bury no one until his debts are paid.* Until this man's debts are paid by charity we cannot bury him." "What is the use of keeping him here?" he said. "Proclaim that all those whom he owed shall come to me and be paid." Then they issued the proclamation and he paid the debts; and, poor fellow! he did not have a farthing left—not a penny of his capital. So he returned to his father's house. "What news, son? What means your return so soon?" he replied: "On crossing the sea, we encountered pirates; they have robbed me of all my capital!" His father said: "No matter, son; it is enough that they have left you your life. Behold, I will give you more money; but you must not go again in that direction." He gave him another six thousand *scudi.* The son replied: "Yes, father, don't worry; I will change my course." He departed and began his journey. When he was well out at sea he saw a Turkish vessel. He said to himself: "Now it is better for me to summon them on board than for them to summon us." They came on board. He said to them: "Whence do you come?" They answered: "We come from the Levant." "What is your cargo?" "Nothing but a beautiful girl." "How do you come to have this girl?" "For her beauty; to sell her again. We have stolen her from the Sultan, she is so beautiful!" "Let me see this girl." When he saw her he said: "How much do you want for her?" "We want six thousand *scudi.*" The money which his father gave him he gave to those corsairs, and took the girl and carried her away to his ship. But he at once had her become a Christian and married her.

He returned to his father's house; he went up, and his father said to him:

> "Welcome! O my handsome son.
> What merchandise of women have you
> made?"
> "My father, I bring you a handsome ring,
> I bring it for your reward;
> It cost me neither city nor castle,
> But the most beautiful woman you have ever
> seen:
> The daughter of the Sultan, who is in
> Turkey,
> Her I bring for my first cargo!"

"Ah, you miserable knave!" cried his father. "Is this the cargo you have brought?" He ill-treated them both, and drove them from the house. Those poor unfortunate ones did not know where to find shelter. They went away, and at a short distance from their town there were some rooms at a villa. They went to live in one of those. He said: "What shall we do here? I do not know how to do anything; I have no profession or business!" She said: "Now I can paint beautiful pictures; I will paint them, and you shall go and sell them!" He said: "Very well!" "But, remember, you must tell no one that I paint them!" "No, no!" he said.

Now let us go to Turkey. The Sultan, meanwhile, had sent out many vessels in search of his daughter. These ships went here and there in quest of her. Now it happened that one of these vessels arrived in the town near where she lived, and many of the sailors went on land. Now one day the husband said to his wife: "Make many pictures, for to-day we shall sell them!" She made them, and said to him that he should not sell them for less than twenty *scudi* apiece. She made a great many, and he carried them to the public square. Some of the Turks came there; they gave a glance at the paintings, and said to themselves: "Surely, it must be the Sultan's daughter who has painted these." They came nearer, and asked the young man how he sold them. He said they were dear; that he could not let them go for less than twenty *scudi*. They said: " Very well! We will buy them; but we want some more." He answered: "Come to the house of my wife who makes them!" They went there, and when they saw the Sultan's daughter, they seized her, bound her, and carried her far away to Turkey. This husband, then, unhappy, without wife, without a trade, alone in that house, what could he do?

Every day he walked along the beach, to see if he could find a ship that would take him on board; but he never saw any. One day he saw an old man fishing in a little boat; he cried: "Good old man, how much better off you are than I!" The old man asked: "Why, my dear son?" He said: "Good old man, will you take me to fish with you?" "Yes, my son," said he; "If you wish to come with me in this boat, I will take you!" "Thank heaven!" said he. "Good!" said the old man:

"You with the rod, and I with the boat,
Perhaps we shall catch some fish.

I will go and sell the fish, for I am not ashamed, and we will live together!" They ate, and afterward went to sleep; without knowing it, there arose in the night a severe storm, and the wind carried them to Turkey. The Turks, seeing this boat arrive, went on board, seized them, made slaves of them, and took them before the Sultan. He said: "Let one of them make bouquets; let the other plant flowers; put them in the garden!" They placed the old man there as gardener, and the young man to carry flowers to the Sultan's daughter, who with her maids was shut up in a very high tower for punishment. They were very comfortable there. Every day they went into the garden and made friends with the other gardeners. As time went on, the old man made some fine guitars, violins, flutes, clarionets, piccolos—all sorts of instruments he made. The young man played them beautifully when he had time. One day his wife, who was in the tower, hearing his fine songs—Fair Brow had a voice which surpassed all instruments,—said: "Who is playing, who is singing so beautifully?" They went out on the balcony, and when she saw Fair Brow, she thought at once of having him come up. The Sultan's daughter said to one of those who filled the basket with flowers: "Put that young man in the basket and cover him with flowers!" He put him in, and the maids drew him up. When he was up, he came out of the basket, and beheld his wife. He embraced and kissed her and thought about escaping from there. Then she told her damsels that she wished to depart without any one knowing it. So they loaded a large ship with pearls and precious stones, with rods of gold and jewels; then they let down Fair Brow first, then his wife; finally the damsels. They embarked and departed. When they were out at sea the husband remembered that he had forgotten the old man and left him on shore. Fair Brow said: "My sister, even if I thought I should lose my life, I would turn back, for *the word which I have given him is the mother of faith!*" So they turned back, and saw the old man, who was still awaiting them in a cave; they took him with them, and put to sea again. When they were near home, the old man said: "Now, my son, it is fitting for us to settle our accounts and divide things!" "Know, good old man," said Fair Brow to him, "that all the wealth that I have belongs half to you and half to me!" "Your wife, too, belongs half to me!" He said: "Good old man, I will leave you three quarters, and I will take one only, but leave me my wife. Do you want me to divide her in two?" Then the old man said: "You must know that I am the soul of him whom you had buried; and you have had all this good fortune because you did that good action, and converted and baptized your wife!" Then he gave him his blessing and disappeared. Fair Brow, when he heard this, as you can imagine, came near dying of joy. When they reached his city, they fired a salute, for Fair Brow had arrived with his wife, the wealthiest gentleman in the world. He sent for his father and told him all that had happened to him. He went to live with them, and as he was old, he died soon, and all his riches went to Fair Brow.[12]

WE HAVE already stated in the preface that it was not our design to admit into this work (except for occasional reference) any stories that were literary in their character. For this reason we have not drawn on the treasures of Straparola or Basile, or even on the more popular chapbooks, of which there are in Italy, as elsewhere, a great profusion. Of some of the stories contained in the last named class of works there are purely popular versions. As an example of the class, and for purposes of comparison, we give the story of Leombruno, or Lionbruno, one of the oldest and most popular of its kind. The most complete version is the one from the Basilicata, given by Comparetti, No. 41, which is as follows:

❧ *XXXVI. Lionbruno* ❧

There was once a mariner who had a wife and three or four children. He followed the business of a fisherman, and he and his family lived on his fishing. For three or four years there had been a dearth of fish, so that he had not been able to catch even a sardine. Poor mariner! From this misfortune he had been obliged to sell, little by little, all he possessed, to live, and was reduced almost to beggary. One day he was fishing, and as you can imagine, poor fellow! He did not haul in even a shell. He cursed madonnas and saints. All at once a certain person (it was the Enemy) rose in the midst of the sea before his bark. "What is the matter, mariner, that you are so angry?" "What should the matter be? My bad luck. For three or four years I have been ruining myself, body and soul, in this sea with these nets, and I cannot catch even a string to hang myself with." "Listen," said the Enemy. "If you will agree to give me your wife's next child in thirteen years, from now until you deliver it to me I will cause you to catch so much fish that you shall become the richest of men by selling it." Then the mariner understood that this was the Enemy, and said to himself: "My wife has had no children for some years. Will she take it into her head to have another just now when I make this agreement with the Enemy? Oh, come! She is old now, she will have no more." Then turning to the Enemy, he said: "Well, since you wish to make this contract, let us make it. But, remember, you must make me rich." "Don't fear," said the Enemy; "let us make the agreement and then leave the matter to me." "Softly, we must settle another matter first; then we will make the contract." "What is it?" "Listen. Suppose my wife should have no children during these thirteen years?" "Then you will remain rich and give me nothing." "That is what I wanted to know. Now we can make the contract." And they settled everything at once. Then the Enemy disappeared. The mariner began to draw in his nets, and they were full to overflowing of all kinds of fish, and he became richer from day to day. In great joy he said: "I have played a trick on the devil!"—and, poor man! He did not know that it was the devil who had played a trick on him. Now you must know that just when they were making the contract, the mariner's wife, old as she was, expected to become a mother again, and the Enemy knew it. In due time the wife gave birth to a boy so handsome that he seemed a flower. His parents named him Lionbruno. The Enemy suddenly appeared: "Mariner! Mariner!" "How can I serve you?" replied the poor man, all trembling. "The promise is due. Lionbruno is mine." "Yes, you are right. But you must obey the contract. Remember that it is in thirteen years. Now only a few months have passed." "That is true," replied the Enemy; "farewell, then, until the end of the thirteen years." Then he vanished. Meanwhile Lionbruno grew every day, and became constantly handsomer, and his parents sent him to school. But time passes, and behold the end of the thirteen years draws near. One day, before the time agreed upon, the Enemy appeared. "Mariner! Mariner!" "Oh, poor me!" said the wretched man, who recognized him by his horrid voice. But he had to answer. And what could he do? The contract was clear and the time come. The poor mariner, willingly or unwillingly, was obliged to promise to send the boy the next day alone to the sea. The next day the mother sent her son, when he returned from school, to carry something to eat to his father. The unhappy father had, however, gone far out to sea, so that his son could not find him. The poor boy sat down on the beach, and to pass the time, took pieces of wood and made little crosses of them, and stuck them in the sand around him, so that he was surrounded by them, and held one also in his hand, singing all the time.

Behold, the Enemy comes to take him, and says to him: "What are you doing, boy?" "I am waiting for my father," he replied. The Enemy looked and saw that he could not take him, because he was seated in the midst of all those little crosses, and moreover had one in his hand. He regarded the boy with an ugly look, and cried: "Destroy those crosses, miserable boy!" "No, I will not destroy them." "Destroy them at once, or—or"—and he threatened him and frightened him with his ugly face. Then the poor child destroyed the little crosses around him, but still held one in his hand. "Destroy the other, quick!" cried the Enemy, more enraged than ever. "No, no!" The poor child replied, all in tears; "I will not destroy this little cross." The Enemy threatened him again and terrified him with his rolling eyes, but the child was firm, and then a bright light appeared in the air. The fairy Colina, queen of the fairies, came down, took the good boy by the hair, and delivered him from the Enemy. Then if you had seen what lightnings and thunder! What darts! The Enemy shot fire from his eyes, mouth, nose, ears, everywhere! But with all his flames he remained duped, and the fairy carried the good boy away to her splendid palace. There Lionbruno grew up in the midst of the fairies. Imagine how well off he was there! He lacked nothing. Increasing always in beauty, he became a youth whom you should have seen! Some years passed. One day Lionbruno said to the fairy Colina: "Listen. I want to go and see my mother and father a little. You will not refuse me your permission, will you?" "No, I will not refuse you it," said the fairy. "I will give you twenty days to go and see your family. But do not stay any longer. Remember that I have saved you from the Enemy and have brought you up in the midst of great wealth. Now this wealth we are to enjoy together, for you, Lionbruno, are to be my husband." You can imagine whether the youth wished to say no. He replied at once: "I will do your will in all things." Then the fairy said: "My Lionbruno, take this ruby; all that you ask of it you shall have." He took the ruby. Then all the fairies gave him in turn some token. He took them, and thanked them all. Then he embraced his bride and departed. Lionbruno traveled better than a prince, magnificently dressed, on a superb horse, with guards before him. He arrived at his town, went to the square, and a crowd of people surrounded him out of curiosity. He asked his way to the house of the mariner who was his father. He did not reveal himself to his parents, but asked them for a lodging that night. At midnight Lionbruno changed, by virtue of the ruby, the wretched hovel into a magnificent palace, and the next day he changed himself into the thirteen-year-old Lionbruno and revealed himself to his parents, telling them how the fairy Colina had liberated him from the Enemy, brought him up, and made him her husband. "For this reason, dear father and mother," said he, "I cannot remain with you. I have come to see you, to embrace you, to make you rich; but I can stay with you a few days only, and then I must leave you." His father and mother saw that they could do nothing, and had to be contented. One fine morning Lionbruno, by an order to the ruby, which he wore on his finger, brought together a great mass of riches, and then called his parents and said: "I leave you masters of all this wealth and of this palace. You will no longer need anything. Now give me your blessing, for I wish to go." The poor people began to weep, and said: "Bless you, my son!" They embraced each other in tears, and he departed.

He arrived at a great city—like Naples, for example—and went to lodge at the finest inn. Then he went out to walk and heard a proclamation which declared: "Whatever prince or knight, on horse, with spear in hand, shall pierce and carry away a gold star, shall marry the king's daughter." Imagine how many princes and knights entered the lists! Lionbruno, more for braggadocio than for anything else, said to himself: "I wish to go and carry away the star," and he commanded the ruby: "My ruby, to-morrow, I wish to carry away the golden star." The princes and knights began to assemble and try their skill. Every one reached the star and touched it with his spear, but there was no talk of their carrying it away. Lionbruno came, and with a master-stroke carried off the star. Then he quickly escaped with his horse to the inn, so that no one should see him. "Who is he?" "Where is the winner?" No one can give any news of him. The king was ill-humored about it, and issued the proclamation again for the next day. But, to cut the matter short, the same thing occurred the next day. Lionbruno duped them a

second time. Imagine how angry the king was! He issued a third proclamation. But this time what does the crafty king do? He posts a large number of soldiers at all the places by which one could escape. The princes and
knights begin their courses. As usual, no one carries away the star, and
Lionbruno carries it off and rides away. But the soldiers, quicker than he,
seize him, arrest him, and carry him to the king. "What do you take me for,
that, not satisfied with duping me twice, you wish to dupe me a third
time?" Thus spoke the king, who was seated on the throne. "Pardon,
Majesty. I did not dare to enter your presence." "Then you ought not to
have undertaken to carry away the star. Now you have done so, and must
become my daughter's husband." Lionbruno, *nolens volens,* was obliged to
marry the princess. The king prepared a magnificent feast for the wedding,
and invited all the princes, counts, and barons—all sorts of persons. When
the hall was filled with these gentlemen, Lionbruno, before marrying the
princess, said to the king: "Majesty, it is true that your daughter is a very
beautiful girl, but I had a bride by whose side your daughter could not
stand for beauty, grace, everything." Imagine how the king felt when he
heard these words. The poor princess, at this affront in the presence of so
many noblemen, became as red as fire. The king, greatly disturbed, said:
"Well, if it is so, we wish to see your wife, if she is as beautiful as you say."
"Yes, yes!" cried all the noblemen; "We, too, wish to see her; we wish to see
her!" Poor Lionbruno was in a tight place. What could he do? He had
recourse to the ruby. "Ruby mine, make fairy Colina come here." But this
time he was mistaken. The ruby could do everything, but it could not com-
pel the fairy to come, for it was she who had given it its magic power. The
summons, however, reached the fairy Colina; but she did not go. "My
friend has done a pretty thing!" said she. "Bravo! Good! Now I will fix him
as he deserves!" She called the lowest of her servants, and made her suddenly appear in the great hall of the king, where all were assembled for the
wedding. "How beautiful she is! How beautiful she is!" all said as soon as
they saw her. "Is this, then, your first bride?" "What!" answered Lionbruno,
"my first bride! This is the lowest of the servants of my first bride." "Gracious!" exclaimed the noblemen; "If this is the lowest of the servants and is
so beautiful, imagine what the mistress must be!" "Then," said the king, "If
this is not your first bride, I wish you to make her come herself." "Yes, yes,
herself!" cried the others, likewise. Poor Lionbruno! He was obliged to have
recourse again to the ring. But this time, also, the fairy did not go, but sent
instead her next servant. Scarcely had they seen her when they all said:
"This one, oh, this one, is really beautiful! This, now, is certainly your first

bride, is she not, Lionbruno?" "No, no!" replied Lionbruno; "my first bride is a marvel of beauty. Different from this one! This one is only the second servant." Then the king, in a threatening tone, said to him: "Lionbruno, let us put an end to this! I command you to cause your first wife to come here instantly." The matter was growing serious. Poor Lionbruno had recourse for the third time to the ruby, and said to it: "Ruby mine, if you really wish to help me, now is the moment. You must cause the fairy Colina herself to come here." The summons reached her at once, and this time she went. When all those great lords and the king and his daughter saw that marvel of beauty, they became as so many statues. But the fairy Colina approached Lionbruno, pretended to take his hand, and drew off his ring, saying: "Traitor! You cannot find me until you have worn out seven pairs of iron shoes." Then she vanished. The king, in fury, said to Lionbruno: "I understand. The power of carrying off the star was not yours, but your ruby's. Leave my palace!" He had him seized and well beaten and sent away.

And so poor Lionbruno was left without the fairy Colina and the king's daughter, and departed from the city in great grief. When he had gone a few steps, he heard a great noise. It was a smithy. He entered, and called the blacksmith: "Master, I want seven pairs of iron shoes." "I will make you twelve if you wish, but it seems to me that you must have some agreement with the Eternal to live who knows how many hundred years to wear out all these shoes." "What does that matter to you? It is enough if I pay you. Make me the shoes and hold your tongue." He made them for him at once. Lionbruno paid him, put on one pair, and stuck three in one side of his travelling sack and three in the other, and set out. After walking a long time, he arrived late at night in a forest. All at once three robbers came there. " Good man," said they to Lionbruno, "How did you happen here?" "I am a poor pilgrim," he replied; "It grew dark and I stopped here to rest. And who are you, gentlemen?" "We are travelers." And they all stopped there to rest. The next day Lionbruno arose, took leave of the three robbers, and departed. But he had scarcely gone a few steps when he heard them quarrelling. Now you must know that those robbers had stolen three objects of great value, and were now disputing as to how they should divide them. One of them said: "Fools that we are! We had here that pilgrim, who could have acted as judge and made the division, and we have let him go. Let us call him back." "Yes, yes! Let us call him," said the others. They called him, and he came back. "How can I serve you, gentlemen?" said he. "Listen, good man; we have three objects of great value to divide. You must be the judge, and give to each one what belongs to him." "Very well; but what objects are you talking of?" "Here is a pair of boots, a purse, and a cloak. The boots have this virtue, that he who has them on runs faster than the wind. If you say to the purse, 'open and shut,' it at once gives you a hundred ducats. Finally he who puts on the cloak and buttons it up, can see and yet not be seen." "Very good. But to act the judge well, I must first examine these three objects carefully." "Certainly, that is right." Lionbruno put on the boots, tried to run, and went marvelously. "What do you think of these boots?" asked the thieves. "Excellent, indeed," replied Lionbruno, and kept them on. Then he said: "Now let us see the purse." He took it and said: "Purse, open and shut," and at once there came forth a hundred silver ducats. "Now let us see what this cloak is," he said, at last. He put it on and began to button it up. While he was doing so he asked the robbers: "Do you see me now?" They answered: "Yes." He kept on buttoning it and asked again: "Now do you see me?" "Yes." Finally he reached the last button. "Now do you see me?" "No." "If you don't see me now you never will see me again." He threw away the iron shoes and cried: "Now for you, boots!" And away! Faster than the wind. When the three robbers saw themselves duped in that way, what a rage they were in! They thrashed each other soundly, and especially the one who had called Lionbruno back; and at last they all found themselves with broken bones.

Lionbruno, after having cheated the robbers thus, continued his way joyfully. After a long journey, he arrived in the midst of a forest. He saw at a distance a slight smoke, and among frightful rocks, a little old hovel all surrounded by dense wild shrubs, with a little door entirely covered with ivy, so that it could scarcely be seen. Lionbruno approached the door and knocked softly. "Who is knocking?" asked from within an old woman's voice. "I am a poor Christian," replied Lionbruno; "night has overtaken me here, and I am seeking a lodging, if it can be had." The door opened and Lionbruno entered. "Oh, poor youth! How have you been tempted to come and ruin yourself in this remote place?" demanded, in great wonder, the old woman, who was within, and who was Borea.[13] (Do you know who Borea is? No less a person than the mother of the winds.) "Oh, dear little old lady, my aunt," replied Lionbruno, "I am lost in this great forest, for I have been travelling a long time to find my dear bride, the fairy Colina, and I have not yet been able to find any trace of her." "My son, you have made a great mistake! What shall we do now that my sons are coming home? Perhaps, God help you! they will want to eat you." "Oh, wretched me!" cried Lionbruno, then, all trembling; "Who, my aunt, are these sons of yours who so devour Christians?" "My son," replied Borea, "you do not know where you are. Do you not know that this house in the midst of these precipices is the house of the winds? And I, you do not recognize me; I, my son, am Borea, the mother of all the winds." "What shall I do now? Oh, my dear aunt, help me; do not let your sons eat me up!" The old woman finally concealed him in a chest, telling him not to make the slightest noise when her sons returned. Soon a loud noise was heard at a distance: it was the winds returning home. The nearer they approached the louder the noise grew, and a sound of branches and trees broken off was heard. At last the winds arrived, pushed open the door, and entered. "Good evening, mamma." "Welcome, my sons!" replied their mother, all smiling. And so one after the other all the winds entered, and the last to enter was Sirocco, for you must know that Sirocco is the youngest of Borea's sons. Scarcely had they entered when they began to say: "What smell of human flesh is here? Here, Christians, Christians!" "Oh, bad luck to you! What fools you are! Where is there any smell of human flesh here? Who do you think would risk their lives by coming here?" But her sons would not be convinced, especially that obstinate Sirocco. Lionbruno commended his soul to God, for he saw death at his heels. But finally Borea succeeded in convincing her sons. "Oh, mamma, what is there to eat to-night? We have traveled so far, and are so hungry!" "Here, my sons," the mother answered, "come here; for a nice polenta is cooking for you. I will finish cooking it soon, and put it at once on the table." The next day Borea said to her sons: "My sons, when you came you said you smelled human flesh. Tell me, should you really see a man now, what would you do to him?" "Now, we would not do anything to him. Last night, we should have torn him in pieces." "But you would not do anything to him, truly?" "Truly." "Well, if you will give me your promise by St. John not to harm him, I will show you a live man." "Oh! Just see! A man here! Yes, yes, mamma, show him to us at once. We swear by St. John! We will not touch a hair of his head." Then their mother opened the chest and made Lionbruno come forth. If you had heard the winds then! They puffed and blowed around him and asked him, first of all, how he had come to that place, where no living soul had ever penetrated. Lionbruno said: "Would to heaven that my journey ended here! I must go to the palace of the fairy Colina; perhaps one of you can tell me where it is?" Then Borea asked her sons one by one and each replied that he knew nothing of it. Finally she questioned her youngest son: "And you, Sirocco, do you not know anything about it?" "I? Should I not know something about it? Am I perchance like my brothers who never can find a hiding-place? The fairy Colina is love-sick. She says that her lover has betrayed her, and continually weeps, and is so reduced by her grief that she can live but little longer. And I deserve to be hanged, for I have seen her in this condition, and yet I have annoyed her so that I have driven her to despair. I amused myself by making a noise about her palace, and more than once I burst open windows and turned things upside down, even the bed she was resting on." "Oh, my dear Sirocco!" said Lionbruno; "my good Sirocco, you must aid me! Since you have given me news of her, you must also do me the favor to show me the way to my bride's palace. I, dear Sirocco, am the betrothed of the fairy Colina, and it is not true that I have betrayed her; on the contrary, if I do not find her, I shall die of grief." "My son," said Sirocco, "listen; for my part I would take you there with all my heart. But I should have to carry you about my neck. And the trouble is I cannot do so, for I am wind, I am air, and you would slip off. Were you like me the matter would go very well." "Don't worry about that," said Lionbruno, "show me the way, and I will not lag behind." "He is crazy," said Sirocco to himself; then he said to Lionbruno: "Very well, since you feel so strong, to-morrow we will make the trial. Meanwhile let us go to bed, for it is late, and to-morrow, God willing, we will rise early!" And all went to sleep. In the morning early Sirocco arose and cried: "Lionbruno! Lionbruno! Get up quickly!" And Lionbruno put on his boots in a hurry, seized his purse, fixed his cloak carefully, and left the house with Sirocco. "There," said Sirocco, "is the way we must take, be careful! Don't let me out of your sight, and leave the rest to me. If a few hours after sunset tonight I don't make you find your beauty, you may call me an ass." They started. They ran like the wind. Every little while Sirocco called out: "Lionbruno!" And he, who was ahead, answered at once: "Oh! Don't think I am going to lag behind!" And with these questions and answers they finally reached the palace of the fairy Colina about two hours after sunset. "Here we are," said Sirocco. "Here is your fair one's balcony! See how I am going to blow open the window for you. Attention, now! As soon as it is opened you give a jump and spring in." And so he did. Before the servants could run and shut the balcony window, Lionbruno was already under the fairy Colina's bed. Afterwards one of the maids said to the fairy: "My mistress, how do you feel now? Do you not feel a little better?" " Better? I am half dead. That cursed wind has nearly killed me." "But, mistress, will you not take something this evening? A little coffee, or chocolate, or broth?" "I wish nothing at all." "Take something, if you don't, you will not rest to-night, you have eaten nothing for three or four days. Really, you must take something." And the servant said so much that to get rid of her importunity the fairy said: "Well, bring something; if I want it, I will take it." The servant brought a little coffee, and left it by the side of the bed. Lionbruno, in his cloak so that no one could see him, came from under the bed and drank the coffee himself. The servant, believing her mistress had drunk it, brought the chocolate too, and Lionbruno drank that as before. Then the servant brought the fairy some broth and a pigeon. "Mistress," said she, "since, thank God, you have taken the coffee and the chocolate, take this broth and a bit of pigeon, and so you will gain strength and be better to-morrow." The mistress on hearing all this believed that the servants were making fun of her. "Oh, stupid blockheads! What are you saying? Are not the cups still here with the coffee and the chocolate? I have touched nothing." The servants thought that their mistress was out of her mind. Then Lionbruno took off his cloak, came out from under the bed, and said: "My bride, do you know me?" "Lionbruno mine, is it you?" and she rose from the bed and embraced him, "Then it is not true, my Lionbruno, that you have forgotten me?" "If I had forgotten you I should not have suffered so much to find you. But do you still love me?" "My Lionbruno, if I had not always loved you, you would not have found me at the point of death. And now you see I am cured only because I have seen you."

Then they ate and drank together, and summoned the servants and made a great festival. The next day they arranged everything for the wedding and were married with great splendor and joy. In the evening they gave a grand ball and a fine banquet, which you should have seen![14]

THE ABOVE story is extremely popular, and has long circulated among the people as an independent work in the shape of a chap-book. We have, however, given the form which is handed down by oral tradition, purposely avoiding the use of any literary materials. Many similar tales might be added to this chapter, but the most important and best known have been given. To give those tales which cannot be described as fairy tales and which are usually found in the shape of chap-books in prose and poetry would fall without the scope of the present volume, and would belong more appropriately to a work on Italian popular literature.[15]

CHAPTER III

⌇

STORIES OF ORIENTAL ORIGIN

THE GEOGRAPHICAL situation of Italy and its commercial connections during the Middle Ages would lead us to expect a large foreign element in its popular tales. This foreign element, it is hardly necessary to say, is almost exclusively Oriental, and was introduced either by direct communication with the East, or indirectly from France, which received it from Spain, whither it was brought by the Saracens. Although this Oriental element is now perfectly popular, it is, as far as its origin is concerned, purely literary. That is to say, the stories we are about to examine are to be found in the great Oriental collections of tales which were early translated into all the languages of Europe, and either passed directly from these translations into circulation among the people, or became familiar to them from the novelists who made such frequent use of this element.[1] A few stories may have been taken from the French *fabliaux* or from the French translations of the *Disciplina Clericalis*, as we shall afterwards see.[2] The Pentamerone, and especially Straparola's tales, may finally be mentioned as the source from which many Oriental stories have flowed into popular circulation.[3] In this chapter it is proposed to notice briefly only those stories the Oriental origin of which is undoubted, and which may be found in the great collections above mentioned and in some others less known. For convenience, some stories of this class have been referred to chapter VI.

The first of this class which we shall mention is well known from the version in Lafontaine (IX. 1), *Le Dépositaire infidèle*. The only Italian version we have found is Pitrè, No. 194, which is as follows:

⌇ XXXVII. The Peasant and the Master ⌇

A peasant one day, conversing in the farmhouse with his master and others, happened, while speaking of sheep and cheese, to say that he had had a present of a little cheese, but the mice had eaten it all up. Then the master, who was rich, proud, and fat, called him a fool, and said that it was not possible that the mice could have eaten the cheese, and all present said the master was right and the peasant wrong. What more could the poor man say? Talk makes talk. After a while the master said that having taken the precaution to rub with oil his ploughshares to keep them from rusting, the mice had eaten off all the points. Then the friend of the cheese broke forth: "But, master, how can it be that the mice cannot eat my cheese, if they can eat the points of your ploughshares?" But the master and all the others began to cry out: "Be silent, you fool! Be silent, you fool! the master is right!"[4]

THE ABOVE story really belongs to the class of fables of which there are but few of Oriental origin in the Italian collections.[5] The following version of one of the most famous of the Eastern apologues is from Monferrato (Comparetti, No. 67). It is called:

❧ XXXVIII. The Ingrates ❧

There was once a man who went into the forest to gather wood, and saw a snake crushed under a large stone. He raised the stone a little with the handle of his axe and the snake crawled out. When it was at liberty it said to the man: "I am going to eat you." The man answered: " Softly; first let us hear the judgment of some one, and if I am condemned, then you shall eat me." The first one they met was a horse as thin as a stick, tied to an oak-tree. He had eaten the leaves as far as he could reach, for he was famished. The snake said to him: "Is it right for me to eat this man who has saved my life?" The nag answered: "More than right. Just look at me! I was one of the finest horses. I have carried my master so many years, and what have I gained? Now that I am so badly off that I can no longer work they have tied me to this oak, and after I have eaten these few leaves I shall die of hunger. Eat the man, then; for he who does good is ill rewarded, and he who does evil must be well rewarded. Eat him, for you will be doing a good day's work." They afterwards happened to find a mulberry-tree, all holes, for it was eaten by old age; and the snake asked it if it was right to eat the man who had saved its life. "Yes," the tree answered at once, "for I have given my master so many leaves that he has raised from them the finest silk-worms in the world; now that I can no longer stand upright, he has said that he is going to throw me into the fire. Eat him, then, for you will do well." Afterwards they met the fox. The man took her aside and begged her to pronounce in his favor. The fox said: "The better to render judgment I must see just how the matter has happened." They all returned to the spot and arranged matters as they were at first; but as soon as the man saw the snake under the stone he cried out: "Where you are, there I will leave you." And there the snake remained. The fox wished in payment a bag of hens, and the man promised them to her for the next morning. The fox went there in the morning, and when the man saw her he put some dogs in the bag, and told the fox not to eat the hens close by, for fear the mistress of the house would hear it. So the fox did not open the bag until she had reached a distant valley; then the dogs came out and ate her; and so it is in the world; for who does good is ill rewarded and who does evil is well rewarded.[6]

IT WOULD be surprising if we did not find the fascinating stories of the Thousand and One Nights naturalized among the people. It is, of course, impossible to tell whether they were communicated to the people directly from a literary source, or whether the separate stories came to Italy from the Orient by way of oral transmission.[7] These stories have circulated among the people long enough to be treated as their own property and changed to suit their taste. Incidents from other stories have been added and the original story remodeled until it is hardly recognizable. The story of "Aladdin and the Wonderful Lamp," for instance, is found from Sicily to Lombardy; but in no one version are all the features of the original story preserved. In one of the Sicilian versions (Messina) Aladdin does not lose his lamp; in another (Palermo), after Aladdin has lost his lamp he goes in search of it, and on his journey settles the quarrel of an ant, an eagle, and a lion, who give him the power to transform himself into any one of them. He finally discovers the magician, who has his life elsewhere than in his own body, and who is killed after the usual complicated process. In the Roman version the point of the unfinished window in Aladdin's palace is missed, the magician requires to be killed, as in the version from Palermo, and there are some additional incidents not in the Oriental original. In the Mantuan story, instead of a lamp we have a rusty ring, which the youngest brother finds inside of a dead cock bequeathed to three brothers by their father. After the ring has fallen into the possession of the magician and the palace has disappeared, the hero goes in search of his wife and ring. On his way he is assisted by the "King of the Fishes" and the "King of the Birds." The eagle carries a letter to the captive princess, who obtains the ring from the magician, rubs it on a stone, and when it asks what she wishes, answers: "I wish this palace to return where it first was and the magician to be drowned in the sea."[8]

Of almost equal popularity is the story of the "Forty Thieves," who are, however, in the Italian versions, reduced to thirteen, twelve, or six in number. The versions in Pitrè (No. 23 and variants) contain but one incident of the original story, where the robbers are detected in the oil-jars, and killed by pouring boiling oil over them. In one of versions the robbers are hidden in sacks of choral, and the cunning daughter pierces the bags with a red-hot spit. In another, they are hidden in oil-skins, and sold to the abbess of a certain convent for oil. One of the nuns has some suspicion of the trick, and invites her companions to tap the skins with red-hot irons. Another Sicilian version (Gonz. No. 79, "The Story of the Twelve Robbers") contains the first part of the Arabian tale, the robbers' cave which opens and closes by the words, "Open, door!" and "Shut, door!" The story ends with the death of one of the brothers, who entered the cave and was killed by one of the robbers who had remained. It is only in the version from Mantua (Visentini, No. 7, "The Cunning Maid") that we find the story complete; boiling water is used instead of oil in killing the thieves, and the servant girl afterwards kills the captain, who had escaped before. The story of the "Third Calendar" is told in detail in Comparetti (No. 65, "The Son of the King of France") and the "Two Envious Sisters" furnishes details for a number of distinct stories.[9] The story of "The Hunchback" is found in Pitrè and Straparola, and as it is also the subject of an Old-French *fabliau*, it may have been borrowed from the French, or, what is more likely, both French and Italians took it from a common source.[10] The fable of "The Ass, the Ox, and the Peasant," which the Vizier relates to prevent his daughter becoming the Sultan's wife, is found in Pitrè (No. 282) under the title of "The Curious Wife," and is also in Straparola.[11] The beautiful story of "Prince Ahmed and the fairy Peribanu" is found in Nerucci, No. 40, "The Three Presents, or the Story of the Carpets." The three presents are the magic telescope that sees any distance, the carpet that carries one through the air, and the magic grapes that bring to life. The Italian version follows closely the Oriental original. The same may be said of another story in the same collection, No. 48, "The Traveler from Turin," which is nothing but Sindbad's "Fourth Voyage."[12] The last story taken from the Arabian Nights which we shall mention is that of "The Second Royal Mendicant," found in Comparetti (No. 63, "My Happiness") from the Basilicata, and in the collection of Mantuan stories. The latter (No. 8) is entitled: "There is no longer any Devil." The magician is the devil, and the story concludes, after the transformations in which the peasant's son kills the devil in the shape of a hen, with the words: "And this is the reason why there is no longer any devil."[13]

The first collection of Oriental tales known in Europe as a collection was the *Disciplina Clericalis,* that is, Instruction or Teaching for Clerks or Clergymen. It was the work of a converted Spanish Jew, Petrus Alphonsi, and was composed before 1106, the date of the baptism of the author, the time and place of whose death are not known. The *Disciplina Clericalis* was early translated into French prose and poetry, and was the storehouse from which all subsequent story-tellers drew abundant material.[14] Precisely how the *Disciplina Clericalis* became known in Italy we cannot tell; but the separate stories must have become popular and diffused by word of mouth at a very early date. One of the stories of this collection is found in Italian literature as early as the *Cento Novelle Antiche.*[15] Four of the stories in the *Disciplina Clericalis* are found in Pitrè and other collections of popular tales, and although belonging, with one exception, to the class of jests, they are mentioned here for the sake of completeness.

In one of the stories of the *Disciplina Clericalis,* two citizens of a certain town and a countryman were making the pilgrimage to Mecca together, and on the way ran so short of food that they had only flour enough left to make one small loaf. The two citizens in order to cheat the countryman out of his share devised the following scheme: While the bread was baking they proposed that all three should sleep, and whoever should have the most remarkable dream should have the whole loaf. While the citizens were asleep, the countryman, who had divined their plan, stole the half-cooked bread from the fire, ate it, and then threw himself down again. One of the other two pretended to wake up in a fright, and told his companion that he had dreamed that two angels had led him through the gates of heaven into the presence of God. The other declared that he had been led by two angels into the nether-world. The countryman heard all this and still pretended to sleep. When his companions aroused him he asked in amazement: "Who are those calling me?" They answered: "We are your companions." "What," said he, "Have you got back already?" "Where have we been to in order to return?" The countryman replied: "It seemed to me that two angels led one of you to heaven, and afterwards two others conducted the other to hell. From this I imagined that neither of you would return, so I got up and ate the bread."[16]

The same story is told in Pitrè (No. 173) of a monk who was an itinerant preacher, and who was accompanied on his journey by a very cunning lay brother. One day the monk received a present of some fish which he wished to eat himself alone, and therefore proposed to the brother that the one of them who dreamed the best dream should have all the fish. The dreams and the conclusion are the same as in the original.[17]

The next story is well known from the use made of it by Cervantes in Don Quixote (Part I., chap. xx.) where Sancho relates it to beguile the hours of the memorable night when the noise of the fullingmill so terrified the doughty knight and his squire. The version in the *Disciplina Clericalis* is as follows: "A certain king had a story-teller who told him five stories every night. It happened once that the king, oppressed by cares of state, was unable to sleep, and asked for more than the usual number of stories. The storyteller related three short ones. The king wished for more still, and when the story-teller demurred, said: "You have told me several very short ones. I want something long, and then you may go to sleep." The story-teller yielded, and began thus: "Once upon a time there was a certain countryman who went to market and bought two thousand sheep. On his way home a great inundation took place, so that he was unable to cross a certain river by the ford or bridge. After anxiously seeking some means of getting across with his flock, he found at length a little boat in which he could convey two sheep over." After the story-teller had got thus far he went to sleep. The king roused him and ordered him to finish the story he had begun. The story-teller answered: "The flood is great, the boat small, and the flock innumerable; let the aforesaid countryman get his sheep over, and I will finish the story I have begun."[18]

The version in Pitrè (No, 138) lacks all connection and is poor, but we give it here, as it is very brief.

⚬ XXXIX. The Treasure ⚬

Once upon a time there was a prince who studied and racked his brains so much that he learned magic and the art of finding hidden treasures. One day he discovered a treasure in a bank, let us say the bank of Ddisisa: "Oh," he says, "now I am going to get it out." But to get it out it was necessary that ten million million ants should cross one by one the river Gianquadara (let us suppose it was that one) in a bark made of the half shell of a nut. The prince puts the bark in the river and begins to make the ants pass over. One, two, three—and he is still doing it.

Here the person who is telling the story pauses and says: "We will finish this story when the ants have finished passing over."[19]

THE version from Milan is still shorter:

✌ XL. The Shepherd ✌

Once upon a time there was a shepherd who went to feed his sheep in the fields, and he had to cross a stream, and he took the sheep up one by one to carry them over. . . .

What then? Go on!

When the sheep are over, I will finish the story.[20]

IN CHAPTER V. we shall meet two popular figures in Sicilian tales, whose jokes are repeated elsewhere as detached stories. One of these persons is Firrazzanu, the practical joker and knave, who is cunning enough to make others bear the penalty of his own boldness. In the story in Pitrè (No. 156, var. 2) Firrazzanu's master wants a tailor for some work, and Firrazzanu tells him he knows of one who is good, but subject to fits, which always make their approach known by a twitching of the mouth, and the only remedy for them is a sound beating. Of course, when the unlucky tailor begins to cut his cloth, he twists his mouth, and receives, to his amazement, a sudden beating.

In this version there is no reason given why Firrazzanu should play such a joke on the innocent tailor. In the original, however, a motive is given for the trick.[21]

The last story we shall mention from the *Disciplina Clericalis* is the one known in Pitrè (No. 197) as:

✌ XLI. The Three Admonitions ✌

A man once left his country to go to foreign parts, and there entered the service of an abbot. After he had spent some time in faithful service, he desired to see his wife and native land. He said to the abbot: "Sir, I have served you thus long, but now I wish to return to my country." "Yes, my son," said the abbot, "But before departing I must give you the three hundred ounces* that I have put together for you. Will you be satisfied with three admonitions, or with the three hundred ounces?" The servant answered: "I will be satisfied with the three admonitions." "Then listen: First: When you change the old road for the new, you will find troubles which you have not looked for. Second: See much and say little. Third: Think over a thing before you do it, for a thing deliberated is very fine.[22] Take this loaf of bread and break it when you are truly happy."

The good man departed, and on his journey met other travelers. These said to him: "We are going to take the by-way. Will you come with us?" But he remembering the three admonitions of his master answered: "No, my friends, I will keep on this road." When he had gone halfway, bang! bang! He heard some shots. "What was that, my sons?" The robbers had killed his companions. "I have gained the first hundred ounces!" he said, and continued his journey. On his way he arrived at an inn as hungry as a dog and called for something to eat. A large dish of meat was brought which seemed to say: "Eat me, eat me!" He stuck his fork in it and turned it over, and was frightened out of his wits, for it was human flesh! He wanted to ask the meaning of such food and give the innkeeper a lecture, but just then he thought: "See much and say little;" so he remained silent. The innkeeper came, he settled his bill, and took leave. But the innkeeper stopped him and said: "Bravo, bravo! You have saved your life. All those who have questioned me about my food have been soundly beaten, killed, and nicely cooked." "I have gained the second hundred ounces," said the good man, who did not think his skin was safe until then.

When he reached his own country he remembered his house, saw the door ajar and slipped in. He looked about and saw no one, only in the middle of the room was a table, well set with two glasses, two forks, two seats, service for two. "How is this?" He said: "I left my wife alone and here I find things arranged for two. There is some trouble." So he hid himself under the bed to see what went on. A moment after he saw his wife enter, who had gone out a short time before for a pitcher of water. A little after he saw a sprucely dressed young priest come in and seat himself at the table. "Ah, is that he?" and he was on the point of coming forth and giving him a sound beating; but there came to his mind the final admonition

*The ounce is equivalent to nearly thirteen francs (12.75).

of the abbot: "Think over a thing before you do it, for a thing deliberated is very fine," and he refrained. He saw them both sit down at the table, but before eating his wife turned to the young priest and said: "My son, let us say our accustomed Paternoster for your father." When he heard this he came from under the bed crying and laughing for joy, and embraced and kissed them both so that it was affecting to see him. Then he remembered the loaf his master had given him and told him to eat in his happiness; he broke the loaf and there fell on the table all the three hundred ounces, which the master had secretly put in the loaf.[23]

WE NOW turn to some stories taken from a collection more famous in some respects than those previously mentioned, The Seven Wise Masters, which enjoyed during the Middle Ages a popularity second only to that of the Bible. Of this collection there are several Italian translations reaching back to the fourteenth century.[24] From one of these, or possibly from oral tradition, the stories about to be mentioned passed into the popular tales of Italy. The first story we shall cite is interesting because popular tradition has connected it with Pier delle Vigne, the famous chancellor of the Emperor Frederick the Second. The Venetian version (Bernoni, *Trad. pop. venez.* Punt, I. p. 11) is in substance as follows:

ᴄᴄ XLII. *Vineyard I Was and Vineyard I Am* ᴄᴄ

A king, averse to marriage, commanded his steward to remain single. The latter, however, one day saw a beautiful girl named Vigna, and married her secretly. Although he kept her closely confined in her chamber, the king became suspicious and sent the steward off on an embassy. After his departure the king entered the apartment occupied by him, and saw his officer's wife sleeping. He did not disturb her, but, in leaving the room, dropped one of his gloves accidentally on the bed. When the husband returned he found it, but kept a discreet silence, ceasing, however, all demonstrations of affection, believing his wife had been faithless. The king, anxious to see again the beautiful woman, made a feast and ordered the steward to bring his wife. He denied in vain that he had one, but brought her at last, and while every one else was talking gayly at the feast she was silent. The king observed it and asked her the cause of her silence; and she answered with a pun on her name: "Vineyard I was and Vineyard I am, I was loved and no longer am: I know not for what reason the Vineyard has lost its season." Her husband, who heard this, replied: "Vineyard thou wast and Vineyard thou art, loved thou wast and no longer art: the Vineyard has lost its season for the lion's claw." The king, who understood what he meant, answered: "I entered the Vineyard, I touched the leaves, but I swear by my crown that I have not tasted the fruit." Then the steward understood that his wife was innocent, and the two made peace and always after lived happy and contented.[25]

THIS STORY is found only in the Greek and Hebrew versions of The Seven Wise Masters, and in the Arabic Seven Viziers. It did not pass into any of the Occidental versions, although it was known to Boccaccio, who based on it the fifth novel of the first day of the Decameron. Either, then, the story is a late adaptation of the Oriental tale, which is unlikely, or it comes from some now lost, but once popular Italian version of the Oriental form of The Seven Wise Masters.[26]

The three following stories are found only in the Western, or European versions of the collection. The first, technically called "*Vaticinium*" or "The Prophecy," relates that a son who understood the language of birds heard the prediction that his father and mother should come to such want that they would not have bread to eat; but that he, the son, should rise so high that his father should offer him water to wash his hands with. The father, enraged at this prediction, threw his son into the sea. He was rescued, and after many adventures, married the daughter of the king of Sicily. One day, while riding through Messina, he saw his father and mother, meanly dressed, sitting at the door of an inn. He alighted from his horse, entered their house, and asked for food. After his father and mother had brought him water to wash his hands he revealed himself to them and forgave his father for his cruelty.

The only Italian version, and disfigured by some extraneous details, is in the Mantuan tales (Visentini, No. 50): "Fortune aid me." Here the son does not hear the prophecy from the birds, but an angel tells a king, who has long desired a son, that he shall have one whom he shall one day serve. When the child was ten years old the king was so vexed by the prediction that he exposed his son in a wood. The child was found by a magician, who brought him up, and from whom he afterwards escaped. He went to the court of the king, his father, and won the hand of the princess (his own sister) by leaping his horse over a broad ditch. At the marriage banquet the king handed his son a glass of wine, and the latter recognized him and exclaimed: "Behold, the father serves the son." The marriage was of course given up and the previous aversion of the sister explained.[27]

Closely connected with the original story in The Seven Wise Masters is the class of stories where the hero is acquainted with the language of animals, and attains by means of it some high position (generally becoming pope) after he has been driven from home by his father. The following version is from Monferrato (Comparetti, No. 56) and is entitled:

ॐ XLIII. The Language of Animals ॐ

A father once had a son who spent ten years in school. At the end of that time, the teacher wrote the father to take away his son because he could not teach him anything more. The father took the boy home and gave a grand banquet in his honor, to which he invited the most noble gentlemen of the country. After many speeches by those gentlemen, one of the guests said to the host's son: "Just tell us some fine thing that you have learned." "I have learned the language of dogs, of frogs, and of birds." There was universal laughter on hearing this, and all went away ridiculing the pride of the father and the foolishness of the son. The former was so ashamed at his son's answer and so angry at him that he gave him up to two servants, with orders to take him into a wood and kill him and to bring back his heart. The two servants did not dare to obey this command, and instead of the lad they killed a dog, and carried its heart to their master. The youth fled from the country and came to a castle a long way off, where lived the treasurer of the prince, who had immense treasures. There he asked for and obtained a lodging, but scarcely had he entered the house when a multitude of dogs collected about the castle. The treasurer asked the young man why so many dogs had come, and as the latter understood their language he answered that it meant that a hundred assassins would attack the castle that very evening, and that the treasurer should take his precautions. The castellan made two hundred soldiers place themselves in ambush about the castle and at night they arrested the assassins. The treasurer was so grateful to the youth that he wished to give him his daughter, but he replied that he could not remain now, but that he would return within a year and three days. After he left that castle he arrived at a city where the king's daughter was very ill because the frogs which were in a fountain near the palace gave her no rest with their croaking. The lad perceived that the frogs croaked because the princess had thrown a cross into the fountain, and as soon as it was removed the girl recovered. The king, too, wished the lad to marry her, but he again said that he would return within a year and three days. After leaving the king he set out for Rome, and on the way met three young men, who became his companions. One day it was very warm and all three lay down to sleep under an oak. Immediately a great flock of birds flew into the oak and awakened the pilgrims by their loud singing. One of them asked: "Why are these birds singing so joyfully?" The youth answered: "They are rejoicing with the new Pope, who is to be one of us."

And suddenly a dove alighted on his head, and in truth shortly after he was made Pope. Then he sent for his father, the treasurer, and the king. All presented themselves trembling, for they knew that they had committed some sin. But the Pope made them all relate their deeds, and then turned to his father and said: "I am the son whom you sent to be killed because I said I understood the language of birds, of dogs, and of frogs. You have treated me thus, and on the other hand a treasurer and a king have been very grateful for this knowledge of mine." The father, repenting his fault, wept bitterly, and his son pardoned him and kept him with him while he lived.[28]

THE NEXT story is doubly interesting because it is found not only in the mediaeval collection last mentioned, but also in Greek literature, being told of Rampsinitus, King of Egypt, by Herodotus (II. 121), and by Pausanias of the two architects Agamedes and Trophonius who robbed the treasury of Hyrleus.[29] There are four versions in Italian: two from Sicily (Pitrè, Nos. 159, 160), one from Bologna (Coronedi-Berti, No. 2), and one from Monferrato (Comparetti, No. 13). In one of the Sicilian versions (Pitrè, No. 159), and in the other two from Bologna and Monferrato, the thieves are two friends. In the other Sicilian version they are a father and son. We give a translation of the last named version, which is called:

↬ XLIV. The Mason and His Son ↫

There was once a mason who had a wife and son. One day the king sent for the mason to build a country-house in which to put his money, for he was very rich and had no place to keep it. The mason set to work with his son. In one corner they put in a stone that could be taken out and put back, large enough for a man to enter. When the house was finished the king paid them and they went home. The king then had his money carted to the house and put guards around it. After a few days he saw that no one went there and took away the guard. Let us leave the king, who took away the guard, and return to the mason. When his money was gone he said to his son: "Shall we go to the country-house?" They took a sack and went there. When they arrived at the house they took out the stone and the father entered and filled the bag with gold. When he came out he put the stone back as it was before and they departed. The next day the king rode out to his house and saw that his pile of gold had diminished. He said to his servants: "Who has been taking the money?" The servants answered: "It is not possible, your Majesty; for who comes here; where could they get in? It may be that the house has settled, being newly built." So they took and repaired it. After a while the mason said again to his son: "Let us go back there." They took the accustomed sack and went there, arriving as usual they took out the stone and the father entered, filled the sack, and they departed. The same night they made another trip, filled the same sack again, and went away. The next day the king visited the house with his soldiers and councilors. When he entered he went to see the money and it was very greatly diminished; he turned to his councilors and said: "Some one comes here and takes the money." The councilors said: "But, your Majesty, while you are saying so, one thing can be done; take a few tubs, fill them with melted pitch, and place them around the walls on the inside, whoever enters will fall in them, and the thief is found."

They took the tubs and put them inside, and the king left sentinels and returned to the city. The sentinels remained there a week; but as they saw no one, they, too, left.

Let us leave the sentinels, who have departed, and return to the mason. He said to his son: "Let us go to the accustomed place." They took the sack and went. Arriving there, they took out the stone, and the father entered. As he entered he stuck fast in the pitch. He tried to help himself and get his feet loose, but his hands stuck fast. Then he said to his son: "Do you hear what I tell you, my son? Cut off my head, tear my coat to pieces, put back the stone as it was, and throw my head in the river, so that I shall not be known." The son did as he was told, and returned home. When he told his mother what had become of his father, she began to tear her hair. After a few days, the son, who did not know any trade, entered the service of a carpenter, and told his mother not to say anything, as if nothing had happened.

Let us leave these and return to the king, who went the next day with his councilors to the country-house. They entered and saw the body, and the king said: "But it has no head! How shall we find out who it is?" The councilors said: "Take him and carry him through the streets three days; where you see weeping you will know who it is." They took the body, and called Filippu Carruba and Brasi Vuturu,* and made them carry it about. When they passed through the street where the mason's widow lived, she began to weep. The son, whose shop was near by, heard it, and gave himself a blow in the hand with an axe and cut off his fingers. The police arrested the mother, saying: "We have found out who it is." Meanwhile the son arrived there and said: "She is not weeping for that; she is weeping because I have cut off my fingers and can no longer work and earn my bread." The police saw it was so, believed him, and departed. At night they carried the body to the palace and built outside a scaffold to put the body on, because they had to carry it around three days. About the scaffold they placed nine sentinels—eight soldiers and a corporal. Now it was in the winter and was very cold; so the son took a mule and loaded it with drugged wine, and passed up and down. When the soldiers saw him they cried: "Friend, are you selling that wine?" He said: "I am." "Wait until we drink, for we are trembling with the cold." After they had drunk they threw themselves down and went to sleep, and the son took the body, and, after he had buried it outside of the town, returned home.

[In the morning the soldiers awoke and told the king what had happened, and he issued a proclamation that whoever found the body should receive a large sum of money. The body was found and carried about the street again, but no one wept. That night new sentinels were appointed, but the same thing happened as the night before. The soldiers were drugged and dressed in monks' robes, and the corporal had a cross stuck between his legs. The next day another proclamation, the body again found and carried about, but no one detected weeping. The story then continues:]

The mason's son (here called for the first time Ninu) could not rest, and went to Cianedda,** "Will you do me a favor?" "If I can," answered Cianedda; "Not one, but two. What can I do for you?" "Will you lend me your goats this evening?" "I will." Ninu took them, bought four *rotula*† of candles and an old earthen pot, knocked out the bottom and fastened some candles around it. Then he took the goats and fixed two candles to the horns of each one and took them where the body was, and followed with the pot on his head and the candles lighted. The

* Names of two undertakers in Salaparuta, where the story was collected.
** The name of a goatherd in Salaparuta.
† A *rotulu* = .793 kilos.

soldiers ran away in terror, and the son took the body and threw it in the sea.

[The next day the king commanded that the price of meat should be set at twelve *tari** a *rotulu,* and ordered that all the old women of the city should assemble at the palace. A hundred came, and he told them to go begging about the city and find out who was cooking meat; thinking that only the thief could afford to buy meat at that price. Ninu, of course, bought some and gave it to his mother to cook. While it was cooking, and Ninu absent, one of the old women came begging, and the widow gave her a piece of meat. As she was going down-stairs Ninu met her and asked her what she was doing. She explained that she was begging for some bread. Ninu, suspecting the trick, took her and threw her into the well.]

At noon, when the old women were to present themselves to the king, one was missing. The king then sent for the butchers, and found that just one *rotulu* of meat had been sold. When the king saw this, he issued a proclamation to find out who had done all these wonders, and said: "If he is unmarried, I will give him my daughter; if he is married, I will give him two measures of gold." Ninu presented himself to the king and said: "Your Majesty, it was I." The king burst out laughing, and asked: "Are you married or single?" He said: "Your Majesty, I am single." And the king said: "Will you be satisfied with my daughter, or with two measures of gold?" "Your Majesty," he said, "I want to marry; give me your daughter." So he did, and they had a grand banquet.[30]

THE STORY in The Seven Wise Masters, known as "*Inclusa,*" or "The Elopement," is found only in Pitrè (No. 176), where it is told of a tailor who lived next to the king's palace, with which his house communicated by a secret door known only to the king and the tailor's wife. The tailor, while at work in the palace, imagines he sees his wife there, and pretending that he has forgotten his shears, etc., rushes home to find his wife there. She finally elopes with the king, leaving at her window an image that deceives her husband until she is beyond pursuit.[31]

Far more curious than any of the stories above given is the last one we shall mention from The Seven Wise Masters. The story in this collection known as "*Avis,*" or "The Talking Bird," is briefly as follows: A jealous husband has a talking bird that is a spy upon his wife's actions. In order to impair his confidence in the bird, one night while he is absent the wife

* Frs. 5.10.

orders a servant to shower water over the bird's cage, to make a heavy sound like thunder, and to imitate the flashing of lightning with candles. The bird, on its master's return, tells him of the terrific storm the night before, and is killed for its supposed falsehood. This story is found in both the Eastern and Western versions of The Seven Wise Masters, and practically constitutes the framework of another famous Oriental collection, the Çukasaptati (from *çuka*, a parrot, and *saptati*, seventy, The Seventy Tales of a Parrot), better known by its Persian and Turkish name, Tûtî-Nâmeh, Tales of a Parrot.[32] The frame, or groundwork, of the various Oriental versions is substantially the same. A husband is obliged to leave home on business, and while he is absent his wife engages in a love affair with a stranger. A parrot, which the husband has left behind, prevents the wife meeting her lover by telling her stories which interest her so much that she keeps putting off her appointment until her husband returns. In the Turkish version the parrot reconciles the husband and wife; in the Persian versions the parrot relates what has happened, and the faithless wife is killed.

The Italian versions, as will soon be seen, are not derived from The Seven Wise Masters, but from the Çukasaptati; and what is very curious, the framework has been retained and filled with stories that are not in the original.[33] The most simple version is from Pisa (Comparetti, No. I), and is called:

✢ XLV. The Parrot (FIRST VERSION) ✢

There was once a merchant who had a beautiful daughter, with whom the king and the viceroy were both in love. The former knew that the merchant would soon have to depart on business, and he would then have a chance to speak with the girl. The viceroy knew it, too, and pondered on how he could prevent the king succeeding in his plan. He was acquainted with a witch, and promised her immunity and a large sum of money if she would teach him how to change himself into a parrot. This she did, and of course the merchant bought him for his daughter, and departed.

When the parrot thought it was about time for the king to come, he said to the girl: "Now, to amuse you, I will tell you a story; but you must attend to me and not see any one while I am telling it." Then he began his story, and after he had gone a little way in it a servant entered and told her mistress that there was a letter for her. "Tell her to bring it later," said the parrot, "and now listen to me." "I do not receive letters while my father is away," said the mistress, and the parrot continued. After a while another interruption. A servant announces the visit of an aunt. (It was not an aunt, but a woman who came from the king.) The parrot said: "Do not receive her; we are in the finest part of our story," and the young girl sent word that she did not receive any visits while her father was absent, and the parrot went on. When his story was ended the girl was so pleased that she would listen to no one else until her father returned. Then the parrot disappeared, and the viceroy visited the merchant and asked his daughter's hand. He consented, and the marriage took place that very day. The wedding was scarcely over when a gentleman came to ask the girl's hand for the king; but it was too late, and the poor king, who was much in love with her, died of a broken heart, and the girl remained the wife of the viceroy, who had been more cunning than the king.

WE HAVE omitted the story told by the parrot because we shall meet it again in the Sicilian version, and substantially in the following version from Florence, which we give entire on account of the rarity of the work in which it is found, and for its own merits.[34] It is also entitled:

∾ XLVI. The Parrot (SECOND VERSION) ∾

Once upon a time there was a merchant who, having to go on a journey, gave his wife a parrot to amuse her in her loneliness. The wife, vexed that her husband should leave her so soon, threw the bird in a corner and thought no more about it. At evening she went to the window and saw pass a young man, who fell in love with her as soon as he saw her. On the first floor there lived a woman who sold coals, and the young man began to tempt her to help him in his love affair. She would not promise, because the merchant's wife had been married but a few days, and was an honest woman. She added, however, that there was a way; her daughter was to be married shortly, she would invite the young wife to the wedding, and the young man, being there too, could manage the rest. The wife accepted the invitation, dressed herself in her finest clothes, and was on the point of leaving when the parrot cried from its corner: "O mistress, where are you going? I wished to tell you a story; but suit yourself." The wife then dismissed the coal-woman, who, not to spoil matters, promised to put off the wedding and return for her the next day. Then the parrot began:

"Once upon a time there was a king's son whose master was so learned in magic that with certain words he could change himself into various animals. The prince wanted to learn these words, too; but the magician hesitated and refused, although he had to yield at last. Then the prince became a crow and flew far away to a distant country and into the garden of a king, where he saw a beautiful girl with a mirror in which was set her portrait. The crow in wonder snatched the glass from her hands, and flew home and resumed his own form, but he fell so deeply in love with the unknown girl that he became ill.

"She, meanwhile, who was the daughter of a king, seeing the glass taken from her, no longer had any peace of mind, and begged her father until he gave her permission to go in search of it. She dressed herself like a physician and departed. She came to a city and heard a proclamation by the king, that whatever physician should pass that way should be obliged to visit and try to cure his daughter. Then the new physician had to go to the palace, but she could not discover any remedy for the grave disease. At night, while sitting by the princess' bed, the light went out, and she left the room to light it, and saw in a little cottage three old women sitting around a cauldron boiling over a great fire. 'Good women, are you washing?' 'What a washing! These are three heads, and when they are cooked the princess will die.' 'Bravo, my good women; bring the wood and I will help, too.' She remained there some time and promised to return. The brighter the fire burned, the nearer the princess came to death. The physician consoled the king and had a fine supper prepared. The second night she carried food and a great deal of wine to the old women, and when they were drunk threw them into the fire and lifted off the cauldron with the boiling heads. The princess recovered and the king wished to give her to the physician and reward him with gems and gold, but the physician would take nothing, and departed."

"You know, mistress, it is late and I am tired," interrupted the parrot; "I will tell you the rest to-morrow."

The next day the woman who sold coals came again, and the merchant's wife was on the point of accompanying her; but the parrot detained her, promising to finish the story. So the woman went away in anger, and the parrot continued:

"The princess disguised as a physician journeyed until she came to another city, and heard a proclamation by the king, that every physician who passed that way should be forced to visit and attempt to cure his son.

The new physician, too, had to go to court; but could find no remedy for the severe disease. At night, while sitting at the bedside of the prince, she heard a loud noise in the next room: went to the door and saw three old women, who were preparing a banquet. Afterwards they approached the invalid, anointed him from head to foot, and carried him healed to the table; then when they were full of wine and merry, they anointed him again and replaced him on his bed worse than before. The physician comforted the king, and the second night allowed the witches to take the prince to the table, then appeared and frightening the old women with threats of the king's anger drove them from the room and restored the son to his father. The king, well pleased, wished to recompense the physician, who would take nothing, and departed."

"But you know, mistress, it is late and I am weary. I will tell you the rest to-morrow."

The next day the woman who sold coals returned, and the merchant's wife was on the point of following her; but the parrot detained her, promising to finish the story. The woman went away angry, and the parrot continued:

"After a long journey the princess disguised as a physician came to another city, and heard a proclamation by the king, that every physician who passed that way should be compelled to visit and attempt to cure his son. The new physician, too, had to go to court; but she could find no remedy for the severe disease. The prince would speak to no one, but the physician at last made the invalid disclose the secret of his heart, and he told of the mirror and showed the portrait of the unknown lady whom he loved desperately. The physician consoled the king; had garments and ornaments exactly like those of the young girl in the glass prepared; dressed in them, and as she appeared before the prince he leaped from his bed, embracing his betrothed in the midst of rejoicings."

But here the lady hears her husband arriving. Joy makes her beside herself; and she throws from the window the poor parrot, which now seems to her only a tiresome companion. The merchant enters and inquires about the bird; sees the parrot hurt upon the neighboring roof and picks it up kindly. The parrot narrates to him the wiles of the coal-woman and its own prudence; assures the husband that his wife is innocent; but complains of her being so ungrateful; she had promised him a gold vase, and now treats him thus. The merchant consoles the dying bird, and afterwards has him embalmed and placed in the gold vase. As for his wife, he loved her more than ever.

ANOTHER version from Piedmont (Comparetti, No. 2; De Gub. Zoöl. Myth. II. 322) differs materially from the ones just given. A king is obliged to go to war and leave behind him his wife, with whom another king is in love. Before parting he forbids his wife to leave the palace during his absence, and presents her with a parrot. No sooner has the king departed than his rival attempts to obtain an interview with the queen by giving a feast and inviting her to it. The parrot prevents her going by relating the story contained in the first version. They are interrupted in the same manner by an old woman sent by the lover, but to no purpose. When the story is finished, the husband returns, and the parrot becomes a young man, whom the king had engaged to watch over his wife's fidelity.

The Sicilian version of our story is the most interesting as well as the most complete of all; the single story in the continental versions has been expanded into three, and the frame is more artistic. The story is the second in Pitrè, and is as follows:

↝ XLVII. The Parrot Which Tells Three Stories (THIRD VERSION) ↝

Once upon a time there was a rich merchant who wanted to marry, and who happened to find a wife as good as the day was long, and who loved her husband desperately. One day she saw him a little annoyed, and said: "What makes you feel so?" "What should make me feel so! I have important business to attend to, and must go and see to it on the spot." "And are you annoyed about that? Let us arrange matters thus: you will leave me provisions and close up all the doors and windows but one high up; make me a wicket, and then depart." "The advice pleases me," said her husband, and he laid in at once a large provision of bread, flour, oil, coals, and everything; had all the doors and windows closed up but one, to take the air, had a wicket made like those in the convents, and departed, and the wife remained with her maid. The next day a servant called at the wicket to do what was necessary and then went away. After ten days the lady began to be oppressed, and had a great mind to cry. The maid said: "There is a remedy for everything, my mistress; let us draw the table up to the window, and climb up and enjoy the sight of the Corso." They did so, and the lady looked out. "Ah! I thank you, sirs!" As she uttered the ah! opposite her was a notary's office, and there were the notary and a cavalier. They turned and saw this beautiful young woman. "Oh! What a handsome woman! I must speak with her!" said the cavalier. "No: I will speak first," said the notary. And "I first," and "I first." They laid a wager of four hundred ounces as to who would speak with her first. The lady perceived them and withdrew from the window.

The notary and the cavalier thought about the bet, and had no rest running here and there and trying to speak with the lady. At last the notary in despair went out into the fields and began to call his demon. The demon appeared and the notary told him everything, saying: "And this cavalier wishes to have the advantage of speaking with the lady first." "What will you give me?" said the demon. "My soul." "Then see what you have to do; I will change you into a parrot and you must fly and alight on the window of the lady. The maid will take you and have a silver cage made for you and put you in it. The cavalier will find an old woman who is able to make the lady leave the house. But she will not make her leave, you know. You must say: 'My pretty mamma, sit down while I tell you a story.' The old woman will come thrice; you must tear out your feathers and fly into a passion and say always: 'My pretty mamma, don't go with that old woman, she will betray you; sit down while I tell you a story.' And then tell her any story you wish."

The demon ended with: "Man you are, become a parrot!" And the parrot flew away to the window. The maid saw it and caught it with her handkerchief. When the lady saw the parrot she said: "How beautiful you are! Now you will be my consolation." "Yes, pretty mamma, I will love you, too." The lady had a silver cage made, and shut the parrot up in it.

Let us leave the parrot in the cage, and return to the cavalier, who was making desperate efforts to see the lady. An old woman met him, and asked him what the matter was. "Must I tell you what the matter is?" and dismissed her; but the old woman was persistent. At last to get rid of her he told her all about the wager. The old woman said: "I am able to make you speak with the lady. You must have prepared for me two handsome baskets of early fruit." The cavalier was so anxious to see the lady that he had the baskets of early fruit prepared and given to her. With these things the old woman went to the wicket, pretending that she was the lady's grandmother. The lady believed her. One word brings on another. "Tell me, my granddaughter, you are always shut up, but don't you hear mass Sundays?" "How could I hear it shut up?" "Ah, my daughter, you will be damned. No, this is not well. You must hear mass Sundays. To-day is a feast day; let us go to mass."

While the lady was being persuaded, the parrot began to lament. When its mistress opened the clothespress, the parrot said: "My pretty mamma, don't go, for the old woman will betray you. If you don't go I will tell you a story." The lady took an idea into her head. "Now, my grand-mother," she said, "go away, for I cannot come." And the old woman went away. When she had gone, the lady went to the parrot, which related to her this story:

↝ First Story of the Parrot ↝

Once upon a time there was a king who had an only daughter, who was very fond of dolls, and had one that was her delight. She dressed her and undressed her and put her to bed, in short did for her what is done for children. One day the king wished to go into the country, and the princess wished to take the doll. While they were walking about, in a moment of forgetfulness, she left her doll on a hedge. It was meal time, and after they had eaten they got into the carriage and returned to the royal palace. What do you suppose the princess forgot? The doll!

As soon as they arrived at the palace the princess remembered the doll. What did she do? Instead of going up-stairs, she turned round and went to look for the doll. When she got outdoors, she became lost and wandered about like a person bereft of her senses. After a time she came to a royal palace and asked who was the king of that palace. "The King of Spain," they said. She asked for a lodging. She entered; the king gave her lodging and treated her like a daughter. She made herself at home in the palace and began to be the mistress. The king had no daughters and gave her liberty to do as she pleased in spite of twelve royal damsels. Now, as there is envy among equals, the damsels began to oppose her. Said they: "Just see! Who knows who she is? And is she to be our princess? Now this thing must stop!" The next day they said to the princess: "Will you come with us?" "No, because papa does not wish it. If he is willing, I will come." "Do you know what you must do to make him let you come? Tell him: 'By the soul of his daughter he must let you go.' When he hears that, he will let you go at once." The princess did so, but when the king heard her say: "By the soul of his daughter!" "Ah! Wretch," exclaimed the king; "Quick, throw her down the trap-door!" When the princess fell down the trap-door she found a door, then another, and another, always feeling her way along. At a certain point she felt with her hands like the blind, and found tinder and matches. She then lighted a candle which she found there, and saw a beautiful young girl, with a padlock on her mouth, so that she could not speak, but she made signs that the key to open it with was under the pillow of the bed. The princess got it and opened the padlock; then the young girl spoke, and said that she was the daughter of the king whom a magician had stolen. This magician brought her, every day, something to eat, and then locked up her mouth, and she had to wait until the next day to open it again. "But tell me," said the princess, "what way is there to free you?" "How do I know? I can do nothing but ask the magician when he opens my mouth; you hide under the bed and listen, and afterwards think what has to be done." "Good! Good!" The princess locked her mouth, put the key under the pillow, and crawled under the bed. But at midnight a great noise was heard; the earth opened, lightning, smoke, and smell of sulphur, and the magician appeared in a magician's robe. With the magician was a giant with a bowl of food, and two servants with two torches. The magician sent away the servants, and locked the doors, took the key, and opened the mouth of the king's daughter. While they were eating, she said: "Magician, I have a thought: out of curiosity I would like to know what it would be necessary for me to do to escape from here." "You want to know a great deal, my daughter!" "Never mind, I don't care to know." "However, I will tell you. It would be necessary to make a mine all around the palace, and precisely at midnight, when I am on the point of entering, to explode the mine: you will find yourself with your father, and I will fly up in the air." "It's as if you had not told any one," said the young girl. The magician dressed himself and went away. After a few hours the princess came out from under the bed, took leave of her little sister, for she already called her "little sister," and departed.

She went back to the trap-door and, at a certain point, stopped and called for help. The king heard her, and had a rope lowered. The princess climbed up and related everything to the king. He was astounded, and began the mine, which he had filled with shot, powder, and balls. When it was full to the brim, the princess descended with a watch and went to the king's daughter: "Either both dead, or both alive!" When she entered the room, she said: "It is I," took the lock from her mouth, talked with her, and then concealed herself under the bed. At midnight the magician came, and the king was on the lookout, with his watch in his hand. As the clock struck twelve, the princess fired the mine: boom! And a great noise was heard: the magician vanished, and the two young girls found themselves free and in each other's arms. When the king saw them, he exclaimed: "Ah! My daughters! Your misfortune was your good fortune. My crown belongs to you," said he to the princess whom he had adopted. "No, your Majesty, for I am a king's daughter, and I, too, have a crown."

This matter spread over the world, and her fame passed through all the kingdoms, and every one talked of nothing but the great courage and goodness of this princess who had delivered the other princess from the magician. And they remained happy and always enjoyed holy peace.

"What do you think, pretty mamma, of this story?" "It is very fine," said the lady to the parrot.

A week passed after the story; the old woman again came with two other baskets of fruit to her granddaughter: "Pretty idea!" said the parrot, "Take care, pretty mamma; the old woman is coming." The old woman said: "Come, my daughter, are you going to mass?" "Yes, my grandmother;" and the lady began dressing herself. When the parrot saw her dressing herself it began to tear out its feathers and weep: "No, pretty mamma, don't go to mass; that old woman will ruin you. If you will stay with me, I will tell you another story." "Now go away," said the lady to the old woman, "for I cannot kill my dear little parrot, for the sake of the mass." "Ah! Wicked woman! To lose your soul for an animal!" The old woman went away and the parrot told this story:

ᖇ Second Story of the Parrot ᖇ

Well then, my lady, there was once upon a time a king who had an only daughter as beautiful as the sun and moon. When she was eighteen a Turkish king wished to marry her. When she heard that it was a Turkish king she said: "What do I want of Turks!" and refused him. Shortly after she became very ill, convulsions, twisting of the body, rolling of her eyes to the back of her head, and the doctors did not know what was the matter. The poor father in confusion called his council together, and said: "Gentlemen, my daughter is losing ground every day; what advice do you give me?" The sages said: "Your Majesty, there is a young girl who found the daughter of the King of Spain; * find her and she will tell you what must be done for your daughter." "Bravo! The council has been favorable." The king ordered vessels to go for this young girl: "And if the King of Spain will not let her go, give him this iron glove and declare war!" The vessels departed and reached Spain one morning. They fired a salute, the ambassador landed, presented himself to the king, and gave him a sealed letter. The king opened it and after reading it began to weep and said: "I prefer war, and I will not give up this girl." Meanwhile the girl entered: "What is the matter, your Majesty? (and she saw the letter). What are you afraid of? I will go at once to this king." "How, my daughter, will you then leave me thus?" "I will return. I will go and see what is the matter with this young girl and then come back."

She took leave of her half-sister and departed. When she arrived the king went to meet her: "My daughter, if you cure this sick daughter of mine, I will give you my crown!" "That makes two crowns!" she said to herself. "I have a crown, your Majesty. Let us see what the matter is, and never mind the crowns." She went and saw the princess all wasted away. She turned to the king and said: "Your Majesty! Have some broth and substantial things made," and they were prepared at once. "I am going to shut myself up with your daughter, and you must not open the door, for in three days I will give her to you alive or dead. And listen to what I say: even if I should knock you must not open." Everything was arranged and the door was fastened with chains and padlocks, but they forgot the tinder to light the candle with at night. In the evening there was great confusion. The young girl did not wish to knock, and as she looked out of the window she saw a light at a distance. So she descended by a ladder of silk, taking with her a candle. When she drew near the light she saw a large cauldron placed on some stones and a furnace under it, and a Turk who was stirring it with a stick. "What are you doing, Turk?" "My king wanted the daughter of the king, she did not want him, he is bewitching her," "My poor little Turk! You are tired, are you not? Do you know what you must do? Rest yourself a little while I stir." "I will, by Mahomet!" He got down; she got up and began to stir with the stick. "Am I doing it all right thus?" "Yes, by Mahomet." "Well then, you take a nap, and I will stir." When he was asleep, she came down, seized him, and threw him into the boiling cauldron, where he died. When she saw that he was dead, she lighted her candle and returned to the palace. She entered the room and

* The princess of the last story.

found the invalid had fainted on the floor. She brought her to with cologne water (*acqua d' oduri*) and in three days she had recovered. Then she knocked at the door and the king entered, beside himself at finding his daughter cured. "Ah! My daughter," he said to the young girl who had healed her, "How much we owe you! You must remain here with me." "It is impossible; you threatened my father with war if he did not allow me to come; now my father declares war with you if you do not let me return to him." She remained there a fortnight, then departed, and the king gave her quantities of riches and jewels. She returned to the king of Spain's palace.

And so the story ends.

"What did you think of the story, pretty mamma?" said the parrot. "Beautiful, beautiful." "But you must not go with the old woman, because there is treason."

After a week the old woman came with her baskets. "My daughter, you must do me this pleasure to-day, come and hear the holy mass." "I will." When the parrot heard that, he began to weep and tear out his feathers: "No, my pretty mamma, don't go with the old woman. If you will stay, I will tell you another story." "Grandmother mine," says she, "I can't come, for I don't wish to lose the parrot for your sake." She closed the wicket and the old woman went away grumbling and cursing. The lady then seated herself near the parrot, which told this story:

﹌ Third Story of the Parrot ﹌

Once upon a time there was a king and a queen who had an only son, whose sole diversion was the chase. Once he wished to go hunting at a distance, and took with him his attendants. Where do you think he happened to go? To the country where the doll was.* When he saw the doll he said: "I have finished my hunt, let us return home!" He took the doll and placed it before him on the horse, and exclaimed every few minutes: "How beautiful this doll is! Think of its mistress!" When he reached the palace he had a glass case made in the wall, and put the doll in it, and kept looking at it continually and saying: "How beautiful the doll is! Think of the mistress!"

The young man would not see any one and became so melancholy that his father summoned the physicians, who said: "Your Majesty, we know

* The doll of the first story.

nothing of this illness; see what he does with his doll." The king went to see his son and found him gazing at the doll, and exclaiming: "Oh! How beautiful the doll is! Think of the mistress!" The physicians departed as wise as when they came. The prince meanwhile did nothing but sit and look at the doll, and draw deep breaths, and sigh, and exclaim: "How beautiful the doll is! Think of the mistress!" The king at last, in despair, summoned his council, and said: "See how my son is reduced! He has no fever, or pain in his head, but he is wasting away, and some one else will enjoy my kingdom! Give me advice." "Majesty, are you perplexed? Is there not that young girl who found the King of Spain's daughter, and cured the other princess? Send for her. If her father will not let her come, declare war with him."

The king sent his ambassadors with the message that the young girl should be sent *nolens volens*. While the ambassadors were in the king's presence, his daughter entered, the one who had done the wonders, and found her father perplexed: "What is the matter, your Majesty?" "Nothing, my daughter. Another occasion has arrived, another king wants you. Does he mean that I am no longer your master?" "Never mind, your Majesty; let me go; I will soon return."

So she embarked with all her attendants and began her journey. When she arrived where the prince was, she saw him drawing such deep breaths that it seemed as if he would swallow himself, and always exclaiming: "Oh! How beautiful the doll is! Think of the mistress!" She said: "You have called me none too soon! However, give me a week: bring me ointments, food, and in a week, alive and well, or dead."

She shut herself up with him and listened to hear what the prince said, for she had not yet heard what he was saying, he was so feeble. When she heard him whisper: "Oh! How be-au-ti-ful is the doll, consider," and saw the doll, she cried: "Ah! Wretch! It was you who had my doll! Leave it to me, I will cure you." When he heard these words he came to himself and said: "Are you the doll's mistress?" "I am." Just think! He returned to life and she began to give him broth until she had restored him. When he was restored she said: "Now tell me how you got the doll," and the prince told her everything. To make the matter short, in a week the prince was cured, and they declared that they would marry each other. The king, beside himself with joy because his son was healed, wrote several letters: one to the King of Spain to tell him that his daughter had found her doll, another to the other king, her father, to tell him that his daughter was found, and another to the king whose daughter she had cured. Afterwards all these monarchs came together and made great festivals, and the prince married the princess, and they lived together in great peace.

"Has this story pleased you, pretty mamma?" "Yes, my son." "But you must not go with the old woman, you know."

After the story was ended a servant came: "My lady, my lady, the master is coming!" "Truly!" said the lady. "Now, parrot, listen; I will have a new cage made for you." The master arrived, the windows were all opened, and he embraced his wife. At dinner they placed the parrot in the middle of the table, and when the joy was at its height the bird threw some soup in its master's eyes. The master, when he felt it, put his hands to his eyes, and the parrot darted at his throat, strangled him, and flew away.

He flew away to the country, and saying, "I am a parrot, and I become a man," he was changed into a handsome, cunning, and well-kempt man on the Corso. He met the cavalier: "Do you know," said this one, "that the poor lady's husband is dead? A parrot strangled him!" "Truly? Poor woman! Poor woman!" said the notary, and went his way without speaking of the wager. The notary learned that the lady had a mother, and went to her to ask her daughter in marriage. After hesitating, the lady finally said yes, and they were married. That evening the notary said to the lady: "Now tell me, who killed your husband?" "A parrot." "And what about this parrot?" The lady told him everything to where the parrot dashed the broth in its master's eyes, and then flew away. "True! True!" said the notary. "Was I not the parrot?" "It was you! I am amazed." "It was I, and I became a parrot for your sake!"

The next day the notary went to the cavalier to get the four hundred ounces of the wager, which he enjoyed with his wife.

THE THREE stories related by the parrot are, as has been seen, in reality one story, and they are, in fact found as such independent of the frame.[35] It has also been seen that the story or stories related by the parrot are, substantially, the same in all the versions. The Florentine version alone does not contain the episode of the doll. The story, as a whole, has no parallels, although it bears a slight resemblance to the story in the Pentamerone (II. 2), "Green Meadow." The princess as physician, and the seeret malady of the prince or princess, are traits which abound in all the popular tales of Europe.[36]

Many single stories of Oriental origin will be found in the chapters following. We shall close this one with a story which was popular in Europe during the Middle Ages, being found in one of the great collections of that period, the Gesta Romanorum. Of the various Italian versions we shall select one from Pomigliano d'Areo called:

ᕭ *XLVIII. Truthful Joseph* ᕬ

One time there was a mother who had a son named Joseph; and because he never told a lie she called him Truthful Joseph. One day when she was calling him, the king happened to pass by, and hearing her call him thus, asked her: "Why do you call him Truthful Joseph?" "Because he never tells a lie." Then the king said that he would like to have him in his service, and set him to keeping his cows. Every morning Joseph presented himself to the king, and said: "Your Majesty's servant." The king answered: "Good morning, Truthful Joseph. How are the cows?" "Well and fat." "How are the calves?" "Well and handsome." "How is the bull?" "The same." So he did every morning. The king praised him so highly in the presence of all his courtiers that they became angry at him; and one day, to make Joseph a liar, they sent to him a lady, who was to induce him by her words to kill the bull. Joseph was urged so strongly that he consented; but afterwards he was in great perplexity as to what he should tell the king. So he put his cloak on a chair and pretended that it was the king, and said: "Your Majesty's servant. Good morning, Truthful Joseph. How are the cows? Well and fat. How are the calves? Well and handsome. How is the bull ? The same. But no; that will not do! I am telling a lie! When the king asks me how the bull is, I will tell him that it is dead."

He presented himself to the king and said: "Your Majesty's servant." "Good morning, Truthful Joseph. How are the cows?" "Well and fat." "How are the calves?" "Well and handsome." "How is the bull?" "Your Majesty, a lady came and with her manners made me kill the bull. Pardon me." The king answered:

"Bravo, Truthful Joseph!" He summoned his courtiers and showed them that Joseph had not yet told any lie. And so Joseph remained always with the king, and the courtiers were duped, because they gained nothing that they had expected.[37]

CHAPTER IV

ॐ

LEGENDS AND GHOST STORIES

THE ITALIAN people possess an inexhaustible store of legends which they have inherited from the Middle Ages. With the great mass of these stories—legends of the saints or local legends—we have at present nothing to do. It is enough to say that they do not differ materially from the legends of the other Catholic peoples of Europe. The class to which we shall devote our attention in this chapter is that of popular legendary stories which have clustered around the person of our Lord and his disciples, and around other favorite characters of mediaeval fancy, such as Pilate, The Wandering Jew, etc. To these may be added tales relating to the other world and stories which are of a legendary nature. The first stories which we shall mention are those referring to mythical journeys of our Lord and his apostles.

The first, "St. Peter and the Robbers" (Pitrè, No. 121), relates that once while the Master was journeying with the apostles they found themselves at night out in the fields, and took shelter in a cabin belonging to some shepherds, who received them very inhospitably and gave them nothing to eat. Soon after, a band of robbers attacked the flock and robbed the shepherds, who ran away. The robbers came to the cabin, and when they heard from the apostles how shabbily they had been treated, gave them the supper that the shepherds had prepared for themselves, and went their way. "Blessed be the robbers!" said St. Peter, "for they treat the hungry poor better than the rich do." "Blessed be the robbers!" said the apostles, and ate their fill.

This story, as can easily be seen, is a tradition of the robbers who pretend to have been blessed by Christ. St. Peter is the hero of several stories, in which he plays anything but a dignified rôle. In one (Pitrè, No. 122), he is sent to buy some wine, and allows himself to be persuaded by the wine merchant to eat some fennel-seed. After this he cannot distinguish between good and bad wine, and purchases an inferior kind. When the Master tasted it he said: "Eh! Peter! Peter! You have let yourself be deceived."* Peter tasted it again and saw that it was sour. Another apostle was sent to get some good wine, and "hence it is that when you have to taste wine to see whether it is good, you must not eat fennel-seed."

L. The Lord, St. Peter, and the Apostles

Once, while the Master was on a journey with the thirteen apostles, they came to a village where there was no bread. The Master said: "Peter, let each one of you carry a stone." They each took up a stone—St. Peter a little bit of a one. The others were all loaded down, but St. Peter went along very easily. The Master said: "Now let us go to another village. If there is any bread there, we shall buy it; if there is none, I will give you my blessing and the stones will become bread."

They went to another town, put the stones down, and rested. The Master gave them his blessing, and the stones became bread. St. Peter, who had carried a little one, felt his heart grow faint. "Master," he said, "how am I going to eat?" "Eh! My brother, why did you carry a little stone? The others, who loaded themselves down, have bread enough."

Then they went on, and the Master made them each carry another stone. St. Peter was cunning this time and took a large one and all the others carried small ones. The Lord said to the others: "Little ones, we will have a laugh at Peter's expense." They arrived at another village, and all the apostles threw away their stones because there was bread there; and St. Peter was bent double, for he had carried a paving-stone with him to no purpose.

On their journey they met a man; and as St. Peter was in advance of the others, he said: "The Lord is coming shortly; ask Him a favor for your soul." The man drew near and said: "Lord, my father is ill with old age. Cure him, Master." The Lord said: "Am I a physician? Do you know what you must do? Put him in a hot oven and your father will become a boy again." They did so, and his father became a little boy.

The idea pleased St. Peter, and when he found himself alone he went about seeking to make some old men young. By chance there met him one who was seeking the Master because his mother was at the point of

---

*This story is an attempt to explain the origin of the word *'nfinucchiari (infinocchiare)* to impose on one, by the word *finocchio,* fennel-seed.

death and he wanted her cured. St. Peter said: "What do you want?" "I want the Master, for I have an old mother who is very ill, and the Master alone can cure her." "Fortunately Peter is here! Do you know what you must do? Heat an oven and put her in it, and she will be cured." The poor man believed him, for he knew that the Lord loved St. Peter, so he went home and immediately put his mother in the hot oven. What more could you expect? The old woman was burned to a coal. "Ah! *Santu di ccà e di ddà!*"* cried the son; "that scurvy fellow has made me kill my mother!" He hastened to St. Peter. The Master was present, and when he heard the story could not control his laughter, and said: "Ah, Peter! what have you done?" St. Peter tried to excuse himself, but the poor man kept crying for his mother. What must the Master do? He had to go to the house of the dead, and with a blessing which he there pronounced he brought the old woman to life again, a beautiful young girl, and relieved St. Peter of his great embarrassment.

THE LAST anecdote is quite popular, and is found in a number of popular stories, as well as in the *Cento Novelle Antiche.*[1] A very amusing version is from Venice (Widter-Wolf, No. 5), and is entitled:

❧ LI. The Lord, St. Peter, and the Blacksmith ❧

In a little town about as large as Sehio or Thiene once lived a mastersmith,—a good, industrious, and skilful man, but so proud of his skill that he would not deign to reply to any one who did not address him as "Professor." This pride in a man otherwise so blameless gave universal dissatisfaction. One day our Lord appeared in the blacksmith's shop, accompanied by St. Peter, whom He was always in the habit of taking with Him on such excursions. "Professor," said the Lord, "will you be so good as to permit me to do a little work at your forge?" "Why not? It is at your service," replied the flattered smith. "What do you wish to make?" "That you will soon see," said the Lord, and took up a pair of tongs, with which he seized Peter and held him in the forge until he was red-hot. Then he drew him out and hammered him on all sides, and in less than ten minutes the old bald-headed apostle was forged anew into a wonderfully handsome youth with beautiful hair. The

---

*This is the strongest imprecation in Sicily.

blacksmith stood speechless with astonishment, while the Lord and St. Peter exchanged the most courteous thanks and compliments. Finally the master-smith recovered himself and ran straight up to the second story, where his sick old father lay in bed. "Father," he cried, "come quickly! I have just learned how to make a strong young man of you." "My son, have you lost your senses?" said the old man, half terrified. "No; only believe me. I have just seen it myself." Finding that the old man protested against the attempt, his son seized him forcibly, carried him to the shop, and in spite of his shrieks and entreaties, thrust him into the forge, but brought nothing out but a piece of charred leg, which fell to pieces at the first blow of the hammer. Then he was seized with anguish and remorse. He ran quickly in search of the two men, and fortunately found them in the market-place. "Sir," he cried, "what have you done? You have misled me. I wanted to imitate your skill, and I have burned my father alive! Come with me quickly, and help me, if you can!" Then the Lord smiled graciously, and said: "Go home comforted. You will find your father alive and well, but an old man again." And so he did find him, to his great joy. From that time his pride disappeared, and whenever any one called him "Professor" he would exclaim: "Ah, what folly that is! There are gentlemen in Venice and professors in Padua, but I am a bungler."

THE VERSION in Knust is different. It is called "A Journey of Our Saviour on Earth," and is, in substance, as follows: A father whose son is a gambler, makes him become a soldier. The son deserts during a stormy night and takes refuge in an inn. There he meets a man who seems acquainted with his whole life and whose name is Salvatore (Saviour). He knows that Peter has deserted and is pursued, but he will save him. To gain a livelihood, he proposes to him to travel together and heal the sick. An opportunity to do this is soon offered. A rich man is ill, and Salvatore promises to heal him in three days. He makes every one withdraw, prepares a potion from herbs, and cures the patient. The relatives of the rich man offer in their gratitude all manner of costly things to Salvatore, who, however, accepts only enough to support life. Such an unreasonable proceeding enrages his companion to such a degree that he parts from him. He wishes to cure people independently, and promises a king to heal his sick daughter at once. But although he does everything exactly like Salvatore, the only effect of the potion is to kill the princess. As soon as the king learns this, he has Peter thrown into prison. On his way there he meets Salvatore, who is ready to help him at his request. The latter goes to the king and promises to raise his daughter if he will release to him the prisoner. The king consents, but threatens Salvatore with death in case of failure. The dead, however, comes to life, and in gratitude offers her hand, through her father, to Salvatore, who declares that it is his vocation to wander over the earth. He asks that the maiden be given to his companion.[2]

In a story from Venice our Lord and St. Peter are hospitably received by a poor woman who has no bed to offer them, but makes up one for them from some straw and five ells of linen which she has bought that day. When the Lord departs the next morning he bestows on the woman the power of doing all day the first thing she does in the morning. She begins by taking the linen from the bed of her guests, and pulls off piece after piece of linen. A friend of hers learns this and determines to do the same, but is punished by the Lord for her selfishness.[3]

﹏ LII. In This World One Weeps and Another Laughs ﹏

Once the Lord, while he was making the world, called one of the apostles and told him to look and see what the people were doing. The apostle looked and said: "How curious! The people are weeping." The Lord answered: "It is not the world yet!" The next day he bade the apostle look again and see what the people were doing. The apostle looked and saw the people laughing, and said: "The people are laughing." The Lord answered: "It is not the world yet." The third day he made him look again, and the apostle saw that some were weeping, and some were laughing, and said: "Some of the people are weeping, and some are laughing." The Lord said: "Now it is the world, because in this world one weeps and another laughs."

THE NEXT legend accounts for the ass' long ears.

﹏ LIII. The Ass ﹏

It is related that when the Lord created the world, he also made all the animals, and gave each its name. He also created the ass, which said: "Lord, what is my name?" "Your name is ass!" The ass went away well pleased. After a while it forgot its name, and went back to the Lord.

"Lord, what is my name?" "Ass!" After a while it came back again. "Excuse me, Lord, what is my name?" "Ass, ass!" The ass turned and went away, but forgot it another time, and came back. "Lord, I have forgotten my name." The Lord could not stand it any longer, but seized its ears and pulled them sharply, exclaiming: "Ass! Ass! Ass!" The ears were pulled so hard that they became long, and that is why the ass has long ears, and why we pull a person's ears to keep him from forgetting a thing.

ANOTHER legend relates that when Christ was journeying through the world he happened, dying with thirst, to enter a town. He saw a woman combing her hair, and said: "Will you give me a drink of water? For I am dying of thirst." "I am busy; it is not the time for water!" Christ said at once:

> "Cursed be the braid
> That is braided Friday."

And continued his journey. After a time he saw a woman making dough for bread. "Good woman, will you give me a drink of water?" "As much as you will!" and went and drew some water and gave him. Christ said:

> "Blessed be the dough
> That is kneaded on Friday."

Hence it is that certain women are accustomed not to comb their hair on Friday.

There is a satirical legend, called "The Lord's Will," which relates that when Christ came to leave the world, he was in doubt as to whom to leave all on the earth. If he left it to the gentlemen, what would the nobility do? if to the nobility, what would become of the gentry, and the workmen, and the peasants? While He was reflecting, the noblemen came and asked the Lord to give them everything, which he did. Then the priests came; and when they were told that everything had been given to the nobility, "Oh! the devil!" they exclaimed. "Then I leave you the devil," said the Lord. To the monks, who, when they heard what had been done, exclaimed, "Patience!" patience was left. The workmen cried: "What a fraud!" and received that for their share. Finally the peasants came and said, with resignation: "Let us do the will of God;" and that was their portion. And this is the reason why in this world the noblemen command, the priests are helped by the devil, the monks are patient, workmen fraudulent, and the peasants have to do many things they don't want to, and are obliged to submit to the will of God.[4]

St. Peter's mother is the subject of a story which has given rise to a widespread proverb. She was, so runs the story, an avaricious woman, who never was known to do good to any one. In fact, during her whole life she never gave anything away, except the top of an onion to a beggar woman. After her death St. Peter's mother went to hell, and the saint begged our Lord to release her. In consideration of her one charitable act, an angel was sent to draw her from hell with an onion-top. The other lost spirits clutched hold of her skirts, in order to escape with her, but the selfish woman tried to shake them off, and in her efforts to do so broke the onion-top, and fell back into hell. This story has given rise to the saying, "Like St. Peter's mamma," which is found, with slight variations, all over Italy.[5]

A curious version of this story is given in Bernoni (*Leggende font.* No. 8): After the onion-top was broken and St Peter's mother had fallen back into hell, the story continues: "Out of regard, however, for St. Peter, the Lord permitted her once a year, on St. Peter's day, to leave hell and wander about the earth a week; and, indeed, she does so every year, and during this week she plays all sorts of pranks and causes great trouble."[6]

St. Peter's sisters are the subject of a story with a moral, contained in Schneller, p. 6.

❧ LIV. St. Peter and His Sisters ❧

St. Peter had two sisters—one large, the other small. The little one entered a convent and became a nun. St. Peter was delighted at this and tried to persuade his big sister to become a nun also. She would not listen to him, however, and said: "I would rather marry." After St. Peter had suffered martyrdom, he became, as is well known, Porter of Heaven. One day the Lord said to him: "Peter, open the gate of heaven to-day as wide as you can, and get out all the heavenly ornaments and decorations, for to-day a very deserving soul is going to arrive here." St. Peter did as he was told with great joy, and thought: " Certainly my little sister is dead, and is coming to heaven to-day." When everything was ready, there came the soul of—his big sister, who had died and left many children, who bitterly lamented her loss. The Lord gave her an exalted place in heaven, much to the astonishment of St. Peter, who thought: "I never should have imagined this; what shall I have to do when the soul of my little sister comes?"

Not long after, the Lord said to him: "Peter, open the gate of heaven to-day a little way, but a very little,—do you hear?" St. Peter did so and wondered: "Who is coming to-day?" Then came the soul of his little sister, and had so much trouble to squeeze through the gate that she hurt herself; and she received a much lower place in heaven than the big sister. At first St. Peter was amazed; afterwards he said: "It has happened differently from what I imagined; but I see now that every profession has its merits, and every one, if he only wishes, can enter heaven."

THE CYCLE of stories referring to our Lord would not be complete without legends of Pilate, Judas, and the Wandering Jew. A powerful story is told of the first in Pitrè, No. 119, which is as follows:

✧ LV. Pilate ✧

It is said that the following once took place at Rome: A wagon loaded with stones was crossing a solitary spot in the country when one of the wheels sank into the ground and it was impossible to extricate it for some time. Finally they got it out, but there remained a large hole that opened into a dark room under ground. "Who wishes to descend into this hole?" "I," said the carter. They soon procured a rope and lowered the carter into the dark room. We will suppose that this carter's name was Master Francis. Well, then. Master Francis, when he was let down, turned to the right and saw a door, which he opened, and found himself in darkness that you could cut. He turned to the left, the same; he went forward, the same; he turned once more and when he opened the door what did he see? He saw a man seated before a table; before him, pen, ink, and a written paper that he was reading; and when he finished it he began over again, and never raised his eyes from the paper. Master Francis, who was of incomparable courage, went up to him and said: "Who are you?" The man made no answer, but continued to read. "Who are you?" said Master Francis again; but not a word. The third time, the man said: "Turn around, open your shirt, and I will write who I am on your back. When you leave this place, go to the Pope and make him read who I am. Remember, however, that the Pope alone must read it." Master Francis turned about, opened his shirt, the man wrote on his back, and then sat down again. Master Francis was courageous, it is true; but he was not made of wood, and in that moment he was frightened to death. He fixed his shirt and then asked: "How long have you been here?" but could get no answer from him. Seeing that it was time lost to question him, he gave the signal to those outside and was drawn up. When they saw him they did not recognize him; he had grown entirely white and seemed like an old man of ninety. "What was it? What happened?" they all began to say. "Nothing, nothing," he replied; "take me to the Pope, for I must confess." Two of those who were present conducted him to the Pope. When he was with him he related what had happened and taking off his shirt, said to him: "Read, your Holiness!" His Holiness read: "I AM PILATE." And as he tittered these words the poor carter became a statue. And it is said that that man was Pilate, who was condemned to stay in a cave, always reading the sentence that he had pronounced on Jesus Christ, without ever being able to take his eyes from the paper. This is the story of Pilate who is neither saved nor damned.[7]

JUDAS IS believed to have hanged himself on a tamarind-tree, which, before that time, was a tall, beautiful tree. After Judas's death it became the diminutive, shapeless shrub called *vruca*, which is a synonym for all that is worthless. The soul of the traitor is condemned to wander through the air, and every time it sees this shrub it pauses, and imagines it sees its miserable body dangling from it, the prey of birds and dogs.[8] This popular legend is told in the following words:

↜ LVI. The Story of Judas ↝

You must know that Judas was the one who betrayed Jesus Christ. Now when Judas betrayed him, his Master said: "Repent, Judas, for I pardon you." But Judas, not at all! He departed with his bag of money, in despair and cursing heaven and earth. What did he do? While he was going along thus desperate he came across a tamarind-tree. (You must know that the tamarind was formerly a large tree, like the olive and walnut.) When he saw this tamarind a wild thought entered his mind, remembering the treason he had committed. He made a noose in a rope and hung himself to the tamarind. And hence it is (because this traitor Judas was cursed by God) that the tamarind-tree dried up, and from that time on it ceased growing up into a tree and became a short, twisted, and tangled bush; and its wood is good for nothing, neither to burn, nor to make anything out of, and all on account of Judas, who hanged himself on it.

Some say that the soul of Judas went to the lowest hell, to suffer the most painful torments; but I have heard, from older persons who can know, that Judas's soul has a severer sentence. They say that it is in the air, always wandering about the world, without being able to rise higher or fall lower; and every day, on all the tamarind shrubs that it meets, it sees its body hanging and torn by the dogs and birds of prey. They say that the pain he suffers cannot be told, and that it makes the flesh creep to think of it. And thus Jesus Christ condemned him for his great treason.[9]

AN INTERESTING legend (Pitrè, No. 120) is told of the Jew who struck our Lord with the palm of his hand (St. John xviii. 22), and whom the popular imagination has identified with the Malchus mentioned by St. John, xviii. 10. It is called

∽ LVII. Desperate Malchus ∽

This Malchus was one of those Jews who beat our Lord; a Jew more brutal than can be told. When Christ was taken to Pilate's house, this Malchus, with an iron glove, gave him a blow so heavy that it knocked out all his teeth. For the sacrilegious act, the Lord condemmed him to walk constantly, without ever resting, around a column in an underground room. This column is in a round room, and Malchus walks and walks without ever having peace or rest. They say that he has walked so much that he has worn the ground down many yards and made the column seem higher than it was, for this Malchus has led this life ever since our Lord's passion and death. It is said that this Malchus is desperate from his remorse, and while he walks he beats the column, strikes his head against the wall, and rages and laments; but notwithstanding he does not die, for the sentence of God is that he must live until the day of judgment.[10]

THE SAME legend is found in Bernoni as follows:

∽ LVIII. Malchus at the Column ∽

Malchus was the head of the Jews who killed our Lord. The Lord pardoned them all, and likewise the good thief, but he never pardoned Malchus, because it was he who gave the Madonna a blow. He is confined under a mountain, and condemned to walk around a column, without resting, as long as the world lasts. Every time that he walks about the column he gives it a blow in memory of the blow he gave the mother of our Lord. He has walked around the column so long that he has sunk into the ground. He is now up to his neck. When he is under, head and all, the world will come to an end, and God will then send him to the place prepared for him. He asks all those who go to see him (for there are such) whether children are yet born; and when they say yes, he gives a deep sigh and resumes his walk, saying: "The time is not yet!" for before the world comes to an end there will be no children born for seven years.[11]

THIS LEGEND recalls the Wandering Jew, who is known in Sicilian tradition under the name of *Buttadeu* (from *buttari*, to thrust away, and *deu*, God) or more commonly as "The Jew who repulsed Jesus Christ." He is reported to have appeared in Sicily, and the daughter of a certain Antonino Caseio, a peasant of Salaparuta, gives the following account of her father's encounter with *Buttadeu:*

ᔰLIX. *The Story of Buttadeu* ᔰ

It was in the winter, and my good father was at Scalone, in the warehouse, warming himself at the fire, when he saw a man enter, dressed differently from the people of that region, with breeches striped in yellow, red, and black, and his cap the same way. My good father was frightened. "Oh!" he said, "what is this person?" "Do not be afraid," the man said. "I am called *Buttadeu.*" "Oh!" said my father, "I have heard you mentioned. Be pleased to sit down a while and tell me something." "I cannot sit, for I am condemned by my God always to walk." And while he was speaking he was always walking up and down and had no rest. Then he said: "Listen. I am going away; I leave you, in memory of me, this, that you must say a *credo* at the right hand of our Lord, and five other *credos* at his left, and a *salve regina* to the Virgin, for the grief I suffer on account of her son. I salute you." "Farewell." "Farewell, my name is *Buttadeu.*"[12]

WE HAVE only a few legends of the saints to mention. Undoubtedly a large number are current among the people (Busk, pp. 196, 202, 203, 213–228, gives a good many), but they do not differ materially from the literary versions circulated by the Church. Those which we shall cite are purely popular and belong to the great mediæval legend-cycle.

The first is the legend of "Gregory on the Stone," which was so popular in the mediæval epics. There are several Italian versions, but we select as the most complete the one in Gonzenbach, No. 85, called:

⤳ LX. The Story of Crivòliu ⤳

Once upon a time there was a brother and sister who had neither father nor mother, and lived alone together. They loved each other so much that they committed a sin which they should not have committed. When the time came the sister gave birth to a boy, which the brother had secretly baptized. Then he burnt into his shoulders a cross, with these words: "Crivòliu, who is baptized; son of a brother and sister." After the child was thus marked, he put it in a little box and threw it into the sea.

Now it happened that a fisherman had just gone out to fish, and saw the box floating on the waves. "A ship must have sunk somewhere," he thought. "I will get the box, perhaps there is something useful in it." So he rowed after it and got it. When he opened it and saw the little child in it, he had pity on the innocent child, took it home to his wife, and said: "My dear wife, our youngest child is already old enough to wean; nurse in its place this poor innocent child." So his wife took little Crivòliu and nursed him, and loved him as though he were her own child. The boy grew and thrived and became every day larger and stronger.

The fisherman's sons, however, were jealous because their parents loved the little foundling as well as them, and when they played with Crivòliu and quarrelled, they called him a "foundling." The boy's heart was saddened by this and he went to his foster-parents and said: "Dear parents, tell me, am I truly not your son?" The fisherman's wife said: "How should you not be my son? Have I not nursed you when you were a baby?" The fisherman forbade his children very strictly to call little Crivòliu a "foundling."

When the child was larger, the fisherman sent him to school with his sons. The children, when they were out of their father's hearing, began again to mock little Crivòliu and to call him "foundling," and the other children in the school did the same. Then Crivòliu went again to his foster-parents and asked them if he was not their son. They persuaded him out of it, however, and put him off until he was fourteen. Then he could no longer stand being called "foundling," and went to the fisherman and his wife, and said: "Dear parents, I entreat you to tell me whether I am your child or not." Then the fisherman told him how he had found him and what was written on his shoulders. "Then I will go forth, and do penance for the sins of my parents," said Crivòliu. The fisherman's wife wept and lamented and would not let him go; but Crivòliu would not be detained and wandered out into the wide world.

After he had wandered about a long time, he came one day to a lonely place where there was only an inn. He asked the hostess: "Tell me, good woman, is there a cave near by, to which you alone know the entrance?" She answered: "Yes, my handsome youth, I know such a cave and will take you to it willingly." Then Crivòliu took two *grani*'s worth of bread and a little pitcher of water with him and had the hostess show him the cave. It was some distance from the inn, and the entrance was so covered with thorns and bushes that he could scarcely penetrate into the cave. He sent the hostess back, crept into the cave, put the bread and water on the ground, knelt with folded arms, and so did penance for the sins of his parents.

Many, many years passed, I know not how many, but so many, that his knees took root and he grew fast to the ground.

Now it happened that the Pope died at Rome, and a new one was to be chosen. The cardinals all assembled, and a white dove was let loose; for he on whom it should alight was to be Pope. The white dove made several circles in the air, but alighted on no one. Then all the archbishops and bishops were summoned, and the dove was again let loose, but it did not settle on any one. Then all the priests and monks and hermits were collected, but the white dove would not choose any of them. The people were in great despair, and the cardinals had to wander forth and search the whole country to see whether another hermit was yet to be found, and a crowd of people accompanied them.

At last they came to the inn in the lonely neighborhood, and asked the hostess whether she knew of any hermit or penitent who was yet unknown to the world. The hostess answered: "Many years ago a sorrowful youth came here and made me conduct him to a cave to do penance. He is surely dead long ago, for he took with him only two *grani*'s worth of bread and a pitcher of water." The cardinals said: "We will look, however, and see whether he is still alive; take us to him." Then the hostess conducted them to the cave; the entrance was scarcely to be recognized, so overgrown was it with brambles, and before they could enter the attendants had to cut away the brambles and bushes with axes. After they had forced their way in, they saw Crivòliu kneeling in the cave, with crossed arms, and his beard had grown so long that it touched the ground, and before him lay the bread, and by it the pitcher of water; for in all those years he had not eaten or drunken. When they let the white dove loose now, it flew about in a circle for a moment and then alighted on the head of the penitent. Then the cardinals perceived that he was a saint, and begged him to come with them and be their Pope. As they were going to raise him up, they noticed that his knees had grown fast, and they had to cut the roots. Then they took him to Rome with them and he was made Pope.

Now it happened that at the same time the sister said to her brother: "Dear brother, when we were young, we committed a sin that we have not yet confessed, for the Pope alone can absolve us from it. Let us go, then, to Rome, before death overtakes us, and confess there our sin." So they started on their journey to Rome, and when they arrived there they entered the church where the Pope sat in the confessional.

When they had confessed in a loud voice, for one always confesses openly to the Pope, the Pope said: "Behold, I am your son, for on my shoulder is the mark you speak of. I have done penance many years for your sin, until it has been forgiven you. I absolve you, therefore, from your sin, and you shall stay with me and live in comfort." So they remained with him, and when their time came, the Lord called them all three to his kingdom.[13]

AN IMPORTANT episode of the original legend is omitted in the above version, but preserved in those in Pitrè (No. 117) and Knust (No. 7). The youth after discovering his origin sets out on his wanderings and comes by chance to the country where his mother is living. They meet and, not knowing their relation, marry. In the Sicilian story this relationship is disclosed the day of the marriage by the son showing his mother the box in which he was exposed as a child. In the version of Knust (from Leghorn), the child leaves his foster-father and goes in search of his parents. He encounters them without knowing it of course, and they, supposing him to be a beggar boy, give him shelter and care for him until he has grown up. Then he marries his mother, who recognizes him by a lock of red hair. At the conclusion of the story, after the Pope has heard the confession of his parents he reveals himself, they all three embrace, and die thus united. The story adds, "their tomb is still preserved in St. Peter's at Rome."

Another Pope, Silvester I., is the subject of a legend in Pitrè (No. 118) which contains the well-known myth of Constantine's leprosy healed by his baptism at the hands of St. Silvester.

Of greater interest is a legend of St. James the Elder, the patron-saint of Spain, a pilgrimage to whose shrine at Santiago in Galicia was so popular during the Middle Ages. The only popular version which we have found is in a Sicilian story in Gonzenbach, No. 90.

✄ LXI. The Story of St. James of Galicia ✄

There was once a king and queen who had no children, and who longed to have a son or daughter. The queen prayed to St. James of Galicia, and said: "O St. James! if you will grant me a son, he shall make a pilgrimage to your shrine when he is eighteen years old." After a time the queen had, through the favor of God and the saint, a beautiful boy who was as handsome as if God had made him. The child grew rapidly and became larger and fairer every day. When he was twelve years old, the king died, and the queen remained alone with this son, whom she loved as dearly as her eyes. Many years passed and the time drew near when the prince should be eighteen. When the queen thought that she must soon part from him to send him alone on the long pilgrimage, she became very sorrowful and wept and sighed the whole day.

One day the prince said to her: "Mother, why do you sigh all day?" "It is nothing, my son, only some cares of mine," she answered. "What are you concerned about?" asked he. "Are you afraid that your farms in the Plain (of Catania) are badly tilled? Let me go and look after them and bring you news of them." The queen consented and the prince rode to the Plain, to the property that belonged to them. He found everything in good order, and returned to his mother and said: "Dear mother, rejoice, and cease your care, for everything is going well on your property; the cattle are thriving; the fields are tilled, and the grain will soon be ripe." "Very well, my son," answered the queen, but she was not cheerful, and the next day began to sigh and weep again. Then the prince said to her: "Dear mother, if you do not tell me why you are so sad, I will depart, and wander out in the wide world." The queen answered: "Ah, my dear son, I am sad because you must now part from me. For before you were born, when I longed for you so much, I vowed to St. James of Galicia, that if he would grant you to me, you should make a pilgrimage to his shrine when you were eighteen years old. And now you will soon be eighteen, and I am sad because you must wander away alone, and be gone so many years; for to reach the saint, one must journey a whole year." "Is it nothing but that, dear mother?" asked her son. "Be not so sorrowful. Only the dead return not. If I live, I will soon come back to you."

So he comforted his mother, and when he was eighteen he took leave of the queen, and said: "Now farewell, dear mother, and, God willing, we shall meet again." The queen wept bitterly, and embraced him with many tears; then she gave him three apples, and said: "My son, take these three apples and give heed to my words. You shall not make the long journey alone. When, however, a youth joins you and wishes to accompany you, take him with you to the inn, and let him eat with you. After the meal cut an apple in two halves, one large and the other small, and offer them to the young man. If he takes the larger half, part from him, for he will be no true friend to you; but if he takes the smaller half, regard him as your brother, and share everything that you have with him." After these words she embraced her son and blessed him, and the prince departed.

He had already travelled a long time, and no one had met him. One day, however, he saw a youth coming along the road who joined him and asked: "Where are you going, handsome youth?" "I am making a pilgrimage to St. James of Galicia;" and he told him of his mother's vow. "I must go there, too," said the other, "for the same thing happened to my mother as to yours; if we have the same journey to make, we can make it together." They continued their journey together, but the prince was not confidential towards his companion, for he thought: "I must first make the trial with the apple."

As they were passing an inn, the prince said: "I am hungry: shall we not have something to eat?" The other was willing, so they went in and ate together. After they had eaten, the prince took out the apple, cut it in two unequal halves, and offered them to the other, who took the larger half. "You are no true friend," thought the prince; and to get rid of him, he pretended to be ill, and obliged to remain there. The other said: "I cannot wait for you, for I have far to go yet; so farewell." "Farewell," said the prince, and was glad to be rid of him.

When he continued his journey again, he thought: "Ah, if God would only send me a true friend, so that I should not have to travel alone!"

Not long after, another youth joined him and asked: "Handsome young man, where are you going?" The prince answered him as he had done before, and everything happened the same as with the first young man.

After the prince had got rid of him he resumed his journey and thought: "O God, let me find a true friend who shall be to me a brother on the long journey!" While he was uttering this prayer he saw a youth coming along the way, who was a handsome lad, and appeared so friendly that he liked him at once, and thought: "Ah, may this be the true friend!" The youth joined him, and everything passed as before, except that this time the youth took the smaller half of the apple, and the prince rejoiced that he had found a true friend. "Fair youth," said he to him, "we must consider ourselves as brothers now, what is mine shall be yours also, and what is yours, shall be mine. We will travel together, until we come to the shrine of the saint; and if one of us dies on the way, the other must carry his body there. We will both promise this." They did so, and regarded each other as brothers, and continued their journey together.

To reach the shrine of the saint requires a whole year; imagine, then, how long the two must travel. One day when they came, weary and exhausted, to a large, beautiful city, they said: "We will stay here and rest a few days, and afterwards continue our journey." So they took a small house, and dwelt in it. Now opposite it was the royal palace, and one morning as the king was standing on the balcony, he saw the two handsome youths, and thought: "Oh! How handsome these two youths are! one is, however, much handsomer than the other. I will give him my daughter in marriage." Now the prince was the handsomer of the two. In order to attain his aim, the king invited them both to dinner, and when they came to the palace received them in a very friendly manner and had his daughter called, who was more beautiful than the sun and moon. When they retired for the night, the king had a poisonous drink given to the prince's companion, who fell down dead; for the king thought: "If his friend dies, the other will remain here willingly, and think no more of his pilgrimage, but marry my daughter."

The next morning, when the prince awoke, he asked: "Where is my friend?" "He died suddenly last night, and is to be buried at once," answered the servants. The prince said: "If my friend is dead, I cannot remain here longer, but must depart this very hour." "Ah! Do remain here," begged the king. "I will give you my daughter for your wife." "No," said the prince, "I cannot stay here. If you will grant me a wish, give me a horse, and let me depart in peace; and when I have completed my pilgrimage, I will return and marry your daughter." The king then gave him a horse, which the prince mounted, and took his dead friend before him on the saddle, and thus completed his journey. The young man, however, was not dead, but lay only in a deep sleep.

When the prince reached the shrine of St. James of Galicia, he dismounted, took his friend in his arms like a child, and entered the church and laid the body on the steps of the altar before the saint, and prayed: "O St. James of Galicia! Behold, I have kept my vow. I have come to you and have brought you my friend, also. I confide him now to you; if you will restore him to life, we will laud your mercy; but if he is not to come to life again, he has at least kept his vow." And behold, while he was still praying, his dead friend rose, and became again alive and well. Both thanked the saint, and gave him costly presents, and then started on their journey home.

When they reached the city where the king lived, they occupied again the little house opposite the royal palace. The king was greatly rejoiced to see the handsome prince there again, and much handsomer than before; he arranged great festivities, and had a splendid marriage celebrated, and thus the prince married the fair princess. After the wedding they remained several months with her father, and then the prince said: "My mother is expecting me at home with great anxiety; therefore I cannot stay longer here, but will return to my mother with my wife and my friend." The king consented and they prepared for the journey.

Now the king had a deadly hatred against the poor, innocent youth, to whom he had before given the fatal drink, and who had nevertheless returned alive, and in order to cause him sorrow, he sent him in great haste on the morning of the departure into the country with an errand. "Hasten," he said. "Your friend will not start until you return." The youth hastened away, without taking leave, and performed the king's errand. The king, meanwhile, said to the prince: "Hasten your departure, otherwise you cannot reach your quarters for the night before evening." "I cannot depart without my friend," answered the prince. The king, however, said: "Set out on your journey; he will be here within an hour, and will soon overtake you on his swift horse." The prince allowed himself to be persuaded, took leave of his father-in-law, and departed with his wife. The poor friend could not fulfil the king's commission before several hours, and when he finally returned, the king said to him: "Your friend is already far from here; see how you can overtake him."

So the poor youth had to leave the palace, and did not even receive a horse, and began to run, and ran day and night until he overtook the prince. From his great exertions, however, he contracted leprosy, so that he looked ill, wretched, and dreadful. The prince, nevertheless, received him in a friendly manner and cared for him like a brother.

They finally reached home, where the queen had awaited her son with great anxiety, and now embraced him with perfect joy. The prince had a bed prepared at once for his sick friend and summoned all the physicians of the town and state, but no one could help him. When the poor youth grew no better the prince addressed himself to St. James of Galicia and said: " O St. James of Galicia! You raised my friend from the dead; help him now this time also, and let him recover from his leprosy." While he was praying, a servant entered and said: "A strange physician is without, who will make the poor youth well again." This physician was St. James of Galicia himself, who had heard the prayer of the prince and had come to help his friend. You must know now that the prince's wife had had a little girl who was a pretty, lovely child.

When the saint approached the bed of the sick youth, he first examined him, and then said to the prince: "Do you really wish to see your friend well again at any price?" "At any price," answered the prince; "only tell me what can help him." "This evening, take your child," said the saint, "open all her veins, and anoint with her blood your friend's wounds, and he will be healed at once."

The prince was horrified when he heard that he himself must kill his dear little daughter, but he answered: "I have promised my friend to treat him like my brother; and if there is no other remedy, I will sacrifice my child."

At evening he took the child and opened her veins and anointed with the blood the sores of the sick youth, who was at once cleansed from his foul leprosy. The child became pale and weak, and looked as if it were dead. Then they laid it in its cradle and the poor parents were deeply grieved, for they believed they had lost their child.

The next morning the physician came and asked after the patient. "He is well and sound," answered the prince. "And where have you put your child?" asked the saint, "There it lies dead in its cradle," said the poor father, sadly. "Just look at her once and see how she is," said the saint; and when they hastened to the cradle, they saw the child in it alive and well again. Then the saint said: "I am St. James of Galicia, and have come to help you, because I have seen what true friendship you have displayed. Continue to love one another, and when you are in trouble turn to me and I will come to your aid." With these words he blessed them and disappeared from their sight. They lived piously and did much good to the poor, and were happy and contented.[14]

THERE are several interesting legends found only in Gonzenbach's collection. They can be mentioned but briefly here. The first (No. 87) is entitled: "The Story of St. Onirià or Nerià." Two huntsmen lost their way in a wood and found at night a hut in which was a table set for supper, and a fire which emitted a heavenly odor. They examined it and found in the coals a heart, which they took with them when they departed, the next morning. After they had travelled a while, they stopped at an inn, and the pious and virtuous daughter of the innkeeper waited on them, and noticed the odor which came from the jacket that one of the huntsmen had laid aside on account of the heat. In the pocket she found the heart, which she kept for a time on a table in her room. One day she was seized with a great longing to eat it. She did so, and it soon was evident that she was about to become a mother. Her father treated her cruelly, for the shame she was going to bring on the family, but her godmother interfered, and one night had a strange dream. There appeared to her a saint, who said: "I am St. Onirià, and was consumed by fire. Only my heart was left, so that I might be born again. This heart the host's daughter has eaten, and she will, in due time, give birth to me." The child was born as predicted, and grew handsomer every day. The grandfather, however, could not endure him, and ill-treated him as well as his mother.

One day, when the child was five years old, the grandfather took him to the city. On the way they passed a place where there was much filth, and the child said to his grandfather: "I wish you might wallow in it." Afterwards they saw a poor man being carried to the grave on a ladder, without any coffin. The child here wished that his grandfather, when he died, might be like this one. Next they met the long funeral procession of a rich man, and the child wished that his grandfather might not be like this rich man. The grandfather, of course, in each case was very angry, and was only restrained from beating the child by the mother's godfather, who had accompanied them.

After they had finished their business in the city they set out for home; and when they came to the spot where they had met the rich man's funeral procession, the child made his grandfather put his ear to the ground, when he heard a great noise, as if of iron pestles and lamentations. The child explained that what he heard were the devils tormenting the rich man's soul. When they came where they had seen the poor man on the ladder, the grandfather listened again and heard the rejoicings of the angels on receiving the poor man's soul.

When they came to the place where the filth was, the child made his grandfather dig and find a pot of money which he told him to use better than he had done his own. The child then said he was St. Onirià, exculpated his mother, and said his grandfather would see him again when the dead spoke with the living. Then he was taken up into heaven.

Years after, two men spent the night in the inn, and one murdered the other and hid the body under the straw, where it was afterwards found by other travellers, and the innkeeper accused of the murder. He was condemned and was on the scaffold when a beautiful youth came riding in hot haste, crying: "Pardon!" The youth led the people into the church, before the coffin of the murdered man, and cried: "Rise, dead one, and speak with the living, and tell us who murdered you." The dead man replied: "The innkeeper is innocent; my treacherous companion killed me." Then the youth accompanied the innkeeper home, revealed himself as St. Onirià, blessed them, and disappeared.[15]

Another legend (No. 92), "The Story of the Hermit," has as its subject the mystery of God's Providence, and is familiar to English readers in the form of Parnell's Hermit. The substance of the Sicilian version is as follows: A hermit sees a man wrongfully accused of theft and shockingly maltreated. He thereupon concludes that God is unjust to suffer such things, and determines to return to the world. On his way back a handsome youth meets him and they journey together. A muleteer allows them to ride his beasts, and in return the youth abstracts the muleteer's money from his wallet and drops it in the road. A woman who keeps an inn receives them hospitably, and on leaving the next morning, the youth strangles her child in the cradle. All at once the youth becomes a shining angel, and says to the hermit: "Listen to me, O man who has been bold enough to murmur against God's decrees;" and then explains that the person who had been wrongfully accused of theft had years before murdered his father on that very spot; the muleteer's money was stolen money, and the child of the hostess, had it lived, would have become a robber and murderer. Then the angel says: "Now you see that God's justice is more far-sighted than man's. Return, then, to your hermitage, and repent if so be that your murmuring be forgiven you." The angel disappears and the hermit returns to his mountain, does severer penance, and dies a saint.[16]

The legend in Gonzenbach (No. 91) entitled "Joseph the Just" is nothing but the story of Joseph and his Brethren, taken from the Bible. In the Sicilian version Joseph has only three brothers; otherwise the story follows the account in Genesis very closely. Another legend in the same collection (No. 89), "The Story of Tobià and Tobiòla," is the story of Tobit and Tobias, taken from the apocryphal book of Tobit. The Sicilian story differs in the names only.

There are several other Sicilian legends the heroes of which are pious, simple youths, the religious counterparts of Giufà. One (Pitrè, No. 112), called "The Poor Boy," tells the story of a simple youth who asked the priest the way to paradise, and was told he must follow the strait and narrow way. He took the first one he came to, and reached a convent church during a festival, and imagined he had reached paradise. He was found in the church when all had departed; but he persisted in remaining, and the superior sent him a bowl of soup, which he put on the altar; and when he was alone he began to converse confidentially with the Lord on the crucifix, and said: "Lord, who put you on the cross?" "Your sins!" and so the Lord responded to all his questions. The youth, in tears, promised he would sin no more, and invited the Lord to descend and partake of his repast with him. The Lord did so, and commanded him to tell the monks in the convent that they would be damned unless they sold all their property and bestowed it on the poor. If they would do so and come and confess to the Lord himself, he would hear their confession and give them the communion, and when it was finished they would all die, one after the other, and enter the glory of paradise. The poor youth went to the superior and gave him the Lord's message. The superior sold the property of the convent, and everything turned out as the Lord had said. The monks all confessed and died, and all who were present or heard of the event were converted and died in the grace of God.[17]

This legend leads quite naturally to another, in which intercourse with the other world is represented as still occasionally permitted to mortals. It is found only in Sicily, having, curiously enough, parallels in the rest of Europe, but none in Italy. It is called:

ᴥ LXII. The Baker's Apprentice ᴥ

There was once a baker who every morning loaded an ounce-worth of bread on a horse that came to his shop. One day he said: "I give this ounceworth of bread to this horse and he renders me no account of it." Then he said to his apprentice: "Vincenzo, the horse will come to-morrow and I will give him the bread, but you must follow him and see where he goes." The next day the horse came and the baker loaded him, and gave the apprentice a piece of bread for himself. Vincenzo followed the horse, and after a while came to a river of milk, and began to eat bread and milk, and could not overtake the horse again. He then returned to his master, who, seeing him return to no purpose, said: "To-morrow the horse will come again; if you cannot tell me where he goes I will no longer have you for my apprentice." The next day the apprentice followed the horse again, and came to a river of wine, and began to eat bread and wine, and lost sight of the horse. He returned to his master in despair at having lost the horse. His master said: "Listen. The first time, one pardons; the second time, one condones; the third time, one beats. If to-morrow you do not follow the horse I will give you a good thrashing and send you home." What did poor Vincenzo do? He followed the horse the next day with his eyes open. After a while he came to a river of oil. "What shall I do? The horse will get away from me now!" So he tied the horse's reins to his girdle and began to eat bread and oil. The horse pulled, but Vincenzo said: "When I finish the bread I will come." When he had finished the bread he followed the horse, and after a time he came to a cattle-farm where the grass was long and thick and the cattle so thin that they could scarcely stand on their feet. Vincenzo was astonished at seeing the grass so long and the cattle so lean. Then he came to another farm, and saw that the grass was dry and short, and the cattle fatter than you can believe. He said to himself: "Just see! There, where the grass was long, the cattle were lean; here, where you can hardly see the grass, the cattle are so fat!" The horse kept on, and Vincenzo after him. After a while he met a sow with her tail full of large knots, and wondered why she had such a tail. Farther on he came to a watering-trough, where there was a toad trying to reach a crumb of bread, and could not. Vincenzo continued his way, and arrived at a large gate. The horse knocked at the gate with his head, and the door opened and a beautiful lady appeared, who said she was the Madonna. When she saw the youth she asked: "And what are you here for?" Vincenzo replied; "This horse comes constantly to my master's to get an ounceworth of bread, and my master never has been able to find out where he carries it." "Very well; enter," said the lady; "I will show you where he carries it." Then the lady began to call all the souls in purgatory: "My children, come hither!" The souls then descended; and to some she gave the worth of a *grano* of bread, to some the worth of a *baiocco*, and to others the worth of five *grani*, and the bread was gone in a moment. When the bread had disappeared, the lady said to Vincenzo: "Did you see nothing on your way? " "Yes, lady. The first day that my master sent me to see where the horse went, I saw a river of milk." The lady said; "That is the milk I gave my son." "The second day I saw a river of wine." "That," said the lady, "is the wine with which my son was consecrated." "The third day I saw a river of oil." "That is the oil that they ask of me and of my son. What else did you see the third day?" "I saw," answered Vincenzo, "a farm with cattle. There was plenty of grass, but the cattle were lean. Afterwards I saw another farm, where you could scarcely see the grass, and the cattle were fine and fat." "These, my son, are the rich, who are in the midst of wealth; and no matter how much they eat, it does no good; and the fat ones, that have no grass to eat, are the poor, for my son supports and fattens them. What else did you see?" "I saw a sow with her tail full of knots." "That, my son, is those who repeat their rosaries and do not offer their prayers to me or to my son; and my son makes knots in them." "I also saw a water-ing-trough, with a toad that was reaching after a crumb of bread, and could not get it." She said: "A poor person asked a woman for a bit of bread, and she gave his hand such a blow that she made him drop it. And what else did you see, my son?" "Nothing, lady." "Then come with me, and I will show you something else." She took him by the hand and led him into hell. When the poor youth heard the clanking of chains and saw the darkness, he came near dying, and wanted to get out. "You see," said the lady, "those who are lamenting and in chains and darkness are those who are in mortal sin. Now come, and I will take you to purgatory." There they heard nothing, and the darkness was so great that they could see nothing. Vincenzo wished to depart, for he felt oppressed by anguish. "Now," said the lady, " I will take you to the church of the Holy Fathers. Do you see it, my son? This is the church of the Holy Fathers, which first was full and now is empty. Come; now I will take you to limbo. Do you see these little ones? These are those who died unbaptized." The lady wished to show him paradise, but he was too confused, so the lady made him look through a window. "Do you see this great palace? There are three seats there; one for you, one for your master, and one for your mistress." After this she took him to the gate. The horse was no longer there. "Now," said Vincen-zo, "how shall I find my way back? I will follow the tracks of the horse, and so will get home." The lady answered: "Close your eyes!" Vincenzo closed his eyes, and found himself behind his master's door. When he entered he told all that had occurred to his master and mistress. When he had finished his story all three died and went to paradise.[18]

The most famous story of the class we are now considering is, however, the one best known by its French title, *"Bonhomme Misère."* The French version was popular as a chap-book as early as 1719, running through fifteen editions from that date. The editor of the reprint referred to in the note, as well as Grimm (II. 451), believed the story to be of Italian origin and that the original would some day be discovered.[19] This has proved to be the case, and we have now before us a number of versions. These may be divided into two classes: one independent, the other constituting a part only of some other story. The latter class is generally connected with the cycle of our Lord's journeys upon earth, and is represented by "The Master Thief" and "Brother Lustig" in Germany, and "Beppo Pipetta" from Venice. The Sicilian versions which we shall mention first, although independent stories, are connected with the cycle of our Lord's journeys upon earth. We give first two versions from Pitrè (Nos. 124, 125).

⁓LXIII. Occasion ⁓

Once upon a time there was a father and a mother who had a little boy. They died and the child was left in the street. One of the neighbors had pity upon him and took him in. The boy throve well and when he had grown up, the one who had sheltered him said: "Come now, Occasion (for this was the boy's name), you are a man; why do you not think about supporting yourself and relieving us from that care?" So the lad made up a bundle and departed. He journeyed and journeyed until his clothes were worn out and he was almost dead from hunger. One day he saw an inn and entered it, and said to the innkeeper: "Do you want me for a servant? I wish only a piece of bread for my wages." The host said to his wife: "What do you say, Rosella? We have no children; shall we take this lad?" "Yes;" and so they took him.

The boy was very attentive and did willingly whatever was commanded him, and at last his master and mistress, who had grown to love him like a son, went before the judge and adopted him.

Time passed and the innkeeper and his wife died and left all their property to the young man, who, when he saw himself in possession of it, made known: "That whoever should come to Occasion's inn could have food for nothing." You can imagine the people that went there!

Now the Master and his apostles happened once to pass that way, and when St. Thomas read this announcement he said: "Unless I see and touch with my hands I shall not believe it. Let us go to this inn." They went there and ate and drank and Occasion treated them like gentlemen. Before leaving St. Thomas said: "Occasion, why don't you ask a favor of the Master?" Then Occasion said: "Master, I have before my door this fig-tree, and the children do not let me eat one of the figs. Whoever goes by climbs up and pulls off some. Now I would like this favor, that when any one climbs this tree, he must stay there until I permit him to come down." "Your request is granted," said the Lord, and blessed the tree.

It was a fine thing! The first who climbed up for figs stuck fast to the tree without being able to move; another came, the same thing; and so on; all stuck fast, one by the hand, another by the foot, another by the head. When Occasion saw them he gave them a sound scolding and let them go. The children were frightened and touched the figs no more.

Years passed and Occasion's money was coming to an end; so he called a carpenter and told him to cut up the fig-tree and make him a bottle out of it. This bottle had the property that Occasion could shut up in it whoever he wished. One day Death went to fetch him, for Occasion was now very old. Occasion said: "At your service; we will go. But see here, Death, first do me a favor. I have this bottle of wine, and there is a fly in it, and I don't like to drink from it; just go in there and take it out for me, and then we will go." Death very foolishly entered the bottle, when Occasion corked it and put it in his wallet, saying: "Stay a bit with me."

While Death was shut up no one died; and everywhere you might see old men with such long white beards that it was a sight. The apostles, seeing this, went to the Master about it several times, and at last he visited Occasion. "What is this? Here you have kept Death shut up so many years, and the people are falling down from old age without dying!" Master," said Occasion, "do you want me to let Death out? If you will give me a place in paradise, I will let him out." The Lord thought: "What shall I do? If I don't grant him this favor, he will not leave me in peace." So he said: "Your request is granted!" At these words Death was set at liberty; Occasion was permitted to live a few years longer, and then Death took him. Hence it is "That there is no death without Occasion."

↜ *LXIV. Brother Giovannone* ↝

Once upon a time there was a convent at Casteltermini which contained many monks, one of whom was named Brother Giovannone. At the time when the Lord and all his apostles were on their travels they visited this convent, and all the monks asked the Lord to pardon their souls; Brother Giovannone asked nothing. St. Peter said to him: "Why do you not ask pardon for your soul, like the others?" "I don't wish anything." St. Peter said: "Nothing? When you come to paradise we will talk about it." When the Master had taken his departure and had gone some distance, Brother Giovannone began to cry out: "Master, Master, wait! I want a favor, and it is that any one I command must get into my pouch." The Master said: "This request is granted."

Brother Giovannone was old and one day Death came and said to him: "Giovannone, you have three hours to live!" Brother Giovannone replied: "When you come for me you must let me know half an hour before." After a while Death came and said: "You are a dead man!" Brother Giovannone replied: "In the name of Brother Giovannone, into my pouch with you, Death!" Then he carried his pouch to a baker and asked him to hang it up in the chimney until he came for it. For forty years no one died. At the end of that time Brother Giovannone went and set Death free, so that he might himself die, for he was so old he could do no more. The first one that Death killed when he was free was Brother Giovannone, and then he destroyed all those who had not died in the forty years.

After he was dead Brother Giovannone went and knocked at the gate of paradise and St. Peter said to him: "There is no room for you here." "Where must I go, then?" asked Brother Giovannone. "To purgatory," answered St. Peter. So he knocked at purgatory and they told him: "There is no place for you here." "Where must I go, then?" "To hell." He knocked at hell and Lucifer asked: "Who is there?" "Brother Giovannone." Then Lucifer said to his devils: "You take the mace; you, the hammer; you, the tongs!" Brother Giovannone asked: "What are you going to do with these instruments?" "We are going to beat you." "In the name of Brother Giovannone, into my pouch with you, all you devils!" Then he hung the pouch about his neck and carried all the devils to a smith who had eight apprentices, and the master, nine." Master-smith, how much do you want to hammer this pouch eight days and nights?" They agreed upon forty ounces, and hammered day and night and the pouch was not reduced to powder, and Brother Giovannone was always present. The last day the smiths said: "What the devil are these; for they cannot be pounded fine!" Brother Giovannone answered: "They are indeed devils! Pound hard!" After they were through hammering, he took the pouch and emptied it out in the plain; the devils were so bruised and mangled that they could hardly drag themselves back to hell. Then Brother Giovannone went and knocked again at paradise. "Who is there?" "Brother Giovannone." "There is no room for you." "Peter, if you don't let me in I will call you baldhead." "Now that you have called me baldhead," said St. Peter, "you shall not enter." Brother Giovannone said: "Ah, what is that you say? I will be even with you!" So he stood near the gate of paradise and said to all the souls who were going to enter: "In the name of Brother Giovannone, into my pouch, all you souls!" and no more souls entered paradise. One day St. Peter said to the Master: "Why do no more souls enter?" The Lord answered: "Because Brother Giovannone is behind the gate putting them all in his pouch." "What shall we do?" said St. Peter. The Lord answered: "See if you can get hold of the pouch and bring them all in together." Brother Giovannone heard all this outside. What did he do? He said: "Into the pouch with myself!" and in a moment was in his own pouch. When St. Peter looked Brother Giovannone was not to be seen, so he seized the pouch and dragged it into paradise and shut the gate at once, and opened the pouch. The first one who came out was Brother Giovannone himself, who began at once to quarrel with St. Peter because St. Peter wished to put him out, and Brother Giovannone did not want to go. Then the Lord said: "When one once enters the house of Jesus, he does not leave it again." [20]

THESE stories have close parallels in two Roman legends collected by Miss Busk. In the first, the innkeeper asks first for the faculty of always winning at cards; and second, that any one who climbs his fig-tree must stay there. When Death comes the host asks her (Death is feminine in Italian) to climb the tree and pick him a few figs. When once up the tree, the host refuses to let her down until she promises him four hundred years of life. Death has to consent and the host in turn promises to go quietly with her when she comes again. At the end of the four hundred years Death takes the host to paradise. They pass by hell on the way and the host proposes to the devil to play for the newly received souls. The host wins fifteen thousand, which he carries with him to paradise. St. Peter objects to letting the "rabble" in, and Jesus Christ himself says: "The host may come in himself, but he has no business with the others." Then the host says that he has made no difficulty about numbers when Christ has come to his inn with as many as he pleased. "That is true! That is right!" answered Jesus Christ. "Let them all in! Let them all in!"[21]

In the other story, a priest, Pret' Olivo, received from the Lord, in reward for his hospitality, the favor of living a hundred years, and that when Death came to fetch him he should be able to give her what orders he pleased, and that she must obey him. Death called at the end of the hundred years, and Pret' Olivo made her sit by the fire while he said a mass. The fire grew hotter and hotter, but Death could not stir until Pret' Olivo permitted her to, on condition that she should leave him alone a hundred years. The second time Death called, Pret' Olivo asked her to gather him some figs and commanded her to stay in the tree. So Death a second time was obliged to promise him a respite of a hundred years. The next time Death called, Pret' Olivo put on his vestments and a cope, and took a pack of cards in his hand and went with Death. She wanted to take him directly to paradise, but he insisted on going around by the way of hell and playing a game of cards with the Devil. The stakes were souls, and as fast as Pret' Olivo won, he hung a soul on his cope until it was covered with them; then he hung them on his beretta, and at last was obliged to stop, for there was no more room to hang any souls. Death objected to taking all these souls to paradise, but could not take Pret' Olivo without them. When they arrived at paradise St Peter made some objection to admitting them, but the Master gave his permission and they all got in.[22]

THE TUSCAN version, which contains some of the traits of the last story, is as follows:

ᕤ LXV. Godfather Misery ᕤ

Godfather Misery was old,—God knows how old! One day Jesus and St. Peter, while wandering through the world to name the countries, came to Godfather Misery's, who offered his visitors some polenta, and gave them his own bed. Jesus, pleased with this reception, gave him some money, and granted him these three favors: that whoever sits on his bench near the fire cannot get up; that whoever climbs his fig-tree cannot descend; and finally, out of regard to St. Peter, the salvation of his soul. One day Death came to Godfather Misery, and wanted to carry him off. Godfather Misery said: "It is too cold to travel." Death pressed him; then he asked her to sit by the fire and warm herself a moment, and he would soon be ready. Meanwhile he piled wood on the fire. Death felt herself burning, and tried to move, but could not; so she had to grant Godfather Misery another hundred years of life. Death was released; the hundred years passed, and Death returned. Godfather Misery was at the door, pretending to wait for her, and looking at his fig-tree in sorrow. He begged Death to pick him a few figs for their journey. So Death climbed up, but could not descend until she granted Godfather Misery another hundred years. Even these passed, and Death reappeared. This time there was no help, he must go. Death gave him time only to recite an Ave Maria, and a Paternoster. Godfather Misery, however, could not find this time, and said to Death, who was hurrying him: "You have given me time, and I am taking it." Then Death had recourse to a stratagem, and disguised herself like a Jesuit, and went where Godfather Misery lived, and preached. Godfather Misery at first did not attend these sermons, but his wife finally persuaded him to go to the church and hear a sermon. Just as he entered, the preacher cried out that whoever said an Ave Maria should save his soul. Godfather Misery, who recognized Death, answered from a distance: "Go away! you will not get me." Then Death went away in despair, and never got hold of him again. Godfather Misery still lives, since misery never ends.[23]

In another Tuscan story, similar gifts are bestowed upon a smith, who had always been a good Christian, to enable him to avoid a contract he had made with the Devil, to sell him his soul for two years of life. The first time the Devil comes he sits on the bench near the fire, and cannot rise again until he extends his contract two years. The next time he comes he does not enter the house, but looks in at a window that has the power to detain any one who looks through it. Again the contract is extended. The third time the Devil is caught in the fig-tree, and then a new contract is drawn up, that the Devil and the smith are never to see each other again.[24]

The second class of versions of the story of *"Bonhomme Misère"* is where the legend is merely an episode of some other story. This class comprises two stories from the territory of Venice. The first is entitled "Beppo

Pipetta," from the hero who saved the king's life, which is threatened by some robbers. The king was in disguise, and Beppo did not know who he was until he was summoned to the palace to be rewarded. The king told Beppo that he need not be a soldier any longer, but might remain with him or wherever he pleased, and offered to pay for all he needed; for he had saved his life. We give the rest of the story in the words of the original.

↷ LXVI. Beppo Pipetta ↷

When his first joy at this good fortune was over, Beppo decided to visit his relations. There he met a man in the street who entered into conversation with him, and they chatted for a long time, until they finally went into an inn to refresh themselves with something to eat and drink. "How happens it," asked his new friend, who was vastly entertained by Beppo's conversation, "that you, a soldier, carry no knapsack?" "Hm!" said Beppo, "I don't care to weigh myself down on a march with unnecessary things. I have no effects, and if I need anything, I have a good master who pays all my bills." "Now," said the stranger," I will give you a knapsack, and a very valuable one too; for if you say to any one, 'Jump in,' he will jump into the sack." With these words the stranger took his leave.

"Wait," thought Beppo; " I will put this to the proof." And, indeed, a favorable opportunity offered itself, for just then the landlord appeared to demand the payment of his bill. "What do you want?" asked Beppo. "My money; you might know that of yourself." "Let me alone! I have no money." "What? You ragged soldier"—"Jump in!" said Beppo; and the landlord went over his ears into the sack. Only after long entreaty, and on condition that he would never again present his bill, would Beppo let him out again. "Just wait, fellow! I'll teach you how to insult soldiers," said he to the landlord, as he went out.

Tired and hungry after a long walk, Beppo again turned into an inn. There he saw a man who was continually emptying a purse, but never finished, for it always became full again. He quickly snatched the purse out of the man's hand, and ran out of the inn, but no less quickly did the owner run after him; and since he had not walked as far as Beppo, who had been wandering about all day, he soon caught up with him. Then Beppo cried: "Jump in!" and the owner was in the sack. " Listen," said Beppo, after he had somewhat recovered his breath, "listen and be reasonable. You have had the purse long enough; give it to me now, or else you shall always stay in the sack." What could the man do? Willingly or unwillingly, he had to give up the purse in order to get out of the accursed sack.

For two years Beppo stayed at home, doing much good with the purse, and much mischief with the sack, until at last he began to long for the capital again, and returned there; but what was his astonishment at seeing everything hung with black, and everybody in mourning. "Do you not know what the trouble is?" he was asked, in reply to his questions as to the cause of this sorrow; " don't you know that to-morrow the Devil is going to carry away the king's daughter, on account of a foolish vow that her father once made?" Then he went directly to the king, in order to console him, but the latter would not put any faith in him. "Your Majesty," said he, "you do not know what Beppo Pipetta can do. Only let me have my own way."

Then he prepared, in a room of the palace, a large table, with paper, pen, and ink, while the princess, in the next room, awaited her sad fate in prayer. At midnight a fearful noise was heard, like the roaring of the tempest; and at the last stroke of the clock, the Devil came through the window into— the sack which Beppo held open for him, crying, "Jump in!" "What are you doing here?" asked Beppo of the raging Devil. "How does that concern you?" "I have my reasons," was the bold reply. "Wait a little, you rascal!" cried Beppo, "I'll teach you manners!" and he seized a stick and belabored the sack until the Devil in anguish called upon all the saints. "Are you going to carry off the princess, now?" "No, no; only let me out of this infamous sack!" "Do you promise never to molest her?" "I promise, only let me out!" "No," said Beppo; "you must repeat your promise before witnesses, and also give it in writing." Then he called some gentlemen of the court into the room, had the promise repeated, and permitted the Devil to stretch one hand out of the sack, in order to write as follows: "I, the very Devil, herewith promise that I will neither carry away H. R. H., the Princess, nor ever molest her in the future. SATAN, SPIRIT OF HELL."

"Good!" said Beppo; "the affair of the princess is now ended. But now, on account of your previous impoliteness, allow me to give you a few blows that may serve as reminders of me on your journey." When he had done this, he opened the sack, and the Devil went out as he had come in, through the window.

Then the king gave a great feast, at which Beppo sat between him and the princess; and there was joy throughout the whole kingdom.

After a while Beppo took a pleasure trip and came to a place that pleased him so much that he decided to remain there; but the police must needs go through certain ceremonies and wanted to know who he was, whence he came, and a multitude of other things. Then he answered: "I am myself; let that suffice you. If you want to know anything more, write to the king." Accordingly they wrote to the king, but he commanded them to treat him with respect and not to disturb him.

When he had lived for many years in this place and had grown old, Death came and knocked at his door. Beppo opened it and asked: "Who are you?" "I am Death," was the answer. "Jump in!" cried Beppo, in great haste, and behold! Death was in the sack. "What!" he exclaimed, "shall I, who have so much to do, loiter my time away here?" "Just stay where you are, you old villain," replied Beppo, and did not let him out for a year and a half. Then there was universal satisfaction throughout the world, the physicians being especially jubilant, for none of them ever lost a patient. Then Death begged so humbly and represented so forcibly what would be the consequences of this disorder, that Beppo agreed to let him out, on condition that Death should not come back for him unless he was willing. Death departed and sought by means of a few wars and pestilences to make up for lost time.

At length Beppo grew so old that life became distasteful to him. Then he sent for Death, who, however, would not come, fearing that Beppo might change his mind. So the latter decided to go himself to Death. Death was not at home; but remembering his vacation in the sack, had prudently left the order that in case a certain Beppo Pipetta should come, he was to be beaten soundly; an order which was executed punctiliously. Beaten and cast out by Death, he went sadly to hell; but there the Devil had given the porter orders to show him the same attention that he had received at Death's abode, and that command also was conscientiously obeyed.

Smarting from the blows he had received, and vexed that neither Death nor the Devil wanted him, he went to paradise. Here he announced himself to St. Peter, but the saint thought that he had better first consult the Lord.

Meanwhile Beppo threw his cap over the wall into paradise. After he had waited a while, St Peter reappeared and said: "I am very sorry, but our Lord doesn't want you here." "Very well," said Beppo, "but you will at least let me get my cap," and with that he slipped through the gate and sat down on the cap. When St. Peter commanded him to get up and begone, he replied, composedly: "Gently, my dear sir! At present I am sitting on my own property, where I do not receive orders from any one!"

And so he remained in paradise.[25]

The story known to our readers from the Grimm collection, "Godfather Death," is found in Sicily and Venice. The version from the latter place given in Bernoni *(Trad. pop.,* p. 6) is as follows:

➳ LXVII. The Just Man ➳

Once upon a time there was a peasant and his wife who had a child that they would not baptize until they could find a just man for his godfather. The father took the child in his arms and went into the street to look for this just man. After he had walked along a while, he met a man, who was our Lord, and said to him: "I have this child to baptize, but I do not want to give him to any one who is not just; are you just?" The Lord answered: "But—I don't know whether I am just." Then the peasant passed on and met a woman, who was the Madonna, and said to her: "I have this child to baptize and do not wish to give him to any one who is not just; are you just?" "I don't know," said the Madonna; " but go on, for you will find some one who is just." He went his way and met another woman, who was Death, and said to her: "I have been sent to you, for I have been told that you are just, and I have this child to baptize, and do not wish to give it to one who is not just; are you just?" Death said: "Yes, I believe I am just! Let us baptize the child, and then I will show you whether I am just." Then they baptized the child, and afterwards Death led the peasant into a very long room, where there were many lights burning. "Godmother," said the man, astonished at seeing all the lights, "what are all these lights?" Death said: "These are the lights of all the souls in the world. Would you like to see, friend? This is yours and this is your son's." When the peasant saw that his light was about to expire, he said: "And when the oil is all consumed, godmother?" "Then," answered Death, "you must come with me, for I am Death." "Oh! For mercy's sake," cried the peasant, "let me at least take a little oil from my son's lamp and put it in mine!" "No, no, godfather," said Death, "I don't do anything of that sort; you wished to see a just person, and a just person you have found. And now go home and arrange your affairs, for I am waiting for you."[26]

We can mention but briefly another Venetian legend which, like several of those already given, reaches back to the Middle Ages. A wealthy knight, who has led a wicked life, repents when he grows old, and his confessor enjoins on him a three years' penance. The knight refuses, for he might die at the end of two years and lose all that amount of penance. He refuses in turn a penance of two years, of one year, and even of a month, but agrees to do penance for one night. He mounts his horse, takes leave of his family, and rides away to the church, which is at some distance. After he has ridden for a time, his daughter comes running after him and calls him back, for robbers have attacked the castle. He will not be diverted from his purpose, and tells her that there are servants and soldiers enough to defend the house. Then a servant cries out that the castle is in flames, and his own wife calls for help against violence. The knight calmly continues his way, leaving his servants to act for him, and simply saying: "I have no time for it now."

Finally he enters the church and begins his penance. Here he is disturbed by the sexton, who bids him depart, so that he can close the church; a priest orders him to leave, as he is not worthy to hear a mass; at midnight twelve watchmen come and order him to go with them to the judge, but he will not move for any of them; at two o'clock a band of soldiers surround him and order him to depart, and at five o'clock a wild throng of people burst into the church and cry: "Let us drive him out!" Then the church begins to burn, and the knight finds himself in the midst of flames, but still he moves not. At last, when the appointed hour comes, he leaves the church and rides home to find that none of his family had left the castle, but the various persons who had tried to divert him from his penance were emissaries of the Devil. Then the knight sees how great a sinner he was and declares that he will do penance all the rest of his life.[27]

Bernoni in his *Leggende fantastiche* gives nine legends, one of which is the story of St. Peter's mother, mentioned above. Of the remaining ones, several may be classed under ghost stories, and two illustrate the great sanctity attached by the Italian to the spiritual relationship contracted by godmothers and godfathers, and by groomsmen and the bride. It is well known that in the Romish Church a godfather or godmother contracts a spiritual relationship with the godson or goddaughter and their parents which would prevent marriage between the parties. This relationship the popular imagination has extended to the godfather and godmother, and any improper intimacy between the two is regarded as the most deadly sin. The first of Bernoni's legends is entitled:

ꜱ LXVIII. Of a Godfather and a Godmother of St. John Who Made Love ꜱ

Here in Venice, heaven knows how many centuries ago, there was a gentleman and a lady, husband and wife, who were rich people. Well, there frequented their house a *compare* (godfather) of St. John; and it came to pass that he and his *comare* (godmother, *i.e.* the one who had been godmother to the same child to which he had been godfather), the lady of the house, made love to each other in secret. This lady had a maid, and this maid knew everything. So one day this lady said to the maid: "Hold your tongue, and you'll see that you will be satisfied with me. When I come to die, you shall have an allowance of a dollar a day." So this maid kept always on good terms with the lady. It happened that the *compare* fell very ill. The lady was so desperately sorry, that her husband kept saying to her: "Come, will you make yourself ill too? It's no use fretting, for it's what we must all come to." At last the *compare* died. And she took it so to heart, that she fell ill in earnest. When her husband saw her giving way to such low spirits, he began to suspect that there had been something between her and the *compare;* but he never said a word about it to annoy her, but bore it like a philosopher. The maid was always by her mistress' bedside, and the mistress said to her: "Remember that, if I die, you must watch by me quite alone, for I won't have any one else." And the maid promised her that she would. Well, that day went by, and the next day, and the next, and the lady got worse and worse, until at last she died. You can fancy how sorry her husband was. And the maid and the other servants were very sorry, too, for she was a very good lady. The other servants offered to sit up and watch with the maid; but she said: "No; I must sit up by myself, for my mistress said she would have no others." And they said: "Very well. If you want anything, ring the bell, and we shall be ready to do anything you want." Then the maid had four tapers lighted, and placed at the foot of the bed, and she took the Office for the Dead in her hand and began to read it.

Just at midnight the door of the room burst open, and she saw the figure of the *compare* come in. Directly she saw him she felt her blood turn to water. She tried to cry out, but she was so terrified that she couldn't make a sound. Then she got up from her chair and went to ring the bell; and the dead man, without saying a word (because, of course, dead folks can't talk), gave her a sharp blow on the hand to prevent her from ringing. And he signed her to take a taper in her hand, and come with him to her mistress' bed. She obeyed. When the dead man got to the bedside, he took the lady, and sat her up on the bed, and he began to put her stockings on her feet, and he dressed her from head to foot. When she was dressed, he pulled her out of bed, took her by the arm, and they both went out at the door, with the maid going before them to light the way. In this palace there was an underground passage—there are many like it in Venice—and they went down into it. When they got to a certain part of it, he gave a great knock to the taper that the maid had in her hand, and left her in the dark. The maid was so terrified that she fell down on the ground, all rolled up together like a ball, and there she lay.

At daybreak the other servants thought they would go and see how the maid was getting on, as she had not called them all night. So they went and opened the door of the room, and saw nobody there at all, either living or dead. They were frightened out of their wits, and ran to their master, and said: "Oh, mercy on us, there's nobody left, neither the dead woman nor the live one! The room's quite empty." Said the master: "You don't say so!" Then he dressed himself as fast as he could, and went and looked, and found nobody. And he saw that the clothes his wife wore to go out in were gone too. Then he called the servants, and said to them: "Here, take these torches, and let us go and look in the underground passage." So all the people went down there with lighted torches; and after searching about a bit, they found the poor maid, who gave no sign of life. The servants took her by one arm; but it was all bent up stiff, and wouldn't move. And they tried the other arm, and that was the same, and all her body was knotted together quite stiff. Then they took up this ball of a woman, and carried her up-stairs, and put her on her bed. The master sent for the doctors, to see if they could bring back life to her. And by degrees she began to open her eyes and move her fingers. But she had had a stroke and couldn't speak. But by the movements of her fingers they could make out nearly everything she wanted to say. Then the master had the torches lighted again, and went down again into the underground passage, to see if he could find any trace of the dead woman. They looked and looked, but they could find nothing but a deep hole. And the master understood directly that that was where his wife and her *compare* had been swallowed up. And upon that he went up-stairs again; but he wouldn't stay any longer in that palace, nor even in Venice, and he went away to Verona. And in the palace he left the maid, with her dollar a day and people to take care of her and feed her, for to the end of her days she was bedridden and couldn't speak. And the master would have every one free to go and see that sight, that it might be a warning to all people who had the evil intention of not respecting the baptismal relationship.[28]

THE SECOND of Bernoni's legends turns on the peculiar sanctity of the relation of a groomsman (*compare de l'anelo*) to the bride. The full title is: "About a *compare de l'anelo* who pressed the bride's hand with evil intent." It is as follows:

ᔜ LXIX. The Groomsman ᔜ

You must know that we Venetians have a saying that the groomsman is the godfather of the first child. Well, in the parish of the Angel Raphael it happened that there was a young man and woman who were in love with each other. So they agreed to be married, and the bridegroom looked out for his best man. According to custom, directly he had chosen his best man, he took him to the bride's house, and said to her: "Look here, this is your groomsman." Directly the groomsman saw the bride he fell so much in love with her that he consented more than willingly to be the best man. Well, the wedding day came, and this man went into the church with evil thoughts in his heart. When they came out of the church they had a collation, according to custom, and then in the afternoon they had a gondola to go to the tavern, as people used to do on such days. First the bride got into the gondola, with the best man, and then the bridegroom and the relations. When they were getting into the boat the groomsman took the bride's hand to help her in, and he squeezed it, and squeezed it so hard that he hurt her severely.

As time went on he saw that the bride thought nothing about him, and he began not to care for her, either. But by and by he began to have a sort of scruple of conscience about what he had done to his *comare* on the wedding day. And the more he thought of it, the more he felt this scruple. So he made up his mind to go to confession, and to tell his confessor what he had done, and with what evil intention. "You have committed a great sin, my son," said the priest; "I shall give you a penance,—a heavy penance. Will you do it?" "Yes, father," said he; "tell me what it is." The priest answered: "Listen. You must make a journey in the night-time to a place that I shall tell you of. But mind; whatever voices you hear, you must never turn back for an instant! And take three apples with you, and you will meet three noblemen, and you must give one apple to each of them." Then the priest told him the place he was to go to, and the groomsman left him. Well, he waited until night-fall, and then he took his three apples and set out. He walked and walked and walked, until at last he came to the place the priest had told him of, and he heard such a talking and murmuring, you can't think! One voice said one thing, and one another. These were all folks who had committed great sins against St. John; but he knew nothing about that. He heard them calling out: "Turn back! turn back!" But not he! No; he went straight on, without ever looking round, let them call ever so much. After he had gone on a while he saw the three noblemen, and he saluted them and gave them an apple apiece. The last of the three had his arm hidden under his cloak, and the *compare* saw that the gentleman had great difficulty in stretching his arm out to take the apple. At length he pulled his arm from under his cloak, and showed a hand swelled up to such a huge size that the *compare* was frightened to look at it. But he gave him the apple, the same as to the others, and they all three thanked him and went away. The *compare* returned home again, and went to his confessor and told him all that had happened. Then the priest said: "See, now, my son, you are saved. For the first of the three noblemen was the Lord, the second was St. Peter, and the third was St. John. You saw what a hand he had. Well, that was the hand you squeezed on the wedding day; and so, instead of squeezing the bride's hand, you really hurt St. John!"[29]

THE THIRD legend is entitled: "Of two *compari* of St. John who swore by the name of St. John." Two *compari* who had not seen each other for some time met one day, and one invited the other to lunch and paid the bill. The other declared that he would do the same a week hence. When he said this they happened to be standing where two streets crossed. "Then we meet a week from to-day at this spot and at this hour!" "Yes." "By St. John, I will not fail!" "I swear by St. John that I will be here awaiting you!" During the week, however, the *compare* who had paid for the lunch died. The other did not know he was dead, and at the appointed time he went to the place to meet him. While there a friend passed, who asked: "What are you doing here?" "I am waiting for my *compare* Tony." "You are waiting for your *compare* Tony! Why, he has been dead three days! You will wait a long time!" "You say he is dead? There he is coming!" And, indeed, he saw him, but his friend did not. The dead man stopped before his *compare* and said: "You are right in being here at this spot, and you can thank God; otherwise, I would teach you to swear in the name of St. John!" Then he suddenly disappeared and his *compare* saw him no more, for his oath was only to be at that spot.

The sanctity of an ordinary oath is shown in the fourth story: "Of two lovers who swore fidelity in life and death." Two young persons made love, unknown to the girl's parents. The youth made her swear that she would love him in life and death. Some time after, he was killed in a brawl. The girl did not know it, and the young man's ghost continued to visit her as usual, and she began to grow pale and thin. The father discovered the state of the case, and consulted the priest, who learned from the girl, in confession, how matters stood, and came with a black cat, a stole, and book, to conjure the spirit and save the girl.

The fifth legend is entitled: "The Night of the Dead"; *i. e.* the eve of All Saints' Day. A servant girl, rising early one morning as she supposed (it was really midnight), witnesses a weird procession, which she unwittingly disturbs by lowering her candle and asking the last passer-by to light it. This he does; but when she pulls up her basket she finds in it, besides the lighted candle, a human arm. Her confessor tells her to wait a year, until the procession passes again, then hold a black cat tightly in her arms, and restore the arm to its owner. This she does, with the words: "Here, master, take your arm; I am much obliged to you." He took the arm angrily, and said: "You may thank God you have that cat in your arms, otherwise, what I am, that you would be also."

The sixth legend is of an incredulous priest, who believes that where the dead are, there they stay. It is as follows:

↗ LXX. *The Parish Priest of San Marcuola* ↗

Once upon a time there was a parish priest at San Marcuola, here in Venice, who was a very good man. He couldn't bear to see women in church with hats or bonnets on their heads, and he had spirit enough to go and make them take them off. "For," said he, "the church is the house of God; and what is not permitted to men ought not to be permitted to women." But when a woman had a shawl over her shoulders he would have her throw it over her head, that she might not be stared at and ogled. But this priest had one fault: he did not believe in ghosts; and one day he was preaching a sermon, and in this sermon he said to the people: "Listen, now, dearly beloved brethren. This morning, when I came into the church here, there comes up to me one of my flock, and she says to

me, all in a flutter: 'Oh, Father, what a fright I have had this night! I was
asleep in my bed, and the ghosts came and twitched away my coverlet!'
But I answered her: 'Dear daughter, that is not possible; because *where the
dead are, there they stay.*'" And so he declared before all the congregation
that it was not true that the dead could come back and be seen and heard.
In the evening the priest went to bed as usual, and about midnight he
heard the house-bell ring loudly. The servant went out on to the balcony
and saw a great company of people in the street, and she called out:
"Who's there?" and they asked her if the Priest of San Marcuola was at
home. And she said Yes; but he was in bed. Then they said he must come
down. But the priest, when he heard about it, refused to go. They then
began to ring the bell again and tell the servant to call her master; and
the priest said he wouldn't go anywhere. Then all the doors burst open,
and the whole company marched up-stairs into the priest's bedroom, and
bade him get up and dress himself and come with them; and he was
obliged to do what they said. When they reached a certain spot they set
him in the midst of them, and they gave him so many knocks and cuffs
that he did n't know which side to turn himself; and then they said: "This
is for a remembrance of the poor defunct;" and upon that they all vanished away and were seen no more, and the poor priest went back home,
bruised from head to foot. And so the ghosts proved plain enough that it
isn't true to say: *"Where the dead are, there they stay."*[30]

THE STORY of Don Juan appears in the seventh legend, entitled:

ᘒ *LXXI. The Gentleman Who Kicked a Skull* ᘒ

There was once a youth who did nothing but eat, drink, and amuse himself, because he was immensely wealthy and had nothing to think about.
He scoffed at every one; he dishonored all the young girls; he played all
sorts of tricks, and was tired of everything. One day he took it into his
head to give a grand banquet; and thereupon he invited all his friends and
many women and all his acquaintances.

While they were preparing the banquet he took a walk, and passed
through a street where there was a cemetery. While walking he noticed on
the ground a skull. He gave it a kick, and then he went up to it and said
to it in jest: "You, too, will come, will you not, to my banquet to-night?"
Then he went his way, and returned home. At the house the banquet was

ready and the guests had all arrived. They sat down to the table, and ate and drank to the sound of music, and diverted themselves joyfully.

Meanwhile midnight drew near, and when the clock was on the stroke a ringing of bells was heard. The servants went to see who it was, and beheld a great ghost, who said to them: "Tell Count Robert that I am the one he invited this morning to his banquet." They went to their master and told him what the ghost had said. The master said: "I? All those whom I invited are here, and I have invited no one else." They said: "If you should see him! It is a ghost that is terrifying." Then it came into the young man's mind that it might be that dead man; and he said to the servants: "Quick! Quick! Close the doors and balconies, so that he cannot enter!" The servants went to close everything; but hardly had they done so when the doors and balconies were thrown wide open and the ghost entered. He went up where they were feasting, and said: "Robert! Robert! Was it not enough for you to profane everything? Have you wished to disturb the dead, also? The end has come!" All were terrified, and fled here and there, some concealing themselves, and some falling on their knees. Then the ghost seized Robert by the throat and strangled him and carried him away with him; and thus he has left this example, that it is not permitted to mock the poor dead.[31]

THE NINTH and last of Bernoni's legends is a story about Massariol, the domestic spirit of the Venetians. A man of family, whose business takes him out at night, finds in the street a basket containing an infant. The weather is very cold, so the good man carries the foundling home, and his wife, who already has a young child, makes the little stranger as comfortable as possible. He is cared for and put in the cradle by the side of the other child. The husband and wife have to leave the room a moment; when they return the foundling has disappeared. The husband asks in amazement: "What can it mean?" She answers: "I am sure I don't know; can it be Massariol?" Then he goes out on the balcony and sees at a distance one who seems like a man, but is not, who is clapping his hands and laughing and making all manner of fun of him, and then suddenly disappears.

The same mischievous spirit plays many other pranks. Sometimes he cheats the ferrymen out of their toll; sometimes he disguises himself like the baker's lad, and calls at the houses to take the bread to the oven, and then carries it away to some square or bridge; sometimes, when the washing is hung out, he carries it off to some distant place, and when the owners have at last found their property, Massariol laughs in their faces and disappears. The woman who related these stories to Bernoni added: "Massariol has never done anything bad; he likes to laugh and joke and fool people. He, too, has been shut up, I don't know where, by the Holy Office, the same as the witches, fairies, and magicians."

Pitrè's collection contains little that falls under the second heading of this chapter. The following story, however, is interesting from its English parallels:

﹌ LXXIII. Saddaedda ﹌

Once upon a time there was a girl called Saddaedda, who was crazy. One day, when her mother had gone into the country and she was left alone in the house, she went into a church where the funeral service was being read over the body of a rich lady. The girl hid herself in the confessional. No one knew she was there; so, when the other people had gone, she was left alone with the corpse. It was dressed out in a rose-colored robe and everything else becoming, and it had ear-rings in its ears and rings on its fingers. These the girl took off, and then she began to undress the body. When she came to the stockings she drew off one easily, but at the other she had to pull so hard that at last the leg came off with it. Saddaedda. took the leg, carried it to her lonely home, and locked it up in a box. At night came the dead lady and knocked at the door. "Who's there?" said the girl. "It is I," answered the corpse. "Give me back my leg and stocking!" But Saddaedda paid no heed to the request. Next day she prepared a feast and invited some of her playfellows to spend the night with her. They came, feasted, and went to sleep. At midnight the dead woman began to knock at the door and to repeat last night's request. Saddaedda took no notice of the noise, but her companions, whom it awoke, were horrified, and as soon as they could, they ran away. On the third night just the same happened. On the fourth she could persuade only one girl to keep her company. On the fifth she was left entirely alone. The corpse came, forced open the door, strode up to Saddaedda's bed, and strangled her. Then the dead woman opened the box, took out her leg and stocking, and carried them off with her to her grave.[32]

THIS chapter would be incomplete without reference to treasure stories. A number of these are given by Miss Busk in her interesting collection. A few are found in Pitrè, only one of which needs mention here, on account of its parallels in other countries. It is called *Lu Vicerrè Tunnina*, "Viceroy Tunny " (*tunnina* is the flesh of the tunny-fish). There was at Palermo a man who sold tunny-fish. One night he dreamed that some one appeared to him and said: "Do you wish to find your Fate? Go under the bridge *di li Testi* (of the Heads, so the people call the *Ponte dell' Ammiraglio,* a bridge now abandoned, constructed in 1113 by the Admiral Georgios Antiochenos); there you will find it." For three nights he dreamed the same thing. The third time, he went under the bridge and found a poor man all in rags. The fish-seller was frightened and was going away, when the man called him. It was his Fate. He said: "To-night, at midnight, where you have placed the barrels of fish, dig, and what you find is yours."

The fish-dealer did as he was told; dug, and found a staircase, which he descended, and found a room full of money. The fish-dealer became wealthy, lent the king of Spain money, and was made viceroy and raised to the rank of prince and duke.[33]

CHAPTER V

꒰ꔛ꒱

Nursery Tales

THE TALES we have thus far given, although they may count many young people among their auditors, are not distinctly children's stories. The few that follow are, and it is greatly to be regretted that their number is not larger. That many more exist, cannot be doubted; but collectors have probably overlooked this interesting class. Even Pitrè in his large collection gives but eleven (Nos. 130–141), and those in the other collections are mostly parallels to Pitrè's.

We will begin with those that are advantages taken of children's love for stories. The first is from Venice (Bernoni, Punt. II. p. 53) and is called:

꒰ LXXIV. Mr. Attentive ꒱

"Do you want me to tell you the story of Mr. Attentive?"
"Tell me it."
"But you must not say 'tell me it,' for it is

> The story of Mr. Attentive,
>   Which lasts a long time,
> Which is never explained:
>   Do you wish me to tell it, or relate it?"

"Relate it"
"But you must not say 'relate it,' for it is

> The story of Mr. Attentive,
>   Which lasts a long time,
> Which is never explained:
>   Do you wish me to tell it, or relate it?"

"But come! tell me it."

"But you must not say," etc., etc.[1]

THE FOLLOWING are intended to soothe restless children, and are so short that they may be given entire.

ᴔLXXV. The Story of the Barber ᴔ

Once upon a time there was a barber. . . . Be good and I will tell it to you again.[2]

THE next is from the same source.

Once upon a time there was a king, a pope, and a dwarf. . . . This king, this pope, and this dwarf. . . .

(Then the story-teller begins again).

BUT it is time to give some of the stories that are told to the good children. The first is from Pitrè (No. 130) and is called:

ᴔLXXVI. Don Firriulieddu ᴔ

Once upon a time there was a farmer who had a daughter who used to take his dinner to him in the fields. One day he said to her: "So that you may find me I will sprinkle bran along the way; you follow the bran, and you will come to me."

By chance the old ogre passed that way, and seeing the bran, said: "This means something." So he took the bran and scattered it so that it led to his own house.

When the daughter set out to take her father his dinner, she followed the bran until she came to the ogre's house. When the ogre saw the young girl, he said: "You must be my wife." Then she began to weep. When the father saw that his daughter did not appear, he went home in the evening, and began to search for her; and not finding her, he asked God to give him a son or a daughter.

A year after, he had a son whom they called *"Don Firriulieddu."* When the child was three days old it spoke, and said: "Have you made me a cloak? Now give me a little dog and the cloak, for I must look for my sister." So he set out and went to seek his sister.

After a while he came to a plain where he saw a number of men, and asked: "Whose cattle are these?" The herdsman replied: "They belong to the ogre, who fears neither God nor the saints, who fears *Don Firriulied-du*, who is three days old, and is on the way, and gives his dog bread and says: 'Eat, my dog, and do not bark, for we have fine things to do.'"

Afterwards he saw a flock of sheep, and asked: "Whose are these sheep?" and received the same answer as from the herdsman. Then he arrived at the ogre's house and knocked, and his sister opened the door and saw the child. "Who are you looking for?" she said. "I am looking for you, for I am your brother, and you must return to mamma."

When the ogre heard that *Don Firriulieddu* was there, he went and hid himself up-stairs. *Don Firriulieddu* asked his sister: "Where is the ogre?" "Up-stairs." *Don Firriulieddu* said to his dog: "Go up-stairs and bark, and I will follow you." The dog went up and barked, and *Firriulieddu* followed him, and killed the ogre. Then he took his sister and a quantity of money, and they went home to their mother, and are all contented.

CERTAIN traits in the above story, as the size of the hero and the bran serving to guide the girl to her father, recall, somewhat faintly, it is true, our own "Tom Thumb." It is only recently that a Tuscan version of "Tom Thumb" has been found.[3] It is called:

ᴔ LXXVII. *Little Chick-Pea** ᴔ

Once upon a time there was a husband and wife who had no children. The husband was a carpenter, and when he came home from his shop he did nothing but scold his wife because she had no children, and the poor woman was constantly weeping and despairing. She was charitable, and had festivals celebrated in the church; but no children. One day a woman knocked at her door and asked for alms; but the carpenter's wife answered: "I will not give you any, for I have given alms and had masses said, and festivals celebrated for a long time, and have no son." "Give me alms and you will have children." "Good! In that case I will do all you wish." "You must give me a whole loaf of bread, and I will give you something that will bring you children." "If you will, I will give you two loaves." "No, no! Now, I want only one; you can give me the other when you have the children." So she gave her a loaf, and the woman said: "Now

---

*Cecino, dim. of *Cece,* chick-pea.

I will go home and give my children something to eat, and then I will bring you what will make you have children." "Very well."

The woman went home, fed her children, and then took a little bag, filled it with chick-peas, and carried it to the carpenter's wife, and said: "This is a bag of peas; put them in the kneading-trough, and to-morrow they will be as many sons as there are peas." There were a hundred peas, and the carpenter's wife said: "How can a hundred peas become a hundred sons?" "You will see to-morrow." The carpenter's wife said to herself: "I had better say nothing about it to my husband, because if by any mischance the children should not come, he would give me a fine scolding."

Her husband returned at night and began to grumble as usual; but his wife said not a word and went to bed repeating to herself: "To-morrow you will see!" The next morning the hundred peas had become a hundred sons. One cried: "Papa, I want to drink." Another said: "Papa, I want to eat." Another: "Papa, take me up." He, in the midst of all this tumult, took a stick and went to the trough and began to beat, and killed them all. One fell out (imagine how small they were!) and ran quickly into the bedroom and hid himself on the handle of the pitcher. After the carpenter had gone to his shop his wife said: "What a rascal! He has grumbled so long about my not having children and now he has killed them all!" Then the son. who had escaped said: "Mamma, has papa gone?" She said: "Yes, my son. How did you manage to escape? Where are you?" "Hush! I am in the handle of the pitcher; tell me: has papa gone?" "Yes, yes, yes, come out!" Then the child who had escaped came out and his mamma exclaimed: "Oh! how pretty you are! How shall I call you?" The child answered. "Cecino." "Very well, bravo, my Cecino! Do you know, Cecino, you must go and carry your papa's dinner to him at the shop." "Yes, you must put the little basket on my head, and I will go and carry it to papa."

The carpenter's wife, when it was time, put the basket on Cecino's head and sent him to carry her husband's dinner to him. When Cecino was near the shop, he began to cry: "O papa! Come and meet me; I am bringing you your dinner."

The carpenter said to himself: "Oh! Did I kill them all, or are there any left?" He went to meet Cecino and said: "O my good boy! How did you escape my blows?" "I fell down, ran into the room, and hid myself on the handle of the pitcher." "Bravo, Cecino! Listen. You must go around among the country people and hear whether they have anything broken to mend." "Yes."

So the carpenter put Cecino in his pocket, and while he went along the way did nothing but chatter; so that every one said he was mad, because they did not know that he had his son in his pocket. When he saw some countrymen he asked: "Have you anything to mend?" "Yes, there are some things about the oxen broken, but we cannot let you mend them, for you are mad." "What do you mean by calling me mad? I am wiser than you. Why do you say I am mad?" "Because you do nothing but talk to yourself on the road." "I was talking with my son." "And where do you keep your son?" " In my pocket." "That is a pretty place to keep your son." "Very well, I will show him to you;" and he pulls out Cecino, who was so small that he stood on one of his father's fingers.

"Oh, what a pretty child! You must sell him to us." "What are you thinking about! I sell you my son who is so valuable to me!" "Well, then, don't sell him to us." What does he do then? He takes Cecino and puts him on the horn of an ox and says: "Stay there, for now I am going to get the things to mend." "Yes, yes, don't be afraid; I will stay on my horn." So the carpenter went to get the things to mend.

Meanwhile two thieves passed by, and seeing the oxen, one said: "See those two oxen there alone. Come, let us go and steal them." When they drew near, Cecino cried out: "Papa, look out! There are thieves here! They are stealing your oxen!" "Ah! Where does that voice come from?" And they approached nearer to see; and Cecino, the nearer he saw them come, the more he called out: "Look out for your oxen, papa; the thieves are stealing them!"

When the carpenter came the thieves said to him: "Good man, where does that voice come from?" "It is my son." "If he is not here, where is he?" "Don't you see? There he is, up on the horn of one of the oxen." When he showed him to them, they said: "You must sell him to us; we will give you as much money as you wish." "What are you thinking about! I might sell him to you, but who knows how much my wife would grumble about it!" "Do you know what you must tell her? That he died on the way."

They tempted him so much that at last he gave him to them for two sacks of money. They took their Cecino, put him in one of their pockets, and went away. On their journey they saw the king's stable. "Let us take a look at the king's stable and see whether we can steal a pair of horses." "Very good." They said to Cecino: "Don't betray us." "Don't be afraid, I will not betray you."

So they went into the stable and stole three horses, which they took home and put in their own stable.

Afterwards they went and said to Cecino: "Listen. We are so tired! Save us the trouble, go down and give the horses some oats." Cecino went to do so, but fell asleep on the halter and one of the horses swallowed him. When he did not return, the thieves said: "He must have fallen asleep in the stable." So they went there and looked for him and called: "Cecino, where are you?" "Inside of the black horse." Then they killed the black horse; but Cecino was not there. "Cecino, where are you?" "In the bay horse." So they killed the bay horse; but Cecino was not there. "Cecino, where are you?" But Cecino answered no longer. Then they said: "What a pity! That child who was so useful to us is lost." Then they dragged out into the fields the two horses that they had cut open.

A famished wolf passed that way and saw the dead horses. "Now I will eat my fill of horse," and he ate and ate until he had finished and had swallowed Cecino.* Then the wolf went off until it became hungry again and said: "Let us go and eat a goat."

When Cecino heard the wolf talk about eating a goat, he cried out: "Goat-herd, the wolf is coming to eat your goats!"

[The wolf supposes that it has swallowed some wind that forms these words, hits itself against a stone, and after several trials gets rid of the wind and Cecino, who hides himself under a stone, so that he shall not be seen.]

Three robbers passed that way with a bag of money. One of them said: "Now I will count the money, and you others be quiet or I will kill you!" You can imagine whether they kept still! for they did not want to die. So he began to count: "One, two, three, four, and five." And Cecino: "One, two, three, four, and five." (Do you understand? he repeats the robber's words.) "I hear you! You will not keep still. Well, I will kill you; we shall see whether you will speak again." He began to count the money again: "One, two, three, four, and five." Cecino repeats: "One, two, three, four, and five." "Then you will not keep quiet! now I will kill you!" and he killed one of them. "Now we shall see whether you will talk; if you do I will kill you too." He began to count: "One, two, three, four, and five." Cecino repeats: "One, two, three, four, and five." "Take care. If I have to tell you again I will kill you!" "Do you think I want to speak? I don't wish to be killed." He begins to count: "One, two, three, four, and five." Cecino repeats: "One, two, three, four, and five." "You will not keep quiet either; now I will kill you!" and he killed him. "Now I am alone and can count by

---

*It appears from this that Cecino had been in one of the horses all the time, but the thieves had not seen him because he was so small.

myself and no one will repeat it." So he began again to count: "One, two, three, four, and five." And Cecino: "One, two, three, four, and five." Then the robber said: "There is some one hidden here; I had better run away or he will kill me." So he ran away and left behind the sack of money.

When Cecino perceived that there was no one there, he came out, put the bag of money on his head, and started for home. When he drew near his parents' house he cried: "Oh, mamma, come and meet me; I have brought you a bag of money!"

When his mother heard him she went to meet him and took the money and said: "Take care you don't drown yourself in these puddles of rain-water." The mother went home, and turned back to look for Cecino, but he was not to be seen. She told her husband what Cecino had done, and they went and searched everywhere for him, and at last found him drowned in a puddle.[4]

THE NEXT story is one that has always enjoyed great popularity over the whole of Europe, and is a most interesting example of the diffusion of nursery tales. It is also interesting from the attempt to show that it is of comparatively late date, and has been borrowed from a people not of European extraction.[5] The story belongs to the class of what may be called "accumulative" stories, of which "The House that Jack built" is a good example. It is a version of the story so well known in English of the old woman who found a little crooked sixpence, and went to market and bought a little pig. As she was coming home the pig would not go over the stile. The old woman calls on a dog to bite pig, but the dog will not. Then she calls in turn on a stick, fire, water, ox, butcher, rope, rat, and cat. They all refuse to help her except the cat, which promises help in exchange for a saucer of milk. "So away went the old woman to the cow. But the cow said to her: 'If you will go to yonder hay-stack and fetch me a handful of hay, I'll give you the milk.' So away went the old woman to the hay-stack; and she brought the hay to the cow. As soon as the cow had eaten the hay, she gave the old woman the milk; and away she went with it in a saucer to the cat.

"As soon as the cat had lapped up the milk, the cat began to kill the rat; the rat to gnaw the rope; the rope began to hang the butcher; the butcher began to kill the ox; the ox began to drink the water; the water began to quench the fire; the fire began to burn the stick; the stick began to beat the dog; the dog began to bite the pig; the little pig in a fright jumped over the stile, and so the old woman got home that night."[6]

The Italian versions may be divided into two classes: first, where the animals and inanimate objects are invoked to punish some human being; second, where all the actors are animals. The first version of the first class that we shall give is from Sicily, Pitrè, No. 131, and is called:

↝ LXXVIII. Pitidda ↝

Once upon a time there was a mother who had a daughter named Pitidda. She said to her: "Go sweep the house." "Give me some bread first." "I cannot," she answered. When her mother saw that she would not sweep the house, she called the wolf. "Wolf, go kill Pitidda, for Pitidda will not sweep the house." "I can't," said the wolf. "Dog, go kill the wolf," said the mother, "for the wolf will not kill Pitidda, for Pitidda will not sweep the house." "I can't," said the dog. "Stick, go kill the dog, for the dog will not kill the wolf, for the wolf won't kill Pitidda, for Pitidda won't sweep the house." "I can't," said the stick." "Fire, burn stick, for stick won't kill dog, for dog won't kill wolf, for wolf won't kill Pitidda, for Pitidda won't sweep the house." "I can't," said the fire. "Water, quench fire, for fire won't burn stick, for stick won't kill dog, for dog won't kill wolf, for wolf won't kill Pitidda, for Pitidda won't sweep the house." "I can't." "Cow, go drink water, for water won't quench fire, for fire won't burn stick, for stick won't kill dog, for dog won't kill wolf, for wolf won't kill Pitidda, for Pitidda won't sweep the house." "I can't," said the cow. "Rope, go choke cow," etc.

[Then the mother calls on the mouse to gnaw the rope, the cat to eat the mouse, and the story ends.]

The cat runs and begins to eat the mouse, the mouse runs and begins to gnaw the rope, the rope to choke the cow, the cow to drink the water, the water to quench the fire, the fire to burn the stick, the stick to kill the dog, the dog to kill the wolf, the wolf to kill Pitidda, Pitidda to sweep the house, and her mother runs and gives her some bread.[7]

THE ITALIAN story, it will be seen, has a moral. The animals, etc., are invoked to punish a disobedient child. In the Neapolitan version a mother sends her son to gather some fodder for the cattle. He does not wish to go until he has had some macaroni that his mother has just cooked. She promises to keep him some, and he departs. While he is gone the mother eats up all the macaroni, except a small bit. When her son returns, and sees how little is left for him, he begins to cry and refuses to eat; and his mother calls on stick, fire, water, ox, rope, mouse, and cat to make her son obey, and eat the macaroni.[8] The disobedient son is also found in two Tuscan versions, one from Siena, and one from Florence, which are almost identical.[9]

In the Venetian version, a naughty boy will not go to school, and his mother invokes dog, stick, fire, water, ox, butcher, and soldier.[10]

The Sicilian story of "The Sexton's Nose" (Pitrè, No. 135) will serve as the connecting link between the two classes above mentioned. Properly speaking, only the second part of it belongs here; but we will give a brief analysis of the first also.

ꝯ LXXIX. The Sexton's Nose ꝯ

A sexton, one day in sweeping the church, found a piece of money (it was the fifth of a cent) and deliberated with himself as to what he would buy with it. If he bought nuts or almonds, he was afraid of the mice; so at last he bought some roasted peas, and ate all but the last pea. This he took to a bakery near by, and asked the mistress to keep it for him; she told him to leave it on a bench, and she would take care of it. When she went to get it, she found that the cock had eaten it. The next day the sexton came for the roast pea, and when he heard what had become of it, he said they must either return the roast pea or give him the cock. This they did, and the sexton, not having any place to keep it, took it to a miller's wife, who promised to keep it for him. Now she had a pig, which managed to kill the cock. The next day the sexton came for the cock, and on finding it dead, demanded the pig, and the woman had to give it to him. The pig he left with a friend of his, a pastry-cook, whose daughter was to be married the next day. The woman was mean and sly, and killed the pig for her daughter's wedding, meaning to tell the sexton that the pig had run away. The sexton, however, when he heard it, made a great fuss, and declared that she must give him back his pig or her daughter. At last she had to give him her daughter, whom he put in a bag and carried away. He took the bag to a woman who kept a shop, and asked her to keep for him this bag, which he said contained bran. The woman by chance kept chickens, and she thought she would take some of the sexton's bran and feed them. When she opened the bag she found the young girl, who told her how she came there. The woman took her out of the sack, and put in her stead a dog. The next day the sexton came for his bag, and putting it on his shoulder, started for the seashore, intending to throw the young girl in the sea. When he reached the shore, he opened the bag, and the furious dog flew out and bit his nose. The sexton was in great agony, and cried out, while the blood ran down his face in torrents: "Dog, dog, give me a hair to put in my nose, and heal the bite."* The dog answered: "Do you want a hair? Give me some bread." The sexton ran to a bakery, and said to the baker: "Baker, give me some bread to give the dog; the dog will give a hair; the hair I will put in my nose, and cure the bite." The baker said: "Do you want bread? Give me some wood." The sexton ran to the woodman. "Woodman, give me wood to give the baker; the baker will give me bread; the bread I will give to the dog; the dog will give me a hair, the hair I will put in my nose, and heal the bite." The woodman said: "Do you want wood? Give me a mattock." The sexton ran to a smith. "Smith, give me a mattock to give the woodman; the woodman will give me wood; I will carry the wood to the baker; the baker will give me bread; I will give the bread to the dog; the dog will give me a hair; the hair I will put in my nose, and heal the bite." The smith said: "Do you want a mattock? Give me some coals." The sexton ran to the collier. "Collier, give me some coals to give the smith; the smith will give me a mattock; the mattock I will give the woodman; the woodman will give me some wood; the wood I will give the baker; the baker will give me bread; the bread I will give the dog; the dog will give me a hair; the hair I will put in my nose, and heal the bite." "Do you want coals? Give me a cart." The sexton ran to the wagon-maker. "Wagon-maker, give me a cart to give the collier; the collier will give me some coals; the coals I will carry to the smith; the smith will give me a mattock; the mattock I will give the woodman; the woodman will give me some wood; the wood I will give the baker; the baker will give me bread; the bread I will give to the dog; the dog will give me a hair; the hair I will put in my nose, and heal the bite."

The wagon-maker, seeing the sexton's great lamentation, is moved to compassion, and gives him the cart. The sexton, well pleased, takes the cart and goes away to the collier; the collier gives him the coals; the coals he takes to the smith; the smith gives him the mattock; the mattock he takes to the woodman; the woodman gives him wood; the wood he carries to the baker; the baker gives him bread; the bread he carries to the dog; the dog gives him a hair; the hair he puts in his nose, and heals the bite.[11]

THE SECOND class contains the versions in which all the actors are animals or personified inanimate objects The first example we shall give

* As with us the hair of a dog is supposed to heal the bite the same dog has inflicted.

is from Avellino in the Principato Ulteriore (Imbriani, p. 239), and is called:

✁ LXXX. The Cock and the Mouse ✁

Once upon a time there was a cock and a mouse. One day the mouse said to the cock: "Friend Cock, shall we go and eat some nuts on yonder tree?" "As you like." So they both went under the tree and the mouse climbed up at once and began to eat. The poor cock began to fly, and flew and flew, but could not come where the mouse was. When it saw that there was no hope of getting there, it said: "Friend Mouse, do you know what I want you to do? Throw me a nut." The mouse went and threw one and hit the cock on the head. The poor cock, with its head broken and all covered with blood, went away to an old woman. "Old aunt, give me some rags to cure my head." "If you will give me two hairs, I will give you the rags." The cock went away to a dog. "Dog, give me some hairs; the hairs I will give the old woman; the old woman will give me rags to cure my head." "If you will give me a little bread," said the dog, "I will give you the hairs." The cock went away to a baker. "Baker, give me bread; I will give the bread to the dog; the dog will give hairs; the hairs I will carry to the old woman; the old woman will give me rags to cure my head." The baker answered: "I will not give you bread unless you give me some wood!" The cock went away to the forest. "Forest, give me some wood; the wood I will carry to the baker; the baker will give me some bread; the bread I will give to the dog; the dog will give me hairs; the hairs I will carry to the old woman; the old woman will give me rags to cure my head." The forest answered: "If you will bring me a little water, I will give you some wood." The cock went away to a fountain. "Fountain, give me water; water I will carry to the forest; forest will give wood; wood I will carry to the baker; baker will give bread; bread I will give dog; dog will give hairs; hairs I will give old woman; old woman will give rags to cure my head." The fountain gave him water; the water he carried to the forest; the forest gave him wood; the wood he carried to the baker; the baker gave him bread; the bread he gave to the dog; the dog gave him the hairs; the hairs he carried to the old woman; the old woman gave him the rags; and the cock cured his head.[12]

THERE are other versions from Florence (*Nov. fior.* p. 551), Bologna (Coronedi-Berti, X. p. 16), and Venice (Bernoni, Punt. III. p. 74), which do not call for any detailed notice. In the Florentine version a cock gives a peck at a mouse's head and the mouse cries out: "Where must I go to be cured?" Then follow the various objects which are almost identical with those in the other versions. The mouse, however, is killed by the ox, to which he goes last. The Venetian version is the most elaborate; in it the cock and mouse go nutting together, and while the former flies up into the tree and throws the nuts down, the mouse eats them all up. When the cock comes down he flies into a passion and gives the mouse a peck at his head. The mouse runs off in terror, and the rest of the story is as above until the end. The last person the mouse calls on is a cooper, to make him a bucket to give to the well, to get water, etc. The cooper asks for money, which the mouse finds after a while. He gives the money to the cooper and says: "Take and count it; meanwhile I am going to drink, for I am dying of thirst." As he is going to drink he sees Friend Cock coming along. "Ah, poor me," says he to himself, "I am a dead mouse!" The cock sees him and goes to meet him and says: "Good day, friend, are you still afraid of me? Come, let us make peace!" The mouse then takes heart and says: "Oh, yes, yes! Let us make peace!"

So they made peace, and Friend Mouse said to Friend Cock: "Now that you are here you must do me the favor to hold me by the tail while I hang over the ditch to drink, and when I say *slapo, slapo,* pull me back." The cock said: "I will do as you wish."

Then the mouse went to the ditch and Friend Cock held him by the tail. After the mouse had drunk his fill, he said: "Friend, *slapo, slapo!*" The cock answered: "Friend, and I let you go by the tail!" And in truth he did let go his tail, and the poor mouse went to the bottom and was never seen or heard of more.[13]

The following story from Sicily (Pitrè, No. 132) belongs also to a class of tales very popular and having only animals for its actors. It is called:

LXXXI. Godmother Fox*

Once upon a time there was Godmother Fox and Godmother Goat.† The former had a little bit of a house adorned with little chairs, cups, and dishes; in short, it was well furnished. One day Godmother Goat went out and

Cummari Vurpidda (diminutive of Fox).

†Cummari Crapazza (diminutive of Goat).

carried away the little house. Godmother Fox began to lament, when along came a dog, barking, that said to her: "What are you crying about?" She answered: "Godmother Goat has carried off my house!" "Be quiet. I will make her give it back to you." So the dog went and said to God-mother Goat: "Give the house back to Godmother Fox." The goat answered: "I am Godmother Goat. I have a sword at my side, and with my horns I will tear you in pieces." When the dog heard that, he went away.

Then a sheep passed by and said to the little fox: "What are you cry-ing about?" and she told her the same thing. Then the sheep went to Godmother Goat and began to reprove her. The goat made the same answer she had made the dog, and the sheep went away in fright.

In short, all sorts of animals went to the goat, with the same result. Among others the mouse went and said to the little fox: "What are you crying about?" "Godmother Goat has carried off my house." "Be still. I will make her give it back to you." So the mouse went and said to God-mother Goat: "Give Godmother Fox her house back right away." The goat answered: "I am Godmother Goat, I have a sword at my side, and with my fist and with my horns I will smash you!" The mouse answered at once: "I am Godfather Mouse. By my side I have a spit. I will heat it in the fire and stick it in your tail."

THE INFERENCE of course is that Godmother Goat gave back the house. The story does not say so, but ends with the usual formula:

> Story told, story written,
> Tell me yours, for mine is said.

Pitrè (No. 133) gives another version in which a goat gets under a nun's bed and she calls on her neighbors, a dog, pig, and cricket, to put the goat out. The cricket alone succeeds, with a threat similar to that in the last story.

In the Neapolitan version (Imbriani, *Dodici Conti Pomiglianesi*, p. 273) an old woman, in sweeping the church, found a piece of money and, like the sexton in the story of "The Sexton's Nose," did not know what to buy with it. At last she bought some flour and made a hasty-pudding of it. She left it on the table and went again to church, but forgot to close the window. While she was gone a herd of goats came along, and one smelled the pudding, climbed in at the window, and ate it up. When the old woman came back and tried to open the door, she could not, for the goat was behind it. Then she began to weep and various animals came along and tried to enter the house. The goat answered them all: "I am the goat, with three horns on my head and three in my belly, and if you don't run away I will eat you up." The mouse at last replied: "I am Godfather Mouse, with the halter, and if you don't run away, I will tear your eyes out." The goat ran away and the old woman went in with Godfather Mouse, whom she married, and they both lived there together.

The Florentine version (*Nov. fior.* p. 556) is called "The Iron Goat." In it a widow goes out to wash and leaves her son at home, with orders not to leave the door open so that the Iron Goat, with the iron mouth and the sword tongue, can enter. The boy after a time wanted to go after his mother, and when he had gone half way he remembered that he had left the door open and went back. When he was going to enter he saw there the Iron Goat. "Who is there?" "It is I; I am the Iron Goat, with the iron mouth and the sword tongue. If you enter I will slice you like a turnip." The poor boy sat down on the steps and wept. A little old woman passed by and asked the cause of his tears; he told her and she said she would send the goat away for three bushels of grain. The old woman tried, with the usual result, and finally said to the boy: "Listen, my child. I don't care for those three bushels of grain; but I really cannot send the goat away." Then an old man tried his luck, with no better success. At last a little bird came by and promised for three bushels of millet to drive the goat away. When the goat made its usual declaration, the little bird replied: "And I with my beak will peck your brains out." The goat was frightened and ran away, and the boy had to pay the little bird three bushels of millet.[14]

The next story affords, like "Pitidda," a curious example of the diffusion of nursery tales.

Our readers will remember the Grimm story of "The Spider and the Flea." "A spider and a flea dwelt together in one house and brewed their beer in an egg-shell. One day, when the spider was stirring it up, she fell in and scalded herself. Thereupon the flea began to scream. And then the door asked: "Why are you screaming, flea?" "Because Little Spider has scalded herself in the beer-tub," replied she. Thereupon the door began to creak as if it were in pain, and a broom, which stood in the corner, asked: " What are you creaking for, door?"

"May I not creak?" it replied.

> "The little spicier scalded herself,
> And the flea weeps."

So a broom sweeps, a little cart runs, ashes burn furiously, a tree shakes off its leaves, a maiden breaks her pitcher, and a streamlet begins to flow until it swallows up the little girl, the little tree, the ashes, the cart, the broom, the door, the flea, and, last of all, the spider, all together.[15]

The first Italian version of this story which we shall mention is from Sicily (Pitrè, No. 134), and is called:

⁓ LXXXII. *The Cat and the Mouse* ⁓

Once upon a time there was a cat that wanted to get married. So she stood on a corner, and every one who passed by said: "Little Cat, what's the matter?" "What's the matter? I want to marry." A dog passed by and said: "Do you want me?" "When I see how you can sing." The dog said: "Bow, wow!" "Fy! What horrid singing! I don't want you." A pig passed. "Do you want me, Little Cat?" "When I see how you sing." "Uh! Uh!" "Fy! You are horrid! Go away! I don't want you." A calf passed and said: "Little Cat, will you take me?" "When I see how you sing." "Uhm!" "Go away, for you are horrid! What do you want of me?" A mouse passed by: "Little Cat, what are you doing?" "I am going to get married." "Will you take me?" "And how can you sing?" "Ziu, ziu!" The cat accepted him, and said: "Let us go and be married, for you please me." So they were married.

One day the cat went to buy some pastry, and left the mouse at home. "Don't stir out, for I am going to buy some pastry." The mouse went into the kitchen, saw the pot on the fire, and crept into it, for he wanted to eat the beans. But he did not; for the pot began to boil, and the mouse stayed there. The cat came back and began to cry; but the mouse did not appear. So the cat put the pastry in the pot for dinner. When it was ready the cat ate, and put some on a plate for the mouse, also. When she took out the pastry she saw the mouse stuck fast in it. "Ah! my little mouse! Ah! My little mouse!" so she went and sat behind the door, lamenting the mouse.

"What is the matter," said the door, "that you are scratching yourself so and tearing out your hair?"

The cat said: "What is the matter? My mouse is dead, and so I tear my hair."

The door answered: "And I, as door, will slam."

In the door was a window, which said: "What's the matter, door, that you are slamming?"

"The mouse died, the cat is tearing her hair, and I am slamming."

The window answered: "And I, as window, will open and shut."

In the window was a tree, that said: "Window, why do you open and shut?" The window answered: "The mouse died, the cat tears her hair, the door slams, and I open and shut." The tree answered and said: "And I, as tree, will throw myself down."

A bird happened to alight in this tree, and said: "Tree, why did you throw yourself down?" The tree replied: "The mouse died, the cat tears her hair, the door slams, the window opens and shuts, and I, as tree, threw myself down." "And I, as bird, will pull out my feathers." The bird went and alighted on a fountain, which said: "Bird, why are you plucking out your feathers so?" The bird answered as the others had done, and the fountain said: "And I, as fountain, will dry up." A cuckoo went to drink at the fountain, and asked: "Fountain, why have you dried up?" And the fountain told him all that had happened. "And I, as cuckoo, will put my tail in the fire." A monk of St. Nicholas passed by, and said: "Cuckoo, why is your tail in the fire?" When the monk heard the answer he said: "And I, as monk of St. Nicholas, will go and say mass without my robes." Then came the queen, who, when she heard what the matter was, said: "And I, as queen, will go and sift the meal." At last the king came by, and asked: "O Queen! Why are you sifting the meal?" When the queen had told him everything, he said: "And I, as king, am going to take my coffee."

AND THUS the story abruptly ends. In one of Pitrè's variants a sausage takes the place of the mouse; in another, a tortoise.

In the version from Pomigliano d'Arco (Imbriani, p. 244), an old woman, who finds a coin in sweeping a church, hesitates in regard to what she will spend it for, as in the stories above mentioned. She finally concludes to buy some paint for her face. After she has put it on, she stations herself at the window. A donkey passes, and asks what she wants. She answers that she wishes to marry. "Will you take me?" asks the donkey. "Let me hear what kind of a voice you have." *"Ingò! Ingò! Ingò!"* "Away! Away! You would frighten me in the night!" Then a goat comes along, with the same result. Then follows a cat, and all the animals in the world; but none pleases the old woman. At last a little mouse passes by, and says: "Old Aunt, what are you doing there?" "I want to marry." "Will you take me?" "Let me hear your voice." *"Zivuzì! Zivuzì! Zivuzì! Zivuzì!"* "Come up, for you please me." So the mouse went up to the old woman, and stayed with her. One day the old woman went to mass, and left the pot near the fire and told the mouse to be careful not to fall in it. When she came home she could not find the mouse anywhere. At last she went to take the soup from the pot, and there she found the mouse dead. She began to lament, and the ashes on the hearth began to scatter, and the window asked what was the matter. The ashes answered: "Ah! You know nothing. Friend Mouse is in the pot; the old woman is weeping, weeping; and I, the ashes, have wished to scatter." Then the window opens and shuts, the stairs fall down, the bird plucks out its feathers, the laurel shakes off its leaves, the servant girl who goes to the well breaks her pitcher, the mistress who was making bread throws the flour over the balcony, and finally the master comes home, and after he hears the story, exclaims: "And I, who am master, will break the bones of both of you!" And therewith he takes a stick and gives the servant and her mistress a sound beating.[16]

There is a curious class of versions of the above story, in which the principal actors are a mouse and a sausage, reminding one of the Grimm story of "The Little Mouse, the Little Bird, and the Sausage." In the Venetian version (Bernoni, Punt. III. p. 81), the beginning is as follows: Once upon a time there was a mouse and a sausage, and one day the mouse said to the sausage: "I am going to mass; meanwhile get ready the dinner." "Yes, yes," answered the sausage. Then the mouse went to mass, and when he returned he found everything ready. The next day the sausage went to mass and the mouse prepared the dinner. He put on the pot, threw in the rice, and then went to taste if it was well salted. But he fell in and died. The sausage returned home, knocked at the door,—for there was no bell,—and no one answered. She called: "Mouse! mouse!" But he does not answer. Then the sausage went to a smith and had the door broken in, and called again: "Mouse, where are you?" And the mouse did not answer. "Now I will pour out the rice, and meanwhile he will come." So she went and poured out the rice, and found the mouse dead in the pot. "Ah! Poor mouse! Oh! My mouse! What shall I do now? Oh! poor me!" And she began to utter a loud lamentation. Then the table began to go around the room, the sideboard to throw down the plates, the door to lock and unlock itself, the fountain to dry up, the mistress to drag herself along the ground, and the master threw himself from the balcony and broke his neck. "And all this arose from the death of this mouse."

The version from the Marches (Gianandrea, p. 11) resembles the above very closely; the conclusion is as follows: "The mouse, the master of this castle, is dead; the sausage weeps, the broom sweeps, the door opens and shuts, the cart runs, the tree throws off its leaves, the bird plucks out its feathers, the servant breaks her pitcher," etc.

The version from Milan *(Nov. fior.* p. 552) resembles the one from Venice. Instead of the mouse and the sausage we have the big mouse and the little mouse. In the version from Leghorn (Papanti, p. 19) called "Vezzino and Lady Sausage,"* the actors are Lady Sausage and her son Vezzino, who falls into the pot on the fire while his mother is at mass. The rest of the story does not differ materially from the above versions.

In the Grimm story of the "Golden Goose," the goose has the power of causing anything that touches it to stick fast. This same idea is reproduced in several Italian stories. The best is from Venice (Bernoni, *Fiabe,* p. 21) and is called:

ᠵ *LXXXIII. A Feast Day* ᠵ

Once upon a time there was a husband and wife; the husband was a boat-man. One feast day the boatman took it into his head to buy a fowl, which he carried home and said: "See here, wife, to-day is a feast day; I want a good dinner; cook it well, for my friend Tony is coming to dine with us and has said that he would bring a tart." "Very well," she said, "I will prepare the fowl at once." So she cleaned it, washed it, put it on the fire, and said: "While it is boiling I will go and hear a mass." She shut the kitchen door and left the dog and the cat inside. Scarcely had she closed the door when the dog went to the hearth and perceived that there was a good odor there and said: "Oh, what a good smell!" He called the cat, also, and said: "Cat, you come here, too; smell what a good odor there is! See if you can push off the cover with your paws." The cat went and scratched and scratched and down went the cover. "Now," said the dog, "see if you can catch it with your claws." Then the cat seized the fowl and dragged it to the middle of the kitchen. The dog said: "Shall we eat half of it?" The cat said: "Let us eat it all." So they ate it all and stuffed themselves like pigs. When they had eaten it they said: "Alas for us! What shall we do when the mistress comes home? She will surely beat us both." So they both ran all over the house, here and there, but could find no place in which to hide. They were going to hide under the bed. "No," they said, "for she will see us." They were

---

Vezzino e Madonna Salciccia. Vezzino is the dim. of *vezzo*, delight, pastime.

going under the sofa; but that would not do, for she would see them there. Finally the cat looked up and saw under the beams a cobweb. He gave a leap and jumped into it. The dog looked at him and said: "Run away! You are mad! You can be seen, for your tail sticks out! Come down, come down!" "I cannot, I cannot, for I am stuck fast!" "Wait, I will come and pull you out." He gave a spring to catch him by the tail and pull him down. Instead of that he, too, stuck fast to the cat's tail. He made every effort to loosen himself, but he could not and there he had to stay.

Meanwhile the mistress does not wait until the priest finishes the mass, but runs quickly home. She runs and opens the door and is going to skim the pot, when she discovers that the fowl is no longer there, and in the middle of the kitchen she sees the bones all gnawed. "Ah, poor me! the cat and the dog have eaten the fowl. Now I will give them both a beating." So she takes a stick and then goes to find them. She looks here, she looks there, but does not find them anywhere. In despair she comes back to the kitchen, but does not find them there. "Where the deuce have they hidden? "Just then she raises her eyes and sees them both stuck fast under the beams. "Ah, are you there? Now just wait!" and she climbs on a table and is going to pull them down, when she sticks fast to the dog's tail. She tries to free herself, but cannot.

Her husband knocked at the door. "Here, open!" "I cannot, I am fast." "Loosen yourself and open the door! Where the deuce are you fastened?" "I cannot, I tell you." "Open! It is noon." "I cannot, for I am fast." "But where are you fast?" "To the dog's tail." "I will give you the dog's tail, you silly woman!" He gave the door two or three kicks, broke it in, went into the kitchen, and saw cat, dog, and mistress all fast. "Ah, you are all fast, are you? Just wait, I will loosen you." He went to loosen them, but stuck fast himself. Friend Tony comes and knocks. "Friend? Open! I have the tart here." "I cannot; my friend, I am fast!" "Bad luck to you! Are you fast at this time? You knew I was coming and got fast? Come, loosen yourself and open the door!" He said again: "I cannot come and open, for I am fast." Finally the friend became angry, kicked in the door, went into the kitchen, and saw all those souls stuck fast and laughed heartily. "Just wait, for I will loosen you now." So he gave a great pull, the cat's tail was loosened, the cat fell into the dog's mouth, the dog into his mistress' mouth, the mistress into her husband's, her husband into his friend's, and his friend into the mouth of the blockheads who are listening to me.[17]

THE following nonsense story from Venice (Bernoni, Punt. I. p. 18) will give a good idea of a class that is not very well represented in Italy. It is called:

⁓LXXXIV. The Three Brothers ⁓

Once upon a time there were three brothers: two had no clothes and one no shirt. The weather was very bad and they make up their minds to go shooting. So they took down three guns,—two were broken and one had no barrel,—and walked and walked until they came at last to a meadow, where they saw a hare. They began to fire at it, but could not catch it. "What shall we do?" said one of them. They remembered that near by a godmother of theirs lived; so they went and knocked at her door and asked her to lend them a pot to cook the hare they had not caught. The godmother was not at home, but nevertheless she answered: "My children, go in the kitchen and there you will find three pots, two broken and one with no bottom; take whichever you wish." "Thanks, Godmother!" They went into the kitchen and chose the one without a bottom and put the hare in it to cook. While the hare was cooking, one said: "Let us ask our godmother whether she has anything in her garden." So they asked her and she said: "Yes, yes, my children, I have three walnut-trees; two are dead and one has never borne any nuts; knock off as many as you wish." One went and shook the tree that had never borne nuts, and a little nut fell on his hat and broke his heel. Thereupon they picked up the nuts and went to get the hare, which meanwhile was cooked, and said: "What shall we do with so much stuff?" So they went to a village where there were many ill, and they put up a notice in the street that whoever wished might, at such and such a place, get broth given him in charity. Every one went to get some, and they took it in the salad-basket, and it was given to them with a skimmer. One who did not belong to the village, drank so much of this broth that he was at the point of death. Then they sent for three physicians: one was blind, one deaf, and one dumb. The blind man went in and said: "Let me look at your tongue." The deaf man asked: "How are you?" The dumb said: "Give me some paper, pen and ink." They gave them to him and he said:

> "Go to the apothecary,
> For he knows the business;
> Buy two cents' worth of I know not what,

Put it wherever you wish.
He will get well I know not when,
I will leave and commend him to you."[18]

One of the most popular of Italian tales, as the collector tells us, is one of which we give the version from Leghorn (Papanti, p. 25). It is called:

LXXXV. Buchettino

Once upon a time there was a child whose name was Buchettino. One morning his mamma called him and said: "Buchettino, will you do me a favor? Go and sweep the stairs." Buchettino, who was very obedient, did not wait to be told a second time, but went at once to sweep the stairs. All at once he heard a noise, and after looking all around, he found a penny. Then he said to himself: "What shall I do with this penny? I have half a mind to buy some dates . . . but no! For I should have to throw away the stones. I will buy some apples . . . no! I will not, for I should have to throw away the core. I will buy some nuts . . . but no, for I should have to throw away the shells! What shall I buy, then? I will buy—I will buy—enough; I will buy a pennyworth of figs." No sooner said than done: he bought a pennyworth of figs, and went to eat them in a tree. While he was eating, the ogre passed by, and seeing Buchettino eating figs in the tree, said:

"Buchettino,
My dear Buchettino,
Give me a little fig
With your dear little hand,
If not I will eat you!"

Buchettino threw him one, but it fell in the dirt. Then the ogre repeated:

"Buchettino,
My dear Buchettino,
Give me a little fig
With your dear little hand,
If not I will eat you!"

Then Buchettino threw him another, which also fell in the dirt. The ogre said again:

> "Buchettino,
> My dear Buchettino,
> Give me a little fig
> With your dear little hand,
> If not I will eat you!"

Poor Buchettino, who did not see the trick, and did not know that the ogre was doing everything to get him into his net and eat him up, what does he do? He leans down and foolishly gives him a fig with his little hand. The ogre, who wanted nothing better, suddenly seized him by the arm and put him in his bag; then he took him on his back and started for home, crying with all his lungs:

> "Wife, my wife,
> Put the kettle on the fire,
> For I have caught Buchettino!
> Wife, my wife,
> Put the kettle on the fire,
> For I have caught Buchettino!"

When the ogre was near his house he put the bag on the ground, and went off to attend to something else, Buchettino, with a knife that he had in his pocket, cut the bag open in a trice, filled it with large stones, and then:

> "My legs, it is no shame
> To run away when there is need."

When the rascal of an ogre returned he picked up the bag, and scarcely had he arrived home when he said to his wife: "Tell me, my wife, have you put the kettle on the fire?" She answered at once: "Yes." "Then," said the ogre, "we will cook Buchettino; come here, help me!" And both taking the bag, they carried it to the hearth and were going to throw poor Buchettino into the kettle, but instead they found only the stones. Imagine how cheated the ogre was. He was so angry that he bit his hands. He could not swallow the trick played on him by

Buchettino and swore to find him again and be revenged. So the next day he began to go all about the city and to look into all the hiding places. At last he happened to raise his eyes and saw Buchettino on a roof, ridiculing him and laughing so hard that his mouth extended from ear to ear. The ogre thought he should burst with rage, but he pretended not to see it and in a very sweet tone he said: "O Buchettino; just tell me, how did you manage to climb up there?" Buchettino answered: "Do you really want to know? Then listen. I put dishes upon dishes, glasses upon glasses, pans upon pans, kettles upon kettles; afterwards I climbed up on them and here I am." "Ah! is that so?" said the ogre; "wait a bit!" And quickly he took so many dishes, so many glasses, pans, kettles, and made a great mountain of them; then he began to climb up, to go and catch Buchettino. But when he was on the top—*brututum*—everything fell down; and that rascal of an ogre fell down on the stones and was cheated again.

Then Buchettino, well pleased, ran to bis mamma, who put a piece of candy in his little mouth—See whether there is any more![19]

WE WILL end this chapter with two stories in which the chief actors are animals. One of these stories will doubtless be very familiar to our readers. The first is from Venice (Bernoni, Punt. III. p. 65).

‿ LXXXVI. The Three Goslings ‿

Once upon a time there were three goslings who were greatly afraid of the wolf; for if he found them he would eat them. One day the largest said to the other two: "Do you know what I think? I think we had better build a little house, so that the wolf shall not eat us, and meanwhile let us go and look for something to build the house with." Then the other two said: "Yes, yes, yes . . . good! Let us go!" So they went and found a man who had a load of straw and said to him: "Good man, do us the favor to give us a little of that straw to make a house of, so that the wolf shall not eat us." The man said: "Take it, take it!" and he gave them as much as they wanted. The goslings thanked the man and took the straw and went away to a meadow, and there they built a lovely little house, with a door, and balconies, and kitchen, with everything, in short. When it was finished the largest gosling said: "Now I want to see whether one is comfortable in this house." So she went in and said: "Oh! How comfortable it is in this house!

Just wait!" She went and locked the door with a padlock, and went out on the balcony and said to the other two goslings: "I am very comfortable alone here; go away, for I want nothing to do with you."

The two poor little goslings began to cry and beg their sister to open the door and let them in; if she did not, the wolf would eat them. But she would not listen to them. Then the two goslings went away and found a man who had a load of hay. They said to him: "Good man, do us the kindness to give us a little of that hay to build a house with, so that the wolf shall not eat us!" "Yes, yes, yes, take some, take some!" And he gave them as much as they wanted. The goslings, well pleased, thanked the man and carried the hay to a meadow and built a very pretty little house, prettier than the other. The middle-sized gosling said to the smallest: "Listen, I am going now to see whether one is comfortable in this house; but I will not act like our sister, you know!" She entered the house and said to herself: "Oh! How comfortable it is here! I don't want my sister! I am very comfortable here alone." So she went and fastened the door with a padlock, and went out on the balcony and said to her sister: "Oh! How comfortable it is in this house! I don't want you here! Go away, go away!" The poor gosling began to weep and beg her sister to open to her, for she was alone, and did not know where to go, and if the wolf found her he would eat her; but it did no good: she shut the balcony and stayed in the house.

Then the gosling, full of fear, went away and found a man who had a load of iron and stones and said to him: "Good man, do me the favor to give me a few of those stones and a little of that iron to build me a house with, so that the wolf shall not eat me!" The man pitied the gosling so much that he said: "Yes, yes, good gosling, or rather I will build your house for you." Then they went away to a meadow, and the man built a very pretty house, with a garden and everything necessary, and very strong, for it was lined with iron, and the balcony and door of iron also. The gosling, well pleased, thanked the man and went into the house and remained there.

Now let us go to the wolf.

The wolf looked everywhere for these goslings, but could not find them. After a time he learned that they had built three houses. "Good, good!" he said; "wait until I find you!" Then he started out and journeyed and journeyed until he came to the meadow where the first house was. He knocked at the door and the gosling said: "Who is knocking at the door?" "Come, come," said the wolf; "open, for it is I." The gosling said: "I will not open for you, because you will eat me." "Open, open! I will not eat you, be not afraid. Very well," said the wolf, "if you will not open the door I will blow down your house." And indeed he did blow down the house and ate up the gosling. "Now that I have eaten one," he said, "I will eat the others too." Then he went away and came at last to the house of the second gosling, and everything happened as to the first, the wolf blew down the house and ate the gosling. Then he went in search of the third and when he found her he knocked at the door, but she would not let him in. Then he tried to blow the house down, but could not; then he climbed on the roof and tried to trample the house down, but in vain. "Very well," he said to himself, "in one way or another I will eat you." Then he came down from the roof and said to the gosling: "Listen, gosling. Do you wish us to make peace? I don't want to quarrel with you who are so good, and I have thought that to-morrow we will cook some macaroni and I will bring the butter and cheese and you will furnish the flour." "Very good," said the gosling, "bring them then." The wolf, well satisfied, saluted the gosling and went away. The next day the gosling got up early and went and bought the meal and then returned home and shut the house. A little later the wolf came and knocked at the door and said: "Come, gosling, open the door, for I have brought you the butter and cheese!" "Very well, give it to me here by the balcony." "No indeed, open the door!" "I will open when all is ready." Then the wolf gave her the things by the balcony and went away. While he was gone the gosling prepared the macaroni, and put it on the fire to cook in a kettle full of water. When it was two o'clock the wolf came and said: "Come, gosling, open the door." "No, I will not open, for when I am busy I don't want any one in the way; when it is cooked, I will open and you may come in and eat it." A little while after, the gosling said to the wolf: " Would you like to try a bit of macaroni to see whether it is well cooked?" "Open the door! That is the better way." "No, no; don't think you are coming in; put your mouth to the hole in the shelf and I will pour the macaroni down." The wolf, all greedy as he was, put his mouth to the hole and then the gosling took the kettle of boiling water and poured the boiling water instead of the macaroni through the hole into the wolf's mouth; and the wolf was scalded and killed. Then the gosling took a knife and cut open the wolf's stomach, and out jumped the other goslings, who were still alive, for the wolf was so greedy that he had swallowed them whole. Then these goslings begged their sister's pardon for the mean way in which they had treated her, and she, because she was kind-hearted, forgave them and took them into her house, and there they ate their macaroni and lived together happy and contented.[20]

A curious variant of the above story is found in the same collection (p. 69) under the title:

✌ LXXXVII. The Cock ✌

Once upon a time there was a cock, and this cock flew here and flew there, and flew on an arbor, and there he found a letter. He opened the letter and saw: "Cock, steward,"—and that he was invited to Rome by the Pope.

The cock started on his journey, and after a time met the hen: "Where are you going, Friend Cock?" said the hen. "I flew," said he, "upon an arbor and found a letter, and this letter said that I was invited to Rome by the Pope." "Just see, friend," said the hen, "whether I am there too." "Wait a bit." Then he turned the letter, and saw written there: "Cock, steward; Hen, stewardess." "Come, friend, for you are there too." "Very well!"

Then the two started off, and soon met the goose, who said: "Where are you going, Friend Cock and Friend Hen?" "I flew," said the cock, "upon an arbor, and I found a letter, and this letter said that we were invited to Rome by the Pope." "Just look, friend, whether I am there too." Then the cock opened the letter, read it, and saw that there was written: "Cock, steward; Hen, stewardess; Goose, abbess." "Come, come, friend; you are there too." So they took her along, and all three went their way.

[After a time they found the duck, and the cock saw written in the letter: "Cock, steward; Hen, stewardess; Goose, abbess; Duck, countess." They next met a little bird, and found he was down in the letter as "little manservant." Finally they came across the wood-louse, whom they found mentioned in the letter as "maid-servant." On their journey they came to a forest, and saw a wolf at a distance. The cock, hen, goose, and duck plucked out their feathers and built houses to shelter themselves from the wolf. The poor bug, that had no feathers, dug a hole in the ground and crept into it. The wolf came, and as in the last story, blew down the four houses and devoured their occupants. Then he tried to get at the bug in the same way; but blew so hard that he burst, and out came the cock, hen, goose, and duck, safe and sound, and began to make a great noise. The bug heard it and came out of her hole, and after they had rejoiced together, they separated and each returned home and thought no more of going to Rome to the Pope.]

There is a version from the Marches (Gianandrea, p. 21), called, "The Marriage of Thirteen." The animals are the same as in the last story. On their journey they meet the wolf, who accompanies them, although his name is not in the letter. After a time the wolf becomes hungry, and exclaims: "I am hungry." The cock answers: "I have nothing to give you." "Very well; then I will eat you;" and he swallows him whole. And so he devours one after the other, until the bird only remains. The bird flies from tree to tree and bush to bush, and around the wolf's head, until he drives him wild with anger. At last along comes a woman with a basket on her head, carrying food to the reapers. The bird says to the wolf that if he will spare his life he will get him something to eat from the basket. The wolf promises, and the bird alights near the woman, who tries to catch him; the bird flies on a little way, and the woman puts down her basket and runs after him. Meanwhile the wolf draws near the basket and begins eating its contents. When the woman sees that, she cries: "Help!" and the reapers run up with sticks and scythes, and kill the wolf, and the animals that he had devoured all came out of his stomach, safe and sound.[21]

There are two Sicilian versions of the story of "The Cock." One (Pitrè, No. 279), "The Wolf and the Finch," opens like the Venetian. The animals are: Cock, king; Hen, queen; Viper, chambermaid; Wolf, Pope; and Finch, keeper of the castle. The wolf then proceeds to confess the others, and eats them in turn until he comes to the finch, which plays a joke on him and flies away. The conclusion of the story is disfigured, nothing being said of the wolf's punishment or the recovery of the other animals.

The other Sicilian version is in Gonzenbach (No. 66). We give it, however, for completeness and because it recalls a familiar story in Grimm.[22] It is entitled:

ꙮ LXXXVIII. The Cock
That Wished to Become Pope ꙮ

It occurred once to the cock to go to Rome and have himself elected Pope. So he started out, and on the way found a letter, which he took with him. The hen met him, and asked: "Mr. Cock, where are you going?" "I am going to Rome, to be Pope." "Will you take me with you?" she asked. "First I must look in my letter," said the cock, and looked at his letter. "Come along; if I become Pope, you can be the Popess." So Mr. Cock and Mrs. Hen continued their journey and met a cat, who said: "Mr. Cock and Mrs. Hen, where are you going?" "We are going to Rome, and wish to be Pope and Popess." "Will you take me with you?" "Wait until I look in my letter," said the cock, and glanced at it. "Very well; come along; you can be our lady's-maid." After a while they met a weasel, who asked: "Where are you going, Mr. Cock, Mrs. Hen, and Mrs. Cat?" "We are going to Rome, where I intend to become Pope," answered the cock. "Will you take me with you?" "Wait until I look in my letter," said he. When the cock looked in his letter, he said: "Very well; come along."

So the three animals continued their journey together towards Rome. At night-fall they came to a little house where lived an old witch, who had just gone out. So each animal chose a place to suit him. The weasel sat himself in the cupboard, the cat on the hearth in the warm ashes, and the cock and the hen flew up on the beam over the door.

When the old witch came home she wanted to get a light out of the cupboard, and the weasel struck her in the face with his tail. Then she wanted to light the candle, and went to the hearth. She took the bright eyes of the cat for live coals and tried to light the match by them, and hit the cat in the eyes. The cat jumped in her face and scratched her frightfully. When the cock heard all the noise he began to crow loudly. Then the witch saw that they were no ghosts, but harmless domestic animals, and took a stick and drove all four out of the house.

The cat and the weasel had no longer any desire to prolong their journey; but the cock and hen continued their way.

When they reached Rome they entered an open church, and the cock said to the sexton: "Have all the bells rung, for now I will be Pope." "Good!" answered the sexton; "that may be, but just come in here." Then he led the cock and the hen into the sacristy, shut the door, and caught them both. After he had caught them he twisted their necks and put them in the pot. Then he invited his friends, and they ate with great glee Mr. Cock and Mrs. Hen.

CHAPTER VI

やん

Stories and Jests

Until the Reformation, Europe was, by its religion and the culture growing out of it, a homogeneous state. Not only, however, did the legends of the Church find access to the people everywhere, but the stories imported from the Orient were equally popular and widespread. The absence of other works of entertainment and the monotonous character of the legends increased the popularity of tales which were amusing and interesting. We have considered in other places the fairy tales and those stories which are of more direct Oriental origin. In the present chapter we shall examine those stories which are of the character of jests or amusing stories, some of which are also Oriental, but may more appropriately be classed in this chapter. The first story we shall mention is familiar to the reader from the ballad of "King John and the Abbot of Canterbury," in Percy and Bürger's poem of *Der Kaiser und der Abt.* There are two popular versions in Italian, as well as several literary ones. The shortest is from Milan (Imbriani, *Nov. Fior.* p. 621), and is entitled:

✧ XCI. The Cook ✧

There was once a lord whose name was "Abbot-who-eats-and-drinks-without-thinking." The king went there and saw this name on the door, and said that if he had nothing to think of, he would give him something to think of. He told him that he must do in a week the three things which he told him. First, to tell him how many stars there were in heaven, how many fathoms of rope it would take to reach to heaven, and what he, the king, was thinking of. The cook saw that his master was sad, and sat with his head bent over the table, and asked him what was the matter, and his master told him everything. The cook promised to settle the matter if he would give him half of his property. He also asked for the skin of a dead ass, a cartload of rope, and his master's hat and cloak. Then the cook went to the king, who said to him: "Well, how many stars are there in heaven?" The cook answered: "Whoever counts the hairs on this ass' skin will know how many stars there are in heaven." Then the king told him to count them, and he answered that his share was already counted, and that it was for the king to count now. Then the king asked him how many fathoms of rope it would take to reach to heaven, and the cook replied: "Take this rope and go to heaven, and then come back and count how many fathoms there are." Finally the king asked: "What am I thinking of?" "You are thinking that I am the abbot; instead of that, I am the cook, and I have here the stew-pan to try the broth."

THE VERSION in Pitrè (No. 97) is much better. It is called:

ʒ XCII. The Thoughtless Abbot ʒ

There was once in a city a priest who became an abbot, and who had his carriages, horses, grooms, steward, secretary, valet, and many other persons on account of the wealth that he had. This abbot thought only of eating, drinking, and sleeping. All the priests and laymen were jealous of him, and called him the "Thoughtless Abbot."

One day the king happened to pass that way, and stopped, and all the abbot's enemies went to him straightway, and accused the abbot, saying: "Your Majesty, in this town there is a person happier than you, very rich, and lacking nothing in the world, and he is called the 'Thoughtless Abbot.'"

After reflection the king said to the accusers: "Gentlemen, depart in peace, for I will soon make this abbot think." The king sent directly for the abbot, who had his carriage made ready, and went to the king in his coach and four. The king received him kindly, made him sit at his side, and talked about various things with him. Finally he asked him why they called him the "Thoughtless Abbot," and he replied that it was because he was free from care, and that his servants attended to his interests.

Then the king said: "Well, then, Sir Abbot, since you have nothing to do, do me the favor to count all the stars in the sky, and this within three days and three nights; otherwise you will surely be beheaded." The poor "Thoughtless Abbot" on hearing these words began to tremble like a leaf, and taking leave of the king, returned home, in mortal fear for his neck.

When meal-time came, he could not eat on account of his great anxiety, and went at once out on the terrace to look at the sky, but the poor man could not see a single star. When it grew dark, and the stars came out, the poor abbot began to count them and write it down. But it grew dark and light again, without the abbot succeeding in his task. The cook, the steward, the secretaries, the grooms, the coachmen, and all the persons in the house became thoughtful when they saw that their master did not eat or drink, and always watched the sky. Not knowing what else to think, they believed that he had gone mad. To make the matter short, the three days passed without the abbot counting the stars, and the poor man did not know how to present himself to the king, for he was sure he would behead him. Finally, the last day, an old and trusty servant begged him so long, that he told him the whole matter, and said: "I have not been able to count the stars, and the king will cut my head off this morning." When the servant had heard all, he said: "Do not fear, leave it to me; I will settle everything."

He went and bought a large ox-hide, stretched it on the ground, and cut off a piece of the tail, half an ear, and a small piece out of the side, and then said to the abbot: "Now let us go to the king; and when he asks your excellency how many stars there are in heaven, your excellency will call me; I will stretch the hide on the ground, and your excellency will say: 'The stars in heaven are as many as the hairs on this hide; and as there are more hairs than stars, I have been obliged to cut off part of the hide.'"

After the abbot had heard him, he felt relieved, ordered his carriage, and took his servant to the king. When the king saw the abbot, he saluted him, and then said: "Have you fulfilled my command?" "Yes, your Majesty," answered the abbot, "the stars are all counted."

"Then tell me how many they are." The abbot called his servant, who brought the hide, and spread it on the ground, while the king, not knowing how the matter was going to end, continued his questioning.

When the servant had stretched out the hide, the abbot said to the king: "Your Majesty, during these three days I have gone mad counting the stars, and they are all counted." "In short, how many are they?" "Your Majesty, the stars are as many as the hairs of this hide, and those that were in excess, I have had to cut off, and they are so many hundreds of millions; and if you don't believe me, have them counted, for I have brought you the proof."

Then the king remained with his mouth open, and had nothing to answer; he only said: "Go and live as long as Noah, without thoughts, for your mind is enough for you;" and so speaking, he dismissed him, thanking him, and remaining henceforth his best friend.

The abbot returned home with his servant, delighted and rejoicing. He thanked his servant, made him his steward and intimate friend, and gave him more than an ounce of money a day to live on.[1]

IN ANOTHER Sicilian version referred to by Pitrè, vol. IV., p. 437, the Pope, instead of the king, wishes to know from the abbot: "What is the distance from heaven to earth; what God is doing in heaven; what the Pope is thinking of." The cook, disguised as the abbot, answers: "As long as this ball of thread. Rewarding the good, and punishing the wicked. He thinks he is speaking with the abbot, and on the contrary, is talking to the cook."

The following story from Venice (Bernoni, *Fiabe,* No. 6) is a combination of the two stories in Grimm, "Clever Alice" and the "Clever People." It is called:

✌ *XCIII. Bastianelo* ✌

Once upon a time there was a husband and wife who had a son. This son grew up, and said one day to his mother: "Do you know, mother, I would like to marry!" "Very well, marry! Whom do you want to take?" He answered: "I want the gardener's daughter." "She is a good girl; take her; I am willing." So he went, and asked for the girl, and her parents gave her to him. They were married, and when they were in the midst of the dinner, the wine gave out. The husband said: "There is no more wine!" The bride, to show that she was a good housekeeper, said: "I will go and get some." She took the bottles and went to the cellar, turned the cock, and began to think: "Suppose I should have a son, and we should call him Bastianelo, and he should die. Oh! How grieved I should be! Oh! How grieved I should be!" And thereupon she began to weep and weep; and meanwhile the wine was running all over the cellar.

When they saw that the bride did not return, the mother said: "I will go and see what the matter is." So she went into the cellar, and saw the bride, with the bottle in her hand, and weeping, while the wine was running over the cellar. "What is the matter with you, that you are weeping?"

"Ah! My mother, I was thinking that if I had a son, and should name him Bastianelo, and he should die, oh! How I should grieve! Oh! How I should grieve!" The mother, too, began to weep, and weep, and weep; and meanwhile the wine was running over the cellar.

When the people at the table saw that no one brought the wine, the groom's father said: "I will go and see what is the matter. Certainly something wrong has happened to the bride." He went and saw the whole cellar full of wine, and the mother and bride weeping. "What is the matter?" he said; "has anything wrong happened to you?" "No," said the bride, "but I was thinking that if I had a son and should call him Bastianelo, and he should die, oh! How I should grieve! Oh! How I should grieve!" Then he, too, began to weep, and all three wept; and meanwhile the wine was running over the cellar.

When the groom saw that neither the bride, nor the mother, nor the father came back, he said: "Now I will go and see what the matter is that no one returns." He went into the cellar and saw all the wine running over the cellar. He hastened and stopped the cask, and then asked: "What is the matter, that you are all weeping, and have let the wine run all over the cellar?" Then the bride said: "I was thinking that if I had a son and called him Bastianelo and he should die, oh! How I should grieve! Oh! How I should grieve!" Then the groom said: "You stupid fools! Are you weeping at this, and letting all the wine run into the cellar? Have you nothing else to think of? It shall never be said that I remained with you! I will roam about the world, and until I find three fools greater than you I will not return home."

He had a bread-cake made, took a bottle of wine, a sausage, and some linen, and made a bundle, which he put on a stick and carried over his shoulder. He journeyed and journeyed, but found no fool. At last he said, worn out: "I must turn back, for I see I cannot find a greater fool than my wife." He did not know what to do, whether to go on or to turn back. "Oh!" he said, "it is better to try and go a little farther." So he went on and shortly he saw a man in his shirtsleeves at a well, all wet with perspiration and water. "What are you doing, sir, that you are so covered with water and in such a sweat?" "Oh! Let me alone," the man answered, "for I have been here a long time drawing water to fill this pail and I cannot fill it." "What are you drawing the water in?" he asked him. "In this sieve," he said. "What are you thinking about, to draw water in that sieve? Just wait!" He went to a house near by, and borrowed a bucket, with which he returned to the well and filled the pail. "Thank you, good man,

God knows how long I should have had to remain here!" "Here is one who is a greater fool than my wife."

He continued his journey and after a time he saw at a distance a man in his shirt who was jumping down from a tree. He drew near, and saw a woman under the same tree holding a pair of breeches. He asked them what they were doing, and they said that they had been there a long time, and that the man was trying on those breeches and did not know how to get into them. "I have jumped, and jumped," said the man, "until I am tired out and I cannot imagine how to get into those breeches." "Oh!" said the traveler, "you might stay here as long as you wished, for you would never get into them in this way. Come down and lean against the tree." Then he took his legs and put them in the breeches, and after he had put them on, he said: "Is that right?" "Very good, bless you; for if it had not been for you, God knows how long I should have had to jump." Then the traveler said to himself: "I have seen two greater fools than my wife."

Then he went his way and as he approached a city he heard a great noise. When he drew near he asked what it was, and was told it was a marriage, and that it was the custom in that city for the brides to enter the city gate on horseback, and that there was a great discussion on this occasion between the groom and the owner of the horse, for the bride was tall and the horse high, and they could not get through the gate; so that they must either cut off the bride's head or the horse's legs. The groom did not wish his bride's head cut off, and the owner of the horse did not wish his horse's legs cut off, and hence this disturbance. Then the traveler said: "Just wait," and came up to the bride and gave her a slap that made her lower her head, and then he gave the horse a kick, and so they passed through the gate and entered the city. The groom and the owner of the horse asked the traveler what he wanted, for he had saved the groom his bride, and the owner of the horse his horse. He answered that he did not wish anything and said to himself: "Two and one make three! That is enough; now I will go home." He did so and said to his wife: "Here I am, my wife; I have seen three greater fools then you; now let us remain in peace and think about nothing else." They renewed the wedding and always remained in peace. After a time the wife had a son whom they named Bastianelo, and Bastianelo did not die, but still lives with his father and mother.[2]

THERE IS a Sicilian version of this story (Pitrè, No. 148) called, "The Peasant of Larcàra," in which the bride's mother imagines that her daughter has a son who falls into the cistern. The groom (they are not yet married) is disgusted and sets out on his travels with no fixed purpose of returning if he finds some fools greater than his mother-in-law, as in the Venetian tale. The first fool he meets is a mother, whose child, in playing the game called *nocciole,** tries to get his hand out of the hole while his fist is full of stones. He cannot, of course, and the mother thinks they will have to cut off his hand. The traveler tells the child to drop the stones, and then he draws out his hand easily enough. Next he finds a bride who cannot enter the church because she is very tall and wears a high comb. The difficulty is settled as in the former story.

After a while he comes to a woman who is spinning and drops her spindle. She calls out to the pig, whose name is Tony, to pick it up for her. The pig does nothing but grunt, and the woman in anger cries: "Well, you won't pick it up? May your mother die!"

The traveler, who had overheard all this, takes a piece of paper, which he folds up like a letter, and then knocks at the door. "Who is there?" "Open the door, for I have a letter for you from Tony's mother, who is ill and wishes to see her son before she dies." The woman wonders that her imprecation has taken effect so soon, and readily consents to Tony's visit. Not only this, but she loads a mule with everything necessary for the comfort of the body and soul of the dying pig.

The traveler leads away the mule with Tony, and returns home so pleased with having found that the outside world contains so many fools that he marries as he had first intended.

The credulity of the woman in the last version, in allowing Tony to visit his sick mother, finds a parallel in a Neapolitan story (Imbriani, *Pomiglianesi,* p. 226) called:

ᔌ XCIV. Christmas ᔌ

Once upon a time there was a husband who had a wife who was a little foolish. One day he said to her: "Come, put the house in order, for Christmas is coming." As soon as he left the house his wife went out on the balcony and asked every one who passed if his name was Christmas. All said No; but finally, one—to see why she asked—said Yes. Then she

---

* A game played with peach-pits, which are thrown into holes made in the ground and to which certain numbers are attached.

made him come in, and gave him everything that she had (in order to clean out the house). When her husband returned he asked her what she had done with things. She responded that she had given them to Christmas, as he had ordered. Her husband was so enraged at what he heard that he seized her and gave her a good beating.

Another time she asked her husband when he was going to kill the pig. He answered: "At Christmas." The wife did as before, and when she spied the man called Christmas she called him and gave him the pig, which she had adorned with her earrings and necklace, saying that her husband had so commanded her. When her husband returned and learned what she had done, he gave her a sound thrashing; and from that time he learned to say nothing more to his wife.[3]

In the Sicilian version, Pitrè, No. 186, "Long May,"* the wife, who is very anxious to make more room in her house by getting rid of the grain stored in it, asks her husband when they shall clean out the house. He answers: "When Long May comes." The wife asks the passers-by if they are Long May; and at last a swindler says he is, and receives as a gift all the grain. The swindler was a potter, and the woman told him that he ought to give her a load of pots. He did so, and the wife knocked a hole in the bottom of each, and strung them on a rope stretched across the room. It is needless to say that when the husband returned the wife received a beating "that left her more dead than alive."

Another story about foolish people is the following Venetian tale (Bernoni, *Fiabe*, xiii.), entitled:

✌ XCV. The Wager ✌

There was once a husband and a wife. The former said one day to the latter: "Let us have some fritters." She replied: "What shall we do for a frying-pan?" "Go and borrow one from my godmother." "You go and get it; it is only a little way off." "Go yourself; I will take it back when we are done with it." So she went and borrowed the pan, and when she returned said to her husband: "Here is the pan, but you must carry it back." So they cooked the fritters, and after they had eaten, the husband said: "Now let us go to work, both of us, and the one who speaks first shall carry back the pan." Then she began to spin and he to draw his thread—for he was

*There is a Sicilian phrase: "Long as the month of May," to indicate what is very long.

a shoemaker—and all the time keeping silence, except that when he drew his thread he said: "*Leulerò, leulerò;*" and she, spinning, answered: "*Picicì, picicì, picìciò.*" And they said not another word.

Now there happened to pass that way a soldier with a horse, and he asked a woman if there was any shoemaker in that street. She said that there was one near by, and took him to the house. The soldier asked the shoemaker to come and cut his horse a girth, and he would pay him. The latter made no answer but: "*Leulerò, leulerò,*" and his wife: "*Picicì, picicì, picìciò.*" Then the soldier said: "Come and cut my horse a girth, or I will cut your head off!" The shoemaker only answered: "*Leulerò, leulerò*" and his wife: "*Picicì, picicì, picìciò.*" Then the soldier began to grow angry, and seized his sword and said to the shoemaker: "Either come and cut my horse a girth, or I will cut your head off!"

But to no purpose. The shoemaker did not wish to be the first one to speak, and only replied: "*Leulerò, leulerò,*" and his wife: "*Picicì, picicì, picìciò.*" Then the soldier got mad in good earnest, seized the shoemaker's head, and was going to cut it off. When his wife saw that, she cried out: "Ah! Don't, for mercy's sake!" "Good!" exclaimed her husband, "Good! Now you go and carry the pan back to my godmother, and I will go and cut the horse's girth." And so he did, and won the wager.

IN A Sicilian story with the same title (Pitrè, No. 181), the husband and wife fry some fish, and then set about their respective work—shoemaking and spinning—and the one who finishes first the piece of work begun is to eat the fish. While they were singing and whistling at their work, a friend comes along, who knocks at the door, but receives no answer. Then he enters and speaks to them, but still no reply; finally, in anger, he sits down at the table and eats up all the fish himself.[4]

One of our most popular stories illustrating woman's obstinacy is found everywhere in Italy. The following is the Sicilian version:

ᕦ XCVI. *Scissors They Were* ᕤ

Once upon a time there was a husband and a wife. The husband was a tailor; so was the wife, and in addition was a good housekeeper. One day the husband found some things in the kitchen broken—pots, glasses, plates. He asked: "How were they broken?" "How do I know?" answered the wife. "What do you mean by saying 'How do I know?' Who broke them?"

"Who broke them? I, with the scissors," said the wife, in anger. "With the scissors?" "With the scissors!" "Are you telling the truth? I want to know what you broke them with. If you don't tell me, I will beat you." "With the scissors!" (for she had the scissors in her hand). "Scissors, do you say?" "Scissors they were!" "Ah! What do you mean? Wait a bit; I will make you see whether it was you with the scissors." So he tied a rope around her and began to lower her into the well, saying: "Come, how did you break them? You see I am lowering you into the well." "It was the scissors!" The husband, seeing her so obstinate, lowered her into the well; and she, for all that, did not hold her tongue. "How did you break them?" said the husband. "It was the scissors." Then her husband lowered her more, until she was half way down. "What did you do it with?" "It was the scissors." Then he lowered her until her feet touched the water. "What did you do it with?" "It was the scissors!" Then he let her down into the water to her waist. "What did you do it with?" "It was the scissors!" "Take care!" cried her husband, enraged at seeing her so obstinate, "it will take but little to put you under the water. You had better tell what you did it with; it will be better for you. How is it possible to break pots and dishes with the scissors! What has become of the pieces, if they were cut?" "It was the scissors! The scissors!" Then he let go the rope. Splash! His wife is all under the water. "Are you satisfied now? Do you say any longer that it was with the scissors?" The wife could not speak any more, for she was under the water; but what did she do? She stuck her hand up out of the water, and with her fingers began to make signs as if she were cutting with the scissors. What could the poor husband do? He said: "I am losing my wife, and then I shall have to go after her. I will pull her out now, and she may say that it was the scissors or the shears." Then he pulled her out, and there was no way of making her tell with what she had broken all those things in the kitchen.[5]

ANOTHER familiar story is:

ꙅ XCVII. The Doctor's Apprentice ꙅ

Once upon a time there was a doctor who took his apprentice with him when he made his visits. One day while visiting a patient, the doctor said: "Why do you not listen to my orders that you are not to eat anything?" The invalid said: "Sir, I assure you that I have eaten nothing." "That is not true," answered the doctor," for I have found your pulse heating like that of a person who has eaten grapes." The patient, convicted, said: "It is true that I have eaten some grapes; but it was only a little bunch." "Very well; do not risk eating again, and don't think you can fool me."

The poor apprentice, who was with the doctor, was amazed to see how his master guessed from the pulse that his patient had eaten grapes; and as soon as they had left the house he asked: "Master, how did you perceive that he had eaten grapes?" "Listen," said the doctor, "A person who visits the sick must never pass for a fool. As soon as you enter, cast your eyes on the bed and under the bed, too, and from the crumbs that you see you can guess what the patient has eaten. I saw the stalk of the grapes, and from that I inferred that he had eaten grapes."

The next day there were many patients in the town, and the doctor, not being able to visit them all, sent his apprentice to visit a few. Among others, the apprentice went to see the man who had eaten the grapes; and wishing to play the part of an expert like his master, to show that he was a skilful physician, when he perceived that there were bits of straw under the bed, said angrily: "Will you not understand that you must not eat?" The invalid said: "I assure you that I have not even tasted a drop of water." "Yes, sir, you have," answered the apprentice; "you have been eating straw, for I see the bits under the bed." The sick man replied at once: "Do you take me for an ass like yourself?" And so the apprentice cut the figure of the fool that he was.[6]

THERE are two figures in Sicilian folk-lore around whom many jokes have gathered which are, in other parts of Italy, told of some nameless person or attributed to the continental counterparts of the insular heroes. These two are Firrazzanu and Giufà. The former is the practical joker; the second, the typical booby found in the popular literature of all peoples.

The following stories of Firrazzanu (unless otherwise indicated) are from Pitrè, No. 156.

᧞ XCVIII. Firrazzanu's Wife and the Queen ᧞

Firrazzanu was the valet of a prince in Palermo, on whom he also played his tricks; but as Firrazzanu was known and everybody was amused by him, the prince overlooked them.

The queen was once in Palermo, and wished to know Firrazzanu. He went to see her, and amused her somewhat. The queen said: "Are you married, or single?" "Married, your Majesty." "I wish to make your wife's acquaintance." "How can that be, your Majesty, for my wife is deaf?" (Firrazzanu made this up out of his own head, for it was not true.) "No matter; when I speak with her I will scream. Go, have your wife come here."

Firrazzanu went home. "Fanny, the queen wants to know you; but you must remember that she is a little hard of hearing, and if you wish to speak to her, you must raise your voice."

"Very well," said his wife, "let us go." When they arrived at the palace she said to the queen, in a loud voice: "At your Majesty's feet!" The queen said to herself: "You see, because she is deaf, she screams as if everybody else were deaf!" Then she said to her, loudly: "Good day, my friend; how do you do?" "Very well, your Majesty!" answered Firrazzanu's wife, still louder. The queen, to make herself heard, raised her voice and screamed, also, and Fanny, for her part, cried out louder and louder, so that it seemed as if they were quarrelling. Firrazzanu could contain himself no longer, and began to laugh, so that the queen perceived the joke; and if Firrazzanu had not run away, perhaps she would have had him arrested, and who knows how the matter had ended?[7]

THE SECOND story, "The Tailor who twisted his Mouth," has already been mentioned in Chapter III.

On one occasion (No. 7) the viceroy gave a feast, and needed some partridges. Now the word *pirnicana* means both partridge and humpback; so Firrazzanu said he would get the viceroy as many *pirnicani* as he wanted, although they were very scarce. The viceroy said twenty would do. Firrazzanu then collected a score of humpbacks and introduced them into the viceroy's kitchen, sending word to the viceroy that the *pirnicani* were ready. His excellency wished to see them, and Firrazzanu led his troop to his apartment. When they were all in, Firrazzanu said: "Here they are." The viceroy looked around and said: "Where?" "Here. You wanted *pirnicani,* and these are *pirnicani.*" The viceroy laughed, gave each of the humpbacks a present, and dismissed them.[8]

Another time, while the prince was at dinner, Firrazzanu led a number of asses under his window, and made them bray so that the poor prince was driven almost to distraction. The author of the joke, as usual, took to his heels, and escaped.

Once a very wealthy prince, having a great number of rents to collect, and not succeeding, thought of making Firrazzanu collector. "Here," said he to him, "take my authority, and collect for me, and I will give you twenty per cent." Firrazzanu went into the places where the rents were to be collected, and called together all the debtors. What do you suppose he did? He made them pay his share, that is, twenty per cent, and nothing more. "The rest," he said, "you can pay another year to the prince; now you may depart."

Then he went back to the prince. "What have you done, Firrazzanu? Have you collected all the rents?" "What are you talking about collecting! I had hard work to collect my share." "What do you mean?" "I collected with difficulty the twenty percent that belonged to me; your share will be paid next year." The prince was obliged to laugh at last, and Firrazzanu went away happy and satisfied.[9]

Another time the prince went hunting, and ordered Firrazzanu, when it was convenient, to tell the princess that he should not be home to dinner that day. Firrazzanu did not find it convenient to deliver the message for a week, when he said that the prince would not be home to dine that day. On the first occasion, of course, the princess waited for her husband in great anxiety until midnight; on the second she went out to pay visits, and when the prince returned, he found his wife out, and no dinner prepared. Firrazzanu, when scolded, excused himself by saying that the prince told him to deliver the message when convenient.

This recalls the story in Straparola (XIII. 6) where a master orders his lazy servant to go to market and buy some meat, and says to him, sarcastically: "Go and stay a year!" which command the servant obeys to the letter.

The viceroy at last, angry at one of Firrazzanu's jokes, banished him to the town of Murriali. When Firrazzanu grew tired of the place, he had a cart filled with the earth of the town, and rode into Palermo on it. The viceroy had him arrested as soon as he saw him, but Firrazzanu protested that he had not broken the viceroy's command, for he was still on the earth of Murriali.

The same story is told of Gonnella, the Italian counterpart of Firrazzanu, by Sacchetti (Nov. 27), and Bandello (IV. 18).

The prince desired once to give Firrazzanu a lesson that would correct him of his fondness for jokes; so he told the commandant of the castle that he would send him one day a servant of his with a letter, and that he, the commandant, should carry out the orders contained in it.

A week after, the prince called Firrazzanu and said: "Go to the commandant of the castle and ask him to give you what this letter says."

Firrazzanu went, turning over the letter and in doubt about the matter. Just then he met another servant and said to him: "Carry this letter for me to the commandant of the castle, and tell him to give you what he has to give you. When you return, we will have a good drink of wine."

The servant went and delivered the letter to the commandant, who opened it, and read: "The commandant will give my servant, who is a rascal, a hundred lashes, and then send him back to me." The order was carried out, and the poor servant returned to the palace more dead than alive. When Firrazzanu saw him, he burst out laughing, and said: "My brother, for roe and for you, better you than me."

This story is told in Gonzenbach (No. 75) as the way in which the queen tried to punish Firrazzanu for the joke he played on her by telling her his wife was deaf.

There are other stories told of Firrazzanu, but they do not deserve a place here, and we can direct our attention at once to Giufà, the typical booby, who appears in the various provinces of Italy under different names.[10]

The first story told of him in Pitrè's collection (No. 190) is:

✄ XCIX. Giufà and the Plaster Statue ✄

Once upon a time there was a very poor woman who had a son called Giufà, who was stupid, lazy, and cunning. His mother had a piece of cloth, and said one day to Giufà: "Take this cloth, and go and sell it in a distant town, and take care to sell it to those who talk little." So Giufà set out, with the cloth on his shoulder.

When he came to a town, he began to cry: "Who wants cloth?" The people called him, and began to talk a great deal; one thought it coarse, another dear. Giufà thought they talked too much, and would not sell it to them. After walking a long way, he entered a courtyard where he found nothing but a plaster image. Giufà said to it: "Do you want to buy the cloth?" The statue said not a word, and Giufà, seeing that it spoke little, said: "Now I must sell you the cloth, for you speak little;" and he took the cloth and hung it on the statue, and went away, saying: "Tomorrow I will come for the money."

The next day he went after the money, and found the cloth gone. "Give me the money for the cloth." The statue said nothing. "Since you will not give me the money, I will show you who I am," and he borrowed a mattock, and struck the statue until he overthrew it, and inside of it he found a jar of money. He put the money in a bag, and went home to his mother, and told her that he had sold the cloth to a person who did not speak, and gave him no money; that he had killed him with a mattock, and thrown him down, and he had given him the money which he had brought home. His mother, who was wise, said to him: "Say nothing about it, and we will eat this money up little by little."[11]

Another time his mother said to him: "Giufà, I have this piece of cloth to be dyed; take it and leave it with the dyer, the one who dyes green and black," Giufà put it on his shoulder, and went off. On his way he saw a large, beautiful snake, and because it was green he said to it: "My mother has sent me with this cloth which she wants dyed. To-morrow I will come for it." And there he left it.

He went home and told his mother, who began to tear her hair. "Ah! Shameless fellow! How you ruin me! Hasten and see whether it is there still!" Giufà went back, but the cloth had disappeared.[12]

✄ C. Giufà and the Judge ✄

One day Giufà went out to gather herbs, and it was night before he returned. On his way back the moon rose through the clouds, and Giufà sat down on a stone and watched the moon appear and disappear behind the clouds, and he exclaimed constantly: "It appears, it appears! It sets, it sets!"

Now there were near the way some thieves, who were skinning a calf which they had stolen, and when they heard: "It appears, it sets!" They feared that the officers of justice were coming, so they ran away and left the meat. When Giufà saw the thieves running away, he went to see what it was and found the calf skinned. He took his knife and cut off flesh enough to fill his sack and went home. When he arrived there his mother asked him why he came so late. He said it was because he was bringing some meat which she was to sell the next day, and the money was to be kept for him. The next day his mother sent him into the country and sold the meat.

In the evening Giufà returned and asked his mother: "Did you sell the meat?" "Yes, I sold it to the flies on credit." "When will they give you the money?" "When they get it." A week passed and the flies brought no money, so Giufà went to the judge and said to him: "Sir, I want justice. I sold the flies meat on credit and they have not come to pay me." The judge said: "I pronounce this sentence on them: wherever you see them you may kill them." Just then a fly lighted on the judge's nose, and Giufà dealt it such a blow that he broke the judge's head.

THE ANECDOTE of the fly in the latter part of the story is found independently in a version from Palermo. "The flies plagued Giufà and stung him. He went to the judge and complained of them. The judge laughed and said: 'Wherever you see a fly you can strike it.' While the judge was speaking a fly rested on his face and Giufà dealt it such a blow that he broke the judge's nose."

This story, which, as we shall see, has variants in different parts of Italy, is of Oriental origin and is found in the *Pantschatantra*. A king asked his pet monkey to watch over him while he slept. A bee settled on the king's head; the monkey could not drive it away, so he took the king's sword and killed the bee—and the king, too. A similar parable is put into the mouth of Buddha. A bald carpenter was attacked by a mosquito. He called his son to drive it away; the son took the axe, aimed a blow at the insect, but split his father's head in two, in killing the mosquito. In *Anvar-i-Suhaili*, the Persian translation of the *Pantschatantra*, it is a tame bear who keeps the flies from the sleeping gardener by throwing a stone at his head.[13]

The only popular European versions of this story, as far as we know, are found in Italy. Besides those from Sicily, there are versions from Florence, Leghorn, and Venice. The first is called:

↭ CI. The Little Omelet ↭

Once upon a time there was a little woman who had a little room and a little hen. The hen laid an egg and the little woman took it and made a little omelet of it, and put it to cool in the window. Along came a fly and ate it up. Imagine what an omelet that must have been! The little woman went to the magistrate and told him her story. He gave her a club and told her to kill the fly with it wherever she saw it. At that moment a fly lighted on the magistrate's nose, and the woman, believing it to be the same fly, gave it a blow and broke the magistrate's nose.

THE VERSIONS from Leghorn and Venice are in almost the same words.[14]

The literary versions are quite abundant, four or five being found in Italy, and a number in France, the best known of which is La Fontaine's fable of "The Bear and the Amateur Gardener," Book VIII. 10.[15]

One morning, before Giufà was up, he heard a whistle and asked his mother who was passing. She answered that it was the morning-singer. One day Giufà, tired of the noise, went out and killed the man who was blowing the whistle, and came back and told his mother that he had killed the morning-singer. His mother went out and brought the body into the house and threw it into the well, which happened to be dry. Then she remembered that she had a lamb, which she killed and also threw in the well.

Meanwhile the family of the murdered man had learned of the murder and had gone to the judge, with their complaint, and all together went to Giufà's house to investigate the matter. The judge said to Giufà: "Where did you put the body?" Giufà, who was silly, replied: "I threw it in the well." Then they tied Giufà to a rope and lowered him into the well. When he reached the bottom he began to feel around and touched wool, and cried out to the son of the murdered man: "Did your father have wool?" "My father did not have wool." "This one has wool; he is not your father." Then he touched the tail: "Did your father have a tail?" "My father did not have a tail." "Then it's not your father." Then he felt four feet and asked: "How many feet did your father have?" "My father had two feet." Giufà said: "This one has four feet; he is not your father." Then he felt the head and said: "Did your father have horns?" "My father did not have horns." Giufà replied: "This one has horns; he is not your father." Then the judge said: "Giufà, bring him up either with the horns or with the wool." So they drew up Giufà with the lamb on his shoulder, and when the judge saw that it was a real lamb, they set Giufà at liberty.

In a variant of the above story Giufà's mother, to get rid of him, one day tells him to take his gun and go off and shoot a cardinal-bird. Giufà asks what a cardinal is, and his mother tells him that it is one that has a red head. Giufà, of course, shoots a cardinal and carries him home. The remainder of the story is as above. In another variant Giufà's mother has a cock which she cooks one day, and Giufà, who had never eaten anything of the kind before, likes it greatly and asks what it is. His mother tells him it is the night-singer. One evening Giufà saw a poor man singing behind a door, and thinking he was a night-singer, killed him and carried him home. The rest of the story is like the first version.[16]

Giufà is not without an occasional gleam of wit, as is shown in the following story (Pitrè No. 190, § 8), entitled:

༴ CII. Eat, My Clothes! ༴

As Giufà was half a simpleton no one showed him any kindness, such as to invite him to his house or give him anything to eat. Once Giufà went to a farmhouse for something, and the farmers, when they saw him looking so ragged and poor, came near setting the dogs on him, and made him leave in a hurry. When his mother heard it she procured for him a fine coat, a pair of breeches, and a velvet vest. Giufà dressed up like an overseer, went to the same farmhouse, and then you should see what great ceremonies they made! They invited him to dine with them. While at the table all were very attentive to him. Giufà, on the one hand, filled his stomach, and on the other, put into his pockets, coat, and hat whatever was left over, saying: "Eat, my clothes, for you were invited!"

IT IS interesting to note that this story is told of no less a person than Dante, about whom cluster more popular traditions than many are aware of. It is the subject of one of Sercambi's novels, and will be found with many other interesting traditions of the great poet in Papanti's *Dante secondo la Tradizione e i Novellatori*, Leghorn, 1873.[17]

Giufà was not a very safe person to leave alone in the house. Once his mother went to church and told him to make some porridge for his little sister. Giufà made a great kettle of boiling porridge and fed it to the poor child and burned her mouth so that she died. On another occasion his mother, on leaving home, told him to feed the hen that was sitting and put her back on the nest, so that the eggs should not get cold. Giufà stuffed the hen with the food until he killed her, and then sat on the eggs himself until his mother returned.[18]

Giufà's mother went to mass once and said to him: "Pull the door to!" When his mother had gone out Giufà took hold of the door and began to pull it, and pulled and pulled until it came off. Giufà put it on his back and carried it to the church, and threw it down before his mother, saying: "There is the door!"[19]

A number of other stories about Giufà are found in Gonzenbach (No. 37) which we give here for completeness.

◦ CIII. Giufà's Exploits ◦

After Giufà had scalded his little sister to death, his mother drove him from the house, and he entered the service of a priest. "What wages do you want?" asked the priest. "One egg a day, and as much bread as I can eat with it; and you must keep me in your service until the screech-owl cries in the ivy." The priest was satisfied and thought he could not find such a cheap servant again. The next morning Giufà received his egg and a loaf of bread. He opened the egg and ate it with a pin, and every time he licked off the pin he ate a great piece of bread. "Bring me a little more bread," he cried; "this is not enough;" and the priest had to get him a large basket of bread.

So it was every morning. "Alas for me!" cried the priest; "in a few weeks he will reduce me to beggary." It was winter then and would be several months until the screech owl cried in the ivy. In despair the priest said to his mother: "This evening you must hide in the ivy and scream like an owl." The old woman did as she was told and began to cry: " Miu, miu!" "Do you hear, Giufà?" said the priest, "the screech-owl is crying in the ivy; we must part." So Giufà took his bundle and was going to return to his mother.

As he was going by the place where the priest's mother was still crying "Miu, miu," he exclaimed: "O you cursed screech-owl suffer punishment and sorrow!" And threw stones into the ivy and killed the old woman.

Giufà's mother would not allow him to remain at home, and made him take service as a swineherd with a farmer, who sent him into the woods to keep the swine until they were fat and then drive them back. So Giufà lived several months in the woods until the swine were fat. As he was driving them home he met a butcher and said to him: "Would you like to buy these swine? I will sell them to you at half price if you will give me back the ears and tails." The butcher bought the whole herd, and paid Giufà the money, together with the ears and tails.

Giufà then went to a bog near by and planted two ears close together and three spans off a tail, and so with all of them. Then he ran in great trouble to the farmer and cried: "Sir, imagine what a great misfortune has happened to me. I had fattened your swine beautifully and was driving them home when they fell into a bog and are all swallowed up in it. The ears and tails only are still sticking out." The farmer hastened with all his people to the bog, where the ears and tails still stuck out. They tried to pull the swine out, but whenever they seized an ear or a tail it came right off and Giufà exclaimed: "You see how fat the swine were: they have disappeared in the marsh from pure fatness." The farmer was obliged to return home without his swine, while Giufà took the money home to his mother and remained a time with her.

One day his mother said to him: "Giufà, we have nothing to eat to-day; what shall we do?" "Leave it to me," said he, and went to a butcher." Gossip, give me half a *rotulu* of meat; I will give you the money to-morrow." The butcher gave him the meat and he went in the same way to the baker, the oil-merchant, the wine-dealer, and the cheese-merchant and took home to his mother the meat, macaroni, bread, oil, wine, and cheese which he had bought on credit, and they ate together merrily.

The next day Giufà pretended he was dead and his mother wept and lamented. "My son is dead, my son is dead!" He was put in an open coffin and carried to the church and the priests sang the mass for the dead over him. When, however, every one in the city heard that Giufà was dead, the butcher, the baker, the oil-merchant, and the wine-dealer said: "What we gave him yesterday is as good as lost. Who will pay us for it now?" The cheese-dealer, however, thought: "Giufà, it is true, owes me only four *grani*,* but I will not give them to him. I will go and take his cap from him." So he crept into the church, but there was still a priest there praying over Giufà's coffin. "As long as the priest is there, it is not fitting for me to take his cap," thought the cheese-merchant, and hid himself behind the altar. When it was night the last priest departed and the cheese-merchant was on the point of coming out from his hiding-place when a band of thieves rushed into the church. They had stolen a large bag of money and were going to divide it in the dark church. They quarreled over the division and began to cry out and make a noise. Thereupon Giufà sat up in his coffin and exclaimed: "Out with you!" The thieves were greatly frightened when the dead man rose up, and believed he was calling to the other dead, so they ran out in terror, leaving the sack behind. As Giufà was picking up the sack, the cheese-merchant sprang

* About a cent and a half.

from his hiding-place and claimed his share of the money. Giufà, however, kept crying: "Your share is four *grani*." The thieves outside thought he was dividing the money among the dead and said to each other: "How many he must have called if they receive but four *grani* apiece!" And ran away as fast as they could run. Giufà took the money home to his mother, after he had given the cheese-merchant a little to say nothing about what had happened.

Giufà's mother once bought a large stock of flax and said to her son: "Giufà, you can surely spin a little so as to be doing something." Giufà took a skein from time to time, and instead of spinning it put it in the fire and burned it. Then his mother became angry and beat him. What did Giufà do then? He took a bundle of twigs and wound it with flax like a distaff; then he took a broom for a spindle and sat himself on the roof and began to spin. While he was sitting there three fairies came by and said: "Just see how nicely Giufà is sitting there and spinning. Shall we not give him something?" The first fairy said: "I will enable him to spin as much flax in a night as he touches." The second said: "I will enable him to weave in a night as much yarn as he has spun." The third said: "I will enable him to bleach all the linen he has woven in one night." Giufà heard this and at night when his mother had gone to bed, he got behind her stock of flax, and as often as he touched a skein it was at once spun. When the flax was all gone he began to weave, and as soon as he touched the loom the linen began to roll from it. Finally he spread the linen out and had scarcely wet it a little when it was bleached. The next morning Giufà showed his mother the fine pieces of linen, and she sold them and earned much money. Giufà continued this for several nights; finally he grew tired and wanted to go out to service again.

He found a place with a smith, whose bellows he was to blow. He blew them so hard, however, that he put the fire out. The smith said: "Leave off blowing and hammer the iron on the anvil." But Giufà pounded on the anvil so bard that the iron flew into a thousand pieces. Then the smith became angry, but he could not send him away, for he had agreed to keep him a year. So he went to a poor man and said: "I will make you a handsome present if you will tell Giufà that you are Death, and that you have come to take him away." The poor man met Giufà one day, and said what the smith had told him. Giufà was not slow. "What, are you Death?" cried he, seized the poor man, put him in his sack, and carried him to the smithy. There he laid him on the anvil and began to hammer away on him. "How many years shall I yet live?"

he asked, while he was hammering. "Twenty years," cried the man in the sack. "That is not near enough." "Thirty years, forty years, as long as you will," screamed the man; but Giufà kept on hammering until the poor man was dead.

The bishop once announced to the whole town that every goldsmith should make him a crucifix, and he would pay four hundred ounces for the most beautiful one. Whoever brought a crucifix that did not please him must lose his head. So a goldsmith came and brought him a handsome crucifix, but the bishop said it did not please him and had the poor man's head cut off, but kept the crucifix. The next day a second goldsmith came, who brought a still handsomer crucifix, but it went no better with him than with the first. This lasted for some time and many a poor man lost his head. When Giufà heard of this he went to a goldsmith and said: "Master, you must make me a crucifix with a very thick body, but otherwise as fine as you can make it." When the crucifix was done Giufà took it on his arm and carried it to the bishop. Scarcely had the bishop seen it when he cried out: "What are you thinking of, to bring me such a monster? Wait, you shall pay me for it!" "Ah, worthy sir," said Giufà, "just hear me and learn what has happened to me. This crucifix was a model of beauty when I started with it; on the way it began to swell with anger and the nearer your house I came the more it swelled, most of all when I was mounting your stairs. The Lord is angry with you on account of the innocent blood that you have shed, and if you do not at once give me the four hundred ounces and an annuity to each of the goldsmiths' widows, you, too, will swell in the same way, and God's wrath will visit you." The bishop was frightened and gave him the four hundred ounces, and bade him send all the widows to him so that he could give each of them a yearly pension. Giufà took the money and went to each widow and said: "What will you give me if I will procure you an annuity from the bishop?" Each gave him a handsome sum and Giufà took home to his mother a great heap of money.

One day Giufà's mother sent him to another town, where there was a fair. On the way some children met him, who asked: "Where are you going, Giufà?" "To the fair." "Will you bring me back a whistle?" "Yes!" "And me, too?" "Yes!" "Me, too?" "Me, too?" Asked one after the other, and Giufà said "Yes" to all. At last there was a child who said: "Giufà, bring me a whistle, too. Here is a penny." When Giufà came back from the fair, he brought one whistle only and gave it to the last boy. "Giufà, you promised each of us one," cried the other children. "You did not give me a penny to buy it with," answered Giufà.[20]

THE COUNTERPART of Giufà is found in a Venetian story (Bernoni, *Fiabe*, No. II) entitled "The Fool," which is, in substance, as follows:

✣ CIV. The Fool ✣

Once upon a time there was a mother who had a son with little brains. One morning she said: "We must get up early, for we have to make bread." So they both rose early and began to make bread. The mother made the loaves, but took no pains to make them the same size. Her son said to her finally: "How small you have made this loaf, mother!" "Oh!" said she, "it does not matter whether they are big or little; for the proverb says: 'Large and small, all must go to mass.'" "Good, good!"

When the bread was made, instead of carrying it to the baker's, the son took it to the church, for it was the hour for mass, saying: "My mother said that, 'Large and small, all must go to mass.'" So he threw the loaves down in the middle of the church. Then he went home to his mother and said: "I have done what you told me to do." "Good! Did you take the bread to the baker's?" "Oh! mother, if you had seen how they all looked at me!" "You might also have cast an eye on them in return," said his mother. "Wait, wait, I will cast an eye at them, too," he exclaimed, and went to the stable and cut out the eyes of all the animals, and putting them in a handkerchief, went to the church and when any man or woman looked at him he threw an eye at them.

When his mother learned what he had done she took to her bed and sent her son for a physician. When the doctor came he felt her pulse and said: "Oh! How weak this poor woman is!" Then he told the son that he must take good care of his mother and make her some very thin broth and give her a bowlful every minute. The son promised to obey him and went to the market and bought a sparrow and put on the fire a pail of water. When it boiled he put in the sparrow and waited until it boiled up two or three times, and then took a bowl of the broth to his mother, and repeated the dose as fast as he could.

The next day the physician found the poor woman weaker than ever, and told her son he must put something heavy on her so as to throw her into a perspiration. When the doctor had gone the son piled all the heavy furniture in the room on her, and when she could no longer breathe he ran for the doctor again. This time the doctor saw that nothing was to be done, and advised her son to have her confess and prepare for death. So her son dressed her and carried her to church and sat her in the confessional and told the priest that some one was waiting for him and then went home. The priest soon saw that the woman was dead and went to find her son. When the son heard that his mother was dead, he declared that the priest had killed her, and began to beat him.[21]

THERE ARE many stories in Italy which turn on the tricks played by a sharper on his credulous friends; a good specimen of the class is the following from Sicily (Pitrè No. 157):

৵ CV. Uncle Capriano ৵

There was once a husband and wife who had a daughter. The man's name was Uncle Capriano and he owned near the town a piece of property, where he always worked. One day thirteen robbers happened to pass that way, saw Uncle Capriano, dismounted, and began to talk with him, and soon formed a friendship for him. After this they frequently went to divert themselves with him. When they arrived they always saluted him with: "Good day, Uncle Capriano," and he answered; "Your servant, gentlemen; what are your worships doing?" "We have come to amuse ourselves. Go, Uncle Capriano, go and lunch, for we will do the work meanwhile." So he went and ate and they did his work for him. Finally, what do you suppose Uncle Capriano tried to do? He sought to invent some way to get money from the robbers. When he went home he said to his wife: "I am on friendly terms with the robbers and I would like to see whether I can get a little money out of them, and I have invented this story to tell them: that we have a rabbit, which I send home alone every evening with fire-wood and things for soup, which my wife cooks." Then he said to his daughter: "When I come with the thieves, you bathe the rabbit in water and come out of the door to meet me and say: 'Is that the way to load the poor little rabbit so that it comes home tired to death?'"

When the thieves heard that he had a rabbit that carried things, they wanted it, saying: "If we had it we could send it to carry money, food, and other things to our houses." Uncle Capriano said to them one day: "I should like to have you come to my house to-day." There were thirteen of the thieves; one said Yes, another said No. The captain said: "Let us go and see the rabbit." When they arrived at the house the daughter came to the door and said: "Is that the way to load the poor little rabbit so that it comes home tired to death?" When they entered the house all felt of the rabbit and exclaimed: "Poor little animal! Poor little animal! It is all covered with sweat." When the thieves saw this they looked at each other and said: "Shall we ask him to give us this little rabbit?" Then they said: "Uncle Capriano, you must give us the rabbit without any words, and we will pay you whatever you ask." He answered: "Ask me for anything except this rabbit, for if I give you that I shall be ruined." They replied: "You must give it to us without further words, whether you are ruined or not." Finally Uncle Capriano let them have the rabbit for two hundred ounces, and they gave him twenty besides to buy himself a present with. After the thieves had got possession of the rabbit, they went to a house in the country to try it. They each took a bag of money and said: "Let us send a bag to each of our houses." The captain said: "First, carry a bag to mine." So they took the rabbit to load it, and after they had put the bags on it, the rabbit could not move and one of the thieves struck it on the haunch with a switch. Then the rabbit ran away instantly. The thieves went in great anger to Uncle Capriano and said: "Did you have the boldness to play such a trick on us, to sell us a rabbit that could not stir when we put a few bags of money on it?" "But, gentlemen," said the old man, "did you beat it?" "Of course," answered one of the thieves, "my companion struck it with a switch on the haunch." The old man asked: "But where did you strike it, on the right or on the left haunch?" "On the left." "That is why the rabbit ran away," said the old man. "You should have hit it on the right. If you did not observe these conditions, what fault is it of mine?" "This is true," said the thieves, "Uncle Capriano is right; so go and eat and we will attend to the work." And so their friendship was not broken this time.

After a time Uncle Capriano said to his wife: "We must get some more money from the thieves." "In what way?" "To-morrow you must buy a new pot, and then you must cook in an old pot somewhere in the house, and at Ave Maria, just before I come home, you must empty the old pot into the new one, and put it on the hearth without any fire. To-morrow I will tell the thieves that I have a pot that cooks without any fire."

The next evening Uncle Capriano persuaded the thieves to go home with him. When they saw the pot they looked at one another and said: "We must ask him to give it to us." After some hesitation, he sold it to them for four hundred ounces, and twenty over as before.

When the thieves arrived at their house in the country, they killed a fine kid, put it into the pot, and set it on the hearth, without any fire, and went away. In the evening they all ran and tried to see who would arrive first, and find the meat cooked. The one who arrived first took out a piece of meat, and saw that it was as they had left it. Then he gave the pot a kick, and broke it in two. When the others came and found the meat not cooked, they started for Uncle Capriano's, and complained to him that he had sold them a pot that cooked everything, and that they had put meat into it, and found it raw. "Did you break the pot?" asked Uncle Capriano. "Of course we broke it." "What kind of a hearth did you have, high or low?" One of the thieves answered: "Rather high." "That was why the pot did not cook; it should have been low. You did not observe the conditions and broke the pot; what fault is that of mine?" The thieves said: "Uncle Capriano is right; go, Uncle Capriano, and eat, for we will do your work."

Some time after, Uncle Capriano said again to his wife: "We must get some more money out of them." "But how can we manage it?" "You know that we have a whistle in the chest; have it put in order, and to-morrow go to the butcher's, and get a bladder of blood, and fix it about your neck, and put on your mantilla; and when I return home, let me find you sitting down and angry, and the candle not lighted. I will bring my friends with me, and when I find the candle not lighted, I will begin to cry out, and you will not utter a word; then I will take my knife and cut your throat. You will fall down on the floor; the blood will run out of the bladder, and the thieves will believe that you are dead. You" (turning to his daughter)—"what I say I mean, when I tell you: 'Get the whistle'—get it and give it to me. When I blow it three times, you" (speaking to his wife) "will get up from the floor. When the thieves see this operation they will want the whistle, and we will get another six hundred ounces from them."

[Everything took place as Uncle Capriano had arranged; the thieves paid him six hundred ounces, and twenty over as usual, and then went home and killed their wives, to try the whistle on them. The rage of the thieves can be imagined when they found they had been deceived again. In order to avenge themselves, they took a sack and went to Uncle Capriano, and without any words seized him, put him in it, and taking him on a horse, rode away. They came after a time to a country-house, where they stopped to eat, leaving Uncle Capriano outside in the bag.]

Uncle Capriano, who was in the bag, began to cry: "They want to give me the king's daughter, and I don't want her!" There happened to be near by a herdsman, who heard what he was saying about the king's daughter, and he said to himself: "I will go and take her myself." So he went to

Uncle Capriano and said: "What is the matter with you?" "They want to give me the king's daughter, and I don't want her, because I am married." The herdsman said: "I will take her, for I am single; but how can we arrange it?" Uncle Capriano answered: "Take me out, and get into the bag yourself." "That is a good idea," said the herdsman; so he set Uncle Capriano at liberty, and got into the bag himself. Uncle Capriano tied him fast, took his crook, and went to tend the sheep. The herdsman soon began to cry: "They want to give me the king's daughter. I will take her, I will take her!" In a little while the thieves came and put the bag on a horse, and rode away to the sea, the herdsman crying out all the time: "They want to give me the king's daughter. I will take her, I will take her!" When they came to the sea, they threw the bag in, and returned home. On their way back, they happened to look up on the mountain, and exclaimed: "See there! Is that not Uncle Capriano?" "Yes, it is." "How can that be; did we not throw him into the sea, and is he there now?" Then they went to him and said: "How is this, Uncle Capriano, didn't we throw you in the sea?" "Oh! You threw me in near the shore, and I found these sheep and oxen; if you had thrown me in farther out, I would have found many more." Then they asked Uncle Capriano to throw them all in, and they went to the sea, and he began to throw them in, and each said: "Quick, Uncle Capriano, throw me in quickly before my comrades get them all!" After he had thrown them all in, Uncle Capriano took the horses and sheep and oxen, and went home and built palaces, and became very rich, and married off his daughter, and gave a splendid banquet.[22]

A very interesting class of stories is found in Pitrè (Nos. 246–270) illustrating proverbial sayings. The first, on the text "The longer one lives, the more one learns," relates that a child came to an old man and asked for some coals to light a fire with. The old man said he would willingly give them, but the child had nothing to carry them in. The child, however, filled his palm with ashes, put a coal on them, and went away. The old man gave his head a slap, and exclaimed: "With all my years and experience, I did not know this thing. 'The longer one lives, the more one learns.'" And from that time these words have remained for a proverb.

Another (No. 252) recalls one of Giufà's pranks. A husband, to test his wife and friend, who is a bailiff, throws a goat's head into the well, and tells the wife that he has killed a person and cut off the head to prevent the body from being recognized. The wife promises secrecy, but soon tells the story to her friend, who denounces the supposed murderer to the judge. The house is entered by an arbor, from which they climb into a window, and the husband is arrested and taken to the well, which a bailiff descends, and finds the goat's head. The husband explains his trick, which gave rise to the saying: "Do not confide a secret to a woman; do not make a bailiff your friend, and do not rent a house with an arbor."[23]

Another shows how the stories of classic times survive among the people. Nero, a wicked king, goes about in disguise to hear what the people say of him. One day he meets an old woman in the field, and when Nero's name is mentioned, instead of cursing him as others do, she says: "May God preserve him." She explains her words by saying that they have had several kings, each worse than the other, and now they have Nero, who tears every son from his mother, wherefore may God guard and preserve him, for "There is no end to evil."[24]

There was once a whimsical prince who thought he could arrange the world and animals as he pleased and overcome Nature. He taught his horse to devour flesh and his dogs to eat grass. He trained an ass to dance and accompany himself by his braying: in short, the prince boasted that by means of Art one could rule Nature. Among other things he trained a cat to stand on the table and hold a lighted candle while he was eating. No matter what was brought on the table, the cat never moved, but held the candle as if it had been a statue of wood. The prince showed the cat to his friends and said, boastingly: "Nature is nothing; my art is more powerful and can do this and other things." His friends often said that everything must be true to its nature; "Art departs and Nature prevails." The prince invited them to make any trial they wished, asserting that the cat would never forget the art he had taught it. One of his friends caught a mouse one day and wrapped it up in a handkerchief and carried it with him to the prince's. When the cat heard and saw the mouse, it dropped the candlestick and ran after the mouse. The friend began to laugh, and said to the prince, who stood with his mouth wide open with amazement: "Dear prince, I always told you Art departs and Nature prevails!"

This story is told of Dante and Cecco d'Ascoli, the former playing the role of the prince.[25]

To counterbalance the stories of foolish people which have been related above, we will conclude this chapter with some stories of clever people, stories which were popular as long ago as the Middle Ages.

The first is from Sicily (Gonz., No, 50) and is called:

∾ CVII. The Clever Peasant ∾

There was once a king who, while hunting, saw a peasant working in the fields and asked him: "How much do you earn in a day?" "Four *carlini,* your Majesty," answered the peasant. "What do you do with them?" continued the king. The peasant said: "The first I eat; the second I put out at interest; the third I give back, and the fourth I throw away."

The king rode on, but after a time the peasant's answer seemed very curious to him, so he returned and asked him: "Tell me, what do you mean by eating the first *carlino,* putting the second out to interest, giving back the third, and throwing away the fourth?" The peasant answered: "With the first I feed myself; with the second I feed my children, who must care for me when I am old; with the third I feed my father, and so repay him for what he has done for me, and with the fourth I feed my wife, and thus throw it away, because I have no profit from it." "Yes," said the king, "you are right. Promise me, however, that you will not tell any one this until you have seen my face a hundred times." The peasant promised and the king rode home well pleased.

While sitting at table with his ministers, he said: "I will give you a riddle: A peasant earns four *carlini* a day; the first he eats; the second he puts out at interest; the third he gives back, and the fourth he throws away. What is that?" No one was able to answer it.

One of the ministers remembered finally that the king had spoken the day before with the peasant, and he resolved to find the peasant and obtain from him the answer. When he saw the peasant he asked him for the answer to the riddle, but the peasant answered: "I cannot tell you, for I have promised the king to tell no one until I have seen his face a hundred times." "Oh!" said the minister, "I can show you the king's face," and drew a hundred coins from his purse and gave them to the peasant. On every coin the king's face was to be seen of course. After the peasant had looked at each coin once, he said: "I have now seen the king's face a hundred times, and can tell you the answer to the riddle," and told him it.

The minister went in great glee to the king and said: "Your Majesty, I have found the answer to the riddle; it is so and so." The king exclaimed: "You can have heard it only from the peasant himself," had the peasant summoned, and took him to task. "Did you not promise me not to tell it until you had seen my face a hundred times?" "But, your Majesty," answered the peasant, "your minister showed me your picture a hundred times." Then he showed him the bag of money that the minister had given him. The king was so pleased with the clever peasant that he rewarded him, and made him a rich man for the rest of his life.[26]

❧ CVIII. The Clever Girl ❧

Once upon a time there was a huntsman who had a wife and two children, a son and a daughter; and all lived together in a wood where no one ever came, and so they knew nothing about the world. The father alone sometimes went to the city and brought back the news. The king's son once went hunting and lost himself in that wood, and while be was seeking his way it became night. He was weary and hungry. Imagine how he felt! But all at once he saw a light shining at a distance. He followed it and reached the huntsman's house and asked for lodging and something to eat. The huntsman recognized him at once and said: "Highness, we have already supped on our best. But if we can find anything for you, you must be satisfied with it. What can we do? We are so far from the towns, that we cannot procure what we need every day." Meanwhile he had a capon cooked for him. The prince did not wish to eat it alone, but called all the huntsman's family, and gave the head of the capon to the father, the back to the mother, the legs to the son, and the wings to the daughter, and ate the rest himself. In the house there were only two beds, in the same room. In one the husband and wife slept, in the other the brother and sister. The old people went and slept in the stable, giving up their bed to the prince. When the girl saw that the prince was asleep, she said to her brother: "I will wager that you do not know why the prince divided the capon among us in the manner he did." "Do you know? Tell me why." "He gave the head to papa because he is the head of the family, the back to mamma because she has on her shoulders all the affairs of the house, the legs to you because you must be quick in performing the errands which are given you, and the wings to me to fly away and catch a husband." The prince pretended to be asleep; but he was awake and heard these words, and perceived that the girl had much judgment; and as she was also pretty, he fell in love with her.

The next morning he left the huntsman's; and as soon as he reached the court, he sent him, by a servant, a purse of money. To the young girl he sent a cake in the form of a full moon, thirty patties, and a cooked capon, with three questions: "Whether it was the thirtieth of the month in the wood, whether the moon was full, and whether the capon crowed in the night." The servant, although a trusty one, was overcome by his gluttony and ate fifteen of the patties, and a good slice of the cake, and the capon. The young girl, who had understood it all, sent back word to the prince that the moon was not full but on the wane; that it was only the fifteenth of the month and that the capon had gone to the mill; and that she asked him to spare the pheasant for the sake of the partridge. The prince, too, understood the metaphor, and having summoned the servant, he cried: "Rogue! You have eaten the capon, fifteen patties, and a good slice of the cake. Thank that girl who has interceded for you; if she had not, I would have hung you."

A few months after this, the huntsman found a gold mortar, and wished to present it to the prince. But his daughter said: "You will be laughed at for this present. You will see that the prince will say to you: 'The mortar is fine and good, but, peasant, where is the pestle?'" The father did not listen to his daughter; but when he carried the mortar to the prince, he was greeted as his daughter had foretold. "My daughter told me so," said the huntsman. "Ah! If I had only listened to her!" The prince heard these words and said to him: "Your daughter, who pretends to be so wise, must make me a hundred ells of cloth out of four ounces of flax; if she does not I will hang you and her." The poor father returned home weeping, and sure that he and his daughter must die, for who could make a hundred ells of cloth with four ounces of flax. His daughter came out to meet him, and when she learned why he was weeping, said: "Is that all you are weeping for? Quick, get me the flax and I will manage it." She made four small cords of the flax and said to her father: "Take these cords and tell him that when he makes me a loom out of these cords I will weave the hundred ells of cloth." When the prince heard this answer he did not know what to say, and thought no more about condemning the father or the daughter.

The next day he went to the wood to visit the girl. Her mother was dead, and her father was out in the fields digging. The prince knocked, but no one opened. He knocked louder, but the same thing. The young girl was deaf to him. Finally, tired of waiting, he broke open the door and entered: "Rude girl! Who taught you not to open to one of my rank? Where are your father and mother?" "Who knew it was you? My father is where he should be and my mother is weeping for her sins. You must leave, for I have something else to do than listen to you." The prince went away in anger and complained to the father of his daughter's rude manners, but the father excused her. The prince, at last seeing how wise and cunning she was, married her.

The wedding was celebrated with great splendor, but an event happened which came near plunging the princess into misfortune. One Sunday two peasants were passing a church; one of them had a hand-cart and the other was leading a she-ass ready to foal. The bell rang for mass and they both entered the church, one leaving his cart outside and the other tying the ass to the cart. While they were in the church the ass foaled, and the owner of the ass and the owner of the cart both claimed the colt. They appealed to the prince, and he decided that the colt belonged to the owner of the cart, because, he said, it was more likely that the owner of the ass would tie her to the cart in order to lay a false claim to the colt than that the owner of the cart would tie it to the ass. The owner of the ass had right on his side, and all the people were in his favor, but the prince had pronounced sentence and there was nothing to say. The poor man then applied to the princess, who advised him to cast a net in the square when the prince passed. When the prince saw the net, he said: "What are you doing, you fool? Do you expect to find fish in the square?" The peasant, who had been advised by the princess, answered: "It is easier for me to find fish in the square than for a cart to have foals." The prince revoked the sentence, but when he returned to the palace, knowing that the princess had suggested the answer to the peasant, he said to her: "Prepare to return to your own home within an hour. Take with you what you like best and depart." She was not at all saddened by the prospect, but ate a better dinner than usual, and made the prince drink a bottle of wine in which she had put a sleeping potion; and when he was as sound asleep as a log, she had him put in a carriage and took him with her to her house in the wood. It was in January, and she had the roof of the house uncovered and it snowed on the prince, who awoke and called his servants: "What do you wish?" said the princess. "I command here. Did you not tell me to take from your house the thing I liked best? I have taken you, and now you are mine." The prince laughed and they made peace.[27]

THE NEXT story is the Italian version of the tale familiar to the readers of Grimm by the title of "Doctor Knowall." There is a Sicilian version in Pitrè, No. 167, in which our story forms one of several episodes. It is found, however, independently in the Mantuan collection from which we take it, changing the name slightly to suit the conclusion of the story.

‑ CIX. Crab ‑

There was once a king who had lost a valuable ring. He looked for it everywhere, but could not find it. So he issued a proclamation that if any astrologer could tell him where it was he would be richly rewarded. A poor peasant by the name of Crab heard of the proclamation. He could neither read nor write, but took it into his head that he wanted to be the astrologer to find the king's ring. So he went and presented himself to the king, to whom he said: "Your Majesty must know that I am an astrologer, although you see me so poorly dressed. I know that you have lost a ring and I will try by study to find out where it is." "Very well," said the king, "And when you have found it, what reward must I give you?" "That is at your discretion, your Majesty." "Go, then, study, and we shall see what kind of an astrologer you turn out to be."

He was conducted to a room, in which he was to be shut up to study. It contained only a bed and a table on which were a large book and writing materials. Crab seated himself at the table and did nothing but turn over the leaves of the book and scribble the paper so that the servants who brought him his food thought him a great man. They were the ones who had stolen the ring, and from the severe glances that the peasant cast at them whenever they entered, they began to fear that they would be found out. They made him endless bows and never opened their mouths without calling him "Mr. Astrologer." Crab, who, although illiterate, was, as a peasant, cunning, all at once imagined that the servants must know about the ring, and this is the way his suspicions were confirmed. He had been shut up in his room turning over his big book and scribbling his paper for a month, when his wife came to visit him. He said to her: "Hide yourself under the bed, and when a servant enters, say: 'That is one;' when another comes, say: 'That is two;' and so on." The woman hid herself. The servants came with the dinner, and hardly had the first one entered when a voice from under the bed said: "That is one." The second one entered; the voice said: "That is two;" and so on. The servants were frightened at hearing that voice, for they did not know where it came from, and held a consultation. One of them said: "We are discovered; if the astrologer denounces us to the king as thieves, we are lost." "Do you know what we must do?" said another. "Let us hear." "We must go to the astrologer and tell him frankly that we stole the ring, and ask him not to betray us, and present him with a purse of money. Are you willing?" "Perfectly."

So they went in harmony to the astrologer, and making him a lower bow than usual, one of them began: "Mr. Astrologer, you have discovered that we stole the ring. We are poor people and if you reveal it to the king, we are undone. So we beg you not to betray us, and accept this purse of money." Crab took the purse and then added: "I will not betray you, but you must do what I tell you, if you wish to save your lives. Take the ring and make that turkey in the court-yard swallow it, and leave the rest to me." The servants were satisfied to do so and departed with a low bow. The next day Crab went to the king and said to him: "Your Majesty must know that after having toiled over a month I have succeeded in discovering where the ring has gone to." "Where is it, then?" Asked the king. "A turkey has swallowed it." "A turkey? Very well, let us see."

They went for the turkey, opened it, and found the ring inside. The king, amazed, presented the astrologer with a large purse of money and invited him to a banquet. Among the other dishes, there was brought on the table a plate of crabs. Crabs must then have been very rare, because only the king and a few others knew their name. Turning to the peasant the king said: "You, who are an astrologer, must be able to tell me the name of these things which are in this dish." The poor astrologer was very much puzzled, and, as if speaking to himself, but in such a way that the others heard him, he muttered: "Ah! Crab, Crab, what a plight you are in!" All who did not know that his name was Crab rose and proclaimed him the greatest astrologer in the world.[28]

$\mathcal{Z}$

Notes

Introduction

1. THERE are some popular tales, chiefly Oriental in their origin, in the *Cente novelle antiche* (see the notes to Chapter III.), and Boccaccio and his imitators undoubtedly made use of popular material. These popular elements, however, are almost exclusively of the class of jests. The fairy tale, which constitutes by far the largest and most important class of popular tales, is not found in European literature until Straparola. For a few earlier traces of fairy tales in mediæval literature, see an article by the writer, "Two Mediæval Folk-Tales," in the *Germania,* XVIII. [New Series], p. 203.

2. The little that is known of Straparola and a very complete bibliography of his *Piacevoli Notti* will be found in an excellent monograph entitled, *Giovan Francesco Straparola da Caravaggio,* Inaugural-Dissertation von F. W. J. Brakelmann aus Soest, Göttingen, 1867. Straparola's work, especially the unexpurgated editions, is scarce, and the student will ordinarily be obliged to consult it in the French translation of Louveau and Larivey, of which there is an excellent edition in the *Bibliothèque Elzevirienne* of P. Jannet, Paris, 1857. There is a German translation with valuable notes of the *Märchen* contained in the *Piacevoli Notti* by F. W. Val. Schmidt, Berlin, 1817. Schmidt used, without knowing it, an expurgated edition, and translated eighteen instead of twenty-two popular tales.

3. The reader will find all the necessary references to Straparola's borrowed materials in Liebrecht's translation of Dunlop's History of Fiction, pp. 283, 493; in Brakelmann's dissertation above cited; in the French version in the *Bib. Elsevir.;* and in Grimm, II. 477.

4. A comparison of Straparola's tales with those of Grimm, and an analysis of those lacking in Schmidt's translation, will be found in Grimm, II. 477–481.

5. The imitations of Straparola will be found in Dunlop-Liebrecht, p. 284. It is impossible to say with absolute certainty that Perrault borrowed his "*Chat Botté*" and "*Peau d'Ane*" from Straparola. It is, however, quite likely. Perrault's stories appeared 1694–97, and twelve editions of the French translation of Straparola had been issued before that date.

6. The few details of Basile's life will be found in Grimm, II. 481, Liebrecht's translation, II. p. 316, and Taylor's translation, p. v. An article in a recent number of the periodical named from Basile, vol. II. p. 17, gives the conflicting testimony of a number of Italian writers as to Basile's birth and death. The writer has discovered a mention of Basile's burial in the church of St. Sophia at Giugliano, near Naples, and in a

record of deaths kept in the same town, an entry stating that Basile died there on the 23d of February, 1632. The following are all the editions of which I can find mention: Naples, 1637, 8vo, 1644, 12mo, 1645, 1674, 1694 (Graesse), 1697 (Pitrè), 1714, 1722, 1728, 1747, 1749 (Liebrecht), 1788, *Collezione di Tutti i Poemi*, etc.; Rome, 1679, 1797 (Pitrè). Italian translations appeared at Naples in 1754, 1769, 1784, and 1863, and in Bolognese at Bologna, 1742, 1813, 1872, and at Venice in 1813. The editions used in the preparation of this work will be found in the Bibliography. In spite of the numerous editions above cited, the *Pentamerone* is a very scarce work, and the scholar will usually have to content himself with Liebrecht's excellent translation. Thirty-one of the fifty stories have been admirably translated by John Edward Taylor, London, 1848, 1850. The *Pentamerone* suffered the same fate as the *Piacevoli Notti*. It was not known, for instance, in Germany, until Fernow described it in his *Römische Studien*, Zürich, 1808, vol. III. pp. 316, 475, although Wieland had taken the material for his "Pervonte" from the third story of the first day.

7. The frame of the *Pentamerone* is the story of the "False Bride:" See Gonz., Nos. 11, 12; Pitrè, No. 13; Imbriani, "*'E Sette Mane-Mozze;*" and Hahn, Nos. 12, 49. Grimm, II. p. 483, gives the stories in the *Pent.* which have parallels among his own *Kinder- und Hausmärchen*. The notes to Liebrecht's translation are to be supplemented by the same author's additional notes in his translation of Dunlop, p. 515.

8. This story is usually printed with Perrault's tales, but its author was really Mlle. Lhéritier. See the latest edition of Perrault's tales, *Les Contes de Charles Perrault*, par Andre Lefèvre, Paris, Lemerre, 1875, p. xli.

9. See Dunlop-Liebrecht, p. 408 *et seq.;* and Grimm, II, p. 489 *et seq.*

10. References to four of the five stories will be found as follows: I., Pitrè, vol. IV. pp. 372, 375; II., Pitrè, *ibid.* p. 381; III., *Nov. fior.* pp. 93, 112, Pitrè, No. 36; V., Pitrè, vol. IV. p. 391. The two editions of Naples, 1684 and 1751, are extremely scarce and the student will be obliged to have recourse to the edition of 1789, contained in the *Collezione di tutti li poeti in lingua Napoletana.*

11. Pitrè, vol. I. p. xliii, mentions some other names, as, *rumanzi* by the inhabitants of Termini, and *pugaret* by the Albanian colonists. To these may be added another Milanese appellation, *panzanega.*

12. Other endings are given by Imbriana, *Pomiglianesi*, p. 129:—

> Cuccurucù,
> No' nce n' è cchiù.

(Cuccurucù, there is no more.)

> Cuccurucù.
> Ss' 'o vuo' cchiù bello, t' o dice tu.

(Cuccurucù, if you want it finer, tell it yourself.) See also Pitrè, vol. I. p. 196, note 2. The most curious introductions and endings are those in De Nino, *Usi e Costumi abruzzesi*, vol. III. There is no general formula, but each *fiaba* has one of its own. Some are meaningless jingles, but others are quite extensive poems on religious subjects. Among these may be found legends of various saints, St. Nicholas, p. 335, etc.

13. An interesting article might be written on the Italian story-tellers, generally illiterate women, from whose lips the stories in the modern collections have been

taken down. Some details may be found in Pitrè, vol. I. p. xvii. (repeated in Ralston's article in *Fraser's Magazine*).

14. Any attempt at an explanation of these facts would lead into the vexed question of the origin and diffusion of popular tales in general. We cannot refrain, however, from calling attention to a remark by Nerucci in the preface to his *Nov. pop. montalesi*, p. v. He thinks that the Italian popular tale will be found to have much the same origin as the Italian popular poetry, that is, that very much is of a literary origin which has usually been deemed popular. This is undoubtedly true of many stories; but may not two versions of a given story, a popular and a literary one, have had a source common to both? A very interesting study might be made of the Italian popular tales in their relation to literary versions which may be the originals.

The most valuable contributions to the question of the origin of Italian popular tales are those by Pitrè in the first volume of his *Fiabe*, pp. xli.–cxlv., and in the same author's *Nov. pop. tosc.* pp. v.–xxxviii.

Chapter I. *Fairy Tales*

1. This story is a variant of Pitrè, No. 17, *Marvizia* (the name of the heroine who was as small as a *marva*, the mallow plant), in which the introduction is wanting. The heroine falls in love with a green bird she sees in her garden, and goes in search of it. After many adventures, she restores the bird to its former human shape and marries it. Other Italian versions of the story in the text are: Sicilian, Pitrè, No. 281, *Nuovo Saggio*, V.; Gonz., No. 15; Neapolitan, *Pent.* II. 9, V. 4; Comp., No. 33 (from the Basilicata); Roman, Busk, p. 99; Tuscan, De Gub., *Sto. Stefano*, No. 14; and Tyrolese, Schneller, No. 13.

An important trait in the above clash is "Tasks set Wife." Besides in the above stories, this trait is also found in those belonging to other classes: see De Gub., *Sto. Stefano*, No. 2, and *Nov. fior.* p. 209.

Another important trait is the following: When after a long search the wife discovers her husband, it is only to find him in the power of a second wife, who, however, by various bribes, is induced to permit the first wife to spend a night in her husband's chamber. She is unable to awaken her husband, who has been drugged by the second wife. The third night she succeeds, makes herself known to him, and they escape. As an example of this trait, we give in full De Gub., *Sto. Stefano*, No. 14, referred to above.

XX. SIR FIORANTE, MAGICIAN

A woodman had three daughters. Every morning one after the other, in turn, carried him his bread to the wood. The father and the daughters noticed in a thicket a large snake, which one day asked the old man for one of his daughters in marriage, threatening him with death if none of them would accept such an offer. The father told his daughters of the snake's offer, and the first and second immediately refused. If the third had refused too, there would have been no hope of salvation for the father; but for his sake she declared at once that snakes had always pleased her, and she thought the snake proposed by her father very handsome. At this the snake shook his tail in token of great joy, and making his bride mount it, carried her away to the midst of a beautiful meadow, where he caused a splendid palace to arise while he himself became a handsome man, and revealed himself as Sir Fiorante with the red and white stockings. But woe to her if she ever disclosed to any one his existence and name! She would lose him forever, unless, to obtain possession of him again, she wore out a pair of iron shoes, a staff and a hat, and filled with her tears seven bottles. The maiden promised; but she was a woman; she went to visit her sisters; one of them wished to know her husband's name, and was so cunning that at last her sister told her, but when the poor girl went back to see her husband, she found neither husband nor palace. To find him again, she was obliged in despair to do penance. She walked and walked and walked, and wept unceasingly. She had already filled one bottle with tears, when she met an old woman who gave her a fine walnut to crack in time of need, and disappeared. When she had filled four bottles, she met another old woman, who gave her a hazel-nut to crack in time of need, and disappeared. She had filled all seven bottles when a third old woman appeared to her, and left her an almond to be cracked in a third case of need, and she, too, disappeared. At last the young girl reached the castle of Sir Fiorante, who had taken another wife. The girl broke first the walnut, and found in it a beautiful dress which the second wife wanted herself. The young girl said: "You may have it if you will let me sleep with Sir Fiorante." The second wife consented, but meanwhile she gave Sir Fiorante some opium. In the night, the young girl said: "Sir Fiorante with the red and white stockings, I have worn out a pair of iron shoes, the staff and the hat, and filled seven bottles with tears, wherefore you must recognize your first wife."

He made no answer, for he had taken opium. The next day the girl opened the hazel-nut, and out came a dress more beautiful than the first; Sir Fiorante's second wife wanted this, and obtained it on the same condition as the first, but took care that Sir Fiorante should take some opium before going to bed. The third day, a faithful servant asked Sir Fiorante if he had not heard in the night the cries that were uttered near him. Sir Fiorante replied, No, but was careful not to take any opium the third night, when, having broken the almond and found in it a dress of unapproachable beauty, the young girl obtained the second wife's consent to sleep anew with Sir Fiorante. The latter pretended this time to take the opium, but did not. Then he feigned to be asleep, but remained awake in order to hear the cries of his abandoned wife, which he could not resist, and began to embrace her. The next day they left that palace to the second wife, and departed together and went to live in happiness at another more wonderful castle.

This episode is found in the *Pent.* V. 3, otherwise not belonging to this class; and in Comp., No. 51, and *Nov. fior.* p. 168, which properly belong to the formula of "Animal Children."

Hahn's formula No. 6, in which a maiden sells herself for three costly presents, and is obliged to marry the buyer, is sufficiently illustrated by Gonz., No. 18, Pitrè, No. 105, and Nerucci, No. 50. In the last story the person to whom the maiden has sold herself refuses to marry her.

The wedding torch is found also in Pitrè, No. 17, and is clearly a survival of the classic custom. The episode in which the birth of the child is hindered recalls the myths of Latona and Alcmene, see Köhler's notes to Gonz., No. 12 (II. p. 210). Other cases of malicious arrest of childbirth in popular literature may be found in Child's *English and Scottish Pop. Ballads*, Part I. p. 84. Pandora's box is also found in *Pent.* V. 4.

Copious references to other European versions of our story will be found in Köhler's notes to Gonz., No. 15 (II. 214), and to Bladé, *Contes pop. rec. en Agenais,* p. 145, to which may be added the notes to the Grimm stories Nos. 88, 113, 127 ("The Soaring Lark," "The Two Kings' Children," and "The Iron Stove"), and Benfey, *Pant.* I. p. 255.

2. The lamp lighted at night to enable the wife to see her husband is found in Pitrè, No. 82, and in a Calabrian story in De Gub., *Zoöl. Myth,* II. 286–287, where the drop of wax falls on the mirror of the sleeping youth. The same incident occurs in the curious story of "The Enchanted Palace," in Comp., No. 27, which is simply a reversal of the Cupid and Psyche myth, and in which the husband is the curious one, and the drop of wax falls on the sleeping wife, and awakens her.

The "iron shoes" are found in Comp., No. 51; Pitrè, No. 56; *Pent.* V. 4; De Gub., *Sto. Stefano,* No. 14; Gradi, *Vigilia,* p. 26; and Ortoli, p. 8. See also Hahn, Nos. 73, 102, and *Basque Legends,* p. 39.

3. See Köhler to Gonz., No, 16; Dunlop-Liebrecht, p. 406 (*Anmerkung.* 475, and *Nachtrag,* p. 544); Graesse, *Sagen-Kreise,* p. 380; Benfey, I, 254; and Simrock, *D. M.* pp. 332, 391, 427.

4. Other Italian versions of this story are: Nerucci, Nos. 33, 59; Comparetti, No. 27 (Monferrato), mentioned already in Note 2; and Schneller, No. 13. Pitrè, No. 27, has some points of contact also with our story.

5. Nerucci, No. I, and *Nov. fior.* p. 319. For the story of "Beauty and the Beast" in general, see Ralston's article with this title in the *Nineteenth Century,* No. 22, December, 1878; and notes to Schiefner's *Tibetan Tales,* London, 1882, p. xxxvii.

6. The following versions all contain the episodes of the father asking his daughters what gifts he shall bring them, and daughter's tardy return to the monster: Busk, p. 115; Gradi, *Saggio,* p. 189; Comparetti, No. 64 (Montale); and *Zoöl. Myth.* II. p. 382 (Leghorn), with which compare *Indian Fairy Tales,* p. 292. In *Fiabe Mant.* No. 24, we have father's gifts and sympathetic ring; but the danger to monster does not depend on the tardiness of his bride. In *Zoöl. Myth.* II. p. 381 (Piedmont), we have father's gift; but danger to monster results from wife's revealing his name to her sisters. Schneller, No. 25, contains the usual introduction (father's gifts), but the monster, a snake, accompanies his bride on her visit home, and while they are dancing together she steps on his tail and crushes it, whereupon the snake becomes a handsome young man. A Sicilian story, "Zafarana" (Gonz., No. 9), contains both episodes above mentioned, but otherwise differs from the class of stories we are now examining.

Closely allied with the formula of "Beauty and the Beast" is that of "Animal Children." In the latter class the introduction (father's gift) is wanting, and also the episode of visit of wife and tardy return. The "animal child" is usually born in accordance with a rash wish of childless mother that she might have a son, even if he were like one of the animals which she happens to see (Hahn, Formula No. 7). When the "animal child" is grown up his parents attempt to obtain a wife for him; two of three sisters show their disgust and are killed; the third is more prudent, and ultimately disenchants her husband, usually by burning his skin, which he puts on and off at pleasure. The typical story of this class is Pitrè, No. 56, "The Serpent." To Pitrè's copious reference may be added: Comparetti, No. 9 (Monferrato), in which the prince resumes his shape after his third marriage without any further means of disenchantment; No 66 (Monferrato), the prince takes off seven skins, and from a dragon becomes a handsome youth. In both these stories the prince is enchanted and not born in accordance with mother's wish. Gianandrea, p. 15, is a version of Comp., No. 9. Corazzini, p. 429 (Benevento), belongs more properly to "Beauty and the Beast;" the husband disappears on wife's revealing to his mother the secret of his being a handsome youth by night. A somewhat similar version is in Prato, No. 4, "*Il Re Serpente.*" See also Finamore, *Nov. pop. abruzzesi,* Nos. 6, 21, and *Archivio,* I. 424 (Piedmont), 531 (Tuscany); II. 403 (Marches); III. 362 (Abruzzi).

For other references to this class see Köhler's notes to Widter-Wolf, *Jahrb.* VII. p. 249; Benfey, *Pant.* I. p. 265 *et seq.;* and notes to Grimm, Nos. 108 ("Hans the Hedgehog") and 144 ("The Little Ass").

7. Other Italian versions may be found in Pitrè, No. 38; Gonz., No. 27; *Pent.* II. 2; Busk, pp. 46, 57, and 63; *Fiabe Mant.* Nos. 3 and 17; *Nov. tosc.* 4; and Schneller, No. 21. *Pent.* II. 5, contains many points of resemblance, although it belongs to the class of "Animal Children."

Two very close non-Italian versions are Asbj., No. 84, "The Green Knight" [*Tales from the Fjeld,* p.311, "The Green Knight"], and Hahn, No. 7, "The Golden Wand."

An important episode in the above stories is "sick prince and secret remedy." This is found in stories belonging to other classes, as for example in Schneller, 9, 10, 11; in 10 the princess is ill, in 11 there is simply the "overheard council of witches;" *Nov. fior.* pp. 599, 601 (princess ill), and Comp., No. 8 (sick prince).

The above trait is found in the class of stories which may be named "True and Untrue," and of which Grimm, No. 107, "The Two Travellers," is a good example. Italian versions may be found in Widter-Wolf, No. 1 (*Jahrb.* VII. p. 3); Nerucci, No. 23; Ive, *Nozze Ive-Lorenzetto,* p. 31, "*La Curona del Gran Giegno.*" Non-Italian versions will be found in Köhler's notes to Widter-Wolf, and Ive's notes to above cited story.

8. This class is named by Hahn from Geneviève de Brabant, whose legend may be found in *Dict. des Légendes,* p. 396, and, with copious references, in D'Ancona's *Sacre Rappresentazioni,* III. p. 235.

9. The title of the original is "*Li figghi di lu Cavuliciddaru,*" "The Herb-gatherer's Daughters."

10. Another Sicilian version is "*Re Sonnu,*" in Pitrè, *Nuovo Saggio,* No. 1. To the references in Pitrè, No, 36, and Gonz., No. 5, may be added; *Fiabe Mant.* No. 14, only as far as abstraction of children are concerned and accusation of murder against the mother; No. 46, a poor version, the beginning of which is lost; Comparetti, Nos. 6 (Basilicata), and 30 (Pisa); No. 17 (Pisa) is a defective version, the search for the marvellous objects being omitted; another distorted version from Monferrato is found in the same collection, No. 25. See also Prato, *Quattro nov. pop. livornesi,* No. 2, and Finamore, No. 39. Two of the traits of our story are found in many others; they are: "Sympathetic objects," ring, etc., and "Life-giving ointment or leaves." For the former, see notes to next two stories, and in general, Brueyre, p. 93; for the latter, see Gonz., No. 40, Comparetti, No. 33 (see Note 12); Bernoni, *Punt.* III. p. 84. In these stories the life-restoring substance is an ointment; leaves possessing the same power are found in Pitrè, No. 11, *Pent.* I. 7, *La Posillechejata,* No. 1, and Coronedi-Berti, No. 14. See also Grimm, No. 16, "The Three Snake-Leaves;" *Basque Legends,* p. 117; Benfey, *Pant.* I. 454, Cox, *Aryan Myth.* I. 160; and

Germania, XXI. p. 68. For non-Italian versions of the story in the text see Köhler's notes in *Mélusine,* p. 213, to a Breton version, and *Indian Fairy Tales,* pp. 242, 277.

In the above formula are embraced several somewhat different stories in which the persecution of innocent wife proceeds from various persons. For instance, in the Italian legends Sta. Guglielma is persecuted by her brother-in-law; Sta. Ulila by her father and mother-in-law; and Stella by her stepmother. See D'Ancona, *op. cit.,* pp. 199, 235, 317. A popular version, somewhat distorted, of the second of the above-mentioned legends may be found in Nerucci, No. 39; of the third in Gonz., No. 24.

More commonly, however, the persecution is on the part of envious sisters or wicked stepmother. The important role played by the last in tales of the North of Europe has its counterpart in those of the South. The following story from Siena (Pitrè, *La Scatola di Cristallo*) will sufficiently illustrate this class.

XXI. THE CRYSTAL CASKET

There was once a widower who had a daughter. This daughter was between ten and twelve years old. Her father sent her to school, and as she was all alone in the world commended her always to her teacher. Now, the teacher, seeing that the child had no mother, fell in love with the father, and kept saying to the girl: "Ask your father if he would like me for a wife." This she said to her every day, and at last the girl said: "Papa, the school-mistress is always asking me if you will marry her." The father said: "Eh! my daughter, if I take another wife, you will have great troubles." But the girl persisted, and finally the father was persuaded to go one evening to the school-mistress' house. When she saw him she was well pleased, and they settled the marriage in a few days. Poor child! How bitterly she had to repent having found a stepmother so ungrateful and cruel to her! She sent her every day out on a terrace to water a pot of basil, and it was so dangerous that if she fell she would go into a large river.

One day there came by a large eagle, and said to her: "What are you doing here?" She was weeping because she saw how great the danger was of falling into the stream. The eagle said to her: "Get on my back, and I will carry you away, and you will be happier than with your new mamma." After a long journey they reached a great plain, where they found a beautiful palace all of crystal; the eagle knocked at the door and said: "Open, my ladies, open! for I have brought you a pretty girl." When the people in the palace opened the door, and saw that lovely girl, they were amazed, and kissed and caressed her. Meanwhile the door was closed, and they remained peaceful and contented.

Let us return to the eagle, who thought she was doing a spite to the stepmother. One day the eagle flew away to the terrace where the stepmother was watering the basil. "Where is your daughter?" asked the eagle. "Eh!" she replied, "perhaps she fell from this terrace and went into the river; I have not heard from her in ten days." The eagle answered: "What a fool you are! I carried her away; seeing that you treated her so harshly I carried her away to my fairies, and she is very well." Then the eagle flew away.

The stepmother, filled with rage and jealousy, called a witch from the city, and said to her: "You see my daughter is alive, and is in the house of some fairies of an eagle which often comes upon my terrace; now you must do me the favor to find some way to kill this stepdaughter of mine, for I am afraid that some day or other she will return, and my husband, discovering this matter, will certainly kill me." The witch answered: "Oh, you need not be afraid of that: leave it to me."

What did the witch do? She had made a little basketful of sweetmeats, in which she put a charm; then she wrote a letter, pretending that it was her father, who, having learned where she was, wished to make her this present, and the letter pretended that her father was so glad to hear that she was with the fairies.

Let us leave the witch who is arranging all this deception, and return to Ermellina (for so the young girl was named). The fairies had said to her: "See, Ermellina, we are going away, and shall be absent four days, now in this time take good care not to open the door to any one, for some treachery is being prepared for you by your stepmother." She promised to open the door to no one: "Do not be anxious, I am well off, and my stepmother has nothing to do with me." But it was not so. The fairies went away, and the next day when Ermellina was alone, she heard a knocking at the door, and said to herself: "Knock away! I don't open to any one." But meanwhile the blows redoubled and curiosity forced her to look out of the window. What did she see? She saw one of the servant girls of her own home (for the witch had disguised herself as one of her father's servants). "O my dear Ermellina," she said, "your father is shedding tears of sorrow for you, because he really believed you were dead, but the eagle which carried you off came and told him the good news that you were here with the fairies. Meanwhile your father, not knowing what civility to show you, for he understands very well that you are in need of nothing, has thought to send you this little basket of sweetmeats." Ermellina had not yet opened the door; the servant begged her to come down and take the basket and the letter, but she said: "No, I wish nothing!" but finally, since women, and especially young girls, are fond of sweetmeats, she descended and opened the door. When the witch had given her the basket, she said: "Eat this," and broke off for her a piece of the sweetmeats which she had poisoned. When Ermellina took the first mouthful the old woman disappeared. Ermellina had scarcely time to close the door, when she fell down on the stairs.

When the fairies returned they knocked at the door, but no one opened it for them; then they perceived that there had been some treachery, and began to weep. Then the chief of the fairies said: "We must break open the door," and so they did, and saw Ermellina dead on the stairs. Her other friends who loved her so dearly begged the chief of the fairies to bring her to life, but she would not, "for," said she, "she has disobeyed me;" but one and the other asked her until she consented; she opened Ermellina's mouth, took out a piece of the sweetmeat which she had not yet swallowed, raised her up, and Ermellina came to life again.

We can imagine what a pleasure it was for her friends; but the chief of the fairies reproved her for her disobedience, and she promised not to do so again.

Once more the fairies were obliged to depart. Their chief said: "Remember, Ermellina; the first time I cured you, but the second I will have nothing to do with you." Ermellina said they need not worry, that she would not open to any one. But it was not so; for the eagle, thinking to increase her stepmother's anger, told her again that Ermellina was alive. The stepmother denied it all to the eagle, but she summoned anew the witch, and told her that her stepdaughter was still alive, saying: "Either you will really kill her, or I will be avenged on you." The old woman, finding herself caught, told her to buy a very handsome dress, one of the handsomest she could find, and transformed herself into a tailoress belonging to the family, took the dress, departed, went to poor Ermellina, knocked at the door and said: "Open, open, for I am your tailoress." Ermellina looked out of the window and saw her tailoress, and was, in truth, a little confused (indeed, any one would have been so). The tailoress said, "Come down, I must fit a dress on you." She replied, "No, no, for I have been deceived once." "But I am not the old woman," replied the tailoress, "you know me, for I have always made your dresses." Poor Ermellina was persuaded, and descended the stairs; the tailoress took to flight while Ermellina was yet buttoning up the dress, and disappeared. Ermellina closed the door, and was mounting the stairs; but it was not permitted her to go up, for she fell down dead.

Let us return to the fairies, who came home and knocked at the door; but what good did it do to knock! There was no longer any one there. They began to weep. The chief of the fairies said: "I told you that she would betray me again; but now I will have nothing more to do with her." So they broke open the door, and saw the poor girl with that beautiful dress on; but she was dead. They all wept, because they really loved her. But there was nothing to do; the chief struck her enchanted wand, and commanded a beautiful rich casket all covered with diamonds and other precious stones to appear; then the others made a beautiful garland of flowers and gold, put it on the young girl, and then laid her in the casket, which was so rich and beautiful that it was marvellous to behold. Then the old fairy struck her wand as usual and commanded a handsome horse, the like of which not even the king possessed. Then they took the casket, put it on the horse's back, and led him into the public square of the city, and the chief of the fairies said: "Go, and do not stop until you find some one who says to you: 'Stop, for pity's sake, for I have lost my horse for you.'"

Now let us leave the afflicted fairies, and turn our attention to the horse, which ran away at full speed. Who happened to pass at that moment? The son of a king (the name of this king is not known); and saw this horse with that wonder on its back. Then the king began to spur his horse, and rode him so hard that he killed him, and had to leave him dead in the road; but the king kept running after the other horse. The poor king could endure it no longer; he saw himself lost, and exclaimed: "Stop, for pity's sake, for I have lost my horse for you!" Then the horse stopped (for those were the words). When the king saw that beautiful girl dead in the casket, he thought no more about his own horse, but took the other to the city. The king's mother knew that her son had gone hunting; when she saw him returning with this loaded horse, she did not know what to think. The son had no father, wherefore he was all powerful. He reached the palace, had the horse unloaded, and the casket carried to his chamber; then he called his mother and said: "Mother, I went hunting, but I have found a wife." "But what is it? A doll? A dead woman?" "Mother," replied her son, "don't trouble yourself about what it is, it is my wife." His mother began to laugh, and withdrew to her own room (what could she do, poor mother?).

Now this poor king no longer went hunting, took no diversion, did not even go to the table, but ate in his own room. By a fatality it happened that war was declared against him, and he was obliged to depart. He called his mother, and said: "Mother, I wish two careful chambermaids, whose business it shall be to guard this casket; for if on my return I find that anything has happened to my casket, I shall have the chambermaids killed." His mother, who loved him, said: "Go, my son, fear nothing, for I myself will watch over your casket." He wept several days at being obliged to abandon this treasure of his, but there was no help for it, he had to go.

After his departure he did nothing but commend his wife (so he called her) to his mother in his letters. Let us return to the mother, who no longer thought about the matter, not even to have the casket dusted, but all at once there came a letter which informed her that the king had been victorious, and should return to his palace in a few days. The mother. called the chambermaids, and said to them: "Girls, we are ruined." They replied: "Why, Highness?" "Because my son will be back in a few days, and how have we taken care of the doll?" They said: "True, true; now let us go and wash the doll's face." They went to the king's room and saw that the doll's face and hands were covered with dust and fly-specks, so they took a sponge and washed her face, but some drops of water fell on her dress and spotted it. The poor chambermaids began to weep, and went to the queen for advice. The queen said: "Do you know what to do! Call a tailoress, and have a dress precisely like this bought, and take off this one before my son comes." They did so, and the chambermaids went to the room and began to unbutton the dress. The moment that they took off the first sleeve, Ermellina opened her eyes. The poor chambermaids sprang up in terror, but one of the most courageous said: "I am a woman, and so is this one; she will not eat me." To cut the matter short, she took off the dress, and when it was removed Emellina began to get out of the casket to walk about and see where she was. The chambermaids fell on their knees before her and begged her to tell them who she was. She, poor girl, told them the whole story. Then she said: "I wish to know where I am?" Then the chambermaids called the king's mother to explain it to her. The mother did not fail to tell her everything, and she, poor girl, did nothing but weep penitently, thinking of what the fairies had done for her.

The king was on the point of arriving, and his mother said to the doll: "Come here; put on one of my best dresses." In short, she arrayed her like a queen. Then came her son. They shut the doll up in a small room, so that she could not be seen. The king came with great joy, with trumpets blowing, and banners flying for the victory. But he took no interest in all this, and ran at once to his room to see the doll; the chambermaids fell on their knees before him saying that the doll smelled so badly that they could not stay in the palace, and were obliged to bury her. The king would not listen to this excuse, but at once called two of the palace servants to erect the gallows. His mother comforted him in vain: "My son, it was a dead woman." "No, no, I will not listen to any reasons; dead or alive, you should have left it for me." Finally, when his mother saw that he was in earnest about the gallows, she rang a little bell, and there came forth no longer the doll, but a very beautiful girl, whose like was never seen. The king was amazed, and said: "What is this!" Then his mother, the chambermaids, and Ermellina, were obliged to tell him all that had happened. He said: "Mother, since I adored her when dead, and called her my wife, now I mean her to be my wife in truth." "Yes, my son," replied his mother, "do so, for I am willing." They arranged the wedding, and in a few days were man and wife.

Sicilian versions of this story may be found in Pitrè, Nos. 57, s8; Gonz., Nos. 2–4. To the copious references in the notes to the stories just mentioned may be added: *Fiabe Mant.* No. 28; *Tuscan Fairy Tales,* No. IX.; *Nov. fior.* pp. 232, 239; De Nino, XLI., XLIX., L.; *Nov. tosc.* 9. Other European versions are: Grimm, No. 53, "Little Snow-White;" Hahn, No. 103; *Lo Rondallayre,* No. 46: see also Köhler's notes to Gonz., Nos. 2–4.

The last class of "stepmother" stories which we shall mention is Hahn's Formula 15, "Phryxos and Helle," in which both brother and sister are persecuted by stepmother. A good example of this class is Pitrè, No. 283.

XXII. The Stepmother

T*here was once* a husband and a wife who had two children, a son and a daughter. The wife died, and the husband married a woman who had a daughter blind of one eye. The husband was a farmer, and went to work in a field. The stepmother hated her husband's children, and to get rid of them she baked some bread, and sent it by them to her husband, but directed them to the wrong field, so that they might get lost. When the children reached a mountain they began to call their father, but no one answered. Now the girl was enchanted; and when they came to a spring and the brother wanted to drink, she said to him: "Do not drink of this fountain, or you will become an ass." Afterwards they found another spring, and the brother wanted to drink; but his sister said to him: "Do not drink of it, or you will become a calf." However, the boy would drink, and became a calf with golden horns. They continued their journey, and came to the seashore, where there was a handsome villa belonging to the prince. When the prince saw the young girl, and beheld how beautiful she was, he married her, and afterwards asked her what there was about the little calf, and she replied; "I am fond of him because I have brought him up."

Let us now return to her father, who, from the great grief he had on account of his children's disappearance, had gone out to divert himself, and wandered away, gathering fennel. He arrived at last at the villa, where was his daughter who had married the king. His daughter looked out of the window and said to him: "Come up, friend." His daughter had recognized him, and asked: "Friend, do you not know me?" "No, I do not recognize you." Then she said: "I am your daughter, whom you believed lost." She threw herself at his feet, and said: "Pardon me, dear father; I came by chance to this villa, and the king's son was here and married me." The father was greatly consoled at finding his daughter so well married. "Now, my father," said she, "empty this sack of fennel, for I will fill it with gold for you." And then she begged him to bring his wife, and the daughter blind of one eye. The father returned home with his bag full of money, and his wife asked in terror: "Who gave you this money?" He answered: "O wife! Do you know that I have found my daughter, and she is the king's wife, and filled this bag with money?" She, instead of being happy, was angry at hearing that her stepdaughter was still alive, however, she said to her husband: "I will go and take my daughter." So they went, the husband, the wife, and the blind daughter, and came to the husband's daughter, who received her stepmother very kindly. But the latter, seeing that the king was away, and that her stepdaughter was alone, seized her and threw her from a window into the sea; and what did she do then? She took her blind daughter and dressed her in the other's clothes, and said to her: "When the king comes and finds you here weeping, say to him: 'The little calf has blinded me with his horn, and I have only one eye!'" Then the stepmother returned to her own house. The king came and found her daughter in bed weeping, and said to her: "Why you weeping?" "The little calf struck me with his horn and put out one of my eyes." The king cried at once: "Go call the butcher to kill the calf!" When the calf heard that he was to be killed, he went out on the balcony and called to his sister in the sea:—

> "Oh! sister,
> For me the water is heated,
> And the knives are sharpened."

The sister replied from the sea:—

> "Oh! brother, I cannot help you,
> I am in the dog-fish's mouth."

When the king heard the calf utter these words, he looked out of the window, and when he saw his wife in the sea, he summoned two sailors, and had them take her out and bring her up and restore her. Then he took the blind girl and killed her and cut her in pieces and salted her like tunny-fish, and sent her to her mother. When her husband found it out he left her and went to live with his daughter.

It may not be amiss to mention here another class of stories which come under the formula of "Persecuted Maiden." The class resembles in some respects the history of King Lear. The youngest daughter is persecuted by her father because he thinks she does not love him as much as her older sisters. A good example of this class is Pitrè, No. 10, *L'Acqua e lu Sali.*

XXIII. WATER AND SALT

A very fine story is related and told to your worships. Once upon a time there was a king with three daughters. These three daughters being at table one day, their father said: "Come now, let us see which of you three loves me." The oldest said: "Papa, I love you as much as my eyes." The second answered: "I love you as much as my heart." The youngest said: "I love you as much as water and salt." The king heard her with amazement: "Do you value me like water and salt? Quick! Call the executioners, for I will have her killed immediately." The other sisters privately gave the executioners a little dog, and told them to kill it and rend one of the youngest sister's garments, but to leave her in a cave. This they did, and brought back to the king the dog's tongue and the rent garment: "Royal Majesty, here is her tongue and garment." And his Majesty gave them a reward. The unfortunate princess was found in the forest by a magician, who took her to his house opposite the royal palace. Here the king's son saw her and fell desperately in love with her, and the match was soon agreed upon. Then the magician came and said: "You must kill me the day before the wedding. You must invite three kings, your father the first. You must order the servants to pass water and salt to all the guests except your father." Now let us return to the father of this young girl, who the longer he lived the more his love for her increased, and he was sick of grief. When he received the invitation he said: "And how can I go with this love for my daughter?" And he would not go. Then he thought: "But this king will be offended if I do not go, and will declare war against me some time." He accepted and went. The day before the wedding they killed the magician and quartered him, and put a quarter in each of four looms, and sprinkled his blood in all the rooms and on the stairway, and the blood and flesh became gold and precious stones. When the three kings came and saw the golden stairs, they did not like to step on them. "Never mind," said the prince, "go up; this is nothing." That evening they were married: the next day they had a banquet. The prince gave orders: "No salt and water to that king." They sat down at table, and the young queen was near her father, but he did not eat. His daughter said: "Royal Majesty, why do you not eat? Does not the food please you?" "What an idea! It is very fine." "Why don't you eat then?" "I don't feel very well." The bride and groom helped him to some bits of meat, but the king did not want it, and chewed his food over and over again like a goat (as if he could eat it without salt!). When they finished eating they began to tell stories, and the king told them all about his daughter. She asked him if he could still recognize her, and stepping out of the room put on the same dress she wore when he sent her away to be killed. "You caused me to be killed because I told you I loved you as much as salt and water: now you have seen what it is to eat without salt and water." Her father could not say a word, but embraced her and begged her pardon. They remained happy and contented, and here we are with nothing.

A Venetian version (Bernoni, No. 14) is translated in the *Cornhill Magazine*, July, 1875, p. 80, a Bolognese version may be found in Coronedi-Berti, No. 5, and from the Abruzzi in Finamore, Nos. 18, 26. Compare also *Pomiglianesi*, p. 42. For transmutation of magician's body see *Zoöl. Myth.* I. p. 123, Benfey, *Pant.* I. pp. 477, 478, Ralston, *R. F. T.* p. 223, and *Indian Fairy Tales*, p. 164.

Other Sicilian versions are in Gonz., Nos. 48, 49. A Neapolitan is in *Pent.* V. 8; a Mantuan, in *Fiabe Mant.* No. 16; a Tuscan, in *Archivio per le Trad. pop.* I. p. 44, and one from the Abruzzi in *Archivio*, III. 546. The same story is in Grimm, Nos. 11 and 141. "The Little Brother and Sister" and "The Little Lamb and the Little Fish." See also Hahn, No. 1. The latter part of the story is connected with "False Bride." See note 21 of this chapter.

11. Other Italian versions are: Pitrè, No. 20; *Pent.* II. 1; *Pomiglianesi*, pp. 121, 130, 136, 188, 191; Busk, p. 3; *Nov. fior.* p. 209; Gargiolli, No. 2; *Fiabe Mant.* No. 20; Bernoni, No. 12; *Archivio*, I. 525 (Tuscan), III. 368 (Abruzzi), and De Nine, XX. Some points of resemblance are found also in *Pent.* V. 4; Coronedi-Berti, No. 8; and Finamore, *Trad. pop. abruzzesi*, No. 12.

Other stories in which children are promised to ogre, demon, etc., are to be found in Pitrè, No. 31, Widter-Wolf, No. XIII., and in the various versions of the story of "Liombruno." See Chap. II., note 13.

For other European versions of the story in the text, see Ralston's *R. F. T.* p. 141; Grimm, No. 12, "Rapunzel," and *Basque Legends*, p. 59. For child promised to demon, see *Romania*, No. 28, p. 531; Grimm, Nos. 31 ("The Girl Without Hands") 55, ("Rumpelstiltskin") 92, ("The King of the Golden Mountain"), and 181 ("The Nix of the Mill-Pond"). See also Hahn, I. p. 47, No. 8.

Some of the incidents of this story are found in those belonging to other classes. The girl's face changed to that of dog, etc., is in Comparetti, No. 3 (furnished with a long beard), and Finamore, *Trad. pop. abruzzesi*, No. 1, *Pent.* I. 8 (goat), Nerucci, Nos. 30 (sheep's neck), 37 (buffalo), and *Nov. pop. toscani*, in *Archivio per la Trad. pop.* No. 1 (goat). For "flight and obstacles," see *Nov. fior.* pp. 12, 415, *Pent.* II. 1, and stories cited by Pitrè in his notes to No. 13, also note 25 to this chapter, *Basque Legends*, p. 120, *Orient und Occident*, II. p. 103, and Brueyre, p. 111. For "ladder of hair," see *Pomiglianesi*, p. 126.

12. Other Italian versions are: *Pent.* I. 9; Gonz., Nos. 39, 40; Comparetti, No. 46 (Basilicata); De Gub., *Sto. Stefano*, Nos. 17, 18; Finamore, *Trad. pop. abruzzesi*, No. 22; De Nino, LXV.; *Nov. fior.* pp. 375, 387 (Milan); Coronedi-Berti, No. 16; *Fiabe Mant.* No. 19; and Schneller, No. 28. This story, as far as the two brothers (not born miraculously) and liberation of princess are concerned, is in *Pent.* I. 7, and Widter-Wolf, No. 8.

References to other European versions may be found in the *Romania*, Nos. 19, pp. 336, 339; 28, p. 563; 32, p. 606: *Orient und Occident*, II. p. 115 (Köhler to Campbell, No. 4), and Bladé, *Agenais*, No. 2 (p. 148).

As regards the separate traits, as usual many of them are found in other classes of stories: the cloud occurs in Comp., No. 40; children born from fish, De Gub., *Zoöl. Myth.* II. 29; for sympathetic objects and life-giving ointment, see last two stories. For "kindness to animals," and "thankful beasts," see *Fiabe Mant.* Nos. 37, 26, Gonz., No. 6, and the stories belonging to the class "Giant with no heart in his body" mentioned below. The gratitude and help of an animal form the subject of some independent stories, *e.g.*, Strap. III. 1; *Pent.* I. 3; and Gonz., No. 6, above mentioned; and are also found in the formula "Animal Brothers-in-law." See note 23. For European versions see *Orient und Occident*, II. p. 101; Brueyre, p. 98; Ralston, *R. F. T.* p. 98; Benfey, *Pant,* I. p. 193 *et seq.*; *Basque Legends*, p. 81, and *Zoöl. Myth.* I. p. 197; II. 45. For transformation into statues, see stories mentioned in note 10, Bernoni, *Punt.* III. p. 89, *Nov. fior.* p. 112, and Ortoli, pp. 10, 34.

The most interesting episode, however, is that of "Magician (or Giant) with no heart in his body" (see Chap. III., note 8), which is in the following Italian tales: Pitrè, No. 81, Busk, p. 158; *Nov. fior.* pp. 7, 347; Gonz., Nos. 6, 16; *Fiabe Mant.* No. 37; and *Pomiglianesi*, No. 2, p. 21 (v. p. 41). For other references, see *Basque Legends*, p. 83; Brueyre, pp. 81–83; Ralston, *R. F. T.*, Am. ed., pp. 119–125; *Orient und Occident*, II. p. 101; Hahn, I. p. 56, No. 31; and *Romania*, No. 22, p. 234. See also note 18 of this chapter.

The story in our text is not a good example of Hahn's Form. 13, "Andromeda, or Princess freed from Dragon." Some of the other stories cited are much better, notably Widter-Wolf, No. 8, Gonz., Nos. 39, 40, and also Strap., X. 3, and Schneller, No. 39. Hahn's Danaë Form. 12 is represented by *Nov. tosc.* No. 30. The allied myth of Medusa by *Nov. tosc.* No. 1, and *Archivio*, I. p. 57.

13. Versions of this wide-spread story are in Pitrè, *Otto Fiabe*, No. 1, Gonz., Nos. 58, 59, 61, 62, 63 (partly), and 64; Köhler, *Italien Volksm.* (Sora) No. 1, "*Die drei Brüder und die drei befreiten Königstöchter*" (*Jahrb.* VIII. p. 241); Widter-Wolf, No. 4 (*Jahrb.* VII. p. 20); Schneller, No. 39; *Nov. fior.* p. 70, and De Gub., *Zoöl. Myth.* II, 187 (Tuscan). Part of our story is also found in Schneller, pp. 188–192, and Pitrè, Nos. 83, 84 (var.). To these references, which are given by Pitrè, may be added the following:

Comparetti, Nos. 19 (Monferrato) partly, 35 (Monferrato), and 40 (Pisa); De Gub. *Sto. Stefano,* No. 19; *Fiabe Mant.* Nos. 18, 32 (the latter part), 49 (partly); *Tuscan Fairy Tales,* No. 3; Finamore, *Trad. pop. abruzzesi,* No. 29; and *Nov. tosc.* No. 3.

The trait "underground world" is also found in Busk, p. 141. These stories illustrate sufficiently Hahn's Form. 40, "Descent into the Nether World."

14. To the stories in Note 13 containing "liberation of hero by eagle" may be added Comparetti, No. 24 (Monferrato). See in general: De Gub., *Zoöl. Myth.* II. 186; Benfey, *Pant,* I. pp. 216, 388; *Rivista Orientale,* I. p. 27; *Orient und Occident,* II. p. 299; and *Basque Legends,* p. 110.

15. Another version from Avellino is in the same collection, p. 201. Other Italian versions are: Pitrè, No. 79; Gonz., No. 51; De Gub., *Sto. Stefano,* No. 20; De Nino, No. 2; Comparetti, No. 28 (Monferrato); Ive, *Fiabe pop. rovignesi,* p. 20; No. 3, "*El Pumo de uoro;*" Schneller, No. 51; and Corazzini, p. 455 (Benevento).

In general see Ive's and Köhler's notes to stories above cited, and *Romania,* No. 24, p. 565. The corresponding Grimm story is No. 28, "The Singing Bone."

16. Other Italian versions are: Pitrè, Nos. 41, 42; *Pent.* I. 6; Busk, pp. 26, 31; Comp., No. 23 (Pisa); *Fiabe Mant.* No. 45; *Nov. fior.* p. 162 (Milan); Finamore, *Trad. pop. abruzzesi,* No. II.; and *Archivio,* II. 185 (Sardinia).

Schneller, No. 24, and Bernoni, No. 8, are connecting links between "Cinderella" and "Allerleirauh." In the former, Cinderella's father asks his three daughters what present he shall make them. Cinderella asks for a sword, and shortly after leaves her home and obtains a situation in a city as servant. In the palace opposite lives a young count, with whom Cinderella falls in love. She obtains a situation in his house. Her sword, which is enchanted, gives her beautiful dresses, and she goes to the balls as in the other versions. The third evening the count slips a costly ring on her finger, which Cinderella uses to identify herself with. Bernoni, No. 8, is substantially the same. After the death of their mother and father Cinderella's sisters treat her cruelly, and she obtains a place as servant in the king's palace, and is aided by the fairies, who take pity upon her. She is identified by means of a ring, and also by her diamond slipper, which she throws to the servants, who are following her to see where she lives.

European versions will be found in the notes to Grimm, No. 21 ("Cinderella"), and W. R. S. Ralston's article, "Cinderella," in the *Nineteenth Century,* November, 1879.

17. Other Italian versions are; Pitrè, No. 43; Gonz., 38; *Pent.* II. 6; Busk, pp. 66, 84, 90, 91; Comparetti, No. 57 (Montale); De Gub., *Sto. Stefano,* No. 3 (see also *Rivista di Lett. Pop.* I. p. 86); Gradi, *Saggio,* p. 141; *Fiabe Mant.* No. 38; *Nov. fior.* p. 158 (Milan), Finamore, *Trad. pop. abruzzesi,* No. 3; De Nino, No. 17, and *Archivio,* I. 190 (Tuscany), II. 26 (Sardinia). Straparola, I. 4, contains the first part of our story, which is also partly found in Coronedi-Berti, No. 3, and Finamore, *Trad. pop. abruzzesi,* No. 13.

The gifts, which in the story in the text are given the day of the wedding, in the other versions are bestowed before marriage by father, in order to overcome daughter's opposition. The recognition by means of ring is found in the last two stories mentioned in Note 16, in *Fiabe Mant.* No. 38, above cited, and *Nov. fior.* p. 158 (Milan). See also Grimm, Nos. 93 ("The Raven"), 101 ("Bearskin"); Hahn, No. 25; Asbj., No. 71 (*Tales from the Fjeld,* p. 130); and *Romania,* No. 23, p. 359.

Other European versions of our story will be found mentioned in the notes to Grimm, No. 65 ("Allerleirauh"), to Gonz., No. 38 (II. 229); *Orient und Occident,* II. 295; D'Ancona, *Sacre Rappresent.* III. 238; *Romania,* No. 24, 571; *Basque Legends,* p. 165, and Ralston's *R. F. T.* p. 159.

18. See Gonz., No. 26, and Widter-Wolf, No. 8 (*Jahrb.* VII. p. 128).

For story in general, see notes to stories just cited, and Cox, *Aryan Myth.* vol. I. p. 224; II, p. 261, "The Myth of Nisos and Skylla;" Hahn, I. p. 52; and De Gub., *Zoöl. Myth,* I. p. 211 *et seq.*

19. Pitrè, in his notes to No. 71, gives two variants of his story, and mentions a Piedmontese version yet unpublished. Comparetti, No. 54, an analysis of which is given in the text, represents sufficiently Hahn's Form. No. 37, "Strong Hans."

20. In the version in *Pent.* IV. 8, after the seven sons have disappeared, their sister goes in search of them, finds them, and they all live happily together until by her fault they are changed into doves, and she is obliged to go to the house of the Mother of Time and learn from her the mode of disenchantment. In a story in Pitrè, No. 73, a husband threatens to kill his wife if she does not give birth to a male child.

For other European versions of our story, see Grimm, No. 9, "The Twelve Brothers;" No. 25, "The Seven Ravens;" and No. 49, "The Six Swans;" *Mélusine,* p. 419, and *Basque Legends,* p. 186. Part of the story in text belongs to the Geneviève formula, see notes 8, 10, of this chapter.

21. The first trait, "Two Sisters," is also found as an independent story, see Chap. II., p. 100, and note 2. "Substitution of false bride" is found without "Two Sisters" in Comp., Nos. 53 (Montale) and 68 (Montale); *Fiabe Mant.* No. 16; and Gradi, *Saggio,* p. 141. See note 10 of this chapter. The best example of "substitution" is, as we have said before, Grimm, No. 89, "The Goose-Girl;" see also *Romania,* No. 24, p. 546. The same trait is found also in a very extensive and interesting class of stories which may be termed, from the usual titles of the stories, "The Three Citrons," some of the versions of which belong to "Forgotten Bride." We give here, however, a version belonging to the class above-mentioned, and which we have taken, on account of its rarity, from Ive, *Fiabe pop. rovignesi,* p. 3.

XXIV. THE LOVE OF THE THREE ORANGES

Once upon a time there was a king and queen who had a half-witted son. The queen was deeply grieved at this, and she thought to go to the Lord and ask counsel of him what she was to do with this son. The Lord told her to try and do something to make him laugh. She replied: "I have nothing but a jar of oil, unfortunately for me!" The Lord said to her: "Well, give this oil away in charity, for there will come many people; some bent, some straight, some humpbacked, and it may happen, that your son will laugh." So the queen proclaimed that she had a jar of oil, and that all could come and take some. And everybody, indeed, hurried there and took the oil down to the last drop. Last of all came an old witch, who begged the queen to give her a little, saying: "Give me a little oil, too!" The queen replied: "Ah, it is all gone, there is no more!" The queen was angry and full of spite because her son had not yet laughed. The old witch said again to the queen: "Let me look in the jar!" The queen opened the jar, and the old woman got inside of it and was all covered with the dregs of the oil; and the queen's son laughed, and laughed, and laughed. The old woman came out, saw the prince laughing, and said to him: "May you never be happy until you go and find the Love of the three Oranges." The son, all eager, said to his mother: "Ah, mother, I shall have no more peace until I go and find the Love of the three Oranges." She answered: "My dear son, how will you go and find the Love of the three Oranges?" But he would go; so he mounted his horse and rode and rode and rode until he came to a large gate. He knocked, and some one within asked: "Who is there?" He replied: "A soul created by God." The one within said: "In all the years that I have been here no one has ever knocked at this gate." The prince repeated: "Open, for I am a soul created by God!" Then an old man came down and opened the gate. He had eyelids that reached to his feet, and he said: "My son, take down those little forks, and lift up my eyelids." The prince did so, and the old man asked: "Where are you going, my son, in this direction?" "I am going to find the Love of the three Oranges." The old man answered: "So many have gone there and never returned! Do you wish not to return, too? My son, take these twigs, you will meet some witches who are sweeping out their oven with their hands; give them these twigs, and they will let you pass." The prince very gratefully took the twigs; mounted his horse and rode away. He journeyed a long time, and at last saw in the distance the witches of immense size who were coming towards him. He threw them the twigs, and they allowed him to pass.

He continued his journey, and arrived at a gate larger than the first. Here the same thing occurred as at the first one, and the old man said: "Well! Since you will go, too, take these ropes, on your way you will encounter some witches drawing water with their tresses; throw them these ropes, and they will let you pass."

Everything happened as the old man said: the prince passed the witches, continued his journey and came to a third gate larger than the second. Here an old man with eyelids longer than the other two gave him a bag of bread, and one of tallow, saying: "Take this bag of bread; you will meet some large dogs; throw them the bread and they will let you pass; then you will come to a large gate with many rusty padlocks; then you will see a tower, and in it the Love of the three Oranges. When you reach that place, take this tallow and anoint well the rusty padlocks; and when you have ascended the tower, you will find the oranges hanging from a nail. There you will also find an old woman who has a son who is an ogre and has eaten all the Christians who have come there; you see, you must be very careful!"

The prince, well contented, took the bag of bread and the tallow and rode away. After a long journey, he saw at a distance, three great dogs with their mouths wide open coming to eat him. He threw them the bread, and they let him pass.

He journeyed on until he came to another large gate with many rusty padlocks. He dismounted, tied his horse to the gate, and began to anoint the locks with the tallow, until, after much creaking, they opened. The prince entered, saw the tower, went up and met an old woman who said to him: "Dear son, where are you going? What have you come here for? I have a son who is an ogre, and will surely eat you up." While she was uttering these words, the son arrived. The old woman made the prince hide under the bed; but the ogre perceived that there was some one in the house, and when he had entered, he began to cry:—

"*Gein gein*, I smell a Christian,
Gein gein, I smell a Christian!"

"Son," his mother said, "there is no one here." But he repeated his cry. Then his mother, to quiet him, threw him a piece of meat, which he ate like a madman; and while he was busy eating, she gave the three oranges to the prince, saying: "Take them, my son, and escape at once, for he will soon finish eating his meat, and then he will want to eat you, too." After she had given him the three oranges, she repented of it, and not knowing what else to do, she cried out: "Stairs, throw him down! lock, crush him!" They answered: "We will not, for he gave us tallow!" "Dogs, devour him!" "We will not, for he gave us bread!" Then he mounted his horse and rode away, and the old woman cried after him; "Witch, strangle him!" "I will not, for he gave me ropes!" "Witch, kill him!" "I will not, for he gave me twigs!" The prince continued his journey, and on the way became very thirsty, and did not know what to do. Finally he thought of opening one of the oranges. He did so, and out came a beautiful girl, who said to him:

"Love, give me to drink!"

He replied:

"Love, I have none!"

And she said:

"Love, I shall die!"

And she died at once. The prince threw away the orange, and continued his journey, and soon became thirsty again. In despair he opened another orange, and out sprang another girl more beautiful than the first. She, too, asked for water, and died when the prince told her he had none to give her. Then he continued his way, saying: "The next time I surely do not want to lose her." When he became thirsty again, he waited until he reached a well; then he opened the last orange and there appeared a girl more beautiful than the first two. When she asked for water, he gave her the water of the well, then took her out of the orange, put her on horseback with himself, and started for home. When he was nearly there, he said to her: "See, I will leave you here for a time under these two trees;" one had leaves of gold and silver fruit, and the other gold fruit and silver leaves. Then he made her a nice couch, and left her resting between the two trees. "Now," said he, "I must go to my mother to tell her that I have found you, then I will come for you and we shall be married!" Then he mounted his horse and rode away to his mother.

Now while he was gone an old witch approached the girl and said: "Ah, dear daughter, let me comb your hair." The young girl replied: "No, the like of me do not wish it." Again she said: "Come, my dear daughter, let me comb you!" Tired of being asked so often by the old woman, the girl at last allowed her to comb her hair, and what did that monster of an old witch take it into her head to do. She stuck a pin through the girl's temples from side to side, and the girl at once was changed into a dove. What did this wretch of an old woman then do? She got into the couch in the place of the young girl, who flew away.

Meanwhile the prince reached his mother's house, and she said to him: "Dear son, where have you been? How have you spent all this time?" "Ah, my mother," said he, "what a lovely girl I have for my wife!" "Dear son, where have you left her?"

"Dear mother, I have left her between two trees, the leaves of one are of gold and the fruit is silver, the leaves of the other are of silver and the fruit gold."

Then the queen gave a grand banquet, invited many guests, and made ready many carriages to go and bring the young girl. They mounted their horses, they entered their carriages, they set out, but when they reached the trees they saw the ugly old woman, all wrinkled, in the couch between the trees, and the white dove on top of them.

The poor prince, you can imagine it! was grieved to the heart, and ashamed at seeing the ugly old woman. His father and mother, to satisfy him, took the old woman, put her in a carriage, and carried her to the palace, where the wedding-feast was prepared. The prince was downhearted, but his mother said to him: "Don't think about it, my son, for she will become beautiful again." But her son could not think of eating or of talking. The dinner was brought on and the guests placed themselves at the round table. Meanwhile, the dove flew up on the kitchen balcony, and began to sing:

> "Let the cook fall asleep,
> Let the roast be burned,
> Let the old witch be unable to eat of it."

The guests waited for the cook to put the roast on the table. They waited, and waited and waited, and at last they got up and went to the kitchen, and there they found the cook asleep. They called and called him, and at last he awoke, but soon became drowsy again. He said he did not know what was the matter with him, but he could not stand up. He put another roast on the spit, however. Then the dove again flew on the balcony and sang:

> "Let the cook fall asleep,
> Let the roast be burned,
> Let the old witch be unable to eat of it."

Again the guests waited until they grew weary, and then the groom went to see what was the matter. He found the cook asleep again, and said: "Cook, good cook, what is the matter with you that you sleep?" Then the cook told him that there was a dove that flew on the balcony and repeated:—

> "Let the cook fall asleep,
> Let the roast be burned,
> Let the old witch be unable to eat of it."

and that he was immediately seized with drowsiness, and fell asleep at once. The bridegroom went out on the balcony, saw the dove, and said to it: "*Cuócula*, pretty *cuócula*, come here and let me see you!" The dove came near him and he caught it, and while he was caressing it he saw the pins planted in its head, one in its forehead, and one in each of its temples. What did he do? He pulled out the pin in the forehead! Then he caressed it again, and pulled out the pins from its temples. Then the dove became a beautiful girl, more beautiful than she was before, and the prince took her to his mother and said: "Here, my mother, this is my bride!" His mother was delighted to see the beautiful girl, and the king, too, was well pleased. When the old witch saw the girl, she cried: "Take me away, take me away, I am afraid!" Then the fair girl told the whole secret how it was. The guests who were present wished to give their opinions as to what should be done with the old woman. One of the highest rank said: "Let her be well greased, and burned!" "Bravo, bravo!" exclaimed the others, "burn her; she must be burned!" So they seized the old woman, had wood brought, and burned her in the midst of the city. Then they returned home, and had a finer wedding than before.

The following are the Italian versions of the above: *Pent.* IV. 9; Pitrè, *Otto Fiabe*, II. "*La Bella di li setti Citri;*" Gonz., No. 13; Busk, p. 15; *Nov. fior.* pp. 305, 308 (Milan); Comparetti, No. 68 (also in Nerucci, p. 111); De Gub., *Sto. Stefano*, Nos. 4, 5; Prato, *Quattro nov. pop. livornesi*, No. 1; *Archivio*, I. 525 (Tuscan); II. 204 (Sardinian); Piedmontese in Mila y Fontanals *Observaciones sobre la poesia popular*, Barcelona, 1853, p. 179; Coronedi-Berti, No. 11; Corazzini (Benevento), p. 467; and Schneller, No. 19. Part of our story is the same as Pitrè, No. 13, "Snow-white-fire-red," given in full in our text. See also Finamore, *Trad. pop. abruzzesi*, No. 15.

Copious references to other European versions will be found in the notes of Ive, Köhler, etc., to the above versions; to these may be added, *Lo Rondallayre*, Nos. 18, 37, Liebrecht to Simrock's *Deut. Märchen* in *Orient und Occident*, III. p. 378 (Kalliopi), No. 3, and *Indian Fairy Tales*, pp. 253, 284.

22. See *Pent.* IV. 7; Gonz., Nos. 33, 34; Pitrè, Nos. 59, 60 (61); *Archivio*, II. 36 (Sardinia); De Nino, No. 19; and Schneller, No. 22. The corresponding Grimm story is No. 135, "The White Bride and the Black One." For other European references, see Köhler to Gonz., Nos. 33, 34 (II. p. 225), and *Romania*, No. 24, pp. 546, 561. See also Chapter II., note 1.

23. The best version is in the *Pent.* IV. 3, where the three daughters are married to a falcon, a stag, and a dolphin, who, as in our story, assist their brother-in-law, but are disenchanted without his aid. Other Italian versions are: Pitrè, No. 16, and *Nov. pop. sicil.* Palermo, 1873, No. 1, Gonz., No. 29; Knust (Leghorn), No. 2 (*Jahrb.* VII. 384), Finamore, *Trad. pop. abruzzesi*, No. 23; *Nov. fior.* p. 266; Comparetti, Nos. 4, 58; *Archivio*, II. p. 42 (Tuscan); *Nov. tosc.* No. 11.

For other European versions see, besides references in notes to above stories, Hahn, No. 25; Grimm, vol. II. p. 510, to Musäus' "*Die drei Schwestern*," and No. 197, "The Crystal Ball;" Benfey, *Pant*, I. p. 534, and Ralston, *R. F. T.* p. 96. See also note 12 of this chapter.

As usual, many of the incidents of our stories are found in those belonging to other classes; among the most important are: Prince hidden in musical instrument, Pitrè, No. 95; finding princess' place of concealment, Pitrè, Nos. 95, 96; Gonz., No. 68; and Grimm, No. 133; "The Shoes which were danced to Pieces;" princess recognized among others dressed alike, or all veiled; *Nov. fior.* p. 411 (Milan); Grimm, No. 62, "The Queen Bee," Ralston, *R. F. T.* p. 141, note; *Basque Legends*, p. 125; *Orient und Occident*, II. pp. 104, 107–114; tasks set hero to win wife, Pitrè, Nos. 21, 95, 96; Gonz., No. 68; De Gub., *Sto. Stefano*, No. 8; *Basque Legends*, p. 120; *Orient und Occident*, II. 103; and *Romania*, No. 28, p. 527. This last incident is found also in "Forgotten Bride," see note 25 of this chapter.

24. For other European references to the first class, "Riddle solved by suitor," see *Jahrb.* V. 13; Grimm, No. 114, "The Cunning Little Tailor," and Hahn, I. p. 54.

Other Italian versions of the second class are: Comparetti, Nos. 26 (Basilicata), 59 (Monferrato); Nerucci, p. 177 (partly); and Widter-Wolf, No. 15 (*Jahrb.* VII. 269).

See also Köhler's notes to last-mentioned story, and also to Campbell, No. 22, in *Orient und Occident*, II. 320; Grimm, No. 22, "The Riddle;" and Prof. F. J. Child, *English and Scottish Popular Ballads*, Part II. p. 414.

For other stories containing riddles belonging to other classes than the above, see Bernoni, *Punt.* II. p. 54; Gradi, *Vigilia*, p. 8; Corazzini, p. 432; Finamore, *Trad. pop. abruzzesi*, No. 7; and Köhler's article, *Das Räthselmärchen von dem ermordeten Geliebten* in the *Rivista di Lett. pop.* I, p. 212. A peculiar version of the second class may be found in Ortoli, p. 123, where a riddle very much like the one in the text is proposed by suitor to princess' father.

25. Other Italian versions are: Gonz., Nos. 14, 54, 55; *Pent.* II. 7, III. 9 (forgets bride on touching shore); *Pomiglianesi*, p. 136 (the first part belongs to the class of "Fair Angiola;") Busk, p. 3 (first part same as last story); De Gub., *Sto. Stefano*, No. 5 (see also *Rivista di Lett. pop.* I. p. 84); Coronedi-Berti, No. 13 (this is one of the few "Three Citrons" stories containing episode of bride forgotten at mother's kiss); Schneller, No. 27; Finamore, *Trad. pop. abruzzesi*, No. 4 (mother's kiss); Pitrè, vol. IV. p. 285, gives an Albanian version of our story. The imprecation and mother's kiss are also found in another of the "Three Citrons" stories, Gonz., No. 13. For obstacles to flight, see Note 11 of this chapter.

For other European versions see Köhler's notes to Gonz., No. 14; to Campbell, No. 2 (*Orient und Occident*, II. 103); to Kreutzwald-Löwe, No. 14; Hahn, I. p. 55; *Romania*, Nos. 19, p. 354, 20, p. 527; Grimm, Nos. 56 ("Sweetheart Roland"), 113 ("The Two Kings' Children"), 186 ("The True Bride"), 193 ("The Drummer;") *Basque Legends*, p. 120; Ralston, *R. F. T.* pp. 119, 131; Brueyre, p. iii; and B. Schmidt, *Griechische Märchen, Sagen und Volkslieder*, Leipzig, 1877, cited by Cosquin, *Romania*, No. 28, p. 543. See also in general, Cox, *Aryan Myth.* I. p. 158.

26. The same incident is found in Gonz., No. 6, and Pitrè, No. 61. See Köhler's notes to Gonz., No. 6; Grimm, No. 193 ("The Drummer"); *Romania*, No. 28, p. 527; and Hahn, No. 15.

27. Another Venetian version is in Bernoni, No. 3. See also *Nov. fior.* p 290; Gradi, *Vigilia*, p. 53; *Fiabe Mant.* No. 39; and Schneller, No. 32.

For other European versions, see Grimm, No. 46 ("Fitcher's Bird"), Köhler's notes to Widter-Wolf, No. 11 (*Jahrb.* VII. 148); and Ralston, *R. F. T.* p. 97.

28. See Pitrè, No. 19, *Nuovo Saggio*, No. 4; *Nov. fior.* pp. 7, 12; and Nerucci, No. 49. Compare also Gonz., Nos. 10 and 22 (already mentioned, "The Robber who had a Witch's Head"), and Comparetti, No. 18 (Pisa).

For other references to this class, see Grimm, No. 40 ("The Robber-Bridegroom") and *Romania*, No. 22, p. 236.

29. See Chap. II., note 4. For other references to this class, see Grimm, No. 3 ("Our Lady's Child"), and *Romania*, No. 28, p. 568.

30. The seventh version is from Bologna and is entitled *La Fola dêl Muretein* ("The Story of the Little Moor"), and was published by Coronedi-Berti in the *Rivista Europea*, Florence, 1873. It is briefly as follows: A queen has no children and visits a witch who gives her an apple to eat, telling her that in due time she will bear a son. One of the queen's maids eats the peel and both give birth to sons; the maid's being called the Little Moor from resembling the dark red color of the apple peel. The two children grow up together, and when the prince goes off on his travels his friend the little Moor accompanies him. They spend the night in an enchanted cas-

tle and the friend hears a voice saying that the prince will conquer in a tournament and marry the king's daughter, but on their wedding night a dragon will devour the bride, and whoever tells of it will become marble. The friend saves the princess' life, but is thrown into prison, and when he exculpates himself becomes marble. He can only be restored to life by being anointed with the blood of a cock belonging to a wild man (*om salvadgh*) living on a certain mountain. The prince performs the difficult feat of stealing the cock and healing his friend.

For other European versions, see Grimm, No 6 ("Faithful John"); Hahn, No. 29; Wolf, *Proben Port. und Cat. Volksm.* p. 52; *Lo Rondallayre,* No. 35 ("*Lo bon criat*"); *Old Deccan Days,* p. 98; and in general, Benfey, *Pant.* I. p. 417, and Köhler in *Weimarische Beiträge sur Lit. und Kunst,* Weimar, 1865, p. 192 *et seq.*

31. See Pitrè, vol. I. pp. xcix., ciii.; IV. pp. 382, 430, and Comparetti, No. 44. A version from the Abruzzi may be found in Finamore, No. 38. See also Grimm, No. 191 ("The Robber and his Sons"); *Basque Legends,* p. 4, *Dolapathos* ed. Oesterley, pp. xxii., 65; and in general, *Orient und Occident,* II. 120, and Benfey, *Pant.* I. 295.

32. Another Sicilian version is in Gonz., No. 83. Other versions are: *Pent.* III. 7, Nerucci, p. 341; De Nino, No. 30; *Fiabe Mant.* No. 4; *Nov. fior.* p. 340 (Milan); and Widter-Wolf, No. 9 (*Jahrb.* VII. p. 134). There are other similar stories in which a person is forced by those envious of him to undertake dangerous enterprises: see Pitrè, Nos. 34, 35; Comparetti, No. 16; *Tuscan Fairy Tales,* No. 8, De Nino, No. 39, etc. Strap., I. 2, also offers many points of resemblance to our story.

For other versions, see Grimm, No. 192 ("The Master-Thief"), and Köhler's notes to Widter-Wolf, No. 9.

33. The version in *Nov. fior.* p. 574, is from Florence, the others, pp. 575 (the story in our text), 577, 578, 579, are from Milan, and closely resemble each other.

34. Compare Pitrè, No. 83, and De Nino, No. 43. Tyrolese versions are in Schneller, Nos. 53, 54. See also Widter-Wolf, No. 2 (*Jahrb.* VII. 13), and *Jahrb.* VIII. p. 246, *Italien. Märchen aus Sora,* No. 2. For additional European versions, see *Jahrb. ut supra,* and V. 7; *Romania,* Nos. 19, p. 350; 24, p. 562; 28, p. 556; and Grimm, Nos. 20 ("The Valiant Little Taylor"), and 183 ("The Giant and the Tailor"). Some of the episodes mentioned in the text may be found in a Corsican story in Ortoli, p. 204, where, however, instead of a giant, a priest is outwitted by his servant.

Chapter II. *Fairy Tales Continued*

1. This story is found in the *Pent.* I. 10. In Schneller, No. 29, the king falls in love with a frog (from hearing its voice without seeing it) which is transformed by the fairies into a beautiful girl. The good wishes of the fairies are found in Pitrè, Nos. 61, 94. See also *Pent.* I. 3; III. 10, and Chap. I. of the present work, note 22. For gifts by the fairies, see Pitrè, vol. I. p. 334, and the following note.

2. This story is often found as an introduction to "False Bride," see Chap. I., note 21. Sicilian versions may be found in Pitrè, Nos. 62, 63; Neapolitan, *Pent.* III. 10; from the Abruzzi in Finamore, No. 48, De Nino, No. 18; Tuscan, Gradi, *Vigilia,* p. 20, De Gub., *Sto. Stefano,* No. 1, *Zoöl. Myth.* II. p. 62, note, *Tuscan Fairy Tales,* pp. 9, 18, Corazzini, p. 409, *Nov. tosc.* No. 8, *La Tinchina dell' alto Mare;* Venetian, Bernoni, XIX.; and Tyrolese, Schneller, Nos. 7, 8.

In several of the Tuscan versions (Gradi, *Zoöl. Myth.*, *Tuscan Fairy Tales*, p. 9, and *Nov. fior.* p. 202, which is composed of "Two Sisters" and "True Bride") instead of fairies the sisters find cats who bestow the varying gifts.

Other European versions of this story will be found in Grimm, No. 24, "Old Mother Holle; "Norwegian in Asbj. & Moe, No. 15; [Dasent, *Pop. Tales from the Norse*, p. 103, "The Two Step-Sisters"] French in Bladé, *Contes agen.* p. 149, and Cosquin, *Contes pop. lorrains*, No. 48 (*Romania*, No. 32, p. 564). The Oriental versions are mentioned by Cosquin in his notes to the last named story; see also Benfey, *Pant.* I. p. 219.

3. Other Tuscan versions are in Gradi, *Saggio di Letture varie*, p. 125, and *Nov. tosc.* No. 22; Sicilian and Roman versions may be found in Pitrè, No. 64, and Busk, p. 96.

French versions will be found in *Mélusine*, pp. 113 (*conte picard*) and 241 (*conte de l'Amiénois*). A Japanese version is given in the same periodical, p. 161. An Irish version is in Croker, *Fairy Legends* etc. (translated in Brueyre, p. 206); and a Turkish version is given in *The Wonder World Stories*, New York, Putnam, 1877, p. 139. Other French and Oriental versions are noticed in *Mélusine*, pp. 161, 241. A somewhat similar German version is in Grimm, No. 182, "The Presents of the Little Folk."

4. This story somewhat resembles Gonz., No. 20, mentioned in Chap. I., note 29. Another Sicilian version is in Pitrè, No. 86. I have been unable to find any other Italian parallels. Personification of one's Fate maybe found in Gonz., Nos. 52, 55, Pitrè, No. 12, and of Fortune in Pitrè, No. 29, and Comparetti, No. 50. See *Indian Fairy Tales*, p. 263.

5. Sicilian versions are in Pitrè, No. 105, and Gonz., No. 18. In the latter version the king drives his daughter from the palace and the rejected suitor disguises himself, follows her, and marries her. A Neapolitan version is in the *Pent.* IV. 10; Tuscan in Gradi, *Vigilia*, p. 97; Nerucci, p. 211; and *Jahrb.* VII. p. 394 (Knust, No. 9).

Other European versions are: Grimm No. 52, "King Thrushbeard;" Norwegian, Asbj. & Moe, No. 45, and Grundtwig, III. [1], French, *Romania*, No. 32, p. 552 (*Contes pop. lorrains*, No. 45); and Greek, Hahn, No. 113. See also *Tibetan Tales*, London, 1882, Ralston's notes, p. lviii.

6. Other versions of this story are: Sicilian, Pitrè, No. 67, and Gonz., No.28; Tuscan, *Archivio*, I. pp. 41, 65, *Nov. tosc.* No. 7, Abruzzi, De Nino, No. 1. For the first part of the story, see *Nov. fior.* pp. 332–333.

7. I have followed in this division Imbriani, *Pomiglianesi*, p. 89.

8. Another Sicilian version, which, however, does not contain the trait "Cure by laughing," is in Pitrè, No. 28. Gonz., No. 30, may be mentioned here, as it contains a part of our story. The magic gifts in it are a carpet that transports the owner wherever he wishes to go, a purse always full, and a horn that when one blows in the little end covers the sea with ships, when one blows in the big end, the ships disappear. Neapolitan versions are in Imbriani, *Pomiglianesi*, pp. 62, 83; Roman in Busk, pp. 129, 136, comp. p. 146, and Tuscan in Frizzi, *Novella montanina*, Florence, A. Ciardelli e C. 1876, Nerucci, p. 471 *Archivio per le Trad. pop.* I. p. 57, and *Nov. tosc.* No. 16. De Gub., *Zoöl. Myth.* I. p. 288, n. 3, gives a version from the Marches, and there is a Bolognese version in Coronedi-Berti, No. 9. Other versions may be found in Finamore, *Trad. pop. abruzzesi*, No. 30, and Bolognini, p. 21. For other European versions, see *Gesta Rom.* ed. Oesterley, cap. cxx.; Grimm, No. 122; Campbell, No. 10, "The Three Soldiers" (see Köhler's notes to this story in *Orient und Occident*, II. p. 124, and Brueyre, p. 138); Cosquin, *Contes pop. lorrains*, Nos. 11 (*Rom.* No. 19, p. 361) and 42 (*Rom.* No. 28, p. 581);

and finally, Kreutzwald, *Ehstnische Märchen*, No. 23. Comp. also De Gub., *Zoöl. Myth.*
I. p. 182, and Ralston's notes to Schiefner's *Tibetan Tales*, p. liv.

9. I have been unable to find any European parallels to this form of the story.

10. Another version of this story is found in the same collection, p. 359. Other
Tuscan versions are found in De Gub., *Sto. Stefano*, No. 21, Gradi, *Saggio di Letture
varie*, p. 181, *Nov. tosc.* No. 29, and Comparetti, No. 7 (Mugello). The other versions
are as follows: Sicilian, Pitrè, No. 29 (comp. No. 30), Gonz., No. 52; Neapolitan,
Pent. I. 1 (Comp. *Pomiglianesi*, p. 116); Abruzzi, Finamore, No. 37; De Nino, No. 6;
Ortoli, pp. 171, 178; Venetian, Bernoni, No. 9; the Marches, Comp., No. 12; and
Tyrolese, Schneller, p. 28.

For the other European parallels, see Grimm, No. 36, "The Table, the Ass, and
the Stick;" *Mélusine (conte breton)*, p. 130; Cosquin, *Contes pop. lorrains*, No. 14 (*Rom.*
No. 19, p. 333); De Gub., *Zoöl. Myth.* II. p. 262 (Russian); Brueyre, p. 48 (B. Gould,
Yorkshire, Appendix to Henderson's *Folk-Lore of the Northern Counties of England*);
Asbj. & Moe, No. 7 [Dasent, *Pop. Tales from the Norse*, p. 261, "The Lad who went
to the North Wind"], and *Old Deccan Days*, No. 12.

11. Another Sicilian version is in Gonz., No. 65, with same title and contents. A
Neapolitan version is in the *Pent.* II. 4, where the fox is replaced by a cat. This is also
the case in the versions from the Abruzzi, Finamore, No. 46, De Nino, No. 53; in the
Florentine versions in *Nov. fior.* p. 145, *Nov. tosc.* No. xii. var.; and in the Tyrolese
given by Schneller, p. 122 ("*Il Conte Martin dalla gatta*"). In another story in
Schneller, p. 124 ("*L'Anello*"), a youth possesses a magic ring and a dog and cat which
recover the ring when stolen from its owner. Older and more interesting than the
above versions is the one in Straparola, XI. 1. We give it here in full in order that our
readers may compare with it the version in our text and Perrault's "Puss in Boots,"
which is the form in which the story has become popular all over Europe. The following translation is from the edition of 1562 (Venice).

XXXIV. PUSS IN BOOTS

Soriana dies and leaves three sons: Dusolino, Tesifone, and Constantine the Lucky,
who, by virtue of a cat, acquires a powerful kingdom.

There was once in Bohemia a very poor lady named Soriana, who had three sons:
one was called Dusolino, the other Tesifone, and the third Constantine the Lucky.
She owned nothing valuable in the world but three things: a kneading-trough, a
rolling-board, and a cat. When Soriana, laden with years, came to die, she made her
last testament, and left to Dusolino, her eldest son, the kneading-trough, to Tesifone the rolling-board, and to Constantine the cat. When the mother was dead and
buried, the neighbors, as they had need, borrowed now the kneading-trough, now
the rolling-board; and because they knew that the owners were very poor, they made
them a cake, which Dusolino and Tesifone ate, giving none to Constantine, the
youngest brother. And if Constantine asked them for anything, they told him to go
to his cat, which would get it for him. Wherefore poor Constantine and his cat suffered greatly. Now the cat, which was enchanted, moved to compassion for Constantine, and angry at the two brothers who treated him so cruelly, said: "Constantine, do not be downcast, for I will provide for your support and my own." And leaving the house, the cat went out into the fields, and, pretending to sleep, caught a hare

that passed and killed it. Thence, going to the royal palace and seeing some of the courtiers, the cat said that she wished to speak with the king, who, when he heard that a cat wished to speak to him, had her shown into his presence, and asked her what she wished. The cat replied that her master, Constantine, had sent him a hare which he had caught. The king accepted the gift, and asked who this Constantine was. The cat replied that he was a man who had no superior in goodness, beauty, and power. Wherefore the king treated the cat very well, giving her to eat and drink bountifully. When the cat had satisfied her hunger, she slyly filled with her paw (unseen by any one) the bag that hung at her side, and taking leave of the king, carried it to Constantine. When the brothers saw the food over which Constantine exulted, they asked him to share it with them; but he refused, rendering them tit for tat. On which account there arose between them great envy, that continually gnawed their hearts. Now Constantine, although handsome in his face, nevertheless, from the privation he had suffered, was covered with scabs and scurf, which caused him great annoyance. But going with his cat to the river, she licked him carefully from head to foot, and combed his hair, and in a few days he was entirely cured.

The cat (as we said above) continued to carry gifts to the royal palace, and thus supported her master. But after a time she wearied of running up and down so much, and feared that she would annoy the king's courtiers; so she said to her master: "Sir, if you will do what I order, I will make you rich in a short time." "How?" said her master. The cat replied: "Come with me, and do not ask any more, for I am ready to enrich you." So they went together to the stream, which was near the royal palace, and the cat stripped her master, and with his agreement threw him into the river, and then began to cry out in a loud voice: "Help! Help! Messer Constantine is drowning." The king hearing this, and remembering that he had often received presents from him, sent his people at once to aid him. When Messer Constantine was taken out of the water and dressed in fine clothes, he was taken to the king, who received him cordially, and asked him why he had been thrown into the river. Constantine could not answer for grief; but the cat, which was always at his side, said: "Know, O king, that some robbers learned from spies that my master was loaded with jewels, which he was coming to present to you. They robbed him of all, and threw him into the river, thinking to kill him, but thanks to these gentlemen he has escaped from death." The king, hearing this, ordered that he should be well cared for; and seeing that he was handsome, and knowing him to be wealthy, he concluded to give him Elisetta, his daughter, for a wife, endowing her with jewels and most beautiful garments. After the wedding festivities had been ended, the king had ten mules loaded with money, and five with costly apparel, and sent his daughter to her husband's home, accompanied by a great retinue. Constantine, seeing that he had become so wealthy and honored, did not know where to lead his wife, and took counsel with his cat, which said: "Do not fear, my master, for we shall provide for everything." So they all set out gayly on horseback, and the cat ran hastily before them; and having left the company some distance behind, met some horsemen, to whom she said: "What are you doing here, wretched men? Depart quickly, for a large band of people are coming, and will take you prisoners. They are near by: you can hear the noise of the neighing horses." The horsemen said in terror: "What must we do, then?" The cat replied: "Do this,—if you are asked whose horsemen you are, answer boldly, Messer Constantine's, and you will not be molested." Then the cat went on, and found a large flock of sheep, and did the same with their owners, and said the same thing to all those whom she found in the road. The people who were escorting Elisetta asked the horsemen: "Whose knights are you," and "whose are so many fine flocks?" and all with one accord replied: "Messer Constantine's." Then those who accompanied the bride said: "So then, Messer Constantine, we are beginning to enter your territory." And he nodded his head, and replied in like manner to all that he was asked. Wherefore the company judged him to be very wealthy. At last the cat came to a very fine castle, and found there but few servants, to whom she said: "What are you doing, good men; do you not perceive the destruction which is impending?" "What?" asked the servants. "Before an hour passes, a host of soldiers will come here and cut you to pieces. Do you not hear the horses neighing? Do you not see the dust in the air? If you do not wish to perish, take my advice and you will be saved. If any one asks you whose this castle is, say, Messer Constantine's." So they did, and when the noble company reached the handsome castle they asked the keepers whose it was, and all answered boldly Messer Constantine the Lucky's. Then they entered, and were honorably entertained. Now the castellan of that place was Signor Valentine, a brave soldier, who, a short time before, had left the castle to bring home the wife he had lately married; and to his misfortune, before he reached the place where his wife was he was overtaken on the way by a sudden and fatal accident, from which he straightway died, and Constantine remained master of the castle. Before long, Morando, King of Bohemia, died, and the people elected for their king Constantine the Lucky because he was the husband of Elisetta, the dead king's daughter, to whom the kingdom fell by right of succession. And so Constantine, from being poor and a beggar, remained Lord and King, and lived a long time with his Elisetta, leaving children by her to succeed him in the kingdom.

For copious references to other European versions, see Köhler's notes to Gonz., No. 65 (II. p. 242), and Benfey, *Pant.* I. p. 222.

12. The earliest Italian versions are in the *Cento nov. ant., Testo Papanti* (*Romania*, No. 10, p. 191), and Straparola, XI. 2. Later popular versions, besides the Istrian one in the text, are: Nerucci, p. 430, and Bernoni, III. p. 91, both of which are much distorted. Some of the episodes are found in other stories, as, for instance, the division of the property, including the wife, which occurs in Gonz., No. 74. "The Thankful Dead" is also the subject of an Italian novel, *Novella di Messer Danese e di Messer Gigliotto*, Pisa, 1868 (privately printed), and of a popular poem, *Istoria bellissima di Stellante Costantina* composta da Giovonni Orazio Brunetto.

The extensive literature of this interesting story can best be found in D'Ancona's notes to the version in the *Cento nov. ant.*, cited above. To these may be added: Ive's notes to the story in the text, Cosquin's notes to No. 19 of the *Contes pop. lorrains* (*Rom.* No. 24, p. 534), and Nisard, *Hist. des Livres pop.* II. p. 450. Basque and Spanish versions have been published recently, the former in Webster's *Basque Legends*, pp. 146, 151, and the latter in Caballero, *Cuentos, oraciones*, etc., Leipzig, 1878, p. 23. A version from Mentone may be found in the *Folk-Lore Record*, vol. III. p. 48, "John of Calais."

13. In the original it is *la Voria*, which in Sicilian means "breeze," but I take it to be the same as *Boria* in Italian (Lat. *Boreas-æ*), the North Wind.

14. Other Italian versions are: *Nov. fior.* p. 440; *Archivio*, III. 542 (Abruzzi); Pitrè, No. 31, *Tuscan Fairy Tales,* No. 10, p. 102; De Nino, No. 69; and Widter-Wolf, No. 10 (*Jahrbuch,* VII. 139). See also Prato, *Una. nov, pop. monferrina,* Como, 1882; and Finamore, *Trad. pop. abruzzesi,* Nos. 17, 19.

References to other European versions will be found in Köhler's notes to Widter-Wolf, No. 10. See also Grimm, No. 92; Ralston's *R. F. T.* p. 132, and Chap, I., note 11, of the present work.

15. A work of this kind, similar in scope to Nisard's *Hist. des Livres populaires,* is greatly to be desired, and ought to be undertaken before the great changes in the social condition of Italy shall have rendered such a task difficult, if not impossible.

Chapter III. *Stories of the Orient*

1. There are three Italian translations of the *Pantschatantra,* all of the XVI. century. Two, *Discorsi degli Animali,* by Angelo Firenzuola, 1548, and *La Filosofia Morale,* by Doni, 1552, represent the Hebrew translation by Rabbi Joel (1250), from which they are derived through the *Directorium humanae vitae* of Johannes de Capua (1263–78); the third, *Del Governo de' Regni,* by G. Nuti, 1583, is from the Greek version of Simeon Seth (1080). A full account of the various translations of the *Pantschatantra* may be found in Max Müller's *Chips,* Vol. IV. p. 165, "The Migration of Fables." See also Benfey, *Pant.* I. pp. 1–19, *Buddhist Birth Stories; or, Jataka Tales,* By V. Fausböll and T. W. Rhys Davids, Boston, 1880, p. xciii., and Landau, *Die Quellen des Decamerone,* mentioned in the following note.

The Seven Wise Masters was also translated into Italian at an early date. One version, *Il Libro dei Sette Savj di Roma,* Pisa, 1864, edited by Prof. A. D'Ancona, is a XIII. century translation from a French prose version (Cod. 7974, *Bib. nat.*); another, of the same date, *Storia d'una crudele Matrigna,* Bologna, 1862, is from an uncertain source, from which is probably derived a third version, *Il Libro dei Sette Savi di Roma tratto da un codice del secolo XIV.* per cura di Antonio Cappelli, Bologna, 1865. The MS. from which the version edited by Delia Lucia in 1833 (reprinted at Bologna, 1862) was taken has been recently discovered and printed in *Operette inedite o rare, Libreria Dante,* Florence, 1883, No. 3. A fourth version of the end of the XIII. or the beginning of the XIV. century is still inedited, it is mentioned by D'Ancona in the *Libro dei Sette Savj,* p. xxviii., and its contents given. The latest and most curious version is *I Compassionevoli Avvenimenti di Erasto,* a work of the XVI. century (first edition, Venice, 1542) which contains four stories found in no other version of the Seven Wise Masters. The popularity of this version, the source of which is unknown, was great. See D'Ancona, *op. cit.,* pp. xxxi.–xxxiv.

The *Disciplina Clericalis* was not known, apparently, in Italy as a collection, but the separate stories were known as early as Boccaccio, who borrowed the outlines of three of his stories from it (VII. 4; VIII. 10; X. 8). Three of the stories of the *Disc. Cler.* are also found in the Ital. trans. of Frate Jacopo da Cessole's book on Chess (*Volgarizzamento del libro de' Costumi e degli offizzi de' nobili sopra il giuoco degli Scachi,* Milan, 1829) and reprinted in *Libro di Novelle Antiche,* Bologna, 1868, Novelle III., IV., and VI. This translation is of the XII. century. Other stories from the *Disc. Cler.* are found in the *Cento nov. ant.,* Gualt., LIII., XXXI., LXVI., Borg.,

LXXIV. (*Cent. nov.*, Biagi, pp. 226, 51, 58); and in Cintio, *Gli Ecatommiti*, I, 3; VII. 6.

2. It has been generally supposed that the Oriental element was introduced into European literature from Spain through the medium of the French. We shall see later that this was the case with the famous collection of tales just mentioned, the *Disciplina Clericalis*. Oriental elements are also found in the French *fabliaux* which are supposed to have furnished Boccaccio with the plots of a number of his novels. See Landau, *Die Quellen des Decamerone*, 2d ed., Vienna, 1884, p. 107. Professor Bartoli in his *I Precursori del Boccaccio e alcune delle sue Fonti*, Florence, 1876, endeavors to show that Boccaccio may have taken the above mentioned novels from sources common to them and the French *fabliaux*. It is undeniable that there was in the Middle Ages an immense mass of stories common to the whole western world, and diffused by oral tradition as well as by literary means, and it is very unsafe to say that any one literary version is taken directly from another. Sufficient attention has not been paid to the large Oriental element in European entertaining literature prior to the Renaissance. In early Italian literature besides Boccaccio, the *Cento novelle antiche* abound in Oriental elements. See D'Ancona, *Le Fonti del Novellino*, in the *Romania*, vol. III. pp. 164–194, since republished in *Studj di Critica e Storia Letteraria*, Bologna, 1880, pp. 219–359.

3. See Introduction, Notes 3, 7.

4. In the *Pantschatantra* (Benfey's trans. vol. II. p. 120) this story is as follows: A merchant confides to a neighbor some iron scales or balances for safe-keeping. When he wishes them back he is told that the mice have eaten them up. The merchant is silent, and some time after asks his neighbor to lend him his son to aid him in bathing. After the bath the merchant shuts the boy up in a cave, and when the father asks where he is, is told that a falcon has carried him off. The neighbor exclaimed: "Thou liar, how can a falcon carry away a boy? The merchant responded: "Thou veracious man! If a falcon cannot carry away a boy, neither can mice eat iron scales. Therefore give me back my scales if you desire your son." See also Benfey, *Pant.* I. p. 283. La Fontaine has used the same story for his fable of *Le Dépositaire infidèle* (livre IX. 1); see also references in *Fables inédites*, vol. II. p. 193.

5. The fables in Pitrè of non-Oriental origin may be mentioned here; they are: No. 271, "*Brancaliuni*," found also in Straparola, X. 2; No. 272, "The Two Mice," compare Aesop. ed. Furia, 198, and Schneller, No. 59; No. 274, "Wind, Water, and Honor," found in Straparola, XI. 2, No. 275, "Godfather Wolf and Godmother Fox"; No. 276, "The Lion, the Wolf, and the Fox," Aesop. ed. Furia, 233; No. 277, "The Fox," see *Roman du Renart*, Paris, 1828, I. p. 129, and *Nov. tosc.* No. 69; No. 278, "L'Acidduzzu (Pretty Little Bird)," compare Asbj. & Moe, No. 42, Bernoni, *Punt.* III. p. 69, "*El Galo*," Nerucci, *Cincelle da Bambini*, p. 38; No. 279, "The Wolf and the Finch," Gonz., No. 66, *Nov. tosc.* No. 52 (add to Köhler's references: Asbj. & M., Nos. 42, 102, [Dasent, *Tales from the Fjeld*, p. 35, "The Greedy Cat,"] and Bernoni, *Punt.* III. p. 69); and finally No. 280, "The Cricket and the Ants," see Aesop. ed. Furia, 121, La Fontaine, *La Cigale et la Fourmi*, livre I. 1: see copious references in Robert, *Fables inédites*, I, p. 2. For Bernoni, III. p. 69, "*El Galo*," and Pitrè, No. 279, see Chap. V. pp. 270, 272.

There are two fables in Coronedi-Berti's collection: No. 20: "*La Fola del Corov*," and No. 21, "*La Fola dla Vôulp*." The first is the well-known fable of the crow in the peacock's feathers; for copious references see Robert, *Fables inédites*, I. p. 247, to La Fontaine's *Le Geai paré des plumes du Paon*, livre IV. fab. IX., and Oesterley to Kirchhof's *Wendunmuth*, 7, 52. In the second fable the fox leaves her little ones at home, bidding them admit no one without a countersign. The wolf learns it from the simple little foxes themselves, gains admission, and eats two of them up. The mother takes her revenge in almost the same way as does the fox in Pitrè's fable, No. 277.

6. This fable is also found in Pitrè, No, 273, "The Man, the Wolf, and the Fox," and in Gonz., No. 69, "Lion, Horse, and Fox:" see Benfey, *Pant.* I. 113, and Köhler's references to Gonz., No. 69.

There is also a version of this fable in Morosi, p. 75, which is as follows:—

XLIX. The Man, the Serpent, and the Fox

There was once a huntsman, who, in passing a quarry, found a serpent under a large stone. The serpent asked the hunter to liberate him, but the latter said: "I will not free you, for you will eat me." The serpent replied: "Liberate me, for I will not eat you." When the hunter had set the serpent at liberty, the latter wanted to devour him, but the hunter said: "What are you doing? Did you not promise me that you would not eat me?" The serpent replied that hunger did not observe promises. The hunter then said: "If you have no right to eat me, will you do it?" "No," answered the serpent. "Let us go, then," said the hunter, "and ask three times." They went into the woods and found a greyhound, and asked him, and he replied: "I had a master, and I went hunting and caught hares, and when I carried them home my master had nothing too good to give me to eat; now, when I cannot overtake even a tortoise, because I am old, my master wishes to kill me; for this reason I condemn you to be eaten by the serpent; for he who does good finds evil." "Do you hear? We have one judge," said the serpent. They continued their journey, and found a horse, and asked him, and he too replied that the serpent was right to eat the man, "For," he said, "I had a master, who fed me when I could travel; now that I can do so no longer, he would like to hang me." The serpent said: "Behold, two judges!" They went on, and found a fox. The huntsman said: "Fox, you must aid me. Listen: I was passing a quarry, and found this serpent dying under a large stone, and he asked aid from me, and I released him, and now he wants to eat me." The fox answered: "I will be the judge. Let us return to the quarry, to see how the serpent was." They went there, and put the stone on the serpent, and the fox asked: "Is that the way you were?" "Yes," answered the serpent. "Very well, then, stay so always!" said the fox.

7. The individual stories of the *Thousand and One Nights* were known in Europe long before the collection, which was not translated into French until 1704–1717. This is shown by the fact that some of the XIII. century *fabliaux* embody stories of the *Thousand and One Nights*. See Note 10. An interesting article by Mr. H. C. Coote on "Folk-Lore, the source of some of M. Galland's Tales," will be found in the *Folk-Lore Record*, vol. III. pp. 178–191.

8. The Sicilian versions are in Pitrè, No. 81. The version from Palermo, of which Pitrè gives only a *résumé*, is printed entire in F. Sabatini, *La Lanterna, Nov. pop. sicil.* Imola, 1878. The Roman version, "How Cajusse was married," is in Busk, p. 158; and the Mantuan in Visentini, No. 35. Tuscan versions may be found in the *Rivista di Lett. pop.* p. 267; De Nino, No. 5; and a version from Bergamo in the same periodi-

cal, p. 288. For the episode of the "Magician with no heart in his body," see Chap. I. note 12.

9. See Pitrè, No. 36, and Gonz., No. 5, with Köhler's copious references. As this story is found in Chap. I. p. 17, it is only mentioned here for the sake of completeness.

There is another complete version of "The Forty Thieves" in Nerucci, No. 54, *Cicerchia, o i ventidua Ladri.* The thieves are twenty-two, and *cicerchia* is the magic word that opens and shuts the robbers' cave. A version in Ortoli, p. 137, has seven thieves.

10. Pitrè, No. 164, "The Three Hunchbacks;" Straparola, V. 3. It is also found in the *fabliau, Les Trois Bossus,* Barbazan-Méon, III. 245; for copious references see Von der Hagen, *Gesammtabenteuer,* III. p. xxxv. *et seq.* Pitrè, No. 165, *"Fra Ghiniparu,"* is a variation of the above theme, and finds its counterpart in the *fabliau* of *Le Sacristain de Cluni:* see *Gesammtabenteuer, ut sup.* Other versions are in Finamore, *Trad. pop. abruzzesi,* No. 9, and *Nov. tosc.* No. 58.

11. The story is, properly speaking, in the introduction to the *Thousand and One Nights:* see Lane, *The Thousand and One Nights,* London, 1865, I. 10. See Straparola, XII. 3, and *Schmipf und Ernst* von Johannes Pauli, herausgegeben von Hermann Oesterley (*Bibliothek des litt. Vereins,* LXXXV.), Stuttgart, 1866, No. 134, *"Ein bösz weib tugenhaft zemachen."*

12. For the first story, see *Thousand and One Nights* (ed. Breslau), IX. 129; *Pent.* V. 7; Gonz., No. 45; Hahn, No. 47; and Grimm, No. 129. For the second, see *Thousand and One Nights* (ed. Breslau), II. 196; ed. Lane, III, 41.

13. See Lane, I. 140, and, for the transformations, p. 156. This story is also in Straparola, VIII. 5. It is well known in the North of Europe from the Grimm tale (No. 68), "The Thief and his Master." To the references in Grimm, II. p. 431, may be added: *Revue Celtique,* I. 132, II.; Benfey, *Pant.* I. p. 410: Brueyre, 253; Ralston, *R. F. T.* 229; Asbj. & M., No. 57 [Dasent, *Pop. Tales,* No. XXXIX.] (comp. Nos. 9, 46 [Dasent, *Pop. Tales,* Nos. XXIII., IX.]); Hahn, No. 68; Bernhauer, *Vierzig Viziere,* p. 195; *Orient und Occident,* II. 313; III. 374; Grandtvig, 1.248; Jülg, *Kalmükische Märchen, Einleitung,* p. 1; and F. J. Child, *English and Scottish Popular Ballads,* Part II. p. 399, "The Two Magicians."

14. The principal sources of information in regard to the *Disciplina Clericalis* and its author are the two editions of Paris and Berlin: *Disciplina Clericalis:* auctore Petro Alphonsi, Ex-Judæo Hispano, Parisiis, MDCCCXXIV. 2 vols. (Société des Bibliophiles français); Petri Alfonsi Disciplina Clericalis, zum ersten Mal herausgegeben mit Einleitung und Anmerkungen von Fr. Wilh. Val. Schmidt, Berlin, 1827. The first edition was edited by J. Labouderie, Vicar-general of Avignon, and as only two hundred and fifty copies were printed, it is now very scarce. Schmidt even had not seen it; and when he published his own edition, three years later, thought it the first. The Paris edition contains the best text, and has besides two Old-French translations, one in prose, the other in verse. The Berlin edition is, however, more valuable on account of the notes.

15. This is the story shortly after mentioned, Pitrè, No. 138, "The Treasure." The date of the *Cento nov. ant.* cannot be accurately fixed; the compilation was probably made at the end of the XIII. cent., although individual stories may be of an earlier date.

16. See *Disciplina. Cler.* ed. Schmidt, pp. 63 and 142. For copious references see Oesterley's *Gesta Rom.* cap. 106.

17. There are several literary Italian versions of this story; one in Casalicchio, VI., I., VI.; and in Cintio, *Ecatommiti*, I. 3. There is another popular version in Imbriani's *Nov. fior*, p. 616, "The Three Friends."

18. See *Disc. Cler.* ed. Schmidt, pp. 50 and 128. The version in the *Cento nov. ant.* ed. Gualt., No. 31, is as follows: Messer Azzolino had a story-teller, whom he made tell stories during the long winter nights. It happened one night that the story-teller had a great mind to sleep, and Azzolino asked him to tell stories. The story-teller began to relate a story about a peasant who had a hundred bezants. He went to market to buy sheep, and had two for a bezant. Returning home with his sheep, a river that he had crossed was greatly swollen by a heavy rain that had fallen. Standing on the bank he saw a poor fisherman with an exceedingly small boat, so small that it would only hold the peasant and one sheep at a time. Then the peasant began to cross with one sheep, and began to row; the river was wide. He rows and crosses. And the story-teller ceased relating. Azzolino said: "Go on." And the story-teller answered: "Let the sheep cross, and then I will tell the story." For the sheep would not be over in a year, so that meanwhile he could sleep at his leisure.

The story passed from the *Disc. Cler.* into the Spanish collection *El Libro de los Enxemplos,* No. 85. A similar story is also found in Grimm, No. 86, "The Fox and the Geese."

19. The word translated bank (*bancu*) is here used to indicate a buried treasure. The most famous of these concealed treasures was that of Ddisisa, a hill containing caves, and whose summit is crowned by the ruins of an Arab castle. This treasure is mentioned also in Pitrè, No. 230, "The Treasure of Ddisisa," where elaborate directions are given for finding it.

20. See Pitrè, vol. IV. p. 401, and *Nov. fior.* p. 572.

21. See *Disc. Cler.* ed. Schmidt, pp. 64 and 147, where the story is as follows: "A certain tailor to the king had, among others, an apprentice named Nedui. On one occasion the king's officers brought warm bread and honey, which the tailor and his apprentices ate without waiting for Nedui, who happened to be absent. When one of the officers asked why they did not wait for Nedui, the tailor answered that he did not like honey. When Nedui returned, and learned what had taken place, he determined to be revenged; and when he had a chance he told the officer who superintended the work done for the king that the tailor often went into a frenzy and beat or killed the bystanders. The officer said that if they could tell when the attack was coming on, they would bind him, so that he could not injure any one. Nedui said it was easy to tell; the first symptoms were the tailor's looking here and there, beating the ground with his hands, and getting up and seizing his seat. The next day Nedui securely hid his master's shears, and when the latter began to look for them, and feel about on the floor, and lift up his seat, the officer called in the guard and had the tailor bound, and, for fear he should beat any one, soundly thrashed. At last the poor tailor succeeded in obtaining an explanation; and when he asked Nedui: "When did you know me to be insane?" the latter responded: "When did you know me not to eat honey?" See also references in Kirchhoff's *Wendunmuth,* I. 243.

22. In the original the admonitions are in the form of a verse, as follows:—

> "*Primu:* Cu' cancia la via vecchia pi la nova,
> Le guai ch' 'un circannu ddà li trova

Secunnu: Vidi assai e parra pocu.
Terzu: Pensa la cosa avanti chi la fai,
    Ca la cosa pinsata è bedda assai."

23. See *Disc. Cler.* ed. Schmidt, pp. 61 and 141. This story is also found in the *Gesta Romanorum,* cap. 103; Gonz., No. 81, where copious references by Oesterley and Köhler may be found; in Nerucci, No. 53; and in a distorted version in Ortoli, p, 118: see also *Giornale Napoletano della Domenica,* August 20, 1882; Pitrè, *"I Tre Pareri,"* and *Notes and Queries,* London, February 7, March 14, 1885.

24. See Note 1 of this chapter.

25. In the original, what the husband, wife, and king, say, is in verse, as follows:—

"Vigna era e Vigna son,
    Amata era e più non son;
E non so per qual cagion,
    Che la Vigna à perso la so stagion."

"Vigna eri e Vigna sei,
    Amata eri e più non sei:
Per la branca del leon
    La Vigna à perso la so stagion."

"Ne la Vigna io son intrato,
    Di quei pampani n' ò tocato;
Ma lo guiro per la corona che porto in capo,
    Che de quel fruto no ghe n' ò gustato."

This story is also found in Pitrè, No. 76, *"Lu Bracceri di manu manca"* ("The Usher on the Left Hand," *i.e.,* of the king, who also had one on his right hand); *Pomiglianesi,* No. 6, *"Villa;"* and, in the shape of a poetical dialogue, in Vigo, *Raccolta amplissima di Canti popolari siciliani.* Secunda ediz. Catania, 1870–1874, No, 5145.

The story is told of Pier delle Vigne by Jacopo d' Aqui (XIII. cent.) in his *Chronicon imaginis mundi,* and of the Marchese di Pescara by Brantôme, *Vie des Dames galantes.* These versions will be found with copious references in Pitrè and Imbriani as cited above: see also, *Cantilene e Ballate, Strambotti e Madrigali nei Secoli XIII. e XIV.,* A cura di Giosuè Carducci, Pisa, 1871, p. 26. The story is discussed in an exhaustive manner by S. Prato in the *Romania,* vol. XII. p. 535; XIV. p. 132, *"L' Orma del Leone."*

26. For the Oriental versions see *Essai sur les Fables indiennes, par* A. Loiseleur Deslongchamps, Paris, 1838, p. 96; *Das Buch von den sieben weisen Meistern,* aus dem Hebräischen und Griechischen zum ersten Male übersetzt von H. Sengelmann, Halle, 1842, p. 40 (*Mischle Sandabâr*), p. 87 (*Syntipas*), *Tausend und Eine Nacht,* Deutsch von Max Habicht, Von der Hagen und Schall, Breslau, 1836, vol. XV. p. 112 (Arabic); *Li Romans des Sept Sages,* nach der Pariser Handschrift herausgegeben von H. A. Keller, Tübingen, 1836, p. cxxxviii.; *Dyocletianus Leben,* von Hans von Bühel, herausgegeben von A. Keller, Quedlinburg und Leipzig, 1841, p. 45. All students of this subject are acquainted with Domenico Comparetti's masterly essay *Ricerche intorno al Libro di Sindibâd,* Milan, 1869, which has recently been made accessible to

English readers in a version published by the English Folk-Lore Society in 1882. The Persion and Arabic texts may be consulted in an English translation, reprinted with valuable introduction and notes in the following work: *The Book of Sindibād; or, The Story of the King, his Son, the Damsel, and the Seven Vazirs*, From the Persian and Arabic, with Introduction, Notes, and an Appendix, by W. A. Clouston. Privately printed, 1884 [Glasgow], pp. xvii.–lvi.

27. For the original version in the various forms of the Western *Seven Wise Masters*, see Loiseleur-Deslongchamps, p. 162; Keller, *Romans*, p. ccxxix., and *Dyocletianus*, p. 63; and D'Ancona, *Il Libro dei Sette Savi di Roma*, p. 121. To the references in D'Ancona may be added: *Deux Rédactions du Roman des Sept Sages*, G. Paris, Paris, 1876, pp. 47, 162; Benfey, in *Orient und Occident*, III. 420; *Romania*, VI. p. 182; *Mélusine*, p. 384; and *Basque Legends*, collected by Rev. W. Webster, London, 1879, pp. 136, 137.

28. See Grimm, No. 33, "The Three Languages;" Hahn, No. 33, *Basque Legends*, p. 137; and *Mélusine*, p. 300. There is a verbose version in the *Fiabe Mantovane*, No. 23, "*Bobo*."

29. See Herodotus, with a commentary by J. W. Blakesley, London, 1854, I. p. 254, n. 343. For the literature of this story, and for various other Italian versions, see *La Leggenda del Tesoro di Rampsinite*, Stanislao Prato, Como, 1882, and Ralston's notes to Schiefner's *Tibetan Tales*, p. xlvii.

30. For the story in the *Seven Wise Masters*, see D'Ancona, *op. cit.* p. 108, Loiseleur-Deslongchamps, p. 146; Keller, *Romans*, p. cxciii., and *Dyoclet*. p. 55.

Besides the popular versions in Italian, the story is also found in Bandello, I., XXV., who follows Herodotus closely.

31. For the story in the *Seven Wise Masters* see D'Ancona, *op. cit.* p. 120; Loiseleur-Deslongchamps, p. 158; Keller, *Romans*, p. ccxxxvii., and *Dyoclet*. p. 61. Literary versions of this story are in Straparola, II. 11; *Pecorone*, II. 2; Malespini, 53; Bandello, I. 3; and Sercambi, XIII. See Pitrè, IV. pp. 407, 442.

32. The literature of this famous collection of tales will best be found in an article by Wilhelm Pertsch, "*Ueber Nachschabi's Papagaeinbuch*" in the *Zeitschrift der deutschen morgenländischen Gesellschaft*, Bd. XXI. pp. 505–551. Prof. H. Brockhaus discovered that the eighth night of Nachschabî's version was nothing but a version of the *Seven Wise Masters* containing seven stories. Nachschabî, in preparing his work, used probably the oldest version of the *Seven Wise Masters* of which we have any knowledge. Professor Brockhaus made this discovery known in a brief pamphlet entitled: *Die Sieben Weisen Meister von Nachschabî*, Leipzig, 1843, of which only twelve copies were printed. The above, except the Persian text, was reprinted in the *Blätt. für lit. Unterhaltung*, 1843, Nos. 242, 243 (pp. 969 *et seq.*); and, in an Italian translation, in D'Ancona's *Il Libro dei Sette Savi di Roma*.

The Persian version of Qâdirî (a compend of Nachschabî's) is the one most frequently translated. The German translation: *Toutinameh*. Eine Sammlung pers. Märchen, von C. J. L. Iken, mit einem Anhange von J. G. L. Kosegarten, Stuttgart, 1822, is easily found. The Turkish version is elegantly translated by G. Rosen: *Tutinameh, das Papagaeinbuch*, eine Sammlung orientalischer Erzählungen nach der türkischen Bearbeitung zum ersten Male übersetzt von G. Rosen, Leipzig, 1858, 2 vols.

33. The preservation of the frame of the *Çukasaptati* in Italian popular tales is only paralleled, to our knowledge, by the preservation of the *Seven Wise Masters* in a Magyar popular tale. See *La Tradizione dei Sette Savi nelle Novelline magiare.* Lettera al Prof. A. D'Ancona di E. Teza, Bologna, 1864.

It is possible that the Italian stories containing the frame of the *Çukasaptati* may have been developed from the story in the *Seven Wise Masters* which is found in both the Oriental and Occidental versions. The spirit of Folk-tales seems to us averse to expansion, and that condensation is the rule. We think it more likely that it was by way of oral tradition, or from some now lost collection of Oriental tales once known in Italy.

34. It is in the work by Teza mentioned in the last note, p. 52.

35. See Pitrè, vol. I. p. 23. The three stories in one are called *Donna Viulanti* (Palermo) and *Lu Frati e lu Soru* (Salaparuta).

36. See Chapter I. note 7.

37. The Italian versions are: Pitrè, No, 78, "*Lu Zu Viritati*" ("Uncle Truth"); Gonz., No. 8, "*Bauer Wahrhaft*" ("Farmer Truth"); *XII. Conti Pomiglianesi,* p. I, "*Giuseppe 'A Veretà*" ("Truthful Joseph," the version translated by us); p. 6, another version from same place and with same name; and in Straparola, III. 5. References to Oriental sources may be found in Köhler's notes to Gonz., No. 8, and Oesterley's notes to *Gesta Rom.* cap. III.

In addition to the Oriental elements mentioned in the third chapter, Stanislao Prato has discovered the story of Nala in a popular tale from Pitigliano (Tuscany), see S. Prato, *La Leggenda indiana di Nala in una novella popolare pitiglianese,* Como, 1881. (Extracted from *I Nuovi Goliardi.*)

Chapter IV. *Legends and Ghost Stories*

1. It is the LXXV. novel of the *Testo* Gualteruzzi (Biagi, p. 108): *Qui conta come Domeneddio s' accompagnò con un giullare.* The Lord once went in company with a jester. One day the former went to a funeral, and the latter to a marriage. The Lord called the dead to life again, and was richly rewarded. He gave the jester some of the money with which he bought a kid, roasted it and ate the kidneys himself. His companion asked where they were, and the jester answered that in that country the kids had none. The next time the Lord went to a wedding and the jester to a funeral, but he could not revive the dead, and was considered a deceiver, and condemned to the gallows. The Lord wished to know who ate the kidneys, but the other persisted in his former answer; but in spite of this the Lord raises the dead, and the jester is set at liberty. Then the Lord said he wished to dissolve their partnership, and made three piles of money, one for himself, another for the jester, and the third for the one who ate the kidneys. Then the jester said: "By my faith, now that you speak thus, I will tell you that I ate them; I am so old that I ought not to tell lies now." So some things are proved by money, which a man would not tell to escape from death. For the sources and imitations of this story see D'Ancona, *Le Fonti del Novellino,* in the *Romania,* No. 10, p. 180, (*Studj,* p. 333). To D'Ancona's references may be added the following: Grimm, 147, "The Old Man made young again"; Asbjørnsen and Moe,

No. 21 [Dasent, *Pop. Tales*, No. XIV.], *Ny Samm.* No. 101 [Dasent, *Tales from the Fjeld*, p. 94, "Peik"]; Ralston, *R. F. T.* p. 350; Simrock's *Deutsche Märchen*, Nos. 31b (p. 148), 32, *Romania*, No. 24, p. 578, "*Le Foie de Mouton*" (E. Cosquin, *Contes pop. lor-rains*, No. 30); Brueyre, p. 330; and an Italian version, which is simply an amplifica-tion of the one in the *Cento nov. ant.*, in the recently published *Sessanta Nov. pop. montalesi*, Nerucci, No. 31.

2. See *Jahrbuch*, VII. pp. 28, 396. The professional pride of the smith finds a par-allel in an Irish story in Kennedy, "How St. Eloi was punished for the sin of Pride." Before the saint became religious he was a goldsmith, but sometimes amused him-self by shoeing horses, and boasted that he had never found his master in anything. One day a stranger stopped at his forge and asked permission to shoe his horse. Eloi consented, and was very much surprised to see the stranger break off the horse's leg at the shoulder, carry it into the smithy and shoe it. Then the stranger put on again the horse's leg, and asked Eloe if he knew any one who could do such a good piece of work. Eloi tries himself, and fails miserably. The stranger, who is Eloi's guardian angel, cures the horse, reproves the smith for his pride, and disappears. See Brueyre, p. 329, and Bladé, *Agenais*, p. 61, and Köhler's notes, p. 157.

3. Bernoni, *Punt.* I. p. 1, "*I cinque brazzi de Tela.*" See Benfey, *Pant.* I. p. 497, where the same story (without the coarseness of the Italian version) is related of Buddha, who tells the hospitable woman that "what she begins shall not end until sunset." She begins to measure linen and it lengthens in her hands so that she continues to measure it all day. The envious neighbor receives the same gift, but before she begins to measure the linen, she thinks she will water the swine; the bucket does not become empty until evening, and the whole neighborhood is inundated. See Ben-fey's parallels, *ut. sup.* pp. 497–98, and Grimm, No. 87, notes.

4. These four legends are in Pitrè, *Cinque Novelline popolari siciliane*, Palermo, 1878. In the third story, "*San Pietru e sò cumpari*," St. Peter gets something to eat from a stingy man by a play on the word *mussu*, "snout," and *cu lu mussu*, "to be angry." For a similar story see Pitrè, III. 312. A parallel to the first of the above legends may be found in Finamore, No. 34, IV., where are also some other legends of St. Peter.

Since the above note was written, some similar legends have been published by Salomone Marino in the *Archivio per lo Studio delle tradizioni popolari*, vol. II. p. 553. One "The Just suffers for the Sinner" ("*Chianci lu giustu pri lu piccaturi*") relates how St. Peter complained to our Lord that the innocent were punished with the guilty. Our Lord made no answer, but shortly after commanded St. Peter to pick up a piece of honey-comb filled with bees, and put it in the bosom of his dress. One of the bees stung him, and St. Peter in his anger killed them all, and when the Lord rebuked him, excused himself by saying: "How could I tell among so many bees which one stung me?" The Lord answered: "Am I wrong then, when I punish men likewise? *Chianci lu giustu pri lu piccaturi.*"

Another legend relates the eagerness of St. Peter's sister to marry. Thrice she sent her brother to our Lord to ask his consent, and thrice the Lord, with characteristic patience, answered: "Tell her to do what she wishes."

A third legend explains why some are rich and some are poor in this world. Adam and Eve had twenty-four children, and one day the Lord passed by the house, and the parents concealed twelve of their children under a tub. The Lord, at the par-ents' request, blessed the twelve with riches and happiness. After he had departed, the parents realized what they had done, and called the Master back. When he heard that they had told him a falsehood about the number of their children, he replied that the blessing was bestowed and there was no help for it. "Oh!" said Adam in anguish, "what will become of them?" The Lord replied: "Let those who are not blessed serve the others, and let those who are blessed support them." "And this is why in the world half are rich and half are poor, and the latter serve the former, and the former support the latter."

The last of these legends which I shall mention is entitled: "All things are done for money." ("*Tutti cosi su' fatti pri dinari.*") There once died a poor beggar who had led a pious life, and was destined for paradise. When his soul arrived at the gate and knocked, St. Peter asked who he was and told him to wait. The poor soul waited two months behind the gate, but St. Peter did not open it for him. Meanwhile, a wealthy baron died and went, exceptionally, to paradise. His soul did not need even to knock, for the gate was thrown open, and St. Peter exclaimed: "Throw open the gate, let the baron pass! Come in Sir Baron, your servant, what an honor!" The soul of the beggar squeezed in, and said to himself: "The world is not the only one who worships money; in heaven itself there is this law, that all things are done for money."

5. Pitrè, No. 126, where other Sicilian versions are mentioned. A version from Siena is in T. Gradi, *Proverbi e Modi di dire*, p. 23, repeated in the same author's *Saggio di Letture varie*, p. 52, and followed by an article by Tommaseo, originally printed in the *Institutore* of Turin, in which Servian and Greek parallels are given. Besides the Venetian variant mentioned in the text, there are versions from Umbria and Piedmont cited by Pitrè, a Tuscan one in *Nov. tosc.* No. 26, and one from the Tyrol in Schneller, No. 4. Pitrè, in his notes to *Nov. tosc.* No. 26, mentions several other versions from Piedmont, Friuli, and Benevento. An exact version is also found in Corsica: see Ortoli, p. 235.

6. This reminds one of the "Sabbath of the Damned:" see Douhet, *Dictionnaire des Légendes,* Paris, 1855, p. 1040.

7. Pitrè, in a note to this story, mentions several proverbial sayings in which Pilate's name occurs: "To wash one's hands of the matter like Pilate," and "To come into a thing like Pilate in the Creed," to express engaging in a matter unwillingly, or to indicate something that is *mal à propos.*

8. Pitrè, I. p. cxxxvii., and Pitrè, *Appunti di Botanica popolare siciliana,* in the *Rivista Europea,* May, 1875, p. 441.

9. Pitrè, I. p. cxxxviii.

10. This legend is mentioned in a popular Sicilian legend in verse, see Pitrè, *Canti pop. sic.* II. p. 368, and is the subject of a chap-book, the title of which is given by Pitrè, *Fiabe,* vol. IV. p. 397.

11. *Preghiere pop. veneziane* raccolte da Dom. Giuseppe Bernoni, p. 18.

12. Pitrè, I, p. cxxxiii. For earlier appearances of the Wandering Jew in Italian literature, see A. D'Ancona, *La Leggenda dell' Ebreo errante, Nuova Antologia,* serie II. vol. XXIII. 1880, p. 425; *Romania,* vol. X. p. 212, *Le Juif errant en Italia au XIIIe siècle,* G. Paris and A. D'Ancona; vol. XII. p. 112, *Encore le Juif errant en Italie,* A. D'Ancona, and *Giornale Storico,* vol. III. p. 231, R. Renier, where an Italian text of the XVIII. cent. is printed for the first time. The myth of the Wandering Jew can best be studied in the following recent works: G. Paris, *Le Juif Errant, Extrait de l'Encyclopedie des Sciences Religieuses,* Paris, 1880; Dr. L. Neubaur, *Die Sage vom ewigen*

Juden, Leipzig, 1884; P. Cassel, *Ahasverus, die Sage vom ewigen Juden,* Berlin, 1885. The name Buttadeu (Buttadæus in the Latin texts of the XVII. cent.) has been explained in various ways. It is probably from the Ital. verb *buttare,* to thrust away, and *dio,* God.

13. Crivòliu is a corruption of Gregoriu, Gregory, and the legend is, as Köhler says, a peculiar transformation of the well-known legend of "Gregory on the Stone." For the legend in general, see A. D'Ancona's Introduction to the *Leggenda di Vergogna e la Leggenda di Giuda,* Bologna, 1869, and F. Lippold, *Ueber die Quelle des Gregorius Hartmann's von Aue,* Leipzig, 1869, p. 50 *et seq.* See also Pitrè's notes to No. 117. An example of this class of stories from Cyprus may be found in the *Jahrb.* XI. p. 357.

14. See Köhler's notes to Gonz., No. 90, and *Sacre Rappresentazioni del Secoli XIV.–XVI,* raccolte e illustrate di A. D'Ancona, Florence, 1872, III. p. 435. There is another legend of St. James of Galicia in Busk, p. 208, entitled "The Pilgrims." A husband and wife make the usual vow to St. James that if he will give them children they will make the pilgrimage to Santiago. When the children are fifteen and sixteen the parents start on the pilgrimage, taking with them the son and leaving the daughter in charge of a priest, who wrote slanderous letters about her, whereupon the son returned suddenly, slew his sister, and threw her body in a ditch. A king's son happened to pass by, found the body, and discovered that it still contained life. He had her cured, and married her, and they afterwards became king and queen. While the king was once at war, the viceroy tempted the queen, and when she would not listen to him, killed her two children and slandered her to the king. The queen took the bodies of the children and wandered about until she met the Madonna, who took the children, and the queen went to Galicia. The king and viceroy also made a pilgrimage to the same place where the queen's parents had dwelt since the supposed death of their daughter. All met at the saint's shrine and forgave each other, and the Madonna restored the children alive and well.

There are two or three other stories in Pitrè and Gonz. in which saints appear in the *rôle* of good fairies, aiding the hero when in trouble. One of these stories, "The Thankful Dead" (Gonz., No. 74), has already been mentioned in Chapter II. p. 131; two others may be briefly mentioned here. The first is Gonz., No. 74, "Of one who by the help of St. Joseph won the king's daughter." A king proclaims that he will give his daughter to any one who builds a ship that will go by land and water. The youngest of three brothers constructs such a vessel by the help of St. Joseph, after his two brothers have failed. The saint, who is not known to the youth, accompanies him on the voyage on the condition that he shall receive the half of everything that the youth receives. During the voyage they take on board a man who can fill a sack with mist, one who can tear up half a forest and carry the trees on his back, a man who can drink up half a river, one who can always hit what he shoots at, and one who walks with such long steps that when one foot is in Catania the other is in Messina. The king refuses to give his daughter to the youth in spite of the ship that goes by land and water. The youth, however, by the help of his wonderful servants and St. Joseph, fulfils all the king's requirements, and carries away the princess. When the youth returned home with his bride and treasures, St. Joseph called on him to fulfil his promise to him. The youth gives him half of his treasures, and even half of the crown he had won. The saint reminds him that the best of his possessions yet remains undivided,—his bride. The youth determines to keep his promise, draws his sword, and is about to cut his bride in two, when St. Joseph reveals himself, blesses the pair, and disappears.

This story is sometimes found as a version of the "Thankful Dead," see Chapter II. note 12. The second story is Pitrè, No. 116, "St. Michael the Archangel and one of his devotees," of which there is a version in Gonz., No. 76, called, "The Story of Giuseppino." In the first version a child, Pippino, is sold by his parents to the king in order to obtain the means to duly celebrate the feast of St. Michael, to whom they were devoted. The child is brought up in the palace as the princess's playmate; but when he grows up the king is anxious to get rid of him, and so sends him on a voyage in an unseaworthy vessel. St. Michael appears to the lad, and tells him to load the ship with salt. They set sail, and the rotten ship is about to go to pieces, when the saint appears and changes the ship into a vessel all of gold. They sell the cargo to a king who has never tasted salt before, and return to their own country wealthy. The next voyage Pippino, by the saint's advice, takes a cargo of cats, which they sell to the king of a country overrun by mice. Pippino returns and marries the king's daughter. In the version in Gonz., Giuseppino is a king's son, who leaves his home to see the world, and becomes the stable-boy of the king whose daughter he marries. The three cargoes are: salt, cats, and uniforms. On the last voyage, Giuseppino captures a hostile fleet, and makes his prisoners put on the uniforms he has in his ship. With this army he returns, and compels the king to give him his daughter. St. Joseph acts the same part in this version as St. Michael in Pitrè's.

The story of "Whittington and his Cat" will at once occur to the reader. See Pitrè's notes to No. 116, and vol. IV. p. 395, and Köhler to Gonz., No. 76.

15. Köhler has no note on this legend, and I have been unable to find in the list of saints any name of which Onirià or Nerià may be a corruption.

16. The references to this story will best be found in Pauli's *Schimpf und Ernst*, ed. Oesterley, No. 682, and in the same editor's notes to the *Gesta Romanorum*, cap, 80. To these may be added a story by De Trueba in his *Narraciones populares*, p. 65, entitled, "*Las Dudas de San Pedro;*" Luzel, *Légendes Chrétiennes*, I. 282, II. 4; *Fiore di Virtù*, Naples, 1870, p. 68; Etienne de Bourbon, No. 396 (*Anecdotes historiques, légendes et apologues tirés du Receuil inédit d'Etienne de Bourbon,* pub. pour la Société de l'Hist. de France par A. Lecoy de la Marche, Paris, 1877.

Since the above was written, several important contributions to the literature of this story have been made. The first in point of time and importance is a paper by Gaston Paris in the *Comptes Rendus* of the Académie des Inscriptions et Belles Lettres, vol. VIII. pp. 427–449 (reprinted in *La Poésie du Moyen Age*, Leçons et Lectures par Gaston Paris, Paris, 1885). Next may be mentioned "*The Literary History of Parnell's Hermit,*" by W. E. A. Axon, London, 1881 (reprinted from the Seventh Volume of the Third Series of *Memoirs of the Manchester Literary and Philosophical Society, Session* 1879–80). An Icelandic version is in *Islendzk Aeventyri, Isländische Legenden, Novellen und Märchen* herausgegeben von Hugo Gering, Halle, 1884, vol. II. p. 247. The legend is clearly shown by Gaston Paris to be of Jewish origin.

17. There is another version of this story in Gonz., No. 86, "*Von dem frommen Kinde*" ("The Pious Child"), Köhler in his notes cites Grimm's *Children's Legends*, No. 9, and Schneller, No. 1. In this last story a pious child is cruelly treated by his step-mother, and leaves his home to live in a convent. One day he notices in a cor-

ner a neglected crucifix covered with dust and cobwebs. He sees how thin the figure is, and at meal-time brings his food where the crucifix is and begins to feed the image, which opens its mouth and eats with appetite. As the image glows stouter the pious child glows thinner. The Superior learns one day the fact, and tells the child to ask the Lord to invite him and the Superior to his table. The next day both die suddenly after mass.

In a story in Gonz., No. 47, "Of the pious youth who went to Rome," the youth talks to the image on the crucifix in a familiar way, and receives information about questions put to him by various persons. The youth also dies suddenly at the end of the story.

18. Pitrè, No. III. Another Sicilian version is in Gonz., No. 88, "The Story of Spadònia." Spadònia is the son of a king, who every day has bread baked and sent to the souls in purgatory by means of an ass sent for that purpose by the Lord. Spadònia becomes king, and sends one of his servants, Peppe, to see where the ass goes. Peppe crosses a river of clear water, one of milk, and one of blood. Then he sees the thin oxen in a rich pasture, and the reverse; in addition he beholds a forest with small and large trees together, and a handsome youth cutting down now a large tree, now a small one, with a single stroke of a bright axe. Then he passed through a door with the ass, and sees St. Joseph, and St. Peter, and all the saints, and among them God the Father. Farther on Peppe sees many saints, and among them the parents of Spadònia. Finally Peppe comes where the Saviour and his Mother are on a throne. The Lord says to him that Spadònia must marry a maiden named Sècula, and open an inn, in which any one may eat and lodge without cost. The Lord then explains what Peppe has seen. The river of water is the good deeds of men which aid and refresh the poor souls in purgatory; the river of milk is that with which Christ was nourished; and the river of blood that shed for sinners. The thin cattle are the usurers, the fat, the poor who trust in God, the youth felling the trees is Death.

Peppe returns and tells his master all he had seen, and Spadònia wanders forth in search of a maiden called Sècula. He finds at last a poor girl so called, and marries her, and opens an inn as he had been directed. After a time the Lord and his Apostles visit the inn, and the king and his wife wait on them, and treat them with the utmost consideration. The next day after they had departed Spadònia and his wife find out who their guests were, and hasten after them in spite of a heavy storm. When they overtake the Lord they ask pardon for their sins, and eternal happiness for all belonging to them. The Lord grants then request, and tells them to be prepared at Christmas, when he will come for them. They return home, give all their property to the poor, and at Christmas they confess, take communion, and die peacefully near each other, together with Sècula's old parents.

This curious legend has no parallels in Italy out of Sicily. It is, however, found in the rest of Europe, the best parallel being *L'Homme aux dents rouges*, in Bladé, *Agenais*, p. 52. Köhler cites Bladé, *Contes et proverbes pop. rec. en Armagnac*, p. 59, and Asbjørnsen, No. 62 [Dasent, *Tales from the Fjeld*, p. 160, "Friends in Life and Death"]. To these may be added the story in Schneller, p. 215, and the references given by Köhler in his notes to Gonz., No. 88.

19. See Champfleury, *De la littérature populaire en France. Recherches sur les origines et les variations de la légende du bonhomme Misère*, Paris, 1861. It contains a reprint of

the oldest yet known edition of the chap-book, that of 1719. The most valuable references to the legend in general will be found (besides the above work, and Grimm's notes to Nos. 81, 82) in the *Jahrb.* V. pp. 4, 23; VII. 128, 268; and in Pitrè's notes, vol. III. p. 63, and IV, pp. 398, 439. All the Italian versions are mentioned in the text or following notes. To the stories from the various parts of Europe mentioned in the articles above cited, may be added Webster, *Basque Legends,* pp. 195, 199. Since this note was written another Tuscan version has been published by Pitrè; in his *Nov. tosc.* No. 28, who cites in his notes: Ortoli, p, 1, § 1, No. XXII. (Corsica); and two literary versions in Cintio de' Fabritii, Venice, 1726, *Origine de' volgari proverbi,* and Domenico Batacchi in his *Novelle galanti: La Vita e la Morte di Prete Ulivo.*

20. See Pitrè, No. 125.

21. See Busk, p. 178.

22. See Busk, p. 183.

23. *Novelline di Sto. Stefano,* No. XXXII. A version from Monferrato is found in Comparetti, No. 34, entitled, *"La Morte Burlata"* ("Death Mocked"), in which a schoolmaster, who is a magician, tells one of his scholars that he will grant him every day any favor he may ask. The first day the scholar asks that any one who climbs his pear-tree must remain there; the second day he asks that whoever approaches his fireplace to warm himself must stay there; and finally he asks to win always with a pack of cards that he has. When the possessor of these favors has lived a hundred years Death comes for him, but is made to climb the tree, and is forced to grant the owner another hundred years of life. The fireplace procures another respite, and then the man dies and goes to paradise; but the Lord will not admit him, for he had not asked for mercy. Hell will not receive him, for he had been a good man; so he goes to the gate of purgatory and begins playing cards, with souls for stakes, and wins enough to form a regiment. Then he goes to paradise, and the Lord tells him he can enter alone. But he persists in going in with all those who are attached to him; so all the souls enter too.

24. *Novelline di Sto. Stefano,* No. 33. A similar story, told in greater detail, is in Schneller, No. 17, *"Der Stöpselwirth"* ("The Tapster"). A generous host ruins himself by his hospitality, and borrows money of the Devil for seven years, if he cannot repay it his soul is to belong to the lender. The host continues his liberality, and at the end of seven years is poorer than before. The Lord, St. Peter, and St. John come to the tavern and tell the landlord to ask three favors. He asks that whoever climbs his fig-tree may remain there; whoever sits on his sofa must stay there; and finally, whoever puts his hands in a certain chest must keep them there. The Devil first sends his eldest son after the money. The host sends him up the fig-tree, and then gives him a sound beating. Then the Devil sends his second son, whom the landlord invites to sit on his sofa, and gives him a sound thrashing too. Finally the Devil himself comes, and the host tells him to get his money himself out of the chest. The Devil sticks fast, and is set free only on condition of renouncing all claims to the landlord's soul.

The conclusion of the story is like that of "Beppo Pipetta."

There is another story about a bargain with the Devil in the *Novelline di Sto. Stefano,* No. 35, *"Le Donne ne sanno un punto più del diavolo"* ("Women know a point more than the Devil"). A fowler sells his soul to the Devil for twelve years of life and plenty of birds. When the time is nearly up the fowler's wife persuades him to alter his bargain with the Devil a little. The latter is to give up his claim if the former can find a bird unknown to the Devil. The Devil consents, and comes the last day and recognizes easily every bird, until finally the fowler's wife, disguised with tar and feathers, comes out of a case and frightens the fowler and the Devil so that he runs away.

The mysterious bird recalls the one in Grimm, No. 46, "Fitcher's Bird."

25. *Jahrbuch,* VII. 121. The wonderful sack occurs in another Venetian story, Widter-Wolf, No. 14, *"Der Höllenpförtner"* ("The Porter of Hell"). The gifts are: a gun that never misses, a violin that makes every one dance, and a sack into which every one must spring when commanded by the owner. See Köhler's notes to this story, *Jahrb.* VII. 268. A Corsican version is in Ortoli, p. 155. The episode of the Devil beaten in the sack is also found in Comparetti, No. 49, *"Il Ramaio."* A wandering smith gives alms to St. Peter and the Lord, and receives in return a pouch like the above. When the Devil comes to fetch him he wishes him in his sack, and gives him a good pounding. When the smith dies he gets into paradise by throwing his bag inside and wishing himself in it.

There are two other stories in which the Devil gets worsted: they are Gianandrea, No. VI., *"Quattordici"* ("Fourteen"), and *Fiabe Mantovone,* No. 11, *"Pacchione."* In these stories a cunning person is sent to the Devil to bring back a load of gold. The cunning person takes a long pair of tongs, catches the Devil by the nose, loads his horse, and returns in safety.

The first part of the story of *"Quattordici"* is found in the Basque Legend of "Fourteen:" see Webster, p. 195.

26. Another Venetian version is in Widter-Wolf, No. 3, *"Der Gevatter Tod"* ("Godfather Death"). There are also two Sicilian versions: Pitrè, No. 109, *"La Morti e sò figghiozzu"* ("Death and her Godson"); and Gonz., No. 19, *"Gevatter Tod,"* which do not differ materially from the version given in our text. References to European parallels maybe found in Köhler's notes to Widter-Wolf, No. 3, *Jahrb.* VII. p. 19; to Gonz., No. 19, and in Grimm's notes to No. 44.

27. Widter-Wolf, No. 16, *"Der standhafter Büsser"* ("The Constant Penitent"), *Jahrb.* VII. p. 273. For parallels, see Köhler's article, *Die Legende von dem Ritter in der Capelle, Jahrb.* VI. p. 326.

28. Bernoni, *Legg. fant.* p. 3. The translation in text, as well as that of the two following stories, I have taken from *The Cornhill Magazine,* July, 1875, "Venetian Popular Legends," p. 86.

Another story illustrating the same point is found in Pitrè, No. 110, *Li Cumpari di S. Giuvanni,* which is translated as follows by Ralston in *Fraser's Magazine,* April, 1876, "Sicilian Fairy Tales," p. 424.

LXXII. THE GOSSIPS OF ST. JOHN

Once upon a time there lived a husband and wife, and they were both bound in gossipry with a certain man. The husband got arrested, and was taken away to prison. Now the gossip was very fond of his cummer, and used often to go and visit her. One day she said to him: "Gossip, shall we go and see my husband?" *"Gnursi, cummari"* ("Certainly, cummer"), said her gossip; so off they went. On the way they bought a large melon—for it was the melon season—to take to the poor prisoner. We are but flesh and blood! The gossip and his cummer sinned against

St. John. In short, they brought things to a pretty pass. St. John wasn't going to let that pass unpunished. When they had come to the prison and had visited the prisoner, before going away they wanted to make a present to the jailer; so they gave him the melon. He cut it open before their eyes. Horror of horrors! When the melon was cut open, there was found in the middle of it a head! Now this was the head of St. John, which had slipped itself in there for the purpose of bringing home their sin to the minds of the gossips. The matter immediately came to the ears of justice, and they were arrested. They confessed the wrong they had done. The husband was set at liberty, and the gossip and his cummer were sent to the gallows.

In regard to Saint John and the relationship of godfather, see Pitrè's note in vol. I, p. 73.

29. Bernoni, p.7; *Cornhill Magazine,* p. 88.

30. Bernoni, p. 17; *Cornhill Magazine,* p. 89.

31. Bernoni, p. 19. There are prose versions of the closely related story of Don Juan in Busk, p. 202, *"Don Giovanni"* and in *Nov. tosc.* No. 21, "Don Giovanni." There are poetical versions of this legend in G. Ferraro, *Canti popolari raccolti a Pontelagoscuro,* No. 19; *"La Testa di Morto"* in *Rivista di Filologia Romanza,* vol. II. p. 204, Ive, *Canti pop. istriani,* Turin, 1877, cap. xxv. No. 6, "*Lionzo;*" Salomone-Marino, *Leggende pop. sicil.* XXVII. "*Lionziu.*"

32. Pitrè, No. 128, The version in the text is Ralston's condensation, taken from *Fraser's Magazine,* p. 433. As Pitrè notes, there is some slight resemblance between this story and that of "*Cattarinetta*" in Schneller, No. 5, which has a close parallel in Bernoni, *Trad. pop. venez. Punt.* III. p. 76, "*Nono Cocon,*" and one not so close in Papanti, *Nov. pop. livor,* No. 1, "*La Mencherina,*" p. 7. There is a close parallel to the Sicilian story in a Tuscan tale, "*La Gamba*" ("The Leg"), in *Novelline pop. toscane,* pubb. da G. Pitrè, p. 12. In a note Pitrè mentions a variant from Pratovecchio in which the leg is of gold. He also gives copious references to versions from all parts of Europe. The English reader will recall at once Halliwell's story of "Teeny-Tiny " (*Nursery Tales,* p. 25). To the above references may be added: "*Le Pendu*" in Cosquin, *Contes pop. lorrains,* No. 41, in *Romania,* No. 28, p. 580. Since the above note was written, another Tuscan version has been published by Pitrè, *Nov. tosc.* No. 19.

33. Pitrè, No. 203. The parallels to this story may best be found in J. Grimm's *Kleinere Schriften,* III, p. 414, *Der Traum von dem Schatz auf der Brücke.* To Grimm's references may be added: Graesse, *Sagenschatz Sachsen's,* No. 587; Wolf, *Hesseche Sagen,* No. 47; Kuhn, *Westfalische Sagen,* No. 169; and *Vierzig Veziere,* p. 270.

CHAPTER V. *Nursery Tales.*

1. The verse in this story is given somewhat differently by Bolza, *Canzoni pop. Comasche,* Vienna, 1866, Note 9:—

> "La storia de Sior Intento,
> Che dura molto tempo,
> Che mai no se destriga:

Volè che ve la diga?"

The story of Mr. Attentive, which lasts a long time, which is never explained, do you wish me to tell it?

There are in Bernoni, *Punt.* II. pp. 53, 54, two or three other rhymes of this class that may be given here.

ONCE UPON A TIME

Once upon a time—that I remember—into a blind-man's eye—a fly went—and I thought—that it was a quail—wretched blind-man—go away from here!

ONE AND ANOTHER

Fiaba, aba—Questa xe una—Muro e malta—Questa xe un' altra. Story, ory—This is one—Wall and mud—This is another.

> "A long one and a short one,
> Do you wish me to tell you a long one?
> This is the finger and this is the nail.
> Do you wish me to tell you a short one?
> This is the finger and this is the end of it."

2. Pitrè, No. 141. In the notes to this story are given some more of this class.

"Once upon a time there was a page who drew three carts: one of wine, one of bread, and one of relishes. . . . And once upon a time there was a page."

Some poetical versions are given in the same place from various parts of Italy.

> "Once upon a time,
> An old man and an old woman
> Were on top of a mountain . . .
> Be quiet, for I am going to tell you it."
> —Naples.

> "Once upon a time there was a man
> Behind the church
> With a basket on his back . . .
> But be still if I am to tell you it!"
> —Milan, *Nov. fior.* p. 570.

Some more rhymes of this class may be found in Papanti, *Nov. pop. livor,* p. 17; "Once upon a time there was a man, whose name was Boccabella, who skinned his wife to make a skirt, and skinned his children to make some towels."

> "Once upon a time there was a man,
> A woman, and a little bottle . . .
> Listen to this!"

> "Once upon a time there was a king
> Who ate more than you;
> He ate bread and cheese,
> Pull, pull this nose."

Here the speaker pulls the child's nose.

> "Once upon a time there was a rich poor man
> Who had seven daughters to marry;
> On one hand there came a felon,
> And on the other seven blisters."

3. *Rivista di Letteratura popolare,* vol. I. p. 161 (1878). *"Una Variante toscana della Novella del Petit Poucet."* Versions from the Marches, the Abruzzi, and Tuscany may now be found in *Giornale di Filologia romanza,* II. p. 23; Finamore, *Tradizioni popolari abruzzesi,* 1882, No. 47, p. 233; and *Nov. tosc.* No. 42.

4. The myth of "Tom Thumb" has been thoroughly examined in an admirable monograph: *Le Petit Poucet et la Grande Ourse* par Gaston Paris, Paris, 1875. The author says in conclusion (p. 52): "Si nous cherchons enfin quels sont les peuples qui nous offrent soit ce conte, soit cette dénomination, nous voyons qu'ils comprennent essentiellement les peuples slaves (lithuanien, esclavon) el germaniques (allemand, danois, suédois, anglais). Les contes des Albanais, des Roumains et des Grecs modernes sont sans doute empruntés aux Slaves, comme une très-grande partie de la mythologie populaire de ces nations. Le nom wallon et le conte forézien nous montrent en France (ainsi que le *titre* du conte de Perrault) la légende de Poucet: mais elle a pu fort bien, comme tant d'autres récits semblables, y être apportée par les Germains. Ni en Italie, ni en Espagne, ni dans les pays celtiques je n'ai trouvé trace du conte ou du nom." This latter statement must now, of course, be modified. To the references in Paris' book may be added: *Romania,* No. 32, p. 59 (Cosquin, No. 53), and Köhler in *Zeit. f. rom. Phil.* III. p. 617.

The transformation of the chick-peas into children has a parallel in the Greek story of "Pepper-Corn" shortly to be mentioned.

5. The discussion of this point may best be found in the following works; Halliwell's *Nursery Rhymes of England* (*Percy Soc.* IV.), London, 1842, pp. 2, 159; *Romania,* I. p. 218; and *Un Canto popolare piemontese e un Canto religioso popolare israelitico.* Note e confronti di Cesare Foa, Padova, 1879. The references to the other European versions of this story may be found in *Romania,* No. 28, p. 546 (Cosquin, No. 34), and Köhler in *Zeit. f. rom. Phil.* III. 156.

6. Halliwell's *Nursery Rhymes,* p. 160.

7. There is a poetical version of this story in Vigo, *Raccolta amplissima di Canti pop. sicil.* 2da ediz. Catania, 1870–1874, No. 4251, beginning:—

> "Susi, Bittudda
> Va Scupa la casa.
> —Signura, non pozzu
> Mi doli lu cozzu," etc.

The ending, however, is incomplete.

8. Imbriani, *Pomiglianesi*, p. 232, "*Micco.*"

9. The version from Siena is in *Saggio di Letture varie per i Giovani* di T. Gradi, Torino, 1865, p. 175, "*La Novella di Petuzzo;*" the Tuscan (Florence) version is in Imbriani, *Nov. fior.* p. 548, "*Petruzzo.*" Another Tuscan version may be found in Nerucci, *Cincelle da Bambini*, No. 7, and one from Apulia in *Archivio*, III. p. 69.

10. Bernoni, *Punt.* III. p. 72, "*Petin-Petele.*"

11. The first part of this story is found also in a Tuscan version given by Corazzini in his *Componimenti minori*, p. 412, "*Il Cecio*" ("The Chick-pea"). The chick-pea is swallowed by a cock, that is eaten by a pig, that is killed by a calf, that is killed and cooked by an innkeeper's wife for her sick daughter, who recovers, and is given in marriage to the owner of the chick-pea.

The sexton's doubt as to how he shall invest the money he has found is a frequent trait in Italian stories, and is found in several mentioned in this chapter. See notes in Papanti, *Nov. pop. livor.* p. 29. Copious references to this class of stories may be found in the *Romania*, Nos. 24, p. 576, and 28, p. 548; Köhler in *Zeitschrift für rom. Phil.* II. 351; Grimm, No. 80; *Orient und Occident*, II. 123; Bladé, *Agenais*, No. 5; *Mélusine*, 148, 218, 426; and Brueyre, p. 376. See also Halliwell, p. 33, "The Cat and the Mouse."

12. This version is a variant of a story in the same collection, p. 236, which cannot well be translated, as it is mostly in rhyme. There is another version from Montella in the *Principato Ulteriore*, p. 241, "*Lo Haddro e lo Sorece*" ("The Cock and the Mouse"), which has a satirical ending. The beginning is like that of the other versions: the cock and the mouse go to gather pears; one falls and wounds the mouse's head. The mouse goes to the physician, who demands rags, the ragman asks for the tail of the dog. The dog demands bread, the baker wood, the mountain an axe; the iron-monger says: "Go to the *galantuomo* (gentleman, wealthy person), get some money, and I will give you the axe." The mouse goes to the *galantuomo*, who says: "Sit down and write, and then I will give you the money." So the mouse begins to write for the *galantuomo*, but his head swells and he dies. A similar story is found in Corsica, see Ortoli, p. 237.

13. It remains to mention two poetical versions: one in Corazzini, from Verona, *op. cit.* p. 139, which begins:—

> "Cos' è questo?
> La camera del Vesco.
> Cos' è dentro?
> Pan e vin," etc.

"What is this? The bishop's chamber. What is in it? Bread and wine. Where is my share? The cat has eaten it. Where is the cat? The stick has beaten him. Where is the stick? The fire has burned it. Where is the fire? The water has quenched it. Where is the water? The ox has drunk it. Where is the ox? Out in the fields. Who is behind there? My friend Matthew. What has he in his hand? A piece of bread. What has he on his feet? A pair of torn shoes. What has he on his back? A whale. What has he in his belly? A balance. What has he on his head? A cap upside down."

The choice of objects is determined by the rhyme, *e.g.:—*

> "Cosa g'àlo in schena?
> Na balena.
> Cosa g'àlo in panza?

Una balanza."

The second poetical version is from Turin, and is given by Foa, *op. cit.* p. 5. It begins:—

1. "A j'era' na crava
C'a pasturava,
A m' a rout 'l bout
Oh 'l bon vin c'a j'era' nt 'l mè bout
L' è la crava c' a' m l' a rout!

2. "A j'è riva-ie l' luv
L' a mangià, la crava
C' a pasturnava
C' a m' ha rout 'l bout," etc. (*ut supra.*)

The following is a literal prose translation of this curious version.
"There was a goat that was feeding, it has broken my bottle. Oh, the good wine that was in my bottle, it is the goat that has broken it! Then came the wolf that ate the goat that was feeding, that broke my bottle, etc. Then came the dog, that barked at the wolf, that ate the goat, etc. Then came the stick that beat the dog, that barked at the wolf, etc. Then came the fire that burned the stick, that beat the dog, etc. Then came the water that quenched the fire, that burned the stick, etc. Then came the ox, that drank the water, that quenched the fire, etc. Then came the butcher that killed the ox, that drank the water, etc. Then came the hangman that hung the butcher, that killed the ox, etc. Then came death, and carried away the hangman, that hung the butcher, etc. Then came the wind, that carried away death, that carried away the hangman," etc.
A variant of this song reminds one more closely of the prose versions.
"Then came the hangman that hung the butcher, etc. Then came the rat that gnawed the cord, that hung the butcher, etc. Then came the cat that ate the rat, that gnawed the cord, etc. Then came the dog that caught the cat, that ate the rat, that gnawed the cord," etc.
The above Italian version, it will be clearly seen, is only a popular rendition of the Jewish hymn in the *Sepher Haggadah.* Foa, in the work above cited, gives another version from Orio Canarese, and also a number of Italian versions of the "Song of the Kid." His conclusion is the same as that of Gaston Paris in the *Romania,* I. p. 224, that the "Song of the Kid" is not of Jewish origin, but was introduced into the *Haggadah* from the popular song or story.
14. A version of this story is found in Morosi's *Studi sui Dialetti greci,* Lecce, 1870.

LXXXIX. The Goat and the Fox

Once upon a time a goat entered the den of the fox while the latter was absent. At night the fox returned home, and finding the goat fled because frightened by the horns. A wolf passed by, and was also terrified. Then came a hedgehog and entered the den, and pricked the goat with its quills. The goat came out, and the wolf killed it, and the fox ate it.

15. Grimm, No. 30. Another version from the North of Europe is in Asbjørnsen, No. 103 [Dasent, *Tales from the Fjeld*, p. 30, "The Death of Chanticleer"]. Several French versions may be found in the *Romania*, No. 22, p. 244, and *Mélusine*, p. 424. There is a Spanish version in Caballero's *Cuentos*, etc., Leipzig, 1878, p. 3, "*La Hormiguita*" ("The Little Ant"). There is a curious version in Hahn's *Griechische und Albanesische Märchen*, Leipzig, 1864, No. 56, "Pepper-Corn." The story is from Smyrna, and is as follows:—

PEPPER-CORN

Once upon a time there was an old man and an old woman who had no children; and one day the old woman went into the fields and picked a basket of beans. When she had finished, she looked into the basket and said: "I wish all the beans were little children." Scarcely had she uttered these words when a whole crowd of little children sprang out of the basket and danced about her. Such a family seemed too large for the old woman, so she said: "I wish you would all become beans again." Immediately the children climbed back into the basket and became beans again, all except one little boy, whom the old woman took home with her.

He was so small that everybody called him little Pepper-Corn, and so good and charming that everybody loved him.

One day the old woman was cooking her soup and little Pepper-Corn climbed up on the kettle and looked in to see what was cooking, but he slipped and fell into the boiling broth and was scalded to death. The old woman did not notice until meal-time that he was missing, and looked in vain for him everywhere to call him to dinner.

At last they sat down to the table without little Pepper-Corn, and when they poured the soup out of the kettle into the dish the body of little Pepper-Corn floated on top.

Then the old man and the old woman began to mourn and cry: "Dear Pepper-Corn is dead, dear Pepper-Corn is dead."

When the dove heard it she tore out her feathers, and cried: "Dear Pepper-Corn is dead. The old man and the old woman are mourning."

When the apple-tree saw that the dove tore out her feathers it asked her why she did so, and when it learned the reason it shook off all its apples.

In like manner, the well near by poured out all its water, the queen's maid broke her pitcher, the queen broke her arm, and the king threw his crown on the ground so that it broke into a thousand pieces; and when his people asked him what the matter was, he answered: "Dear Pepper-Corn is dead, the old man and the old woman mourn, the dove has torn out her feathers, the apple-tree has shaken off all its apples, the well has poured out all its water, the maid has broken her pitcher, the queen has broken her arm, and I, the king, have lost my crown; dear Pepper-Corn is dead."

See also Benfey, *Pant.* I. p. 191. There is also a version in Morosi, *op. cit.*, given by Imbriani in *Pomiglianesi*, p. 268; and mention is made of one from the Abruzzi in Finamore, *Trad. pop. abruzzesi*, p. 244.

16. In addition to the versions mentioned in the text, Imbriani (*Pomiglianesi*, pp. 250, 252) gives two versions from Lecco.

The following version is found in Morosi, p. 73.

XC. THE ANT AND THE MOUSE

There was once an ant who, while sweeping her house one day, found three *quattrini*, and began to say: "What shall I buy? What shall I buy? Shall I buy meat? No, because meat has bones, and I should choke. Shall I buy fish? No, for fish has bones, and I should be scratched." After she had mentioned many other things, she concluded to buy a red ribbon. She put it on, and sat in the window. An ox passed by and said: "How pretty you are! Do you want me for your husband?" She said: "Sing, so that I may hear your voice." The ox with great pride raised his voice. After the ant had heard it, she said: "No, no, you frighten me."

A dog passed by, and the same happened to him as to the ox. After many animals had passed, a little mouse went by and said: "How pretty you are! Do you want me for your husband?" She said: "Let me hear you sing." The mouse sang, and went *pi, pi, pi!* His voice pleased the ant, and she took him for her husband.

Sunday came, and while the ant was with her friends, the mouse said: "My dear little ant, I am going to see whether the meat that you have put on the fire is done." He went, and when he smelled the odor of the meat, he wanted to take a little, he put in one paw and burned it; he put in the other, and burned that too; he stuck in his nose, and the smoke drew him into the pot, and the poor little mouse was all burned. The ant waited for him to eat. She waited two, she waited three hours, the mouse did not come. When she could wait no longer, she put the dinner on the table. But when she took out the meat, out came the mouse dead. When she saw him the ant began to weep, and all her friends; and the ant remained a widow, because he who is a mouse must be a glutton. If you don't believe it, go to her house and you will see her.

17. Other Italian versions are; Pitrè, No. 136, "*Li Vecchi*" ("The Old Folks"); and *Nov. fior.* p. 567, "The Story of Signor Donato."

18. There are two versions of this story in Pitrè, No. 139, and notes. They differ but little from the one we have translated. An Istrian version is in Ive, *Fiabe pop. rovignesi*, 1878, No. 4, "*I tri fardai*," and a Corsican one in Ortoli, p. 278.

19. Other Italian versions are: Coronedi-Berti, p. 49, "*La Fola d' Zanninein*;" and Bernoni, *Trad. pop.* p. 79, "*Rosseto.*"

20. There is another Italian version in *Fiabe Mantovane*, No. 31, "The Wolf." The only parallel I can find to this story out of Italy is a negro story in *Lippincott's Magazine*, December, 1877, "Folk-Lore of the Southern Negroes," p. 753, "Tiny Pig." Allusion is made to the Anglo-Saxon story of the "Three Blue Pigs," but I have been unable to find it.

21. A Sicilian version is in Pitrè, No. 278, "*L'Acidduzzu*" ("Little Bird"), and one from Tuscany in Nerucci, *Cincelle da Bambini*, No. 12.

22. Köhler, in his notes to this story, gives parallels from various parts of Europe. To these may be added Asbjørnsen and Moe, Nos. 42, 102 [Dasent, *Tales from the Fjeld*, p. 35, "The Greedy Cat"]. Comp. Halliwell, p. 29, "The story of Chicken-licken." A French version is in the *Romania*, No. 32, p. 554 (Cosquin, No. 45), where copious references to this class of stories may be found. Add to these those by Köhler in *Zeitschrift für rom. Phil.* III. p. 617.

CHAPTER VI. *Stories and Jests*

1. A well-known literary version of this story is Sachetti, Nov. IV. Copious references to this popular story will be found in Oesterley's notes to Pauli's *Schimpf und Ernst,* No. 55; see also Pitrè, IV. pp. 392, 437. The entire literature of the subject is summed up in a masterly manner by Professor F. J. Child in *English and Scottish Popular Ballads,* Part II. p. 403.

2. There is a version from Siena in Gradi, *Saggio di Letture varie,* p. 179, "*Teà, Tècla e Teopista;*" and from Rome in Busk, pp. 357, 367. References to other European versions of this story may be found in Grimm, Nos. 34, 104; Schneller, No. 56, "*Die närrischen Weiber;*" Zingerle, *Märchen,* I. No. 14; Dasent's *Tales from the Norse,* p. 191, "Not a Pin to choose between Them " (Asbj. & M., No. 10); Ralston, *R. F. T.* pp. 52–54; *Jahrbuch,* V. 3, Köhler to Cénac Moncaut's *Contes pop. de la Gascogne,* p. 32, "*Maître Jean l'habile Homme;*" *Orient und Occident,* II. p. 319; Köhler to Campbell, No. 20, "The Three Wise Men," p. 686, to No. 48, "Sgire Mo Chealag."

3. This story is sometimes found as one of the episodes of the last tale, as for example in Schneller, No. 56, Imbriani, *Pomiglianesi,* p. 227, cites as parallels: Coronedi-Berti, XII. "*La fola dla Patalocca;*" Beroaldo di Verville, *Le Moyen de Parvenir,* LXXVIII.; and a story in *La Civiltà italiana,* 1865, No. 13. See also *Romania,* VI. p. 551 (E. Cosquin, *Contes pop. lorrains,* No. 22), and *Jahrb.* VIII. 267, Köhler to the above cited story in the *Civiltà ital.* from Calabria. It is also the story of "The Miser and his Wife" in Halliwell, p. 31.

4. There is a literary version in Straparola, VIII. 1., Other literary versions are cited in Pitrè, IV. p. 443.

5. Pitrè, No. 257, where references to other Italian versions may be found. See also Pitrè, IV. pp. 412 and 447; and Köhler's notes to Bladé, *Contes pop. recueillis en Agenais,* p. 155, for other European versions. Additional references may be found in Oesterley's notes to Pauli's *Schimpf und Ernst,* No. 595. A similar story is in Pitrè's *Nov. tosc.* No. 67.

6. Pitrè, No. 180. A literary version is in Straparola, VIII. 6. For other references see Schmidt, Straparola, p. 329; and Oesterley's notes to Pauli's *Schimpf und Ernst,* No. 357.

7. This story is found in Gonz., No. 75, "*Von Firrazzanu*" and is (with the queen's attempt to punish him for it) the only joke in that collection relating to Firrazzanu. A literary version is in Bandello, *Novelle,* IV. 27.

8. See Pitrè, No. 156, var. 5 (III. p. 181).

9. Imbriani in his notes to Pitrè (IV. p. 417) gives a French version of this joke entitled: *Un Neveu pratique.*

10. The name Giufà is retained in many localities with slight phonetic changes. Thus it is Giucà in Trapani; Giuxà in the Albanian colonies in Sicily; in Acri, Giuvali, and in Tuscany, Rome, and the Marches, Giucca. Pitrè, III. p. 371, adds that the name Giufà is the same as that of an Arab tribe. The best known continental counterparts of Giufà are Bertoldino and Cacasenno (see Olindo Guerrini, *La Vita e le Opere di Giulio Cesare Croce,* Bologna, 1879, pp. 257–279). Tuscan versions of the stories of Giufà given in the text may be found in *Nov. tosc.* pp. 179–193.

11. The same story is told by Miss Busk, "The Booby," p. 371, and is in the *Pent.* I. 4. It is probably founded on the well-known fable of Æsop, "*Homo fractor simu-*

lacrì" (ed. Furia, No. 21), which seems very widely spread. A Russian version, from Afanasieff, is in De Gub., *Zoöl. Myth.* I. p. 176. See also Benfey, *Pant.* I. p. 478; and Köhler to Gonz., No. 37.

12. In Gonz., No. 37, Giufà takes the cloth, and on his way to the dyer's sits down to rest on a heap of stones in a field. A lizard creeps out from the stones, and Giufà, taking it for the dyer, leaves the cloth on the stones and returns home. His mother, of course, sends him immediately back for the cloth, but it has disappeared, as well as the lizard. Giufà cries: "Dyer, if you don't give me back my cloth I will tear down your house." Then he begins to pull down the heap of stones, and finds a pot of money which had been hidden there. He takes it home to his mother, who gives him his supper and sends him to bed, and then buries the money under the stairs. Then she fills her apron with figs and raisins, climbs upon the roof, and throws figs and raisins down the chimney into Giufà's mouth as he lies in his bed. Giufà is well pleased with this, and eats his fill. The next morning he tells his mother that the Christ child has thrown him figs and raisins from heaven the night before. Giufà cannot keep the pot of money a secret, but tells every one about it, and finally is accused before the judge. The officers of justice go to Giufà's mother and say: "Your son has everywhere told that you have kept a pot of money which he found. Do you not know that money that is found must be delivered up to the court?" The mother protests that she knows nothing about the money, and that Giufà is always telling stupid stories. "But mother," said Giufà, "Don't you remember when I brought you home the pot, and in the night the Christ child rained figs and raisins from heaven into my mouth?" "There, you see how stupid he is," says the mother, "and that he does not know what he says." The officers of justice go away thinking, "Giufà is too stupid!"

Köhler, in his Notes to Gonz., No. 37, cites as parallels to the above, *Pent.* I. 4, and *Thousand and One Nights*, Breslau trans. XI. 144. For the rain of figs and raisins he refers to *Jahrb*, VIII. 266 and 268; and to Campbell, II. 385, for a shower of milk porridge. See Note 16 of this chapter, and *Indian Fairy Tales*, p. 257.

13. See Max Muller's *Chips*, II. p. 229, and Benfey, *Pant.* I, p. 293.

14. See Imbriani, *Nov. fior.* p. 545; Papanti, *Nov. pop. livor.* No. 3; and Bernoni, *Punt.* III. p. 83.

15. See Robert, *Fables inédites*, II. p. 136. The Italian literary versions are: Morlini, XXI., Straparola, XIII. 4; and two stories mentioned by Imbriani in his *Nov. fior.* pp. 545, 546.

16. This episode is in Strap. XIII. 4; Pitrè, IV. p. 291, gives a version from the Albanian colony of Piana de' Greci, sixteen miles from Palermo. In the same vol., p. 444, he gives a variant from Erice in which, after Giufà has killed the "*Canta-la-notti*," his mother climbs a fig-tree and rains down figs into the mouth of Giufà, who is standing under. In this way she saves herself from the accusation of having thrown a murdered man into the well. See Note 12. For another Sicilian version of this episode see Gonz., No. 37 (I. p. 252).

17. Papanti, p. 65. Copious references will be found in Papanti, pp. 72–81; Oesterley to Pauli, *Schimpf und Ernst*, No. 416; and Kirchof, *Wendumnuth*, I. 122; and Köhler's notes to Sercambi's Novels in *Jahrb*. XII. p. 351.

18. Köhler, in his notes to Gonz., No. 37 (II. p. 228), cites for this story; *Thousand and One Days*, V. 119; *Pent.* I. 4; Grimm, II. 382; Morlini, No. 49; Zingerle, I. 255;

Bebelius, *Facetiæ*, I. 21; Bladé, *Contes et Proverbes*, Paris, 1867, p. 21; and Bertoldino (Florence, Salani),p. 31, "*Bertoldino entra nella cesta dell' oca a covare in cambio di lei.*" In the story in the *Fiabe Mant.* No. 44, "*Il Pazzo*" ("The Fool"), the booby kills his own mother by feeding her too much macaroni when she is ill.

19. See Pitrè, No. 190, var. 9; *Jahrb.* V. 18; Simrock, *Deutsche Märchen*, No. 18 (*Orient und Occident*, III. p, 373); Hahn, No. 34; *Jahrb.* VIII. 267; *Mélusine*, p. 89; *Nov. fior.* p. 601; *Romania*, VI. p. 551, Busk, pp. 369, 374; and *Fiabe Mant*, No. 44.

In the Sicilian stories Giufà simply takes the door off its hinges and carries it to his mother, who is in church. In the other Italian versions the booby takes the door with him, and at night carries it up into a tree. Robbers come and make a division of their booty under the tree, and the booby lets the door fall, frightens them away, and takes their money himself.

20. See Köhler's notes to Gonz., II, p. 228. To these may be added, for the story of Giufà, planting the ears and tails of the swine in the marsh: Ortoli, p. 208; *Mélusine*, p. 474; and *Romania*, VII. p. 556, where copious references to parallels from all of Europe may be found. In the story in Ortoli, cited above, the priest's mother is killed, as in text.

21. For the literal throwing of eyes, see: *Jahrb*, V. p. 19; Grimm, No. 32 (I. p. 382); *Nov. fior.* p. 595; Webster, *Basque Legends*, p. 69; *Orient und Occident*, II. 684 (Köhler to Campbell, No. 45).

22. See Gonz., Nos. 70, 71, and Köhler's notes, II. p. 247. Other Italian versions are: De Gub., *Sto. Stefano*, No. 30; Widter-Wolf, No. 18, and Köhler's notes (*Jahrb.* VII. 282); Strap., I. 3: *Nov.fior.* p. 604; *Fiabe Mant.* No. 13. To these may be added: *Romania*, V. p. 357; VI. p. 539; and VIII. p. 570.

23. See Pitrè's notes, IV. pp. 124, 412; and F. Liebrecht in the *Academy*, vol. IV. p. 421.

24. See Pitrè's notes, IV. pp. 140, 448; Wright's *Latin Stories*, pp. 49, 226.

25. Pitrè, No. 290. See Papanti, *op. cit.* p. 197, where other versions are cited. To these may be added the story in Marcolf, see Guerrini, *Vita di G. C. Croce*, p. 215; and *Marcolphus, Hoc est Disputationis*, etc., in *Epistolæ obscuror, vivorum*, Frankf. a. M., 1643, p. 593.

There is another story in Pitrè (No. 200) which is also attributed to Dante. It is called:—

CVI. Peter Fullone and the Egg

Once upon a time Peter Fullone, the stone-cutter, was working at the cemetery, near the church of Santo Spirito; a man passed by and said: "Peter, what is the best mouthful?" Fullone answered: "An egg;" and stopped.

A year later Fullone was working in the same place, sitting on the ground and breaking stones. The man who had questioned him the year before passed by again and said: "Peter, with what?" meaning: what is good to eat with an egg. "With salt," answered Peter Fullone. He had such a wise head that after a year he remembered a thing that a passer-by had said.

The cemetery alluded to, Pitrè says, is beyond the gate of St. Agatha, near the ancient church of Sto. Spirito, where the Sicilian Vespers began. An interesting article on Peter Fullone maybe found in Pitrè, *Studi di Poesia popolare,* p. 109, "*Pietro Fullone e le Sfide popolari siciliane.*"

The sight-seer in Florence has noticed, on the east side of the square in which the cathedral stands, a block of stone built into the wall of a house, and bearing the inscription, "*Sasso di Dante.*" The guide-books inform the traveller that this is the stone on which the great poet was wont to sit on summer evenings. Tradition says that an unknown person once accosted Dante seated in his favorite place, and asked: "What is the best mouthful?" Dante answered: "An egg." A year after, the same man, whom Dante had not seen meanwhile, approached and asked: "With what?" Dante immediately replied: "With salt."

A poet, Carlo Gabrielli, put this incident into rhyme, and drew from it the following moral (*senso*):—

> "L' acuto ingegno grande apporta gloria;
> Maggior, se v'è congiunta alta memoria."

See Papanti, *op. cit.* pp. 183, 205.

26. This story is told in almost the same words in Pitrè, No. 297, "The Peasant and the King." There are several Italian literary versions, the best known being in the *Cento nov. ant.* ed. Borghini, Nov. VI.: see D'Ancona's notes to this novel in the *Romania,* III. p. 185, "*Le Fonti del Novellino.*" It is also found in the *Gesta Romanorum,* cap. 57, see notes in Oesterley's edition; and in Simrock's *Deutsche Märchen,* No. 8, see Liebrecht's notes in *Orient und Occident,* III. p. 372. To the above may, finally, be added Köhler's notes to Gonz., No. 50 (II. p. 234).

27. Comparetti, No. 43, "*La Ragazza astuta*" (Barga). The first part of the story, dividing the fowl, and sending the presents, which are partly eaten on the way, is found in Gonz., No. I, "*Die Kluge Bauerntochter*" ("The Peasant's Clever Daughter"). See Köhler's notes to Gonz., No. I (II. 205); and to Nasr-eddin's *Schwänke* in *Orient und Occident,* I. p. 444. Grimm, No. 94, "The Peasant's Wise Daughter," contains all the episodes of the Italian story except the division of the fowl. An Italian version in the *Fiabe Mant.* No. 36, "*La giovane accorta,*" contains the episode of the mortar. The king sends word to the clever daughter that she must procure for him some *ahimè* (sneeze) salad. She sent him some ordinary salad with some garlic sprinkled over it, and when he touched it he sneezed (and formed the sound represented by the word *ahimè*). The rest of the story contains the episode lacking in the other popular Italian versions, but found in Grimm, and technically known as "*halb geritten.*" For this episode see *Gesta Romanorum,* ed. Oesterley, cap. 124, and Pauli, 423.

Another Italian version from Bergamo may be found in Corazzini, p. 482, "*La Storia del Pestu d' or*" ("The Story of the Gold Pestle"), which is like the version in the text from the episode of the mortar on. In the story from Bergamo it is a gold pestle, and not a mortar, that is found, and the story of "*halb geritten*" is retained. The episode of the foal is changed into a sharp answer made (at the queen's suggestion) by the king's herdsman to his master, who had failed to pay him for his services. A version from Montale, Nerucci, p. 18, "*Il Mortajo d' oro*" ("The Golden Mortar"), contains all the episodes of the story in the text (including "*halb geritten*") except the division of the fowl. The first part of the story is found in a tale from Cyprus, in the *Jahrb.* XI. p. 360.

A parallel to the story in our text may also be found in Ralston's *R. F. T.* p. 30. The literature of the story of "The Clever Girl" may be found in Child's *English and Scottish Popular Ballads*, Part I. p. 6, "The Elfin Knight."

28. *Fiabe Mantovane*, No. 41, "*Gàmbara*" The Italian for crab is *gambero*. There is a Tuscan story (*Nov. pop. tosc.* p. 8), "*Il Medico grillo*" ("Doctor Cricket"), with reference perhaps to the other meaning of *grillo*, whim, fancy, which reminds one of the story in the text. The pretended doctor cures a king's daughter by making her laugh so hard that she dislodges a fish-bone that had stuck in her throat. Doctor Cricket becomes so popular that the other doctors starve, and finally ask the king to kill him. The king refuses, but sets him a difficult task to do, namely, to cure all the patients in the hospital; failing to accomplish this, he is to be killed or dismissed. Doctor Cricket has a huge cauldron of water heated, and then goes into the wards and tells the patients that when the water is hot they are all to be put into it, but if any one wishes to depart he can go away then. Of course they all run away in haste, and when the king comes the hospital is empty. The doctor is then richly rewarded, and returns to his home.

For parallels to our story see Pitrè's notes, vol. IV. p. 442, and to the Tuscan story above-mentioned.

Another Tuscan version has recently been published in *Nov. tosc.* No. 60. See also Grimm, No. 98; Asbjørnsen, *Ny Sam.* No. 82 [Dasent, *Tales from the Fjeld*, p. 139, "The Charcoal Burner"]; Caballero, *Cuentos*, p. 68; *Orient und Occident*, I. 374, and Benfey, *Pant*, I. 374. There is a story in Straparola (XIII. 6) that recalls the story in our text. A mother sends her stupid son to find "good day" (*il boun dè*). The youth stretched himself in the road near the city gate where he could observe all those who entered or left the town. Now it happened that three citizens had gone out into the fields to take possession of a treasure that they had discovered. On their return they greeted the youth in the road with "Good day." The youth said, when the first one saluted him: "I have one of them," meaning one of the good days, and so on with the other two. The citizens who had found the treasure, believing that they were discovered, and that the youth would inform the magistrates of the find, shared the treasure with him.

~

LIST OF WORKS
MOST FREQUENTLY
REFERRED TO IN THE NOTES

(For works relating directly to Italian Popular Tales, see Bibliography.)

Asbjørnsen: Norske Folke-Eventyr fortalte af P. Chr. Asbjørnsen. Ny Samling. Christiania, 1871. 8°. [English version in Tales from the Fjeld. A second series of Popular Tales from the Norse of P. Chr. Asbjörnsen. By G. W. Dasent, London, 1874.]

Asbjørnsen and Moe: Norse Folke-Eventyr fortalte af P. Chr. Asbjørnsen og Jørgen Moe. 5ᵗᵉ Udgave. Christiania, 1874. 8°. [Partly translated by G. W. Dasent in Popular Tales from the Norse. 2d ed. Edinburgh, 1859. New York, 1859.]

Basque Legends: collected, chiefly in the Labourd, by the Rev. Wentworth Webster. London, 2d ed. 1879. 8°.

Benfey, Pantschatantra: Fünf Bücher indischer Fabeln, Märchen und Erzählungen. Aus dem Sanskrit übersetzt mit Einleitung und Anmerkungen von Theodor Benfey. Erster Theil, Einleitung. Leipzig, 1859. 8°.

Bladé: Contes populaires recueillis en Agenais par M. Jean-François Bladé suivis de notes comparatives par M. Reinhold Köhler, Paris, 1874. 8°.

Brueyre: Contes populaires de la Grande-Bretagne par Loys Brueyre. Paris, 1875. 8°.

Cosquin, Emmanuel: Contes populaires lorrains recueillis dans un village du Barrois, à Montiers-sur-Baulx (Meuse), *Romania,* V. 83, 133; VI. 212, 529; VII. 527; VIII. 545; IX. 377; X. 117, 543.

Cox: The Mythology of the Aryan Nations. By G. W. Cox. 2 vols. London, 1870. 8°.

Dunlop-Liebrecht: Geschichte der Prosadichtung. Aus dem englischen von F. Liebrecht. Berlin, 1851. 8°.

Folk-Lore Record, London, 1879–1882. 5 vols. 8°.

Gesammtabenteuer. Von F. H. von der Hagen. 3 vols. Stuttgart and Tübingen, 1850. 8°.

Gesta Romanorum von Herm. Oesterley. Berlin, 1872. 8°.

Graesse, J. G. T.: Die grossen Sagenkreise des Mittelalters. Dresden und Leipzig, 1842. 8°.

Grimm, The Brothers: Grimm's Household Tales. With the Author's Notes translated from the German and edited by M. Hunt. With an Introduction by A. Lang, M. A. In two volumes. London: G. Bell & Sons. 1884. (Bohn's Standard Library.) [This excellent version contains all the stories and notes of the third edition of the original text, Göttingen, 1856, the third volume of which, containing the notes, is rather scarce. The numbers of the stories correspond in the German and English editions, and the latter will be cited for the convenience of the reader.]

Grundtwig: Danske Folkeminder, Viser, Sagn og Eventyr. Udgivne af Svend Grundtwig. Kjøbenhavn, 1861. 1ste –3^{die} Samling. 8°.

Hahn: Griechische und Albanesische Märchen. Gesammelt, übersetzt und erläutert von J. G. von Hahn. Leipzig, 1864. 2 vols. 8°.

Halliwell, J. O.: Popular Rhymes and Nursery Tales. London, 1849. 12°.

Kreutzwald: Ehstnische Märchen. Aufgezeichnet von Friedrich Kreutzwald. Halle, 1869. 8°.

Luzel: Contes bretons recueillis et traduits par F. M. Luzel. Quimperlé, 1870. 8°.

Mélusine: Revue de Mythologie, Litt. pop., Traditions et usages, dirigée par MM. H. Gaidoz et E. Rolland. Paris, 1877, 1884. 4°.

Nisard, Ch.: Histoire des Livres populaires. Paris, 1854. 2 vols. 8°.

Novelle Ant. Biagi. Le Novelle Antiche dei codici Panciatichiano-Palatino 138 e Laurenziano-Gaddiano 193, con una introduzione etc per Guido Biagi. Florence, 1880. 8°.

Novelle Ant. Borg: Le Cento Novelle Antiche secondo l'edizione del MDXXV. corrette ed illustrate con note. Milano, 1825. 8°.

Novelle Ant. Gualt.: Cento Novelle Antiche. Libro di Novelle e di Bel parlar gentile (Gualteruzzi da Fano). Florence (Naples), 1727. 8°.

Novelle Ant. Papanti. *Romania,* vol. III. p. 189.

Old Deccan Days, or Hindoo Fairy Legends. Collected by M. Frere. Philadelphia: Lippincott & Co. 1868.

Orient und Occident insbes. in ihren gegenwärtigen Beziehungen. Forschungen und Mittheilungen. Eine Vierteljahrschrift herausgegeben von Theodor Benfey. Vols I.–III. Gottingen, 1860–1864. 8°.

Ralston: Russian Folk-Tales. By W. R. S. Ralston. London, 1873. 8°. [There is an American reprint, without date.]

Robert: Fables inédites des XIIe, XIIIe, XIVe Siècles et Fables de La Fontaine. Par A. C. M. Robert. 2 vols. Paris, 1825. 8°.

Romania: Recueil Trimestriel consacré à l'étude des langues et des litteratures romanes. Publié par P. Meyer et G. Paris. Paris, 1872, still in course of publication.

Rondallayre, lo: Quentos populars catalans coleccionats per F. Maspons y Labros. Barcelona, 1871. 18°.

Schiefner, F. Anton von: Tibetan Tales, done into English from the German, with an Introduction by W. R. S. Ralston, M. A. London, 1882 (Trübner's Oriental Series).

Stokes, Maive: Indian Fairy Tales. With notes by Mary Stokes, and an Introduction by W. R. S. Ralston, M. A. London, 1880.

Sacre Rappresentazioni dei Secoli XIV., XV., XVI. Raccolte e illustrate per cura di Alessandro D'Ancona. Florence, 1872. 3 vols. 16°.

Schimpf und Ernst: J. Pauli. Herausgegeben von Herm. Oesterley. Bibliothek des Litt. Vereins in Stuttgart. Bd. LXXXV. Stuttgart, 1866. 8°.

Tausend und Eine Nacht. Arabische Erzählungen. Deutsch von M. Habicht, von der Hagen und C. Schall. Breslau, 1836. 15 vols. 8°.

Wendunmuth: Hans Wilhelm Kirchhof, Wendunmuth. Herausgegeben von Herm. Oesterley. Bibliothek des Litt. Vereins in Stuttgart. Bd. XCV.–XCIX. 5 vols. 8°. Tübingen, 1869.

INDEX

Abbatutis, Gian Alesio
  (Giambattista Basile), LI
Academic career, Crane's, XI–XII
Admonitions, The Three (story), 125
Andromeda, or Princess Freed from
  Dragon, 270
Angiola, The Fair (story), 22
Animal
  brothers-in-law, 49
  children, 261
Animals, dispute of, settled by hero,
  26
The Ant and the Mouse (story), 304
Apple
  as magic token, 30
  unequally divided, indicates true
  friend, 164
Arnim, Achim von, XV
The Ass
  that Lays Money (story), 100
  (story), 153

The Baker's Apprentice (story), 170
The Barber, Story of, 194
Basile, Giambattista, LI
Bastianelo (story), 224
Beauty and the Beast, 8
Beppo Pipetta (story), 179
Bernoni, Giuseppe, XVIII
Bierde (story), 55
Bird
  magic, bestowing gifts, 35

transformation into, 4, 12
Blood of children restores uncle to
  life, 70
Bluebeard, 62
Bone
  of hero as musical instrument
    discovering murderers, 34
  human, to be eaten, 66
Bonhomme Misère, 173, 178, 295
Boots, magic, faster than wind, 115
Bottles, seven, filled with tears, 260
Brentano, Clemens, XV
Bride
  the Forgotten, 47, 57
  the True, 47, 58, 83
Brother Giovannone (story), 175
Brothers
  three, born from mother eating
    magic fish, 25
  The Three (story), 212
Buchettino (story), 213
The Bucket (story), 81
Buddha, parable of, 236
Busk, Rachel Harriet, XVIII
Buttadeu, Story of, 159

Calvino, Italo, IX
Capon divided in peculiar manner,
  250
The Cat and the Mouse (story), 207
Catherine and Her Fate, Story of,
  85

Cento Novelle Antiche, 123, 151

Chess, winning at, disposes of princess's hand, 99

Chick-Pea, Little (story), 195

Children

  apple-peel, 277

  born from chick-peas, 196

  born from fish, 25, 270

  promised to witches, 22

  promised to Devil, 110

Christmas (story), 227

Cinderella

  slipper, lost by, 37

  (story), 35

The Cistern (story), 30

The Clever Girl (story), 250

The Clever Peasant (story), 249

Cloak that makes wearer invisible, 99

The Cloud (story), 25

The Cobbler (story), 75

The Cock

  and the Mouse (story), 203

  (story), 218

  That Wished to Become Pope (story), 219

Comparetti, Domenico, XVIII–XIX

Constantine's leprosy healed by St. Silvester, 162

The Cook (story), 221

Cornell, A. B., XI

Cornell, Ezra, XI

Cornell University, XI–XIII

Crab (story), 253

Crivòliu, Story of, 160

Cross protects child against Devil, 111

Crown, as magic token, 30

The Crumb in the Beard (story), 89

The Crystal Casket (story), 263

Çukasaptati, Oriental collection of tales, 134, 290

Cupid and Psyche, 3, 62

The Curse of the Seven Children (story), 44

Cymbal, prince concealed in, 52

Danaë, 270

Dante, 248, 308

Daughters, two, good and bad, 81

De Gubernatis, Angelo, XVII, LII

Der Kaiser und der Abt, Bürger's poem of, 221

The Devil, Married Three Sisters, How (story), 63

Dialects and vernacular, XIX–XX, LI, LII

Disciplina Clericalis of Petrus Alphonsi, 123, 125, 284, 286

The Doctor's Apprentice (story), 230

Dog's face, by witch's imprecation, 24

Dogs substituted for queen's children, 17

Doll

  king's son in love with, 94, 144

  that moves, sews, and dresses itself, 93

Don Firriulieddu (story), 194

Don Joseph Pear (story), 102

Don Juan, 189

Don Quixote, 124

Doves

  indicate future Pope, 161

  recall forgotten bride, 61

Eagle carries hero up from cave, 33

Eat, My Clothes! (story), 238

Education, Crane's, X–XI

Egg that kills fairy, 27

Ethnography, XXI

The Exempla of Jacques Vitry (Crane), XIII

Eyes, diseased, cured by feather of
griffin, 33

Fables, LIV
Fables of Oriental origin, 120, 284
Fabliaux, French, 119, 284
Fair Brow (story), 106
Fairies' gifts, 17, 80, 81, 83
Fairy tales, XV, L–LI, LII
Family history, Crane's, IX–X
Fate personified, 85
A Feast Day (story), 210
Fiabe Italiane (Calvino), IX
Figs producing horns, 98
Fiorita, The Fair (story), 49
Firrazzanu, stories of, 232, 233
Firrazzanu's Wife and the Queen
(story), 231
Flesh of hero given to eagle, 33
Flight of lovers and pursuit by
witch, 24, 60, 270
The Fool (story), 243
Forbidden chamber, 63, 64
Fountain of wine and oil, 58
Fox, as Puss in Boots, 102
French tales, XV

The Gentleman Who Kicked a
Skull (story), 189
German folklore, XV–XVII, XLIX,
LIII–LIV
Gesta Romanorum, 147
Giant
outwitted by men, 71, 76, 77
with no heart in his body, 270,
286
Giufà
and the Judge (story), 235
and the Plaster Statue (story), 234
Giufà's Exploits (story), 239
Goat
and the Fox (story), 302
the Iron (story), 206

A Godfather and a Godmother of
St. John Who Made Love,
Story of, 184
Godfather Misery (story), 177
Godmother Fox (story), 204
Gold, magician's body turned to,
269
Gonzenbach, Laura, XVII, LII
Goslings, Three (story), 215
Gossips of St. John (story), 297
Gozzi, Lippi, Lorenzo, LI
Gradi, Temistocle, LII
Grimm, Brothers, xx, XV–XVI, XLIX
Gregory on the Stone, 160, 293
Griffin (story), 33
Grimm's Tales cited in text
Allerleirauh, 35
Brother Lustig, 173
Clever Alice, 224
Clever People, 224
Doctor Knowall, 252
Faithful John, 68
Feather Bird [Fitcher's Bird],
62
Golden Goose, 210
Goose-Girl, 47
Handless Maiden, 22
King Thrush-Beard, 89
Little Mouse, Little Bird, and the
Sausage, 209
Master Thief, 173
Robber Bridegroom, 62
Spider and the Flea, 206
White and the Black Bride, 47
Woodcutter's Child [Our Lady's
Child], 62
Groomsman, story of the, 186
Guild, Edward Curtis, XI

Hair, tresses used as ladder, 5, 23, 59,
67
Hands, clasped, prevent child's
birth, 7

Hartwig, Otto, XVII
Heart of saint eaten by maiden
  produces child, 168
Herder, Johann Gottfried, XV
Hermit as adviser, 7, 13, 18
Horn that blows out soldiers, 99
House that Jack built, 199
Hump
  added to humpback, 85
  removed by fairies, 84
Humpbacks, The Two (story), 83

Imbriani, Vittorio, XVIII, LIII
In This World One Weeps and
  Another Laughs (story), 153
Ingrates (story), 120
Italian folklore, history of, XVI–XVII
*Italian Social Customs of the Sixteenth
  Century, and Their Influence on
  the Literatures of Europe*
  (Crane), XIV

Joseph and his Brethren, 170
Journal of American Folklore, IX, XII,
  XXI
Journey of Our Saviour on Earth,
  152
Judas, Story of, 157
Just Man (story), 182

King Bean (story), 11
King, The Crystal (story), 7
King John and the Abbot of
  Canterbury, Percy's poem of, 221
King Lear, 268
The King of Love (story), 3
The King Who Wanted a Beautiful
  Wife (story), 79
Kiss of mother makes hero forget
  bride, 58, 60, 277
Köhler, Reinhold, XVII

Lafontaine, fables of, cited, 119, 237

Language of Animals (story), 129
Language studies, Crane's, XII
Laughing, cure by, 96, 279
Leprosy healed by human blood,
  167
Life-giving ointment or leaves, 262
Lionbruno (story), 109
Lippi, Lorenzo, LI
Long May (story), 228
The Lord, St. Peter, and the
  Apostles (story), 150
The Lord, St. Peter, and the Black-
  smith (story), 151
The Lord's Will (legend), 154
The Love of the Three Oranges
  (story), 272

Magic tokens, 30
Malchus at the Column (story),
  58
Malchus, Desperate (story), 158
The Man, the Serpent, and the Fox
  (story), 285
Maria Wood, Fair (story), 39
The Mason and His Son (story),
  130
Massariol, domestic spirit of the
  Venetians, 190
"Medieval Sermon-Books and
  Stories" (Crane), XIII
"Medieval Story-Books" (Crane),
  XIII–XIV
Medusa, 270
Melusina, 3
Mother-in-law
  ill-treats son's wife, 45
  killed by boiling oil, 46
Mr. Attentive (story), 193

Nala (story), in Italian popular tales,
  290
The Nation, XII, XXII
Neapolitan dialect, LI, LII

Nero, 248
Nerucci, Gherardo, XIX
"New Analogues of Old Tales"
 (Crane), XIII

Occasion (story), 173
Old Deccan Days, stories from,
 cited, 68
Omelet, The Little (story), 236
Oral traditions, XIII–XV, XIX,
 XLIX–L
Oraggio and Bianchinetta (story),
 47
Oriental elements in Italian popular
 tales, 119, 283
Oriental source of Italian tales, L,
 XXII
Orlanda, The Fairy (story), 93

Pandora's box, 6
Pantschatantra, Italian versions of,
 283
Parish Priest of San Marcuola
 (story), 188
Parnell's Hermit, 169, 294
The Parrot (story)
 first version, 134
 second version, 135
 third version. *See* The Parrot
  Which Tells Three Stories
  (story)
The Parrot Which Tells Three
 Stories (story), 138
 First Story of the Parrot, 140
 Second Story of the Parrot, 142
 Third Story of the Parrot, 144
The Peasant and the Master (story),
 119
Penance, Knight's, 183
Pepper-Corn (story), 303
Persecution of innocent wife, 263
Peter Fullone and the Egg (story),
 307

Physician
 princess disguised as, 136
 wife disguised as, 14
Pier delle Vigne, 127
Pig, little, that would not go over
 the stile, 199
Pilate (story), 156
Pitidda (story), 200
Pitrè, Giuseppe, XIV, XVIII, XX–XXI,
 LIII
Pomegranate, as magic token, 30
Popular literature, XI, LI
Pot that cooks without any fire,
 245
Proverbial sayings, 248
Purse always full of money, 17, 97,
 115
Puss in Boots (story), 280

Rabbit that carries things, 244
Rain of figs and raisins, 306
Rampsinitus, treasure house of, 130
Riddle
 bride won by solving, 53
 in general, 277
 proposed by suitor, 55
Ring
 as means of recognition, 42
 turns red and stops steamer at
  owner's forgetfulness, 93
 that causes sneezing, 96
Rose that discovers concealed
 princess, 52
Ruby, magic, does all that owner
 asks, 112

Saddaedda (story), 191
St. James of Galicia, Story of, 163
St. Onirià or Nerià, 168
St. Peter and His Sisters (story), 155
St. Peter and the Robbers, 149
St. Peter, stories about mother of,
 155

Sanctuary, privilege of, 32

Scissors They Were (story), 229

Sepher Haggadah, Jewish hymn in, 302

The Seven Wise Masters, 127, 128, 129, 133
in general, 289
Italian versions of, 283
Magyar version, 290

The Sexton's Nose (story), 201

The Shepherd (story), 125

The Shepherd's Daughter Who Made the King's Daughter Laugh (story), 196

Shoes, worn out in search
of husband, 7, 260
of wife, 114

Sicilian folklore, XVII–XVIII, LII, LIV–LVI

Sick prince and secret remedy, 262

Silence of princess disenchants brothers, 44

Sir Fiorante, Magician (story), 259

Sisters' envy, 8, 15

Sisters, Two (story), 47, 272

Skein of silk outweighs king's treasures, 88

Sleep, magic, 66

Slipper, lost by Cinderella, 37

Snake, youngest daughter marries, 259

Snow-White-Fire-Red (story), 58

Star on daughter's brow, 16, 82

Statue
In Love with a (story), 69
transformation into, 20, 29, 69

The Stepmother
persecutes daughter-in-law, 263, 267
(story), 267

Stick, magic, beats thief, 101

Straparola, Giovan Francesco, L–LI

Sultan's daughter, 106

Swan-maidens, 62

Sympathetic objects
fishbone, 26
in general, 262
ring, 11, 17

Tablecloth, magic, producing food, 97, 101

Tasks, 6, 7, 25
set suitor by father-in law, 52

Thankful Dead, episode of, 105, 282, 293

Thirteenth (story), 72

The Thoughtless Abbot (story), 222

Thousand and One Nights
Aladdin and the Wonderful Lamp, 121
The Ass, the Ox, and the Peasant, 122
Forty Thieves, 122
The Hunchback, 122
Prince Ahmed and the Fairy Peribanu, 122
The Second Royal Mendicant, 122
Third Calendar, 122
Two Envious Sisters, 122
Sinbad's Fourth Voyage, 122
stories from, in Italian popular tales, 121

The Three Brothers (story), 212

The Three Goslings (story), 215

Tobit, 170

Tokens, magic (apple, pomegranate, and crown), 30

Tom Thumb, 195, 300

Torches, nuptial, 7

Transformation of hero
into ant, 27
into bird, 4, 12
into eagle, 27

into lion, 28
See also Statue
The Treasure (story), 156
Treasure stories, 191
True and untrue, 262
Truthful Joseph (story), 147
Turk, in Sicilian tales, 3, 142
Turkish corsairs, 106
Tuscan literature, LIV–LVI
Tûtî-Nâmeh, 134, 289

Uncle Capriano (story), 244

Venetian dialect, XVIII, LV
Vineyard I Was and Vineyard I Am
    (story), 127

The Wager (story), 228
Wandering Jew, 159, 292

Water and Salt (story), 268
Water, The Dancing, the Singing
    Apple, and the Speaking Tree
    (story), 16
Water of life, 43
Whistle
    that brings dead to life, 246
    that makes people dance, 97
White, Andrew D., XI
Whittington and his Cat, 294
Widter, Georg, LII
Witches'
    council under tree, 13
    imprecation, 272
Wooden dress, disguise of heroine,
    40
Wolf, Adam, LII

Zelinda and the Monster (story), 8

About the Series
and Volume Editor

Jack Zipes is a professor of German and director of the Center for German and European Studies at the University of Minnesota in Minneapolis.